The Handbook of Policy Practice

The Handbook of
Policy Practice

Ira C. Colby

OXFORD
UNIVERSITY PRESS

Oxford University Press is a department of the University of Oxford. It furthers
the University's objective of excellence in research, scholarship, and education
by publishing worldwide. Oxford is a registered trade mark of Oxford University
Press in the UK and certain other countries.

Published in the United States of America by Oxford University Press
198 Madison Avenue, New York, NY 10016, United States of America.

Library of Congress Cataloging-in-Publication Data
Names: Colby, Ira C. (Ira Christopher), author.
Title: The handbook of policy practice / Ira C. Colby.
Description: New York, NY : Oxford University Press, [2018] |
Includes bibliographical references and index. |
Identifiers: LCCN 2017028688 (print) | LCCN 2017041280 (ebook) | ISBN 9780190858834 (updf) |
ISBN 9780190858841 (epub) | ISBN 9780190858827 (alk. paper)
Subjects: LCSH: Public welfare—United States. | United States—Social policy. |
Social service—United States.
Classification: LCC HV95 (ebook) | LCC HV95 .C5953 2018 (print) | DDC 361.6/10973—dc23
LC record available at https://lccn.loc.gov/2017028688

9 8 7 6 5 4 3 2 1
Printed by Webcom Inc., Canada

CONTENTS

Contents

PERSPECTIVES

This *Handbook* is the product of my experiences in the social work field, and it reflects on what I strongly believe beginning social work practitioners should know and be able to do in policy practice. Quite simply, a social worker, no matter his or her practice setting or practice specialization, must be able to identify a local social problem; apply a sound analytic process; identify realistic, achievable remedies; and finally be skillful in communicating the findings in a clear, effective, and concise manner. Similarly, all social workers should be able to assess the overall effectiveness of an agency's existing program policy and provide recommendations to strengthen or change the policy and resulting services.

The first social policy course I taught was in 1975 in a small BSW program. Over the ensuing years, I continued teaching social policy in all levels of social work education—BSW, MSW, and PhD. To be honest, I was captivated with and by social policy. This was due to a number of factors. Growing up in the 1950s and being a teenager in the 1960s, I was significantly impacted by the civil rights movement; I could not grasp the reasoning behind hateful, prejudicial policies that had been in place since the United States was first organized in the 18th century. The turning point for me was the September 1963 bombing at the 16th Street Baptist Church in Birmingham, Alabama, killing four African American girls. They had gone to their church that fall Sunday morning just as I had done; I was 14 years old, the same age as three of the four victims of hate. I simply did not understand why such a brutal attack had occurred to people who could have been my classmates. The call for change was punctuated with the escalating Viet Nam war, the rebirth of the feminist movement, the rise of the Latino and Native American movements, and, sadly, the murders of President John Kennedy and the Reverend Dr. Martin Luther King, Jr. These and many more events of the era helped fuel my interests to understand social policies and how they could become instruments of change rather than barriers for social justice.

My MSW program at Virginia Commonwealth University introduced me to the world of social policy, and anything policy related became my first go-to course elective. I purposefully chose to continue with my doctoral work at the University of Pennsylvania so I could study with some of the leading social policy experts and social work historians at that time. Those faculty encouraged my work in social policy, and to this day I am fully indebted to them for their help in broadening and deepening my appreciation for the role that social policy plays in day-to-day living and social work practice.

In teaching social policy, I quickly realized that the vast majority of students did not share my enthusiasm for social policy. Students wanted to learn about social work in general but focus their energies on developing clinical skills and studying various practice and human behavior theories. Policy was pretty much viewed as an afterthought, a curriculum requirement that made little or no sense, and was difficult to translate to local-based social work practice.

My typical policy class-written assignments mimicked my master's and doctoral studies. There was a 20- to 25-page comparative analysis paper of two or more social policies; or the assignment would entail analysis of a social problem with an evaluation of the extent a social policy impacted the issue, again 20–25 pages in length. This "major" paper was augmented by two or three "short" papers, five pages in length, exploring an aspect of a social policy or social problem. And, of course, there was the 15-minute individual or group presentation on a social welfare issue using handouts and visuals such as overhead slides and eventually PowerPoint.

Yet what and how I was teaching was not at all congruent with my policy work. Over the years, I was consistently engaging with local and state governments around homelessness, social work student loan forgiveness, and the regulation of social work practice. I testified numerous times to city councils, state legislative committees, work groups, and the like. Not once did a presentation last 15 minutes as most were limited to 3–5 minutes; not once did I ever make a PowerPoint or use some other type of a visual presentation while testifying; not once did I present a 25-page analysis to a committee. Meetings with elected officials or their staffs were short, never more than 1 hour while most lasted 15 to 20 minutes in length. I also had frequent encounters with elected officials and staffers in the hallways of state legislatures or city halls, where I learned the art of giving a quick 30-second to 1-minute "elevator speech" on the issue. I also learned to carry with me a one-page policy brief to give to the individual.

It's no wonder students didn't seem to embrace social policy courses. The in-class experience was not relevant to day-to-day social work practice in the policy world.

My practice experiences also consistently showed that a social worker was seldom tasked to analyze a federal policy, such as the US House of Representatives H.R. 366 Putting Our Veterans Back to Work Act of 2015 (Congress.Gov, n.d.) or the Runaway and Homeless Youth Act (National Alliance to End Homelessness, n.d.) to present to a committee of the US Congress. Unless employed in a national policy advocacy organization, policy practice for most social workers was not taking place in the halls of the US Congress in Washington, DC. Most policy practice occurred in a local agency focusing on local matters that directly impacted the organization's work or their clients.

What follows in this *Handbook* reflects a commonsense approach to analysis within a practice mindset with added attention to the concept of *social justice* and necessary *critical thinking* skills. Social work educator and policy expert Bruce

Jansson (2015) defined this as *policy practice:* "efforts to change policies in legislative, agency, and community settings whether by establishing new policies, improving existing ones, or defeating the policy initiatives of other people" (p. 565).

This *Handbook* encourages the individual reader to develop his or her own unique skills to assess and propose policies and programs, based on social justice principles, which are relevant to the context of the agency and its clients.

At the same time, this *Handbook* does *not* explore advanced analysis techniques such as applied cost–benefit models, creating fiscal notes, multivariate analysis, environmental risk analysis, qualitative methods for policy analysis, or using geographic information systems. Such content is best suited for study in advanced policy courses supplemented with specific, focused textbooks or readings. Nor does this *Handbook* promote one political ideology over another or endorse specific programs, policies, or ideas in creating a stronger, more effective and efficient social welfare system.

A final, unique piece to this *Handbook* is the source materials. All professional writing, be it journal articles, monographs, or textbooks, require supporting documentation to illustrate or back positions and findings; traditionally these sources come from textbooks, professional journals, newspapers, and the like. These resources for the most part are located in libraries. This text, however, relies heavily on sources from the digital world. Today's college students are tech savvy, able to use the digital world in uncanny ways, and are deeply enmeshed in social media and its many virtual rooms. The Web is a comfortable, familiar place for today's college student. Using the web as a primary source builds on the social work profession's long-held belief to *begin where the client is.* Additionally, students, by using the links to the various data and citation sources, will be able to identify and discern the features of a valid website.

Over the years, my students taught me that a textbook is not an end in itself but a means to greater understanding; they also helped me appreciate that true learning rests with them. My role, as the course instructor, was to encourage their personal and professional growth as the pathway to true discovery rests within each individual. *The Handbook of Policy Practice* is but one of many tools to help the student and faculty person find and walk together down that path.

REFERENCES

Congress.gov. (n.d.). H.R.366—Putting our veterans back to work act of 2015, 114th Congress (2015–2016). Retrieved from https://www.congress.gov/bill/114th-congress/house-bill/366/text?q={%22search%22%3A[%22\%22hr366\%22%22]}&resultIndex=1 on May 18, 2016.

Jansson, B. (2015). *The reluctant welfare state, engaging history to advance social work practice in contemporary society* (8th ed.). Stamford, CT: Cengage Learning.

National Alliance to End Homelessness. (n.d.). Homeless youth legislation. Retrieved from http://www.endhomelessness.org/pages/youthlegislation

HANDBOOK *CHAPTERS REFLECTING CSWE 2015 EDUCATIONAL POLICY AND ACCREDITATION STANDARDS (EPAS)*

The Council on Social Work Education's Commission on Accreditation is responsible for the development and oversight of social work educational programs' accreditation standards, formally referred to as *Educational Policy and Accreditation Standards*; the Commission also reviews and grants accreditation to those educational programs that meet each accreditation standard. More detailed information regarding accreditation, including a complete copy of EPAS as well as a listing of current accredited social work programs, can be found at http://cswe.org/Accreditation.

The following chart documents the relationship between the *Handbook*'s content by chapter, including their related suggested activities, with each specific EPAS competency.

2015 EPAS Competencies	Chapters												
	Pers-pectives	1	2	3	4	5	6	7	8	9	10	11	12
Competency 1 Demonstrate Ethical and Professional Behavior	✓	✓	✓	✓	✓	✓	✓	✓	✓	✓	✓	✓	✓
Competency 2 Engage Diversity and Difference in Practice		✓	✓	✓	✓	✓				✓	✓		
Competency 3 Advance Human Rights and Social, Economic, and Environmental Justice	✓	✓	✓	✓	✓	✓	✓	✓	✓	✓	✓	✓	✓
Competency 4 Engage in Practice-Informed Research and Research-Informed Practice		✓	✓		✓	✓	✓	✓	✓	✓	✓		✓
Competency 5 Engage in Policy Practice	✓	✓	✓	✓	✓	✓	✓	✓	✓	✓	✓	✓	✓
Competency 6 Engage With Individuals, Families, Groups, Organizations, and Communities		✓	✓	✓	✓			✓	✓	✓	✓	✓	✓
Competency 7 Assess Individuals, Families, Groups, Organizations, and Communities			✓		✓	✓			✓				✓
Competency 8 Intervene With Individuals, Families, Groups, Organizations, and Communities	✓	✓	✓	✓	✓			✓	✓	✓	✓	✓	✓
Competency 9 Evaluate Practice With Individuals, Families, Groups, Organizations, and Communities		✓	✓	✓	✓	✓				✓	✓	✓	✓

The Handbook of Policy Practice

Context and Framework

INTRODUCTION TO PART 1: CONTEXT AND FRAMEWORK

For a moment, think about a dinner gathering you or your family might have prepared for family and friends, say for 10 to 15 people. A great deal of preparation and work were required prior to the actual dinner itself. The questions seemed endless:

- When is the dinner, a weekday or weekend evening?
- What time do we want people to arrive and leave?
- Who is invited?
- What types of food should be available?
- Should beer, wine, margaritas, or all three be on hand? What should be available for nondrinkers? Maybe there should be no alcohol.
- Does anyone have food allergies?
- Should vegan options be available?
- What will people use to eat and drink from—paper plates with plastic cup and utensils or silverware, formal wine or liquor glasses and china?
- Will guests sit a dining room table or able to eat informally in the house?
- Do we assign seats if people sit at the dining room table, or should they be allowed to sit where they choose?
- Will this be buffet style or family style?
- Will young children be eating and, if so, will they eat with their caretakers or at a special "children's table"?
- Should music be playing throughout the evening?

Once these and other questions are answered, the host makes the final arrangements, including food preparation, the set-up for the dinner, and arranging the chairs and tables in a manner that is comfortable for guests. Then, after hours of thought and preparation, the doorbell rings and the party is on.

In a metaphorical manner, the content in this *Handbook* is similar to planning a dinner get-together. A person just does not jump right into dinner without any thought or preparation. So, too, the social worker engaged in policy practice requires time to think through and fully understand an issue or policy, the concerns and stands of various stakeholders, and develop a strategy that results in a fair and just conclusion. Part 1 of the *Handbook* is the *thinking-through* phase of policy practice. Selected elements of the social work profession's core ideas and beliefs are identified and explored in depth.

A fundamental underlying premise of the *Handbook* is that a series of interdependent social policies govern every social service agency, including nonprofit and public organizations. A social worker cannot arbitrarily select which policy to follow or what he or she will do or under what circumstances—all social work practice from the actual intervention to how payments or reimbursements protocols are regulated by social policies. Some policies seem somewhat simple and straightforward, such as an agency's operating hours. Other policies are complex, excruciatingly detailed, and difficult to understand, such as an insurance company's reimbursement formula for reimbursing mental health counseling. Knowing what comprises a given policy is essential for effective practice, but equally important is understanding how to affect a policy's mandates by applying unique skills that are built on supporting expertise in a manner that reflects the social work profession's shared values and beliefs.

At the outset, let us be clear that this *Handbook for Policy Practice* is a practice-specific textbook; in particular, what can a social worker do to effectively impact social policy in an agency setting or through formal governmental processes? The *Handbook* does not present or argue for one specific model of policy analysis nor set forth a unique macro-practice framework for policy work. Policy analytic models and theories of practice are proposed, discussed, dissected, and examined in numerous other texts. Rather, the *Handbook* helps the beginning and experienced social worker alike develop hands-on policy practice skills that are effective tools in the constantly changing nonprofit, private, and public agencies; private practice settings; and national governmental elective bodies.

Yes, it is tempting and exciting to jump right into the middle of the "*doing*" or the "*how to*" of policy practice, but such a leap is shortsighted and results in minimal success. The Introduction for Part 1 starts at a key beginning point: What are social policy and social work, and what is their relationship with each other? Content in Chapter 1 may sound somewhat familiar, but the discussion outlines the necessary shape and form of social policy by exploring its uniqueness within a *social welfare* framework. Chapter 2 continues delving into social policy and, in particular, social welfare. The reader is introduced to the differences between public and private social policy.

Chapter 3 continues to develop the uniqueness of policy practice within a social work framework by exploring *social justice theory*. Typically, social workers discuss social justice in terms of rights, fairness, and equal opportunities. Social justice takes on differing meanings for others. This chapter explores social justice through a number of different lenses that result in justice-based decisions that literally reflect polar opposite perspectives from a social work standpoint. The *Handbook* explores contractual, feminist, libertarian, socialist, and utilitarian social justice theories. Discussion also includes an examination of how social justice, as a theory and desired goal, permeates the social work profession's numerous policy statements, including the National Association of Social Work Code of Ethics, the Council on Social Work Education's Educational Policy and Accreditation Standards, and the International Federation of Social Workers Global Standards. Suggested activities encourage readers to explore their personal views of social justice and how these influence their work. A simple question guides the reader through this chapter and throughout the text: Is this fair and just?

Chapter 4 draws the reader's attention to a key aspect of social work education as well as a core skill necessary for successful social work policy practice: *critical thinking*. Critical thinking requires a unique skill set to seek out information that may confirm a long-held belief or may redirect the social worker to adopt a differing position. The discussion builds on the precept that critical thinking is not easy and requires an individual to be open to change. For a moment, consider the political environment that led up to and through the 2016 national presidential election. It is safe to say that presidential candidates' policy positions were built mostly on ideologies and long-held beliefs of one form or another rather than looking at an issue through a nonpartisan factually driven lens. Chapter 4 explores how successful critical thinking requires the ability to lay aside personal beliefs to see what research shows. Furthermore, the chapter addresses a basic concern when seeking information: How does one determine what data, website, or report is valid and reliable?

Finally, Part 1 discusses the structures of both issue and policy analysis presentations. Often times, a social worker will be asked to prepare a report with recommendations for an agency to take on an emerging community issue; or the social worker is asked to look at a particular agency policy and offer proposals that strengthen the policy and its resulting programs and services. Although issue and policy analyses share similar components, they are unique in their individual approaches. The discussion reflects the reality that policy practice analysis is far different from writing a 15- to 20-page college term paper; rather, the actual output is a clearly focused practice-specific document that results in a specific recommendation.

Part 1 helps the reader build a solid framework and foundation for practice policy. The five chapters, while offering different perspectives and insights into social policy, require readers to challenge their beliefs and why they subscribe to certain positions. At the same time, readers are encouraged to frame all issue and policy assessments by the simple question: Is this fair and just?

CHAPTER 1

The Intersection of Social Policy, Social Work Practice, and Social Justice

Welcome to the wonderful, perplexing, confusing, energizing world of social policy! There are few topics that engender the level and intensity of emotionally fueled polarizing discussions as much as social policy, in particular as it relates to social welfare and the human condition. Only look back at the 2016 Democratic and Republican presidential primaries and the November 2016 national election; they were filled with national debates, stump speeches, campaign rallies, demonstrations, and social media responses all illustrating the passions that evolve with particular policies aimed at specific social issues. Not a day goes by when a social policy of one type or another does not make the local, state, national, or international news.

Understanding the essence of a particular social policy—its rationale, what it does and does not do, its intended outcomes as well as its unexpected results—is important to each and every social worker. Recognizing and understanding the extent that social policy controls, regulates, and impacts social work practice is as important as appreciating the role that human behavior theory plays in an individual or family counseling situation.

Just what is this hotbed of *social policy* and why should social workers really be concerned with social policy?

Attempting to define social policy is a difficult task, primarily due to its vagueness and its interrelatedness with various forms of public and social welfare policies (Gilbert & Terrell, 2013, p. 2). As a result, there is confusion as to what exactly is and is not a social program and, more specifically, what constitutes a social welfare program. For example, there is probably general agreement that the Supplemental Nutritional Assistance Program, more commonly referred to as "food stamps," is a social welfare program; however, a library card, which pro-vides access to free books, is generally not thought of as a social welfare program. Similarly, medical benefits provided by the Veterans Administration to veterans and their families are not typically construed to be social welfare, but *Medicaid*, a health care program for the poor, is commonly perceived to be a welfare program (see Activity Box 1.1).

So what is *social policy* and how does it specifically relate to social work? Not surprisingly, there are numerous Web-based sources offering a variety of defini-tions; a simple Google search of the phrase "definition of social policy" found 15.8 million possible links. Although many of these links are repetitive, they show the variety of sources and ways to describe or explain social policy. A cautionary note before proceeding: Using Web sources, as in this case, can be problematic due to their accuracy of content; discerning the validity and reliability of Web and social media materials is essential for successful policy practice and is discussed later in the *Handbook*. Social workers also need to recognize that some people, rightly or wrongly, simply will not accept a Web source for any or partial informa-tion and will only accept a definition from a formal or traditional source such as a textbook or encyclopedia.

Activity Box 1.1

In small groups or as a class discussion, determine if the listed programs can be labeled as *social welfare*. Once there is a group consensus on each program, in groups of three, survey 25 non–social work students and ask them the follow-ing: Do you consider the following programs to be social welfare? Be sure not to explain what each program is or the types of services offered. The questioner is seeking a simple "yes" or "no" response.

Note: there is a trick question by including "food stamps" and "Supple-mental Nutrition Program" as these are the same program. The questioner is seeking to determine if a program's more recognizable name influences a response.

Housing vouchers	Medicaid
Supplemental Nutrition Program	Pre-K school
Foster care	Hospital emergency room
Social Security Retirement	Public library
Medicare	Psychiatric hospitals
College loans such as the Pell grant	Food stamps
Nursing homes	Mental health clinics

The following examples of definitions of social policy illustrate the diversity of sources and their definitions at some of the more frequently accessed websites.

- *The Free Dictionary* defines social policy as "a policy of (*sic*) for dealing with social issues . . . a line of argument rationalizing the course of action of a government."
- *Reference* defines social policies as public services that govern the well-being of citizens, and they revolve around the five social maladies of poverty, poor health, inadequate housing, lack of education and unemployment.
- *Wikipedia* defines social policy as "guidelines, principles, legislation and activities that affect the living conditions conducive to human welfare, such as a person's quality of life."
- *Definitions* offers a number of definitions, including "guidelines, principles, legislation and activities that affect the living conditions conducive to human welfare."

Now compare the examples of Web-based definitions of social policy to examples found in traditional textbooks.

- Midgley and Livermore (2009) write that social policy is designed to "enhance peoples' welfare or social being" (p. x) and "are courses of action adopted by formal organizations (that) prescribe, govern, and routinize the activities of these organizations" (p. 3).
- Popple and Leighninger (2015) suggest that policies may be laws, public or private regulations, formal procedures, or simply normative sanctioned patterns of behavior.
- Reisch (2014) seems to capture the importance of social policy when he writes, "social policies can be viewed as the basis for social programs, often in the form of acts of government to effect change around specific issues" (p. 7).

Although the exact wording and definitions of social policy differ between and among Web sources and textbooks, there are common themes in these definitions, which provide a clear purpose for social policy. First, social policy deals with social issues; second, social policy focuses on social welfare; and, third social policy provides mechanisms for specific programs to enrich the human condition.

The crossroads of these three common characteristics reveal some interesting observations. First, social policies are developed around the array of social issues and social problems. Social problems addressed through social policy include but are not limited to:

- poverty (i.e., Medicaid, Supplemental Security Income, housing vouchers);
- illiteracy (i.e., public library, pre-K programs);
- neighborhood safety and security activities (i.e., police and fire departments);

- child welfare (i.e., child protective services);
- mental health (i.e., emergency mental health services, residential treatment programs);
- criminal justice (i.e., probation and parole, detention centers);
- homelessness (i.e., shelters, food and clothing distribution centers);
- social security (i.e., retirement and disability);
- gerontology (i.e., aging in place initiatives, independent care homes);
- health care (i.e., occupational therapy, immunizations);
- housing (i.e., Section 8 housing, tax exemptions for mortgage interest);
- education (i.e., K–12, higher education); and
- immigration (i.e., EB-5 programs, English as a Second Language).

Second, social policy is a broad construct that goes well beyond programs and services for the poor and disadvantaged. Third, as a result, social policies are found in every facet of the public and private social services community and in every phase of the human daily experience. All people, no matter their age, race, ethnicity, or gender identity, are directly impacted by social policies. Four, the federal, state, and local (e.g., city, town, or county) governments all enact social policies. Five, social workers engaged in their own private practice are governed by social policies, some of which practitioners write for their practice or by policies from external sources such as insurance companies or federal programs. In other words, if one wants to practice social work, she or he will be intimately involved with social policy in day-to-day practice.

POLICY'S INFLUENCE ON SOCIAL WORK PRACTICE

To be clear, social policy influences all dimensions of social work practice. Blau and Abramowitz (2014) explicitly state that "every form of social work practice embodies a social policy . . . and (it) pervade(s) every aspect of social work practice" (p. 4). The client population, the types of services provided, the duration of services, and program funding all result from policy directives. Seemingly small, unnoticed organizational practices, such as the availability of toys for small children in waiting room areas, are the direct result of a policy decision. A policy determines the number of nights a person may stay in a homeless shelter or if an individual who is under the influence of alcohol or drugs may stay in a shelter. Whether or a not an individual is eligible for the *Supplemental Nutritional Assistance Program* (*SNAP*) is determined by policy. A policy determines the extent that health issues are covered by an insurance provider, the level of reimbursement, and the type of professional eligible for reimbursement.

Policy establishes the boundaries and direction of practice in both the private and public sectors of social work. A social worker's practice in a nonprofit agency, also referred to as a *nongovernmental organization* (NGO) in the global community, is regulated by the organization's specific policies. As will be explored later in this text (see Chapter 8), a nonprofit agency is governed by a volunteer board of directors whose primary responsibility is to set policy for the agency. Social workers employed in public settings, that is, state agencies such as child or senior protective services, are limited to practice within the confines of a specific public policy that has been enacted by an elected body such as a state legislature.

Policy also controls the individual social worker's ability to practice and the extent that a person can call herself or himself a social worker. People with a baccalaureate or graduate social work degree from a Council on Social Work Education (CSWE) accredited program are not guaranteed that they will be able to practice or even refer to themselves as social workers. This may seem a bit surprising or even at odds with what is taught in BSW or MSW programs; but in all 50 states, the practice of social work is regulated in some form by the state government, usually through state licensing or registration laws. These laws, also referred to as *rules*, differ from state to state, as there is no single, national law that regulates the practice of social work. In each state, the legislative body, more commonly referred to as the state legislature, enacts licensure or registration policy, which in effect states *to practice social work in this state an individual must meet specific standards set forth by this legislative body* (Association for Social Work Boards, n.d.). There are commonalities across the states such as requiring a social work degree from a CSWE accredited program, but there are significant differences as well. Table 1.1

Table 1.1. LICENSING REQUIREMENTS FOR TEXAS AND FLORIDA

Criteria	Texas	Florida
Types of social work licenses	LBSW (BSW)	LCSW (clinical)
	LMSW (MSW)	
	LCSW (clinical)	
	Recognition for *Independent Practice Recognition* or *IPR* of nonclinical social work is available to LMSWs and LBSWs who meet the requirements.	
	LMSWs who meet certain requirements may receive recognition as an *Advanced Practitioner* of nonclinical social work services.	
Reciprocity with other states	Yes	No

(continued)

Table 1.1. CONTINUED

Criteria	Texas	Florida
Post MSW hours in clinical work	3,000 hours	1,500 hours
Specific MSW coursework required	No	A minimum of 24 semester hours of clinically focused human behavior and social work practice methods courses; at least one course should be in psychopathology. There should be clinical fieldwork as well. However, candidates who do attend accredited nonclinical social work programs may make up clinical coursework deficiencies later.
Other required coursework prior to clinical licensing	No	Yes—Completed an 8-hour laws and rules course from a board approved provider; completed a 2-hour prevention of medical errors course from a board approved provider; completed a 3-hour HIV/AIDS course and 2-hour domestic violence course from a board approved provider within 6 months of licensure
Length of time supervised by approved licensed clinical social worker	24–48 months	At least 100 hours of supervision per 1,500 hours of psychotherapy face to face with clients. At least 1 hour of supervision every 2 weeks; at least 1 hour of supervision per 15 hours of psychotherapy, with a minimum of 1 hour of supervision every 2 weeks. If the applicant obtained group supervision, each hour of group supervision must alternate with an hour of individual supervision. Individual supervision is defined as one supervisor supervising no more than two interns, and group supervision is defined as one supervisor supervising more than two but a maximum of six interns in the group.
Supervision plan filed with state regulatory body	Yes	Yes

Source: http://www.socialworklicensure.org/articles/social-work-license-requirements.html; http://www.naswfl. org/licensure.html; http://floridasmentalhealthprofessions.gov/licensing/licensed-clinical-social-worker/; http:// www.dshs.state.tx.us/socialwork/default.shtm. Retrieved January 6, 2016.

compares the clinical social work licensing requirements for two states, Texas and Florida. Both states require a graduate social work degree from a CSWE accredited program, but they share little else. These licensing rules in Texas and Florida are developed by volunteer members of the states' legislative regulatory boards (Florida Board of Clinical Social Work, Marriage & Family Therapy, and Mental Health Counseling, 2016); Texas Department of State Health Services, 2016), which include social workers as well as individuals with non–social work backgrounds. Logically, one would conclude that an individual with a CSWE accredited social work degree should be able to practice social work anywhere in the United States. Yet state-specific policies, as evidenced by the licensure laws in Florida and Texas, can be significantly different from each other while specifying who can and cannot practice social work.

POLICY'S INFLUENCE ON ACHIEVING SOCIAL JUSTICE

Close examination of US-based social welfare programs illustrates the impact that social policy plays in achieving social justice. For example,

- The Personal Responsibility and Work Opportunity Reconciliation Act of 1996 limits cash payments to the poor for a maximum of 5 years (60 months) in one's lifetime, and in July 2013, the maximum monthly benefit for a family of three ranged from $923 in Alaska to $170 in Mississippi (Falk, 2016, p. 11).
- In December 2016, the average monthly Supplemental Nutritional Assistance Program (SNAP), more commonly and incorrectly referred to as "food stamps," was $125.51 per month for an individual (US Department of Agriculture Food and Nutrition Service).
- In November 2016, the average monthly Disability Insurance benefit for a worker was $1,167.63 per month, spouse of a disabled worker was 323.02, and the child of disabled was $353.67 (Social Security, December 2016).
- The average monthly Supplemental Security Income (SSI) was $539.02 per month (Social Security, December 2016).

These programs are the primary income support for some of the most vulnerable persons in our communities—the poor, persons with disabilities, and their spouses and children. SNAP provides on average $1,500 a year in benefits; a person with a disability receives an annual benefit of $14,011 on average, whereas the spouse's annual support totals $3,386 and a child's allocation is $4,244 per year. And SSI, a program targeting low-income people who are either aged 65 or older, blind, or disabled, averages an annual benefit of $6,468. Yet do these amounts achieve the goals of social justice (see Activity Box 1.2)? Do these supports seem *fair and just*?

According to the US Bureau of Labor Statistics, the first quarter of 2016 median weekly salary was $823.00 or $42,796.00 per year. In other words, half of the US workforce between January 1 and April 31, 2016, made less than $823.00 or $42,796.00 per year. And looking at the data by gender, median weekly salary for men was $904.00 compared to $703.00 for women, a 22.2% gap, in the first quarter of 2016 (US Bureau of Labor Statistics).

All advocacy groups and professional associations look at these basic numbers and facts and arrive at different conclusions. Some argue that cash payments or minimum wages are too high, too low, just right, constraining and limiting, create dependency on the government while stifling individual initiative, or provide a much needed support for the poor.

Activity Box 1.2

Look at your home town, city, or where your college/university is located and do the following:

1. Determine the average monthly apartment rent for a three-person family.

2. According to the Center on Budget Policy and Priorities (March 24, 2016), the average monthly SNAP benefit for a three-person family in 2016 was $379 or $87.46 for a week. Go to a supermarket and put together a menu for 1 week for a three-person family; how much additional money does a family need on top of the SNAP benefit to cover the cost of the food?

3. Estimate how much money the family will need on a monthly basis to maintain a car (include gas, oil changes, auto insurance), pay apartment utilities (average electric/gas, and water), and cover other incidentals.

4. The federal minimum wage in 2016 was $7.25 per hour; based on a 40-hour work week, 52 weeks a year (note, no vacation), the individual will earn $15,080 per year. Some states have higher or lower minimum wages; determine your states minimum wage at the following website: http://www.minimum-wage.org/wage-by-state.asp and calculate the annual earnings per year if it is different from the federal wage.

5. Based on the minimum wage for your state, does the minimum income cover the housing rent, additional dollars for food, and other expenses?

6. Based on your findings, what do you believe a fair minimum wage should be for your community?

Social work membership organizations, both national and international, clearly spell out a social worker's responsibility to engage in social justice matters with specific justice-based statements found among the numerous professional social work membership associations. The US-based National Association of Social Workers states in its Code of Ethics that "Social workers promote social justice" and further articulates in an "ethical principle, social workers challenge social injustice"; the National Association of Black Social Workers (NABSW) Code of Ethics includes among its principles, "(NABSW members) will engage in action for improving social conditions."

Globally, the International Federation of Social Workers (IFSSW) and the International Association of Schools of Social Work (IASSW) write in their joint Statement of Ethical Principles (International Federation, 2012), "Social workers have a responsibility to promote social justice, in relation to society generally, and in relation to the people with whom they work." Similarly, social work membership organizations around the world include specific references to social justice. For example, the Canadian Association of Social Workers mission statement as amended in 2013, "The social work profession has a positive impact on public/social justice issues while advancing social justice among its goals and objectives (and) . . . to advance social justice."

THE COUNCIL ON SOCIAL WORK EDUCATION'S MANDATE TO STUDY SOCIAL POLICY

Data collected by the Council on Social Work Education finds that the majority of social work students aspire to work in a clinical or individual/family setting. However, as discussed earlier in this chapter, understanding a particular social policy's nuances, its dimensions, and influences on social work practice creates the pathway for effective work. This aspect of social work, commonly referred to as *policy practice*, has been part of the Council on Social Work Education's (CSWE) accreditation standards dating back to the initial establishment of the Council in the early 1950s (see Box 1.1). These initial accreditation standards required social policy courses be taught as part of the foundation curriculum in a student's first or second semester of study. In fact, the typical MSW curriculum requirements included completion of two social policy courses as well as one elective.

CSWE is the national educational authority in the United States for baccalaureate and graduate social work education and provides a variety of activities for students and faculty alike such as professional development through its Annual Program Meeting (more commonly referred to as APM), publications, and legislative advocacy. The Council's principal function, however, is its accreditation of baccalaureate and master's programs. CSWE is the only social work accrediting body in the United States, and its authority to establish educational standards is granted by the Council for Higher Education (see http://www.chea.org). Through the CSWE

Box 1.1

COUNCIL ON SOCIAL WORK EDUCATION
AND THE EDUCATIONAL POLICY AND
ACCREDITATION STANDARDS

The Council on Social Work Education (CSWE) is the only national social work education accrediting authority in the United States, and this responsibility was granted by the Council for Higher Education Accreditation (CHEA). Accreditation serves an important quality assurance function as a accredited social work program must meet the criterions set forth in Educational Policy and Accreditation Standards, more commonly referred to as EPAS.

Go to the CSWE website to learn more about EPAS as well as other information related to social work accreditation, including a listing of all CSWE accredited social work programs—http://cswe.org/Accreditation.aspx.

Commission on Accreditation (COA), a specific *educational policy* with detailed *standards*, more commonly referred to as EPAS, is established that an accredited social work education program must follow. To be more precise, a CSWE accredited program must meet each EPAS standard; if a program's work does not meet one or more of these standards, then accreditation may be denied, withdrawn, or a program may be placed on probation.

Reflecting the long-standing belief in the importance of policy practice in social work, the 2015 EPAS defines the purpose of social work to:

> promote human and community well-being. Guided by a person and environment construct, a global perspective, respect for human diversity, and knowledge based on scientific inquiry, social work's purpose is actualized through its quest for social and economic justice, the prevention of conditions that limit human rights, the elimination of poverty, and the enhancement of the quality of life for all persons. (Commission on Accreditation, 2015, p. 5)

The manner in which a particular social work program is structured, the specializations and required/elective courses offered, and the field internship requirements are spelled out in EPAS. Both graduate and undergraduate social work programs are built around a competency-based education models. This is an outcome-based approach to study in which a student is required to demonstrate specific behavioral outcomes. The current 2015 EPAS identifies nine basic social work practice behaviors that are attended to in all BSW or MSW programs (see Box 1.1).

EPAS includes a specific policy practice standard, which refers to this work as "policy practice." The criterion reiterates the point that social workers recognize the direct interactions between direct practice, social service programs, and social justice with social policy. This policy practice benchmark also notes that the social worker specifically "actively engages" in policy development in his or her employment setting "to effect change within those settings" (see Table 1.2). Additionally, the standard identifies three explicit practice behaviors that reflect effective policy practice, including

- "the ability to identify social policy at the local, state, and federal level that impacts well-being, service delivery, and access to social services;
- assess how social welfare and economic policies impact the delivery of and access to social services; and
- apply critical thinking to analyze, formulate, and advocate for policies that advance human rights and social, economic, and environmental justice." (Commission on Accreditation, p. 8)

Policy practice directives are also identified and integrated within other competencies. Various aspects of policy practice are included in the following EPAS competencies.

Table 1.2. POLICY PRACTICE BEHAVIORS IDENTIFIED IN EDUCATIONAL POLICY AND ACCREDITATION STANDARDS

Competency 5: Engage in Policy Practice

Social workers understand that human rights and social justice, as well as social welfare and services, are mediated by policy and its implementation at the federal, state, and local levels. Social workers understand the history and current structures of social policies and services, the role of policy in service delivery, and the role of practice in policy development. Social workers understand their role in policy development and implementation within their practice settings at the micro, mezzo, and macro levels and they actively engage in policy practice to effect change within those settings. Social workers recognize and understand the historical, social, cultural, economic, organizational, environmental, and global influences that affect social policy. They are also knowledgeable about policy formulation, analysis, implementation, and evaluation.

Social workers:

- identify social policy at the local, state, and federal level that impacts well-being, service delivery, and access to social services;
- assess how social welfare and economic policies impact the delivery of and access to social services; and
- apply critical thinking to analyze, formulate, and advocate for policies that advance human rights and social, economic, and environmental justice. (p. 8)

Source: Commission on Accreditation (2015). *2015 educational policy and accreditation standards for baccalaureate and master's social work programs* (p. 8). Alexandria, VA: Council on Social Work Education.

Competency 1: Demonstrate Ethical and Professional Behavior
Social workers understand the value base of the profession and its ethical stan-dards, as well as relevant laws and regulations that may impact practice at the micro, mezzo, and macro levels. Social workers understand frameworks of ethical decision-making and how to apply principles of critical thinking to those frame-works in practice, research, and policy arenas. Social workers:

- *demonstrate professional demeanor in behavior; appearance; and oral, written, and electronic communication* (Commission on Accreditation, p. 7).

Competency 3: Advance Human Rights and Social, Economic, and Environmental Justice
Social workers understand that every person regardless of position in society has fundamental human rights such as freedom, safety, privacy, an adequate standard of living, health care, and education . . . are knowledgeable about theories of human need and social justice and strategies to promote social and economic justice and human rights. Social workers understand strate-gies designed to eliminate oppressive structural barriers to ensure that social goods, rights, and responsibilities are distributed equitably and that civil, political, environmental, economic, social, and cultural human rights are pro-tected. Social workers:

- *apply their understanding of social, economic, and environmental justice to advocate for human rights at the individual and system levels; and*
- *engage in practices that advance social, economic, and environmental justice.* (Commission on Accreditation, pp. 7–8)

Competency 4: Engage in Practice-Informed Research and Research-Informed Practice
Social workers understand quantitative and qualitative research methods and their respective roles in advancing a science of social work and in evaluating their practice . . .

- *use and translate research evidence to inform and improve practice, policy, and service delivery.* (p. 8)

Competency 8: Intervene With Individuals, Families, Groups, Organizations, and Communities
Social workers understand that intervention is an ongoing component of the dynamic and interactive process of social work practice with, and on behalf of, diverse individuals, families, groups, organizations, and communities . . .

- *negotiate, mediate, and advocate with and on behalf of diverse clients and con-stituencies.* (Commission on Accreditation, p. 9)

A FEW FINAL THOUGHTS

The purpose of social work is to help individuals, families, groups, communities, and organizations realize their fullest potential and aspirations while promoting fair and just systems that realize this purpose. Most social worker students hope to someday engage in direct practice with individuals, families, or groups. Research shows that students and practitioners favor child welfare and mental health settings as their optimal place for work. Policy practice is often, and incorrectly, viewed as macro or mezzo practices. This inaccurate view ignores a key purpose of social work practice: "(to) promote human and community well-being (which is) actualized through its quest for social and economic justice, the prevention of conditions that limit human rights, the elimination of poverty, and the enhancement of the quality of life for all persons" (Commission on Accreditation, p. 5).

In summary, policy practice is an integral part of social work practice that all practitioners utilize to strengthen their own work while building conditions for others to fully maximize their individual and collective potential. The social worker's primary objective is to ensure the policy and resulting programs and services are *fair and just*.

REFERENCES

Association of Social Work Boards. (n.d.). *Model social work practice act.* Culpeper, VA: Association of Social Work Boards. Retrieved on April 10, 2012, from http://www.aswb.org/pdfs/Model_law.pdf.

Blau, J., & Abramoqitz, M. (2014). *The dynamics of social welfare policy* (4th ed.) New York, NY: Oxford University Press.

Center on Budget Policy and Priorities. (2016, March 24). Policy basics: Introduction to the supplemental nutrition assistance program (SNAP). Retrieved from http://www.cbpp.org/research/policy-basics-introduction-to-the-supplemental-nutrition-assistance-program-snap on December 29, 2016.

Commission on Accreditation. (2015). *2015 educational policy and accreditation standards for baccalaureate and master's social work programs.* Alexandria, VA: Council on Social Work Education.

Definitions. (n.d.). Definitions for social policy. Retrieved from http://www.definitions.net/definition/social%20policy on November 18, 2015.

Falk, G. (2016, March 18). *The temporary assistance for needy families (TANF) block grant: Responses to frequently asked questions.* Congressional Research Services. Washington, DC: Library of Congress.

Florida Board of Clinical Social Work, Marriage & Family Therapy, and Mental Health Counseling. (2016). Licensed clinical social worker. Retrieved from http://floridas-mentalhealthprofessions.gov/licensing/licensed-clinical-social-worker/ on January 23, 2016.

The Free Dictionary by Fairfax. (n.d.). Social policy. Retrieved from http://www.thefreedictionary.com/social+policy on November 18, 2015.

Gilbert, N., & Terrell, P. (2013). *Dimensions of social welfare policy* (8th ed.). Upper Saddle River, NJ: Pearson.

International Federation of Social Welfare. (2012). Statement of ethical principles. Retrieved from http://ifsw.org/policies/statement-of-ethical-principles/ on December 23, 2015.

Midgley, J., & Livermore, M. (2009). *Handbook of social policy* (2nd ed.). Thousand Oaks, CA: Sage.

National Association of Black Social Workers. (n.d.). Code of ethics. Retrieved from http://nabsw.org/?page=CodeofEthics on December 23, 2015.

National Association of Social Workers. (2008). Code of ethics of the National Association of Social Workers. Washington, DC: National Association of Social Workers. Retrieved from http://socialworkers.org/pubs/code/code.asp on December 23, 2015.

Popple, P., & Leighninger, L. (2015). *The policy-based profession: An introduction to social welfare policy analysis for social workers* (6th ed.). Upper Saddle River, NJ: Pearson.

Reference. (2016). What is the definition of social policy? Retrieved from https://www.reference.com/government-politics/definition-social-policy-bc65cf69354f6717 on December 29, 2016.

Reisch, M. (ed.) (2014). *Social policy and social justice*. Thousand Oaks, CA: Sage.

Social Security. (2016, December). Monthly Statistical Snapshot, November 2016. Retrieved from https://www.ssa.gov/policy/docs/quickfacts/stat_snapshot/ on December 29, 2016.

Texas Department of State Health Services. (2016, May 12). Texas state board of social worker examiners home page. Retrieved from http://www.dshs.state.tx.us/socialwork/ on May 28, 2016.

US Bureau of Labor Statistics. (2016, April 19). *Economic news release, Table 1. Median usual weekly earnings of full-time wage and salary workers by sex, quarterly averages, seasonally adjusted*. Washington, DC: Department of Labor. Retrieved from http://www.bls.gov/news.release/wkyeng.t01.htm on May 27, 2016.

US Department of Agriculture Food and Nutrition Service. (2016). Supplemental Nutrition Assistance Program (SNAP). Retrieved from https://www.fns.usda.gov/pd/supplemental-nutrition-assistance-program-snap on December 29, 2016.

Wikipedia, the free encyclopedia. (n.d.). Social policy. Retrieved from https://en.wikipedia.org/wiki/Social_policy on November 18, 2015.

CHAPTER 2

Recognizing the Underpinnings of Social Policy and Social Welfare Policy

The terms *social policy* and *social welfare policy* are commonly used interchangeably. Switching or substituting *social policy* with *social welfare policy* and vice versa is an inaccurate depiction of these constructs and contributes to the confusion regarding social services in general. To further complicate matters, the public at large has a difficult time understanding the breadth, depth, and scope of social policy and social welfare policy because there are no clear-cut definitions for these terms. For example, *social welfare*, according to noted policy experts Neil Gilbert and Paul Terrell (2013, p. 2), is "elusive" to define, and they go on to say in *Dimension of Social Policy* (Gilbert & Terrell, 2013) that they will *not* spend time attempting to clarify or define the term. Noted policy expert and social worker Michael Reisch (2014, p. 6) writes that there is no one, agreed-upon universal definition for *social welfare*. To Reisch's point, Table 2.1 provides a listing of selected definitions of *social welfare*, which highlights the general lack of agreement of what this term constitutes.

Policy practice, however, does require a basic understanding of the differences between social policy and social welfare policy and how they relate to each other. A somewhat dated, though accurate definition of *social policy* was put forth by Tropman (1984), when he wrote that a social policy is "an *idea* reduced to writing, approved by *legitimate authority*, which gives *direction or guidance*" (p. 2). Tropman's approach suggests there are multiple ways a social policy takes form. From Tropman's perspective, a social policy, for example, can be written (*an idea*) by a social worker in a nonprofit agency, approved by the agency's board of directors (*legitimate authority*), and then results in the development of a new program (*sets an agency's direction*). Or a person might advocate for a new approach (*an idea*) with her or his Congressional representative, who in turn translates the idea into legislative language through a proposed law, which if approved by Congress (*legitimate authority*), creates a new governmental program (*sets an agency's direction*).

Table 2.1. SELECTED DEFINITIONS OF SOCIAL WELFARE AND SOCIAL WELFARE POLICY

Social welfare embraces laws, programmes, benefits and services which address social needs accepted as essential to the well-being of a society. It focuses on personal and social problems, both existing and potential.	The Five-Year Plan for Social Development in Hong Kong—1998. Retrieved from www.swd.gov.hk/doc/pubctn_ch/e5yrplan.pdf. on November 9, 2016. p. 3.
... Social welfare, an organization must operate primarily to further the common good and general welfare of the people of the community (such as by bringing about civic betterment and social improvements).	IRS. (2016, August). Social welfare organizations. Retrieved from https://www.irs.gov/charities-non-profits/other-non-profits/social-welfare-organizations.
Social welfare policy is anything a government chooses to do, or not do, that affects the quality of life of its people.	DiNitto, D., & Johnson, D. (2012). (. *Essentials of social welfare, politics and public policy.* Boston, MA: Pearson. p. 2.
Social welfare ... all social interventions intended to enhance or maintain the social functioning of human beings.	Dolgoff, R., & Fieldstein, D. (2013). *Understanding social welfare, a search for social justice* (9th ed.). Boston, MA: Pearson. p. 4.
The goal of social welfare is to fulfill the social, financial, health, and recreational requirements of all individuals in society. Social welfare seeks to enhance the social functioning of all age groups, rich and poor.	Zastrow, C. (2010). *Introduction to social work and social welfare, empowering people* (10th ed.). Belmont, CA: Brooks/Cole. p. 2.
Social welfare in any society has two major purposes: social treatment (helping) and social control.	Day, P., & Schiele, J. (2013). *A new history of social welfare* (7th ed.). Boston, MA: Pearson. p. 4.
... the guarantee of basic income protection to those resident in a society.	Kennett, P. (2004). *A handbook of comparative social policy.* Northampton, MA: Edward Elgar. p. 128.
A nation's system of programs, benefits and services that help people meet those social, economic, educational, and health needs that are fundamental to the maintenance of society.	Barker, R. ed. (2014). *The social work dictionary.* Washington, DC: NASW Press. p. 402.
Social welfare policy refers to the principles, activities, or framework for action adopted by the government to ensure a socially defined level of individual, family, and community well-being.	Blau, J. and Abramowitz, M. (2014). *The dynamics of social welfare policy* (4th ed.). New York, NY: Oxford University Press. p. 21.
A broad concept related to the general well-being of all of society.	Kirst-Ashman, K. (2017). *Introduction to social work & social welfare, critical thinking perspectives* (5th ed.). Boston, MA: Cengage Learning. p. 6.
Collective interventions to meet certain needs of the individual and/or to serve the wider interests of society.	Titmus, R. (1959). *Essays on the welfare state.* New Haven, CT: Yale University Press. p. 42.

Table 2.1. CONTINUED

A social services and institutions, designed to aid individuals and groups to attain satisfying standards of life and health and personal social relationships that permit them to develop their full capacities and promote their well-being in harmony with the needs of their families and community.	Friedlander, W. (1955). *Introduction to social welfare.* Englewood Cliffs, NJ: PrenticeHall. p. 140.
A subset of social policy, which may be defined as the formal and consistent ordering of affairs.	Karger, H. J., & Stoesz, D. (2010). *American social welfare policy: A pluralist approach* (6th ed.). Boston, MA: Pearson Education/Allyn Bacon. p. 3.
An encompassing and imprecise term but most often it is defined in terms of organizational activities, interventions, or some other element that suggests policy and programs to respond to recognized social problems or to improve the well-being of those at risk.	Reid, P. N. (1995). Social welfare history. In R. Edwards & J. G. Hopps (Eds.), *Encyclopedia of social work* (19th ed.). Washington, DC: NASW Press.
A concept that encompasses people's health, economic condition, happiness, and quality of life.	Segal, W., & Brzuzy, S. (1998). *Social welfare policy, programs, and practice.* Itasca, IL: Peacock. p. 8.
Society's organized way to provide for the persistent needs of all people—for health, education, socioeconomic support, personal rights, and political freedom.	Bloom, M. (1990). *Introduction to the social work drama.* Itasca, IL: Peacock. p. 6.

Scores of textbooks and journal authors have argued for one definition of *social policy* over another. Many pages could be dedicated in this text in an attempt to clarify these positions, yet they will still bring us to the same conclusion: There is a general lack of agreement as to what constitutes social policy. Rather than get bogged down in definitions, let's set forth a position and move ahead.

For this *Handbook*'s purpose, *social policy is a broad map that identifies a desired destination that is reached through a set of activities or services.* In effect, social policy designs an approach to address a specific social issue. Just as important, a social policy informs an organization's staff and volunteers on how to interact with the broader social, economic, and political environments in order to achieve the desired outcome (Midgley & Livermore, 2009).

A social policy also is a statement reflecting a broader community's values and what it believes to be true. Some policies are referred to as a *public social policy,* which is a policy enacted by a local, state, or federal governmental entity (Baker, 1995, p. 357). A social policy enacted by an agency or organization is not a public policy. In other words, *all* public policies or public social policies are enacted by governments, but not all social policies are public social policies.

Social welfare policy is a subset of social policy that focuses on systems and services that help individuals and groups to resolve and confront social problems (see Table 2.1). A broad perspective of public social welfare argues that *social welfare policy* is everything the government does: health care, taxation, national defense, housing, public assistance, education, environment, and social insurance (DiNitto & Johnson, 2012, p. 2). This view basically argues that every person—young or old, wealthy or poor, or any other characterizations or groupings of people—is a direct beneficiary of social welfare policies.

Yet many people would not subscribe to such a broad, all-encompassing definition of social welfare. Rather, the more popular belief is that *public social welfare policies* are enacted by government and specifically designed to help people meet their social, economic, educational, and health needs (Baker, 1995, p. 357). This perspective argues that social welfare includes programs that offer assistance to purchase food, provide shelter or housing, and are essentially tapped into only as a last resort when all other sources of help are unavailable or are depleted. Thus, the common statement "They are on welfare" translates to mean "They are poor." The narrow view also reflects the idea that the middle and upper classes do not need social welfare because they are able to provide for themselves, their families, and, if necessary, their friends (see Chapter 1, Activity Box 1.1).

How can there be such differing perspectives of social policy and the resulting social welfare system? Is it possible to determine which viewpoint is correct?

COMPETING SIDES IN THE UNITED STATES— RESIDUAL AND INSTITUTIONAL SOCIAL WELFARE

Social welfare policies are outgrowths of values, beliefs, and principles, and they vary in their commitments and range of services. For example, the primary public assistance program targeting the poor, Temporary Assistance to Needy Families (TANF), is time limited and does not include full, comprehensive services. Social Security Retirement benefits, on the other hand, provide a monthly retirement income based on the worker's lifelong financial contributions through payroll deductions. TANF reflects the centuries-old belief that the poor are the cause of their life situation and public assistance only reinforces their dependence on others. Conversely, retirees contributed to the greater good through their payroll taxes, supported society by working and purchasing goods, and, as a result, are able to make a just claim for retirement benefits.

The dichotomy of social welfare and related benefits between the poor and nonpoor is best conceptualized in the classic work *Industrial Society and Social Welfare* (Wilensky & Leabaux,1965), which examines a basic question: Is social welfare a matter of giving assistance only in emergencies, or is it a frontline activity that society provides all its people? Their analysis developed two contrasting concepts of social welfare—*residual* and *institutional*—that continue to frame and influence social welfare discussions in the 21st century.

Residual Welfare

Residual welfare characterizes social welfare in narrow terms with its focus limited to programs and services targeting the poor. Characteristics of residual programs include the following: an inherent negative stigma for the individual participant; services are time limited, means tested, and emergency based; and programs are generally available when all other forms of support are unavailable. Guided by this conception of welfare, residual structured programs come into play only when all other personal self-help or support systems prove to be inadequate. Programs such as TANF, Supplemental Nutritional Assistance Program (SNAP), Supplemental Security Income (SSI), General Assistance (GA), and Medicaid reflect the residual description.

The residual conception of social welfare rests on the long-held notion of rugged individualism that each person is responsible for himself and his family and the government intervenes only in times of crisis or emergency. Social services are made available to people who meet certain defined criteria through an eligibility procedure that is referred to as means testing. This residual eligibility process requires the individual show that she does not have the financial ability, for example, the means, to meet her specific needs. A residual program typically mandates "recertification" or reapplication for continued program participation; the recertification typically occurs within a 3- to 6-month time frame. The recertification process is designed primarily to ensure that clients are still unable to meet their needs through private or personal sources.

People receiving residual services are generally viewed as being different from people who are "not on welfare." They are often characterized as failures, who are lazy, lacking morals, and inherently dishonest. They are often accused of making bad decisions and of needing constant monitoring because of their untrustworthiness. In short, people in residual programs carry a stigma.

Institutional Welfare

Wilensky and Lebeaux (1965) second concept of social welfare is referred to as *institutional welfare*. This is a far more encompassing perspective compared to the residual definition by broadening the description of welfare to include an array of services that support all people. Institutional welfare builds on the principle that a community shoulders an obligation to assist people because their personal or group social problems are viewed as part of life in a modern society with services going beyond an immediate, short-term basic need response and extend supports to all facets of day-to-day life. Programs and services are available in a manner that stresses both prevention and rehabilitation services.

Eligibility in an institutional program is universal (available to all people), no stigmas are attached to the program, and services are viewed as normal, regular activities in society. Institutional programs are widely accepted in society to the point that most are not viewed as social welfare programs. Social insurance programs such as Social Security Retirement or Survivors Benefits, veterans programs, public education, food and drug regulations, and Medicare are institutional by nature.

Activity Box 2.1

In recent years people throughout the United States experienced many types of disasters, some natural and some human-made. As is often the case following a disaster, the federal government, a variety of nonprofit organizations, and faith-based groups stepped in to provide emergency relief services. Consider each of the following incidents (do a Web search to learn more details of each) and answer the following questions:

1. Were the services provided after the incident "social welfare services"?
2. How would you classify the services as residual or institutional?
3. Do you believe a time limit on the length of services should have been imposed. If so, why; if not, why not?
4. Do you believe the victims of one incident are more deserving of services than others?
5. You have funding to provide services in only three of the listed events. Which three would you fund? What is your rationale for funding one over another?
   - Hurricane Katrina, a category 5 hurricane in August 2005, cost over $100 billion in damages and killed 1,836 people.
   - The September 11, 2001, terrorism airplane attacks in the United States killed 2,977 persons and 19 hijackers.
   - In June 2013, the Black Forest Fire, near Colorado Springs, CO, claimed 486 homes, causing damage valued at slightly more than $85 million; 38,000 persons were evacuated, approximately 14,280 acres burned, and the death toll now stands at two.
   - Upper Big Branch Mine-South, Performance Coal Company, April 2010, explosion of gas or dust resulted in 29 fatalities.
   - In December, 2015, over a five-day period nearly 40 tornadoes, including an EF4 that tracked through parts of Tennessee and Mississippi, caused major damage and killed nine people. A high-end EF3 caused major damage and killed two persons, and an EF2 killed two people while another EF3 destroyed many structures in a small Tennessee community. The Dallas–Fort Worth metroplex was severely impacted when an EF4 devastated parts of the area while killing nine people. An EF3 destroyed many homes, while an EF2 killed two people. An EF1 killed caused a fatality.
   - In April 2010, an oil drilling rig, Deepwater Horizon, exploded off the coast of Louisiana, spilling nearly 200,000 gallons of oil each day.
   - A winter storm in January 2014 caused widespread damage across numerous Midwest, Southeast, and Northeastern states, with $2.2 million in damages and 16 fatalities.
   - Multiple bombs exploded in April 2015 near the finish line of the Boston Marathon. Three people were killed, including an 8-year-old

> boy, while an estimated 264 persons were injured and treated at 27 area hospitals.
> - In 2016, water in Hoosick Falls, NY, was found to be contaminated with perfluorooctanoic acid (PFOA), a chemical that has been linked to kidney and testicular cancer as well as other health issues.
> - A fire in Yonkers, NY, in a suspected crack house spread quickly to more than a dozen buildings in a densely settled square block here, killing two people, critically injuring three others, and leaving 191 persons homeless.

Beyond Residual and Institutional—Broadening the Scope of Social Welfare Policy

The residual and institutional conception of social welfare creates a dichotomous model with programs falling into one of the two categories. Yet a cautionary note is in order—not all programs and services easily fit into a residual or institutional category; some programs include both institutional and residual attributes. British social researcher Richard Titmus (1965) argued that social welfare was much more than aid to the poor and, in fact, represented a broad system of support for the middle and upper classes. The Titmuss model of social welfare includes three separate but very distinct pieces:

- *Fiscal welfare*: Tax benefits and supports for the middle and upper classes
- *Corporate welfare*: Tax benefits and supports for businesses
- *Public welfare*: Assistance to the poor

Social work educator Mimi Abramowitz (1983) applied the Titmus model to American social welfare and concluded that a *shadow welfare state* for the wealthy and the middle class parallels the social service system that is in place for the poor. Both systems provide direct benefits to individuals in order that they have the possibility to live fuller lives. Abramowitz concludes that the poor and nonpoor, that is, all people, benefit from government programs and tax laws that raise their disposable income. In other words, were it not for direct government support—whether through SNAP, a child care tax credit, or home mortgage income tax deductions—people would have fewer dollars to spend and/or the ability to support themselves and their families (See Activity Box 2.1).

This alternative model of welfare, that welfare supports all people not just the poor, reflects the premise that all public and private social services are institutional in nature. Welfare, no matter its form, provides a subsidy to an individual and his or her family that directly benefits the person, which in turn provides direct and indirect benefits to the broader community. So just how does this work?

Let us examine what takes place each year by April 15—tax day in the United States. As people prepare their individual and joint tax filings, they look for ways to reduce their tax bill. A common practice is the deduction of the interest paid on a home loan. While reducing one's tax liability, this tax deduction also encourages people to buy homes. Obviously, the homeowner is the initial beneficiary of the federal tax policy by reducing their federal tax liability. A second beneficiary of the home loan interest tax deduction is the housing building industry, including individual contractors, construction companies, and suppliers of building materials. As more homes are built, more workers are hired to build the homes; in turn, more construction supplies are needed to build the homes, which creates additional work opportunities in the home building supply industry; and the cycle continues. The interest tax deduction is a direct benefit to the homeowner, even though it lowers the federal government's revenues. Yet the initial loss in tax revenue is theoretically replaced by an expanding home construction industry. In other words, the government is subsidizing the individual homeowner for the greater good. Yet this tax deduction is not viewed by the public as a "welfare benefit."

Now let's examine the *Supplemental Nutrition Assistance Program (SNAP)*, which is commonly thought of as a "welfare program." SNAP assists low-income people in buying certain foods and is provided through an electronic benefit transfer (EBT) account. The EBT card is a debit card that is swiped through a point-of-sale terminal in a supermarket's checkout lane with food cost subtracted from the amount of money in the EBT account. The EBT card can be used to buy groceries or plants and seeds to grow food, but it cannot be used to purchase items such as clothes, alcohol, food items that can be eaten in the store, cigarettes, soaps, paper products, household supplies, and grooming items such as toothpaste and cosmetics. SNAP also does not pay sales tax on items bought with SNAP benefits.

SNAP directly helps low-income persons as well as families, especially during periods of unemployment or a family crisis. SNAP also directly influences the broader community. The Center on Budget and Policy Priorities asserts, "SNAP benefits are one of the fastest, most effective forms of economic stimulus because they get money into the economy quickly" (Center on Budget and Policy Priorities, March 24, 2016). According to the Center, low-income persons spend their available dollars on their basic needs such as housing, food, and transportation. According to a 2012 Congressional Budget Office report, SNAP beneficiaries "tend to increase their total spending on food . . . (while freeing) up resources that people can use to purchase other items and services" (Congressional Budget Office, 2012, p. 2). The 2013 White House report *Supporting Families, Strengthening Communities: The Economic Importance of Nutrition Assistance* stated that SNAP offers two significant benefits beyond direct support for low-income individuals and families. First, the White House report noted that SNAP is a significant cost-effective method for stimulating economic growth and increasing the availability of jobs during a weak economy; and, second, every SNAP dollar ($1.00) generates about $1.80 in broader economic opportunities (Executive Office of the President, 2013, p. 3).

As with the previous example describing the relationship between the home interest deduction and the housing industry, there is a direct connection between SNAP purchases and the farm-to-market industry. SNAP recipients directly purchase food, which in turn supports local supermarkets and grocery stores; SNAP ensures that farmers' products are purchased by food wholesale companies, which then prepare the foods and transport them to the various markets around the country. A grocery store encompasses a complex mix of technologies to ensure the food products remain fresh, and these various refrigeration and irrigation systems require skilled specialists to ensure they are working correctly. Through this farm-to-market cycle, a variety of business are impacted and jobs created, salaries paid, and, in effect, an entire industry becomes an indirect beneficiary of the SNAP program. As with the SNAP recipient, grocery store employees and farmers are also "welfare recipients."

Be it a specific federal or state tax deduction or direct cash or an in-kind voucher from a federal program, the Titmus (1965) and Abramowitz (1983) perspectives support the idea that everyone is on welfare in some form or fashion (see Activity Box 2.2).

Activity Box 2.2

To what extent are the following items "welfare programs"? Why do you consider them welfare services, or why do you feel they are not welfare services? Would your family and friends think these activities are social welfare activities, similar to SNAP or TANF?

- The college student who receives a differentiated, subsidized in-state tuition compared to a nonstate resident
- The local library that loans out books, offers a sitting area to read magazines or daily newspapers, or provides free wi-fi use
- The local park where anyone can have a picnic or sit on a hillside without being charged a usage fee
- A 24-hour, toll-free suicide hotline
- The fire department that responds to a house fire
- A local "aging in place" program that brings seniors to a local community room on a weekly basis for coffee conversation with no fees charged
- Towns that offer free auto or motorcycle parking to all people, residents and nonresidents alike
- A local town dump that charges individuals $2.50 to drop off one bag of garbage ($5.00 for two and so on); residents over age 65 pay $7.50 per year for a pass that allows them to drop 104 bags at the dump (an average of two per week)
- Public roads that are maintained throughout the year, with potholes filled during the summer and snow plowed during the winter.

PUBLIC AND PRIVATE SOCIAL WELFARE
STRUCTURES IN THE UNITED STATES

In general, American social welfare policies are sponsored by the governmental public social agencies or private organizations (see Figure 2.1). *Public social welfare,* also referred to as *public policy,* denotes legislation that is introduced to a legislative body, passed by that group, and signed into law. Public social welfare policy is enacted at the local, state, or federal level of government. *Private social welfare policy* is organized and sponsored by both nonprofit and for-profit social service agencies, which are also referred to as *nongovernmental organizations* (NGOs) in the broader global community. A local, state, or national nonprofit/NGO develops its own policy proposal, which in turn is reviewed and approved by the organization's board of directors.

Figure 2.1 illustrates the American public and private social welfare system. The model reflects the residual and institutional dichotomy with policies and resulting programs targeting the so-called worthy poor (e.g., orphans, widows, handicapped, frail elderly), nonpoor (e.g., individuals who worked and saved money for personal needs), and the unworthy poor (e.g., able-bodied workers, offenders, single parents, homeless persons, seniors without savings). The labeling of these classes of traditional welfare recipients can be traced back to the late 16th- and early 17th-century Elizabethan Poor Laws (Hansan, 2011).

Each level of government, through its respective constitution, defines its areas of responsibility and creates its own set of rules and regulations for its own sphere of responsibility. The long-standing principle defining the relationship and responsibilities between the federal, state, and local governments is attributed to the 10th Amendment of the US Constitution that identifies specific responsibilities of the federal government; other powers not specified or prohibited by the Constitution are the responsibility of the states (National Governors Association, 2015).

Local government typically includes two layers: (1) *county* (also referred to as *boroughs* in Alaska and *parishes* in Louisiana) and *municipality,* and (2) *cities* and/or *towns.* In 20 states, counties are divided into *townships* (US Census, n.d.). Counties and municipalities generally are responsible for parks and recreation services, police and fire departments, housing services, emergency medical services, municipal courts, public transportation services, and public works such as street maintenance, sewers, snow removal, and signage (The White House, n.d.).

Social Security retirement, for example, falls under the federal government's responsibility. The US Congress establishes rules and regulations governing Social Security retirement with services provided through the federal Social Security Administration. As a federal program, the rules apply equally across the country. For example, a 66-year-old retiree in Maine is subject to the identical rules and treated the same as a 66-year-old retiree in Alaska.

On the other hand, Child Protective Services (CPS) is governed by a series of federal laws such as the Child Abuse Prevention and Treatment Act; Indian

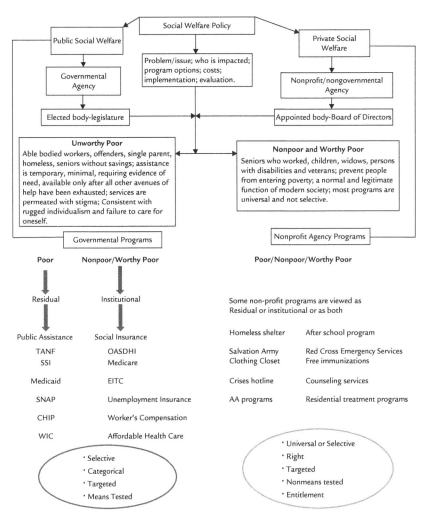

Figure 2.1.
American social welfare, public and private systems.

Child Welfare Act; Multi-Ethnic Placement Act; Adoption and Safe Families Act; Section 504 of the Rehabilitation Act of 1973; and Title II of the Americans with Disabilities Act of 1990, among others. These federal laws create a large, flexible model for CPS initiatives as each state bears responsibility for developing explicit policies and procedures regarding the protection of children. The state CPS protocols are developed by a state's legislature with the resulting program(s) operated directly by a state-based children and family department or contracted to a nonprofit social services organization. Not surprisingly, the rules, procedures, and operational structures for state-based child protection programs reflect a wide variety of approaches and models.

Theoretically, this multilevel model of public welfare differentiated responsibility between the federal, state, and local governments should result in clarity in purpose, coordination of work, and result in minimal duplication or redundancy of efforts. Although an ideal, the alleged clarity of responsibilities between and among the levels of government hardly reflects the reality. It is commonplace for one level of government to argue that a certain social problem does not fall into its sphere of responsibility, whereas another level of government states that it does not have the resources to address a certain issue.

Tensions Between Federal, State, and Local Governments

History shows that there has been a tension between the various levels of government as each challenges the other's authority regarding any number of social issues. In 1963, the Alabama governor, George C. Wallace, literally blocked the door at the University of Alabama's enrollment office to stop African American students from registering for classes in the University; this was in direct violation of the 1954 US Supreme Court decision *Brown v. Board of Education,* which found segregation unconstitutional. Wallace argued that education and its policies was a state's right, whereas the federal government forthrightly stated such actions violated federal law. Federal troops were sent to the University to force its desegregation and its compliance with federal laws (History, n.d.).

In 2012, Colorado became the first state to legalize the possession of small amounts of marijuana for recreational use, and other states soon followed with their own legalization efforts. Yet federal law and the emerging state laws were in conflict with each other, ranging from banks not being able to provide financial services to state-licensed business to the federal government not pressing federal charges against state- officials responsible for licensing marijuana retailers. In September 2013, US Senator Patrick Leahy convened the Senate Judiciary Committee to hold hearings on the growing number of federal–state conflicts over the use of marijuana.

More recently, immigration laws became a flashpoint between many states and the federal government. Based on the 1952 Nationality Act and the 1986 Immigration Reform and Control Act, the US Congress is responsible for establishing immigration rules and reforms, whereas the White House is in control of enforcing the resulting immigration laws. Numerous states have passed laws that severely restrict immigration, including challenging the US Constitution's 14th Amendment that guarantees US citizenship to a person who is born in the United States (FindLaw, n.d.). Other challenges include proof of citizen or legal residence, checking a person's immigration status based on suspicions (e.g., racial profiling), and voter identification laws. The question at hand: Should people be treated differently based on where they live or how they look; or should all people, no matter where they live in the United States, be treated the same?

States challenging the federal government's overreach of power is common. Between 2008 and 2016, the state of Texas sued the federal government on 40 separate occasions on matters ranging from women's health care to voter identification laws to environmental mandates (Aaronson et al., 2013; Satija, McCrimmon, & Aaronson, 2016). In 2015, the state of Ohio along with several of its state universities and one of its counties, sued the federal government over the legality of a tax levied in the Affordable Care Act, commonly called Obamacare (Koff, 2015). Michigan, Virginia, California, and Alaska enacted laws nullifying a measure in the National Defense Authorization Act that gives the federal government the power to indefinitely detain individuals without due process (Chumley, 2014). Kansas passed the Second Amendment Protection Act in 2013, a law that exempts Kansas guns made in Kansas and not having left the state from all federal gun control laws (Celock, 2013). All of these actions are in direct contradiction to federal laws.

Tensions Among Private Social Service Agencies

Private nonprofit social service agencies, typically referred to as a 501(c)(3), are organizations that provide an array of services to promote the public good. Such organizations include, among others, charitable services, faith-based social service agencies, and organizations that work to educate the public on subjects such as abuse and neglect of children and domestic violence (IRS, 2016). Nursing homes, parent–teacher associations, charitable hospitals, homeless shelters, alumni associations, schools, chapters of the Red Cross or Salvation Army, boys and girls clubs, and faith-based organizations such as Jewish Family Services and Catholic Social Services are examples of 501(c)(3) organizations.

Nonprofit social service agencies are often thought to be free from the dogmas of political ideologies. Yet the private nonprofit social welfare system has become increasingly subject to political pressures. Salamon (2012) wrote that "conservative critics, concerned about what they see as an unholy alliance between the once-independent nonprofit sector and the state, have called for a return to the sector's supposed purely voluntary roots. Liberal critics have bewailed the sector's departure from a more socially activist past and its surrender to professionalism" (p. ix) with a "struggle is under way at the present time for the 'soul' of America's nonprofit social services" (p. 3).

In fact, many nonprofit social services agencies adopt an advocacy agenda on behalf of their clients. Expanding health care, ending homelessness, confronting the opioid epidemic, challenging climate change, understanding the Black Lives Matter movement, ending sex trafficking, promoting civil rights, and helping resolve veterans' issues are among the many social problems that various private, nonprofit social service agencies have taken on in a forceful political manner. How these issues are confronted and resolved is directly tied to an organization's mission, values, and interpretation of social justice. An agency's belief system is further reinforced by a larger *groupthink* created and sustained by the organization's staff, its board of directors, donors, and other key stakeholders who all subscribe to similar views and, as a result, further solidify the agency's positions. It is common for one agency's views of an issue to be diametrically opposite from another agency. And, it is at this intersection of conflicting values, beliefs, and resulting programs that politics takes precedence over critical thinking, evidence-based practice.

Planned Parenthood, a focal point of intense philosophical conflict since it was organized in the early 20th century, illustrates the intensity that a social welfare program experiences due to its mission, philosophy, and services. Planned Parenthood, which operates more than 600 health centers across the United States, is one of the nation's leading health care providers for women (Planned Parenthood, 2016b). Nearly 97% of the agency's services include, among other services, pap tests, breast exams, testing and treatments for sexually transmitted diseases, and educational and outreach programs to young people and adults; about 3% of Planned Parenthood health services involve abortion services (Planned Parenthood, 2016b). Even while abortion procedures involve a small amount of the agency's work, Planned Parenthood is under constant political attacks from the conservative wing in state legislatures across the country as well as in the US Congress; clinics have been attacked, burned, and bombed while physicians and patients have been shot and killed (Planned Parenthood, 2016a).

SOCIAL WORK AND POLITICS—MANEUVERING IN A PARTISAN ENVIRONMENT

Politics are difficult, controversial, challenging, and often times disingenuous, but they are a central component that directly influences social work practice and the form and structures of social welfare policies. Social work educator Karen Haynes and practitioner Jim Mickelson (2010) were even more blunt when characterizing all social work practice as "political".

Politics and the political arena are not viewed with the greatest of support. In December 2016, the Gallup Poll found that only 18% of the public approved of the US Congress and this had dropped from 20% in September 2016 (Gallup, 2017). This low approval rating is not a one-time occurrence; the last time the approval rating for Congress was over 30% was in August 2009, and the last time their approval rating was higher than 50% was in August 2003 (Gallup, 2017). In 2013, only 34% of the American public approved of the job Democrats were doing, whereas 26% felt the same about Republicans in Congress (Jones, 2013); in 2014, the approval rating for Congress was 14% (Riffkin, 2014); in September 2015, the vast majority of people believed that the US Congress was "out of touch" (79%) and "corrupt" (52%) (Dugan, 2015); and in spring 2016, Congress's approval rating was only 17% (McCarthy, 2016). These low approval ratings are not an aberration of recent events but reflect a long-standing disapproval of the US Congress (see Table 2.2).

Table 2.2. APPROVAL RATING OF THE US CONGRESS, 1990–2016

Decade	Approve	Disapprove	No Opinion
2011–2016	15.25	81.28	4.90
2000–2010	33.84	58.34	7.80
1990–1999	32.23	58.81	8.85
1980–1989	35.86	45.86	18.29
1974–1979	35.13	50.20	21.33

Notes: Gallup began conducting monthly surveys of the US Congress in 2001; from 1990 to 2001 the number of months surveyed varied from year to year from a low of one (1992) to eleven months surveyed. Between 1980 and 1989, Gallup conducted seven total surveys. Between 1974 and 1979, Gallup conducted 15 surveys. The first Gallup survey of Congress was taken in April 1974.

Source: Gallup (2017). Congress and the public. Retrieved from http://www.gallup.com/poll/1600/Congress-Public.aspx on January 6, 2017.

Given such consistently low approval numbers over the past decades, it is not surprising that the political arena has been the focal point and brunt of many jokes and critics. For example, one definition of *politics* captures a dominate attitude toward this work:

> Politics is rooted in the Greek tradition of governance. Individuals would gather at the Agora, a central meeting place, to debate issues and seek solutions for the greater good. From this grew the concept of politics: *polis*—a gathering of many; and *tics*—blood sucking insects.

A little harsh, yes, but the political arena is generally not held in high regard by the American public. The political world in the 21st century reflects extreme *partisanship*—individual, group, and organization profess a biased, emotional allegiance to a particular issue or cause. Such partisanship results in political gridlock with little accomplished. Social workers, both individuals and the professional associations, must be able to navigate this polarized system of governance if the profession wants to impact public policy in a proactive manner. Adopting a rigid, nonnegotiable partisan stance only contributes to the ongoing governmental stalemate.

Social workers in private settings are not immune from the competing political visions and polarizations found in the public arenas. Agency politics can be just as brutal and hurtful as governmental politics; the agency setting is typically small, and people know each other in special ways as colleagues often become close friends over time. But being criticized by one's colleagues or agency's key stakeholders for advocating a position can be taken as a personal rebuke.

An important key for success in policy practice is the willingness to compromise. Yes, this means giving up part of a position but it also results in getting something that is needed and not yet available. Compromise is a direct result of negotiation and the ability to be flexible in achieving a desired end. It is rare that an initial policy proposal will be fully enacted, word for word.

Though to be clear—there are times when a position is nonnegotiable and the social worker must remain firm and adamant in her or his stance. Issues around civil rights, human equality, and fairness include core social work principles, and these are never negotiable. There has been an escalation in attacks around immigration, race, gender identity, and religious freedom that are front and center in the public debates since 2000. Sadly, the debates sometimes turn violent with people needlessly losing their lives—Orlando GLBT nightclub shootings in June 2016; the December 2015 San Bernardino terrorist attack at a recreation center; the Emanuel AME Church murders in June 2015.

But not all social justice issues are clear cut as most social welfare policy issues reside in a gray area. For example, there is general agreement that the minimum wage should be fair and not take advantage of people in favor of a cheap workforce. In 2016, political support for a minimum wage of $15.00 per hour gained national momentum (Greenhouse, 2016). Yet the federal minimum wage in January 2017 remained at $7.25 per hour. Minimum wage rates varied across the country by states and even in some cities in the same state (see Table 2.3).

The idea that all people should receive a fair, living wage reflects the social work value base. But just what that amount should be is difficult to establish. Should a minimum wage be flexible and based on an actual cost-of-living factor for a specific area? In other words, is it more costly to live in New York City or Waco, Texas? Should a minimum wage reflect such differences?

Once a minimum or living wage is identified, should it go into effect immediately or be implemented over a period of time? Would the social work advocate be doing harm by steadfastly arguing that the wage should go from, for example, the current federal minimum wage of $7.25 to the proposed $15.00 per hour on a certain date? What if the opponents argued that its implementation should be over a 2- to 3-year period? And, what if in this scenario, neither side had the majority votes necessary to pass the bill, thus leaving the minimum wage at $7.25 per hour?

Instead of advocating for an nationwide increase in minimum wage, should activists argue for a living wage or a prevailing wage structure? A living wage is calculated on the income needed to meet basic needs, including food, shelter, and health care, and it accounts for unique cost-of-living variables such as region or area where a person resides, the employee's marital status, number of children, debt, and other cost-of-living considerations.

How does the NASW Code of Ethics, as well as ethic statements of other social work membership associations, inform and guide its members in this situation? Is it best to achieve the desired end over time versus losing it entirely? Is it best to remain steadfast in one's values and beliefs and be nonnegotiable? Or should the advocate adopt an entirely new path and argue for a living wage?

Table 2.3. MINIMUM WAGE BY STATE, AS OF JANUARY 1, 2017

Alabama	**$7.25 (Federal Minimum Wage)**
Alaska	**$9.75* (Indexed Annual Increases will begin on January 1, 2017)**
Arizona	**$10.00* ($10.00 to $12.00 in $0.50 Indexed Annual Increases between 1/1/2017 and 1/1/2020)**
Arkansas	**$8.50**
California	– $10.50 ($11.00 to $15.00 in $1.00 Indexed Annual Increases between 1/1/2018 and 1/1/2022)
	– Emeryville: $12.25 for small businesses with 55 employees, $14.44 companies with more than 55 employers
	– Los Angeles: $10.50 effective July 2016 with increases each year until it reaches $15.00 in 2020
	– Oakland: $12.25
	– Richmond: $12.30, and $13 in 2018 (with exceptions based on employer)
	– San Diego: $11.50
	– San Francisco: $14.00 effective July 2017, $15.00 effective July 2018
	– San Jose: $10.30
Colorado	**$9.30* ($9.30 to $12.00 in $0.90 Indexed Annual Increases between 1/1/2018 and 1/1/2020) Connecticut: $10.10**
Delaware	**$8.25**
District of Columbia	$11.50 ($0.75 Indexed Annual Increases will begin on January 1, 2017)
Florida	**$8.05***
Georgia	$5.15 (if covered by Fair Labor Standards—$7.25)
Hawaii	**$9.25, $10.10 in 2018**
Idaho	**$7.25**
Illinois	$8.25—Chicago $11.00 July 2017, $12.00 July 2018, $13.00 July 2019
Indiana	**$7.25**
Iowa	**$7.25**
Kansas	**$7.25**
Kentucky	**$7.25**
	– Louisville: $9.00 July 2017
	– Kentucky State Workers $10.10
Louisiana	**$7.25 (Federal Minimum Wage)**
Maine	$9.00 ($10.00 to $12.00 in $0.50 Indexed Annual Increases between 1/1/2017 and 1/1/2020)
Maryland	$9.25 July 2017, $10.10 July 2018
Massachusetts	$11.00 ($3.75 for tipped employees), $16.50 per hour for working on a Sunday
Michigan	$8.90, $9.25 by January 2018
Minnesota	Large employers are required to pay workers $9.50/hour and small employers $7.75 (Indexed Annual Increases will begin on January 1, 2018)
Missouri	$7.65 *
	– St. Louis: $10, $11 by January 2018

(continued)

Table 2.3. CONTINUED

Mississippi	$7.25 (Federal Minimum Wage)
Montana	$8.05 * Except $4.00 for businesses with gross annual sales of $110,000 or less
Nevada	$7.25 for employees who receive qualifying health benefits, $8.25 for employees who do not receive qualifying health benefits.*
Nebraska	$9.00
New Hampshire	$7.25 (Federal Minimum Wage, as State Minimum Wage was repealed in 2011)
New Jersey	$8.38*
New Mexico	**$7.50** – Albuquerque: $8.75 ($7.75 with benefits)
New York	$11.00 by 12/31/2016, $13.00 by 12/31/2017, $15 by 12/31/2016 ($9.75 for fast food workers in NYS and $10.50 for fast food workers in New York City, with limitations)
North Carolina	$7.25
North Dakota	**$7.25**
Ohio:	$8.10* ($7:25 for employers grossing $283,000 or less)
Oklahoma	**$7.25**
Oregon	$9.75 (or higher based on county density) (From $10.25 to $13.50 in $0.50 intervals from 7/1/2017 to 7/1/2022)
Pennsylvania	$7.25
Puerto Rico	$7.25
Rhode Island	$9.60
South Carolina	$7.25 (Federal Minimum Wage)
South Dakota	$8.55*
Tennessee	**$7.25 (Federal Minimum Wage)**
Texas	$7.25
Utah	$7.25
Vermont:	**$10.00, $10.50 by January 1, 2018 ***
Virgin Islands	$7.25
Virginia	$7.25
Washington:	$11.00* (From $11.00 to $13.50 in $0.50 intervals from 1/1/2017 to 1/2/2020)—Seattle: $15 (for businesses over 500 employees in 2017 and for all businesses by 2021)
West Virginia	**$8.75**
Wisconsin	$7.25
Wyoming	$7.25

Notes: States indicated by an asterisk (*) adjust their rate annually based on the cost of living. In those cases, the figure listed is an estimate pending that adjustment. In addition, some cities, counties, state governments, and companies have higher minimum wage rates than the state minimum.

Source: 2017 state and federal minim wage rates. Retrieved from https://www.thebalance.com/2017-federal-state-minimum-wage-rates-2061043 on January 3,2017.

A FEW FINAL THOUGHTS

Social policy and social welfare policy are products of the political world. Every policy is a public statement that reflects a community's dominant belief and value system. The political party that controls of majority votes typically will prevail. The Democrats, for example, held the majority of votes in the US House of Representatives and the US Senate in 2009 and 2010; not one Republican in either chamber voted to support the Affordable Care Act (ACA) (i.e., Obamacare). By February 2016, the Republican-led Congress voted 62 times to repeal parts or all of the ACA (Benen, 2016). And one of the early acts of newly elected President Donald Trump in January 2017 was to issue an Executive Order to begin the repeal the Affordable Care Act. The ongoing battle surrounding the ACA is but one example of many that demonstrates the power of a majority and the intense partisanship in the current arena.

A social worker engaged in policy practice can adopt a position of "it's my way or the highway" or, alternatively, seek common ground with others. Finding and enacting points of agreements are achieved through negotiation and compromise. Building partnerships potentially results in long-term collaborations on a variety of issues. Achieving a desired end might not happen in the near future, but it does have a chance of eventually being realized if political rather than enemies are created.

The task for the policy practitioner is to find common ground with others who see things differently. Can it be done? Yes. Should it be done? Well, in most circumstance, yes. How do we know when it should be done? There is no clear answer because policy practice lives in a gray world.

REFERENCES

Aaronson, B., Ura, A., Chang, C., Hasson, B., & Wiseman, T. (2013, July 17). Interactive: Texas vs. the federal government. *The Texas Tribune*. Retrieved from https://www.texas-tribune.org/library/about/texas-versus-federal-government-lawsuits-interactive/#dodd_frank-multi_state-challenge on May 18, 2016.

Abramowitz, M. (1983). Everyone is on welfare: "The role of redistribution in social policy" revisited. *Social Work, 28*(6), 440–445.

Baker, R. (1995). *The social work dictionary* (3rd ed.). Washington, DC: National Association of Social Workers.

Benen, S. (2016, February 2). On groundhog day, republicans seek to repeal Obamacare. MSNBC. Retrieved from http://www.msnbc.com/rachel-maddow-show/groundhog-day-republicans-vote-repeal-obamacare on June 3, 2016.

Celock, J. (2013, April 17). Kansas governor signs strictest "second amendment protection" law in the nation. *The Huffington Post*. Retrieved from http://www.huffingtonpost.com/2013/04/17/kansas-gun-bill_n_3103488.html on June 15, 2016.

Center on Budget and Policy Priorities. (2016, March 24). Policy basics: Introduction to the supplemental nutrition assistance program (SNAP). Retrieved from http://www.cbpp.org/research/policy-basics-introduction-to-the-supplemental-nutrition-assistance-program-snap on November 8, 2016.

Chumley, C. (2014, March 1). Frustrated states fight federal overreach. *Newsmax*. Retrieved from http://www.newsmax.com/Newsfront/federal-government-overreach-obamacare/2014/03/01/id/555476/ on June 14, 2016.

Congressional Budget Office. (2012, April 19). The supplemental nutrition assistance program. Retrieved from https://www.cbo.gov/publication/43173 on November 8, 2016.

DiNitto, D., & Johnson, D. (2012). *Essentials of social welfare, politics and public policy.* Upper Saddle River, NJ: Pearson Education, Inc.

Dugan, A. (2015, September 28). Majority of Americans see Congress out of touch, corrupt. Retrieved from http://www.gallup.com/poll/185918/majority-americans-congress-touch-corrupt.aspx?g_source=COngress&g_medium=search&g_campaign=tiles on March 18, 2016.

Executive Office of the President. (November 2013). *Supporting families, strengthening communities: the economic importance of nutrition assistance.* Washington, DC: The White House. Retrieved from http: //r.search.yahoo.com/_ylt=AwrEWDaKx2tYEwcAHTtXNyoA;_ylu=X3oDMTEyYzJtbmtlBGNvbG8DYmYxBHBvcwMxBHZ0aWQDQjMwMDlfM QRzZWMDc3I-/RV=2/RE=1483487243/RO=10/RU=http%3a%2f%2fwww.white-house.gov%2fsites%2fdefault%2ffiles%2fdocs%2fsnap_report_-_final.pdf/RK=0/RS=0uVqgU2pdmX0rIoR3Goa3h32zWc- on November 8, 2016.

FindLaw. (n.d.). Federal vs. state immigration laws. Retrieved from http://immigration.find-law.com/immigration-laws-and-resources/federal-vs-state-immigration-laws.html on June 16, 2016.

Gallup. (2017). Congress and the public. Retrieved from http://www.gallup.com/poll/1600/Congress-Public.aspx on January 3, 2017.

Gilbert, N., & Terrell, P. (2013). *Dimensions of social welfare policy* (8th ed.). Boston, MA: Pearson.

Greenhouse, S. (2016, April 1). How the $15 minimum wage went from laughable to viable. *New York Times*. Retrieved from http://www.nytimes.com/2016/04/03/sunday-review/how-the-15-minimum-wage-went-from-laughable-to-viable.html?_r=0 on March 18, 2016.

Hansan, J. E. (2011). Poor relief in early America. Retrieved from http://www.socialwelfarehis-tory.com/programs/poor-relief/ on March 18, 2016.

Haynes, K., & Mickelson, J. (2010). *Affecting change: Social workers in the political arena* (7th ed.). Upper Saddle River, NJ: Allyn & Bacon.

History. (n.d.). This date in history, 1963 university of Alabama is desegregated. Retrieved from http://www.history.com/this-day-in-history/university-of-alabama-desegregated on June 16, 2016.

IRS. (2016, April 15). Exemption requirements—501 (c)(3). Retrieved from https://www.irs.gov/charities-non-profits/charitable-organizations/exemption-requirements-section-501-c-3-organizations on June 15, 2016.

Jones, J. (2013, June 26). Americans rate Republicans, Democrats in Congress poorly. Retrieved from http://www.gallup.com/poll/163244/americans-rate-republicans-democrats-congress-poorly.aspx?g_source=COngress&g_medium=search&g_campaign=tiles on March 18, 2016.

Koff, S. (2015, January 26). Ohio, several state universities sue Obama administration over "Obamacare" tax. Retrieved from http://www.cleveland.com/open/index.ssf/2015/01/ohio_several_state_universitie.html on June 14, 2016.

Leahy, P. (2013, August 26). Leahy: SJC will hold hearing on federal and state marijuana laws in september. Retrieved from https://www.leahy.senate.gov/press/leahy-sjc-will-hold-hearing-on-federal-and-state-marijuana-laws-in-september on November 8, 2016.

McCarthy, J. (2016, April 13). U.S. Congress approval rating remains low. Retrieved from http://www.gallup.com/poll/190598/congress-approval-remains-low.aspx?g_source=COngress&g_medium=search&g_campaign=tiles on March 18, 2016.

Midgley, J., & Livermore, M. (2009). *The handbook of social policy.* Thousand Oaks, CA: Sage. Retrieved from http://sk.sagepub.com/reference/the-handbook-of-social-policy-2e/n1.xml on December 8, 2016.

National Governors Association. (2015). Principles for state-federal relations. Retrieved from http://www.nga.org/cms/home/federal-relations/nga-policy-positions/page-ec-policies/col2-content/main-content-list/principles-for-state-federal-rel.html on June 16, 2016.

Planned Parenthood. (2016a). History and successes. Retrieved from https://www.planned-parenthood.org/about-us/who-we-are/history-successes on June 15, 2016.

Planned Parenthood. (2016b). Planned parenthood at a glance. Retrieved from https://www.plannedparenthood.org/about-us/who-we-are/planned-parenthood-at-a-glance on June 15, 2016.

Reisch, M. (2014). *Social policy and social justice.* Thousand Oaks, CA: Sage.

Riffkin, R. (2014, December 15). 2014 U.S. approval of congress remains near all-time low. Retrieved from http://www.gallup.com/poll/180113/2014-approval-congress-remains-near-time-low.aspx?g_source=COngress&g_medium=search&g_campaign=tiles on March 18, 2016.

Salamon, L. (ed). (2012). *The resilient sector: The future of nonprofit America.* Washington, DC: The Brookings Institute.

Satija, N., McCrimmon, R., & Aaronson, B. (2016, May 26). Texas vs. the feds: A look at the lawsuits. *The Texas Tribune.* Retrieved from https://www.texastribune.org/2016/05/26/texas-vs-federal-government/ on June 1, 2016.

Titmus, R. (1965). The role of redistribution in social policy. *Social Security Bulletin,* 28(6), 34–55.

Tropman, J. (1984). *Policy management in the human services.* New York, NY: Columbia University Press.

United States Census. (n.d.). List and structures of governments. Retrieved from https://www.census.gov/govs/go/municipal_township_govs.html on June 18, 2016.

The White House. (n.d.). State and local government. Retrieved from https://www.white-house.gov/1600/state-and-local-government on June 15, 2016.

Wilensky, H., & Lebeaux, C. (1965). *Industrial society and social welfare.* New York, NY: Free Press.

CHAPTER 3

Justice Theory and the Social Work Profession

Is This Fair and Just?

Social justice, in and by itself, is a controversial flashpoint for controversy and hearsay. For example, conservative political commentator Glen Beck said social justice is the "forced redistribution of wealth with a hostility toward individual property rights, under the guise of charity and/or justice. On my radio program, I said if your church is promoting Jeremiah Wright–type 'social or economic justice,' you should run from it or at least get educated on what progressives mean by this" (Jefferson, 2010). There are those who characterize social justice simply as a canard that only results in wasting money that rightfully belongs to those who are taxed. Friedrich Hayek, a leading 20th-century economist and philosopher who, among many honors, was a Nobel Prize recipient in economics in 1974, referred to social justice as a

> mirage . . . (a) will-o'-the-wisp . . . (an) empty formula . . . strictly, necessarily, and entirely empty and meaningless . . . (a phrase that) meant nothing at all . . . has no meaning whatsoever . . . a quasi-religious belief with no content whatsoever . . . (a) primitive . . . anthropomorphism . . . (a) superstition like believing in witches or the philosopher's stone. (Lister, 2011, pp. 1–2)

A very different social justice perspective is set forth by the Center for Economic and Social Justice (2017), which defines social justice as

> a set of universal principles which guide people in judging what is right and what is wrong, no matter what culture and society they live in . . . social institutions, when justly organized, provide . . . access to what is good for the person, both individually and in our associations

with others. Social justice also imposes on each of us a personal responsibility to work with others, at whatever level of the "Common Good" in which we participate, to design and continually perfect our institutions as tools for personal and social development.

Social justice efforts respond to the inequalities that are found throughout the world in day-to-day living. Such inequities include the unfair treatment of a person or groups of people that reduces, hinders, or denies resources and opportunities that others have; or demeaning and hurtful abuse based on cultural differences, personal beliefs, religious affiliation, race/ethnicity, gender/gender identity, sexual orientation, values, nationality, wealth, and/or abilities. Social inequality exists throughout the United States in every region, state, city, town, and village.

Social inequities in the global community are astounding and difficult to fully comprehend or understand. Worldwide,

- 663 million people, 1 in 10 persons, lack access to safe water (World Health Organization, 2015, p. 4);
- 795 million people, or one in nine individuals, suffered from chronic undernourishment in 2014–2016 (Hunger Notes, 2016);
- while down from 1.85 billion people in 1990, in 2013, according to the World Bank (October 2016), 767 million people (about 2.5 times greater than the US population in 2016) lived on less than $1.90 a day;
- UNICEF reports that 14 million children are suffering hardship and trauma from the war in Syria and Iraq, and the head of the United Nations refugee agency has called this the "worst humanitarian crisis of our era" (Cumming-Bruce, 2015); and
- the *New York Times* reported in a January 2017 that the Myanmar military entered villages in northern Rakhine State shooting at random, set houses on fire with rocket launchers, and systematically raped girls and women (Barry, 2017).

The list of human injustices throughout the world is long, wide-ranging, and, sadly, affects every part of the human condition. These social issues reflect the array of situations that profoundly affect, actually limit, the benefits found through social justice. Be it gender identity, age, race and ethnicity, or housing, each is somehow tied to the denial of basic human rights, protections, and assurances that are part of the fabric of social justice. To ignore the connections between social justice and any social issue while proposing a policy or practice strategy intervention essentially is responding to the condition but ignoring the root cause. As such, the cause of the injustice will remain.

SOCIAL JUSTICE AND SOCIAL WORK

Social justice is referenced throughout social work literature and is distinctly embedded in the key documents, positions papers, and fundamental materials among various national and international professional associations. The social work profession has strongly adhered to the belief that social work conceptualizes social justice results in people being treated fairly and justly. Inherent with fair treatment is the belief that universal rights, such as those outlined in the United Nations' *Declaration of Human Rights* and laws of various nations, that is, the US Constitution and Bill of Rights, are strictly followed. Social justice also dictates that all forms of institutional bias, prejudice, and discrimination are unacceptable. A basic guiding question a social worker asks when assessing a social issue or social policy: Is this fair and just?

A review of major social work professional membership associations, both US-based as well as international organizations, finds social justice is a core guiding principle (see Box 3.1). From ethical codes for practice to accreditation standards, various national and international bodies clearly spell out the centrality of social justice in the curricula and resulting practice. Education and practice-specific organizations such as the American-based Council on Social Work Education (CSWE) and the International Association of Schools of Social Work (IASSW) through their respective accreditation protocols direct educators' attention to steadfastly embrace and teach social justice as part of undergraduate and graduate social work programs (International Association of Schools of Social Work, 2004).

Box 3.1

VARIOUS NATIONAL AND INTERNATIONAL SOCIAL JUSTICE STATEMENTS IN SOCIAL WORK

- The NASW Code of Ethics' preamble early on states, "Social workers promote social justice" (National Association of Social Workers, 1999).
- The mission statement of the National Association of Black Social Workers states, "NABSW's vision is guided by the Principles of the Nguzo Saba, which are Unity, Self-determination, Collective Work and Responsibility, Cooperative Economics, Purpose, Creativity, and Faith, and the Seven Cardinal Virtues of Ma'at, which are Right, Truth, Justice, Order, Reciprocity, Balance, and Harmony" (National Association of Black Social Workers, n.d.).
- The International Association of Schools of Social Work and the International Federation of Social Workers include in their Global Standards for Education and Training, "Principles of human rights and social justice are fundamental to social work" (International Association of Schools of Social Work, 2004).
- The Educational Policy and Accreditation Standards for the Council on Social Work Education include in their purpose statement, "the purpose

of social work is actualized through its quest for social and economic justice" (Commission on Accreditation, 2015, p. 4).

- The British Association of Social Workers Code Ethics Principle 2.2 states, "Social workers have a responsibility to promote social justice, in relation to society generally, and in relation to the people with whom they work" (British Association of Social Workers, 2014, p. 9).
- Canadian social work education requires that students "have knowledge and skills to identify negative or inequitable policies and their implications and outcomes, especially for disadvantaged and oppressed groups, and to participate in efforts to change these" (Canadian Association of Social Work, 2014, p. 11).
- The Australian Association of Social Workers Code of Ethics (2010) notes that among the profession's commitment is "promoting policies and practices that achieve a fair allocation of social resources" (p. 8).
- Professionalization of social work in Nigeria will provide the enabling environment to foster the pursuit of social justice, to the attainment of the quality of care of life, and to the development of the full potential of each individual, group, and community in society and improvement in quality of life of the Nigerian citizens, especially the disadvantaged groups (Nigeria Association of Social Workers, 2017).

The roots of social justice in the social work profession are firmly planted in the 19th and 20th centuries, and it is there we find the profession's identification with social justice beginning to form.

- The late 18th-century settlement house movement "focused on the environmental causes of poverty and expanding the working opportunities of the poor. They conducted research, helped establish the juvenile court system, created widows pension programs, promoted legislation prohibiting child labor, and introduced public health reforms and the concept of social insurance" (Tannenubaum & Reisch, 2001, p. 6).
- Social worker and suffragette Janette Rankin was the first woman elected to the US Congress in 1917, three years before the passage of the Constitution's 19th Amendment granting woman the right to vote. An avowed pacifist, Rankin is the only member of Congress to have voted against entry into both World War I and World War II.
- In the 1930s, social worker Frances Perkins, who served as Secretary of Labor during President Franklin Delano Roosevelt's administration, is credited for helping change public laws that created a 40-hour workweek, established workers' compensation, Social Security, and unemployment insurance; and she steadfastly worked to ban child labor. Perkins's advocacy for a universal health program, however, was unsuccessful (Downey, 2010, p. 1).

- Ada Deer, a social worker from Wisconsin, became the first woman to be appointed Assistant Secretary of Indian Affairs, US Department of the Interior; the first Native American woman to run for Congress in Wisconsin; the first native American to lobby Congress successfully to restore tribal rights; and the first chairwoman of her tribe.
- Ronald Dellums, a social worker from California, served in the US Congress from 1970 to 1998 and chaired the Congressional Black Caucus beginning in 1988. Dellums was a key leader in the ongoing effort to reduce military spending and the nuclear arms race while playing a pivotal role in the attempt to cease the United States' support for the apartheid regime in South Africa.

Pages can be devoted to identifying social workers and social work–related organizations who since the mid- to late 18th century have been staunch advocates of social justice. Yet we are getting ahead of ourselves—we need to first understand what the term *social justice* means.

DIFFERING PERSPECTIVES OF SOCIAL JUSTICE

It is fair to say that social justice is synonymous with the social work profession. It is equally fair to say that there is a lack of clarity as to what constitutes social justice. Social justice is much more than passionately arguing a political position or a particular ideology. In fact, it is accurate to conceptualize social justice along a continuum of philosophies ranging from conservative to libertarian to liberal to radical positions. Another way to consider the differences in social justice orientations and beliefs is to recognize that US Presidents Barak Obama, George W. Bush, and Donald Trump each reflects a model of social justice. We can ask a simple question: Do these presidents' individual positions on various social issues differ? The answer, quite obviously, is yes. To think that social justice is unique to a liberal, progressive ideological perspective is simply wrong.

The *Social Work Dictionary* defines social justice as "an ideal condition in which all members of society have the same basic rights, protection, opportunities, obligations, and social benefits" (Baker, 2013). Such conditions that directly result from social justice initiatives might include safe and secure neighborhoods, a living wage, affordable health care for all people, quality public education for children, and fairness in all aspects of life. These conditions, however, reflect only one particular theory of social justice. For example, there are justice theories that suggest a society does not guarantee such benefits to its members; rather, justice reflects a living condition in which there are few, if any, governmental interventions, whereas individual self-reliance and the ability to keep one's own resources is a true benchmark of social justice.

All social policies are extensions of justice theories and reflect particular principles on the human condition. David Miller, a senior research fellow and professor of political theory at Nuffield College, University of Oxford, poses the central question that drives an individual's belief of what constitutes justice:

> What constitutes a fair distribution of rights, resources and opportunities? Is it an equal distribution, in which case an equal distribution of what? . . . Or is it a distribution that gives each person what they deserve, or what they need? Or a distribution that gives everyone an adequate minimum of whatever it is that matters? (Miller, 2005)

Miller focuses on *distributive justice*; that is, how are benefits allocated to a community? Will they be equal or disproportional, or need-based and based on *just desert,* need, or equality? *Just desert* reflects a benefit that an individual gains after participating in an activity. For example, an individual must work for a minimum of 10 years to be eligible for Social Security retirement. *Need* refers to the inability to secure and maintain one or more vital resources such as food, shelter, housing, or health care. *Equality* suggests that every person is entitled to the same resource, no matter who they are or what they did; equality eliminates all forms of discrimination in the distribution of resources. Distributive justice positions are often framed by moral and legal positions, and this most often results in polarizing support or opposition for a particular policy.

Reflecting an individual, group, or organization's values and beliefs, justice theory creates a rationale to support particular policy initiatives and its resulting programs and services. Recognizing and understanding the various, often competing justice theories is essential in creating a successful policy change strategy; such understanding requires, as Morris writes (1987), "to take into account not only its own beliefs and values, but those held by a large number of other non-advocate citizens" (p. 678).

A RANGE OF JUSTICE PHILOSOPHIES— CONTRACTUAL, FEMINIST, LIBERTARIAN, SOCIALIST, AND UTILITARIAN

As has been shown briefly, there are differing social justice theories, each proposing different ways to view social issues and propose social welfare strategies. It is not surprising to find these theories also clothed within a political context. Depending on one's political perspective, there is a corresponding social justice theory that reflects a conservative philosophy while another mirrors a more progressive stance. Policy practitioners should be cautious when labeling or connecting a social justice theory with a political ideology. Yes, classification is easy and quickly accomplished, yet it allows preconceived, and often inaccurate, judgements to be made about a specific person, group, belief system, or policy. Policy negotiation and compromise are most difficult to achieve with the large-scale alignment of people and organizations into political, partisan perspectives. Broad stereotyping fosters a "we–they" strategy with the goal to "win no matter the cost." With that said, we also must recognize that social justice theories are part of political frameworks. The policy practitioner must be able to resist the temptation to be swayed or influenced by a theory's title but in fact understand its particular beliefs, the values it reflects, and the types of programs and services it endorses (see Activity Box 3.1).

Social Justice—Contractual Model

The contractual model of justice theory supports an equal allocation of societal resources while expanding civil and human rights (Reisch, 2014, p. 10). This model builds on the premise that there exists a clear understanding or "contract" between the government and a nation's citizens. The contract calls for the individual to yield or amend some of his or her personal freedoms. The contractual model recognizes that there is a higher authority, for example, government, whose role is to protect the individual's remaining rights. Contract theory essentially legitimizes the government to have authority over the individual and results in preserving the social order.

Political philosopher John Rawls, who was on the faculty of Harvard University, is one of the most recognizable thinkers around the contractual model of social justice. While a prolific scholar, his classic work, *The Theory of Justice* (1971), is the recognized benchmark work for this theory. The essence of Rawls's work is captured by his short characterization: "Justice is fairness."

Rawls notes that birth, status, and family are matters of chance and, as a result, should not influence or bias the benefits one accumulates during his or her lifetime. The contractual model of justice, according to Rawls, allows a society to rectify its inequities with the end product resulting in fairness to all people. Rawls argues that social justice assures equal access to liberties, rights, and opportunities, as well as insures that the least advantaged members of society are cared for. All social goods—liberty, power, opportunities, income, and wealth—are equally distributed; yet the unequal distribution of these goods is appropriate if it favors the least advantaged members of a community. Rawls contends that the inequality of opportunity is permissible if it advantages those who have been set aside. For example, a university's admission criteria that benefit one group, such as race or gender, over another are acceptable if that group has been or remains disadvantaged. Two US Supreme Court cases illustrate this point. The first, in 2003, *Grutter v. Bollinger*, affirmed the University of Michigan Law School affirmative action policy that a race-conscious admissions process may favor "underrepresented minority groups" (Legal Information Institute, n.d.). In 2013, the Supreme Court case of *Fisher v. University of Texas at Austin* challenged the earlier 2003 decision when the litigant, a White female, contended that minority students with less impressive credentials were admitted instead of her (American Psychological Association, n.d.). The US Supreme Court in *Fisher* once again upheld the role of affirmative action as an instrument of social justice.

Rawls's theory also proposes a maximin principle that essentially elevates the place of the least advantaged persons (Oyeshile, 2008). Using the concept of the "veil of ignorance," Rawls reasons if a person does not know or does not consider the impact of a particular policy on oneself, then one will not advantage one group over another. Rather, the outcome will result in what is viewed as the greatest benefit for the largest group of people. A common example to illustrate the maximin principle involves the sizes of a piece of cake. A group of people is going to share a cake; one person is asked to cut the cake so that each person may have a slice. Not knowing which slice he or she may receive, the cake cutter will probably make the slices as even as possible. To do otherwise, the cake slicer may end up with the smaller slice. Thus, making the slices of cake similar in size to each other ensures that no one person will be disadvantaged compared to another. Rawls also believed that inequality is tolerable if and only if it favors or advantages the least advantaged person in a community.

Social Justice–Feminist Model

Feminist theory views the broader community from a perspective that exposes the powers that produce and sustain inequality, oppression, and injustice while promoting equality and justice. It is, as criminologist Kathleen Daley and Julie Stubbs write, "concerned with the ways in which sex/gender structures social institutions, social life, groups, the self, and the body" (Daley & Stubbs, 2007, p. 149). Feminist social justice theory includes three central, interrelated principles:

- First, gender is a socially constructed belief that the attitudes and behaviors of women and men, commonly referred to as femininity and masculinity, are a fundamental organizing element of social life.
- Second, the resulting patriarchal sexism has systematically set aside and marginalized women and girls throughout all corners of society. Consequently, a core principle of feminist theories is to include female perspectives and experiences in all research and practice.
- Third, feminist theories recognize that gender privilege varies across different groups of women and men, including social class, age, and sexual orientation.

Law professors Kristin Kalsem and Verna Williams (2010, pp. 156–157) explain that:

> feminist social justice construes individual liberty more broadly to encompass the moral equality of all persons, regardless of their social location . . .. respecting another person is not just limited to leaving her alone; respecting another person involves attending to the conditions that are necessary for her thriving . . . it also means seeing that she has equally available to her the basic conditions of meaningful self-direction. Thus, under feminist social justice, liberty is not merely a negative concept, in the sense of being free from governmental interference.

Historically, women have been and continue well into the 21st century to be set back by social injustices. Law and ethics professor Martha Nussbaum argues that all women should be guaranteed their protection of equality in the name of justice. Areas such as wage discrimination and employment discrimination, role assignment, and "cultural traditions pose obstacles to women's health and flourishing" (Nussbaum, 1999, p. 29). In her important book, *Sex and Social Justice* (1999), Nussbaum contends that it is possible to redress the inequalities and violations of human dignity based on gender identity provided the tradition transforms itself by responsiveness to arguments concerning the social shaping of preferences and desires.

Social Justice—Libertarian Model

The libertarian model of social justice staunchly supports individual freedoms with a free-marketplace economy. This model builds on the belief that governmental regulations impede growth and stifle initiative; the so-called free-market approach fosters innovation, creates opportunities for all people, and does not benefit one person or group over another. On the one hand, a libertarian justice model supports the rights of the GLBTQ community and opposes the death penalty and anti-immigration laws, yet it favors eliminating the Social Security system and believes that parents should have the freedom to choose what schools their children will attend. Policy proposals such as progressive taxes, affirmative action, regulation of guns, Medicare and Medicaid, drug prohibition, and restrictions on abortion are anathema to the libertarian position. The bottom line for the libertarian justice theory is the protection of individual liberties, property rights, and social/economic order (Reisch, 2014, p. 10).

Philosopher Robert Nozick's writings strongly reflect the libertarian model. His major text, *Anarchy, State, and Utopia* (1974), offers a persuasive perspective for a free-market model that advocates for individuals being able to keep what they earn. His theory is best described as an *entitlement* model. He explicitly states that "Individuals have rights, and there are things no person or group may do to them (without violating their rights)" (Nozick, 1974, p. ix). Nozick's theory includes three key provisions:

- First, a person who justly acquires any item is entitled to keep and use it.
- Second, a person who acquires any item by means of a just transfer of property is allowed to keep and use it. These two principles clearly imply that any product acquired unjustly, for example, theft or fraud, is an illegitimate holding.
- Finally, justice can require the alteration of unjust acquisitions.

The bottom line for Nozick is that the redistribution of social goods is unacceptable and violates a key premise that a person should be able to retain the fruits of one's labor or items that one has lawfully gained. The right to self-ownership is retained at all times.

Additionally, taxation of any form, according to Nozick, is unacceptable as it is akin to forced labor with a portion of one's working time and subsequent wages being taken for another's purpose; taxes are unjust as they force an individual to work for another's benefit. Justice results in respecting the rights of others, particularly their property and self-ownership.

For Nozick (1974) an approach that involves less government is the best model. He asks, "if the state did not exist would it be necessary to invent it? Would one be needed, and would it have to be invented" (p. 3)? Libertarianism stresses that the state's role should be confined to fundamental tasks such as security and safety—police/fire protection, national defense, and the judicial system. Matters related to public education, social welfare, among others are the responsibility of the private sector. Faith-based organizations, nonprofit social services, nongovernmental organizations, and private for-profit groups should provide ongoing welfare services. Social services, according to the libertarian model, are structured within a free market model to encourage efficiency and effectiveness while eliminating unnecessary redundancy and fiscal waste. The government's role is minimal at best with individuals left free to do and act as they wish with their own lives and property as long as their individual actions do not infringe on others. No formal institution can or should interfere with an individual's control of his or her life; the role of the state is to protect from and retaliate against those who use force against an individual. This view is further articulated by Murray Rothbard, an economic and political theorist, who viewed government as the enemy of the people noting, "Taxation is theft, purely and simply even though it is theft on a grand and colossal scale which no acknowledged criminals could hope to match. It is a compulsory seizure of the property of the State's inhabitants, or subjects" (Mises Institute, 2014).

Social Justice–Socialist Model

The socialist model builds on the premise that equality is a more fundamental ideal than individual liberty. According to the socialist model of justice, fairness is achieved by all people contributing to the broader community within their means and ability to do so. Karl Marx believed that all should be required to contribute to society to the extent of their abilities and all should be allowed to receive from society in accordance to their needs. In his *Critique of the Gotha Program*, written in 1875, Marx writes that the economy will distribute goods according to the norm, to each person according to his or her labor contribution (Marx, 2008). He strongly stresses the principles of equality and equity: Each person has the right to receive economic goods that satisfy her needs to the same extent provided she contributes to the economy according to her ability. This philosophy emphasizes the collective of people as a whole, which recognizes the needs of the group over those of the individual. People share and cooperate with each other, even though they do not nor are expected to contribute at the same level, for example, equality; rather, the individual contributes only that which she or he can do, for example, equity.

Philosopher and academician Kai Nielsen, a proponent of the socialist model, argues for equal basic liberties and opportunities, including the opportunities "for meaningful work, for self-determination, and political participation," which he considers important to promote "equal moral autonomy and equal self-respect" (Nielsen, 1979, p. 211). His second principle states that each person has the right to the "most extensive total system of equal basic liberties and they benefit the least advantaged and are part of offices, for example, positions or employment, that every individual has access to (Nielsen, 1979, p. 212). This model prescribes a "classless society . . . without any form of social stratification" (Nielsen, 1979, pp. 223–224).

Social Justice–Utilitarian Model

Utilitarianism holds that the correct course of action is one that produces the maximum balance of benefits over harms for those directly impacted. The goal of utilitarianism is that the greatest level of benefits be available to as many people as possible. In other words, decisions are based on outcomes and consequences. The proponents of this theory subscribe to the overarching principle that a just community must balance the beneficial and harmful consequences of micro and macro conduct. This does lead to an interesting dilemma: If lying results in the most positive outcome, should people then lie to achieve this end? Isn't telling the truth in the best interests of all people? If so, what is more important—reaching a positive outcome for an individual or protecting the interests of the majority of people?

The early 19th-century philosopher John Stewart Mill, recognized as the most influential thinker of the utilitarian model of social justice, builds on the idea that people are inherently fair and adversely react to any form of injustice. This theory strongly approves of actions that increase human happiness, and a utilitarian approach creates the greatest happiness for the largest number of people. A difficulty with this philosophy, however, is a policy that results in a net gain in pleasure for the majority of people is appropriate even at the expense of a minority group. Mills argued that unequal access to happiness is justified only when it is in the best interest of society as a whole. According to (1999), Utilitarianism declares *alternative x* to be better than *alternative y* if and only if total utility is greater in *x* than in *y* (Blackorby, Bossert, & Donaldson, 2002, p. 1). Another way of understanding the utilitarian model is to appreciate that inequality is tolerated in those instances where the majority of people benefit.

The model also asserts that no law should interfere with an individual's private actions as long as they do harm to others. As Mill wrote, " . . ..the only purpose for which power can be rightfully exercised over any member of a civilized community, against his will, is to prevent harm to others" (Mill, 1869, chapter 1, n.p.). Mill goes on to identify five crucial points to the utilitarian model:

1. It is unjust to deprive any one of his personal liberty, his property, or any other thing which belongs to him by law.
2. The legal rights of which he is deprived may be rights which ought not to have belonged to him; in other words, the law which confers on him these rights, may be a bad law.
3. It is universally considered just that each person should obtain that (whether good or evil) which he deserves.
4. It is confessedly unjust to break faith with any one: to violate an engagement, either express or implied, or disappoint expectations raised by our conduct, at least if we have raised those expectations knowingly and voluntarily.
5. Inconsistent with justice to be partial; to show favour or preference to one person over another, in matters to which favour and preference do not properly apply (Mill, chapter 5, n.p.).

The utilitarian approach attempts to find out what is best for society as a whole.

Rogers (2004) writes, "it seems obvious that no system of justice will ever meet the interests of every citizen in its society; so utilitarians say that the best system of justice is that which will bring the greatest total amount of happiness to the society as a whole."

Activity Box 3.1

Based on your understanding of the various theories of social justice, how would each approach the identified social issue or incident? In each situation, identify who is directly impacted and who is indirectly impacted; should the governmental response, if any, be long or short term?

	Contractual	Feminist	Libertarian	Socialist	Utilitarian
Homelessness					
Individual is responsible for condition					
Society is primarily responsible for the condition					
Government must respond to the situation					

The person is responsible for resolving the situation					
How is fairness achieved					
Hunger					
Individual is responsible for condition					
Society is primarily responsible for condition					
Government must respond to the situation					
The person is responsible for resolving the situation					
How is fairness achieved					
Gun violence at Sandy Hook Elementary School					
Individual is responsible for condition					
Society is primarily responsible for condition					
Government must respond to the situation					
The person is responsible for resolving the situation					

How is fairness achieved					
A hurricane strikes the east coast of North Carolina					
Individual is responsible for condition					
Society is primarily responsible for condition					
Government must respond to the situation					
The person is responsible for resolving the situation					
How is fairness achieved					
Low-wage, minimum-wage job					
Individual is responsible for condition					
Society is primarily responsible for condition					
Government must respond to the situation					
The person is responsible for resolving the situation					
How is fairness achieved					

Deportation of undocumented persons				
Individual is responsible for condition				
Society is primarily responsible for condition				
Government must respond to the situation				
The person is responsible for resolving the situation				
How is fairness achieved				
Child Welfare System— abused, neglected, and unwanted children				
Individual is responsible for condition				
Society is primarily responsible for condition				
Government must respond to the situation				
The person is responsible for resolving the situation				
How is fairness achieved				

GLOBAL STATEMENTS REGARDING SOCIAL JUSTICE

There are dozens of international "conventions" and "treaties" focusing on human rights and social justice issues (see Table 3.1). Essentially, these documents detail "activities, conditions, and freedoms" that all people are entitled to due to their status as a human being and, as such, are not granted; furthermore, such rights cannot be taken away and must be respected by all people and governments (International Justice Resource Center, n.d.). The *Preamble* of the United Nations *Declaration of Human Rights*, which is the international overarching statement regarding human rights, captures the purpose of all global human rights' documents when stating *the inherent dignity and of the equal and inalienable rights of all members of the human family is the foundation of freedom, justice and peace in the world* (United Nations, n.d.).

The Declaration includes 30 articles, each addressing one specific aspect of global human rights, including the following precepts among others:

- All human beings are born free and equal in dignity and rights.
- Everyone has the right to life, liberty, and security of person.
- No one shall be held in slavery or servitude; slavery and the slave trade shall be prohibited in all their forms.
- No one shall be subjected to torture or to cruel, inhumane, or degrading treatment or punishment.
- No one shall be subjected to arbitrary arrest, detention, or exile.
- Everyone has the right to freedom of thought, conscience, and religion.
- Everyone has the right to freedom of opinion and expression.
- Everyone, without any discrimination, has the right to equal pay for equal work (United Nations, n.d.).

Unfortunately, these various treaties and conventions, while signed by numerous nations from around the world, are nearly impossible to enforce because of the autonomous rights of countries. These statements are essentially nonbinding recommendations with no legal power to force any nation or government to enact the treaties'/conventions' principles.

A FEW FINAL THOUGHTS

Most assuredly, the concept of social justice is important to the social work profession. Yet defining, understanding, and finding consensus on what constitutes social justice is a difficult task. Some view social justice as a specific product or a service or benefit provided to some persons or groups for a particular reason. Other opinions frame social justice within the context of relationships; how people, groups of

Table 3.1. EXAMPLES OF GLOBAL STATEMENTS ON HUMAN RIGHTS

Treaty	Sponsoring Organization	Website
African Charter on Human and Peoples Rights	African Commission on Human and Peoples' Rights	http://www.achpr.org/instruments/achpr/
American Declaration of the Rights and Duties of Man	Organization of American States	http://www.cidh.oas.org/Basicos/English/Basic2.american%20Declaration.htm
Arab Charter of Human Rights	Council of the League of Arab States	http://www1.umn.edu/humanrts/instree/loas2005.html?msource=UNWDEC19001&tr=y&auid=3337655
ASEAN Human Rights Declaration	ASEAN Intergovernmental Commission on Human Rights	Http://www.ijrcenter.org/regional/asia/#ASEAN_Human_Rights_Declaration
Convention on the Rights of Persons with Disabilities	United Nations	http://www.un.org/disabilities/convention/conventionfull.shtml
Ending Violence and Discrimination Against Lesbian, Gay, Transgender and Intersex People	United Nations	http://www.ohchr.org/EN/Issues/Discrimination/Pages/JointLGBTIstatement.aspx
European Convention for the Protection of Human Rights	European Union	http://www.echr.coe.int/Pages/home.aspx?p=basictexts&c=#n1359128122487_pointer
Indigenous and Tribal Peoples Convention	International Labour Organisation	http://www.ilo.org/dyn/normlex/en/f?p=NORMLEXPUB:12100:0::NO::P12100_ILO_CODE:C169
International Convention on the Elimination of All Forms of Racial Discrimination	United Nations	**treaties.un.org/doc/source/docs/cerd_sp_45-E.pdf**
Universal Declaration of Human Rights	United Nations	http://www.un.org/en/universal-declaration-human-rights/index.html

people, and/or communities stand in relation to each other as well as with institutions and societal structures. Some believe that social justice reflects all people having the same access to the same opportunities; others find that social justice occurs when people are treated the same under all circumstances; social justice for some translates into keeping those goods that one produces or earns; and others argue that justice allows some individuals and groups to have certain advantages over others (see Activity Box 3.2).

Although there are a number of different ways to view social justice, the two prominent schools of thought are the libertarian and contractual models. Rawls, reflecting a contractual conception of social justice, supports the equal distribution of resources and believes that inequality is only acceptable if benefits are provided to the least advantaged. Nozick, a proponent of the libertarian model, points out that people have rights to the things they legally produce and gain through permissible transactions. Clearly, these two distinct philosophies have significant points of disagreement. The most obvious conflict is the redistribution of goods to improve the lives of the least advantaged (Rawls's model) is viewed as unjust as it takes goods/products from those who create them while forcing people to work on behalf of others (Nozick model). The role of government also is a major point of disagreement. The contractual model supports assistance over the long term through an activist government that intervenes with specific laws, public policies, and resulting social service systems; the libertarian model advocates for minimalist government with the individual, family, and other nongovernmental systems being the source for assistance.

Social work, through its professional associations and their specific ethical statements and various policy positions, aligns itself more closely to the Rawls contractual model of justice. From this vantage point, social workers seek fairness and the just and equal treatment of all persons; the social and economic opportunity structures are available to all people no matter who they are, what their beliefs might be, or traditions they hold. The pathway for this to occur is best realized through the development of reasonable social policies, which is referred to as *policy practice* in the social work profession. Social work educator Bruce Jansson (1999) writes that *policy practice* allows the social work profession to promote its values and the well-being of clients while at the same time countering opposition to proactive social welfare (p. 10). From this perspective comes the common question that is applied throughout the policy practice arena: Is this fair and just? It doesn't matter what the policy issue might be—a preschool program, legalization of recreational marijuana, promoting same-sex marriage, expanding health care for elders—the overarching question that drives the policy work remains the same: Is this fair and just?

Social work advocates and educators Karen Haynes and Jim Mickelson (2000) contend that "all social work is political" (p. 23). Although some may disagree with this assertion, there is no doubt that policy practice takes place within a political environment. Policies are enacted at the various levels of government, by nonprofit agencies boards of directors, and by CEOs of for-profit agencies. A policy is the product of a series of social justice–related decisions that specify who is included and excluded from services; what services are provided; how the services are provided; and who provides the services.

Recognizing that the social work profession's view of social justice is one of many theories is imperative in policy practice. Just as important is to appreciate the unique differences and similarities that may exist among the various social justice theories. Knowing an individual or group's beliefs and values and what supports these creates an opportunity to find common ground. Alternatively, such understanding allows for development of a more affective policy practice strategy to unfold. Similarly, social workers engaged in policy practice must remain steadfast to asking the question: Is this fair and just?

Activity Box 3.2

Consider each of the following statements. What is your reaction or response to each? What social justice theory is informing your response?

1. Some argue that civil disobedience is impossible without the distinction between particular and social justice because being civilly disobedient can only take place within a political system. Using Martin Luther King's protests as an example, explain how civil disobedience presupposes a just system.

2. Standing in line may seem like an ethically unchallenging procedure for determining the order in which one is to be seen. But consider each of the following by determining what is being distributed and the order in which individuals are being served and then laying out the harms and benefits to all involved.

   (a) In the emergency room of a hospital, those most severely injured are seen first, regardless of the time of their arrival. Others may sit in the waiting room for hours for what are judged minor injuries by the staff on hand. Those waiting may include elderly individuals who are unable to sit for such long periods without extreme discomfort. Is this just? Is there anything that could be done to mitigate any harms?

   (b) Two social work practitioners in an agency are seeing first-time clients on a first come, first-served basis.

      (1) The clients line up in two lines, one in front of each practitioner, the clients presumably judging which line will move the fastest or deciding which practitioner they want to see.

      (2) This time the clients line up in one line, the first in line going to whichever social work practitioner is free.

      (3) The honor system is used. An elderly woman comes in, asks for a number, and when told that the honor system is used, says, "Good. I'm next."

3. Imagine yourself being queried by a client about why he is being treated in a way he perceives to be unjust and thus harmful. For instance, a client waiting in the office will not see you first when the elderly woman enters (see 2b3 earlier) and announces, "I'm next." The honor system requires

honor, and disputes can readily break out that will need mediating. You will need to have a procedure for mediation and an explanation of how it applies in the situation at hand. The mediation procedure will itself need to be just. With this in mind, craft a just mediation procedure for such disputes and apply it to the case at hand where the elderly woman is taken ahead of others who have been waiting.

4. Disagreements about what to do about so-called welfare cheats focus on where to put the burden of proof. Should we try to ensure that all who need help obtain it? Or should we try to ensure that those who do not need help do not obtain it? The former remedy will let some who do not need help get it, and the latter will not let some who do need help get it. Assess the relative merits of these two remedies and determine which is ethically preferable, if either is.

Source: Robison, W., & Resser, L. (1999). Ethical decision-making in social work. Upper Saddle River, NJ: Allyn and Bacon. pp. 217–221.

REFERENCES

American Psychological Association. (n.d.). Fisher v. University of Texas at Austin. Retrieved from http://www.apa.org/about/offices/ogc/amicus/fisher.aspx on January 8, 2016.

Australian Association of Social Workers. (2010). *Code of ethics*. Canberra, ACT: Author.

Baker, R. (2013). *The social work dictionary*. Washington, DC: NASW Press.

Barry, E. (2017, January 10). "There are no homes left": Rohingya tell of rape, fire and death in Myanmar. *The New York Times*. Retrieved from https://www.nytimes.com/2017/01/10/world/asia/rohingya-violence-myanmar.html?emc=edit_th_20170111&nl=today sheadlines&nlid=72389635&_r=1 on January 10, 2017.

Blackorby, C., Bossert, W., & Donaldson, D. (2002). Utilitarianism and the theory of justice. In K. Arrow, A. Sen, & K. Suzumura, eds., *Handbook of social choice and welfare* (Vol. 1). Amsterdam, Netherlands: Elsevier. Retrieved from https://www.researchgate.net/publication/24138639_Utilitarianism_and_the_Theory_of_Justice on January 3, 2017.

British Association of Social Workers. (2014). The code of ethics for social workers: Statement of principles. Retrieved from https://www.basw.co.uk/codeofethics/ on January 3, 2017.

Canadian Association for Social Work Education, Association Canadienne Pour La Formation en Travil Social. (2014). *Standards for accreditation*. Retrieved from https://caswe-acfts.ca/wp-content/uploads/2013/03/CASWE-ACFTS-Standards-11-2014.pdf on July 26, 2017.

Center for Economic and Social Justice. (2017). Defining economic and social justice. Retrieved from http://www.cesj.org/learn/definitions/defining-economic-justice-and-social-justice/ on January 4, 2017.

Commission on Accreditation. (2015). *2015 Educational policy and accreditation standards for baccalaureate and master's social work programs*. Alexandria, VA: Council on Social Work Education.

Cumming-Bruce, N. (2015, March 12). 14 million children suffering as result of war in syria and iraq, unicef says. *The New York Times.* Retrieved from https://www.nytimes. com/2015/03/13/world/middleeast/iraq-syria-children-unicef-toll.html?_r=0   on December 4, 2016.

Daley, K., & Stubbs, J. (2007). Feminist theory, feminist and anti-racist politics, and restorative justice. In G. Johnstone & D. Van Ness (eds.), *Handbook of restorative justice* (pp. 149–170). Devon, UK: Willian Publishing.

Downey, K. (2010). *The woman behind the new deal: the life and legacy of frances perkins, social security, unemployment insurance, and the minimum wage.* New York, NY: Anchor Books.

Haynes, K., & Mickelson, J. (2000). *Affecting change, social workers in the political arena* (4th ed.). Boston, MA: Allyn and Bacon

Hunger Notes. (2016). 2016 world hunger and poverty facts and statistics. Retrieved from http://www.worldhunger.org/2015-world-hunger-and-poverty-facts-and-statistics/ on December 4, 2016.

International Association of Schools of Social Work (2004). Global standards for the education and training of the social work profession. Retrieved from http://www.iassw-aiets.org on February 6, 2007.

Jansson, B. (1999). *Becoming an effective policy advocate, from policy practice to social justice.* Pacific Grove, CA: Brooks Cole.

Jefferson, T. (2010, March 24). Glen Beck: What is social justice? Retrieved from http://www. glennbeck.com/content/articles/article/198/38320/?utm_source=glennbeck&utm_ medium=contentcopy_link on January 8, 2017.

Kalsem, K., & Williams, V. (2010). Social justice feminism. *UCLA Women's Law Journal, 18,* 131–193.

Legal Information Institute. (n.d.). Grutter v. Bollinger (02-241) 539 U.S. 306 (2003) 288 F.3d 732, affirmed. Retrieved from https://www.law.cornell.edu/supct/html/02-241. ZS.html on January 8, 2016.

Lister, A. (June 2011). The "mirage" of social justice: Hayek against (and for) Rawls. CSSJ Working Papers Series, SJ017. Oxford, UK: Centre for the Study of Social Justice Department of Politics and International Relations, University of Oxford. Retrieved from http://r.search.yahoo.com/_ylt=A0LEVzOqj3JYDygACYNXNyoA;_ ylu=X3oDMTEyYzJtbmtlBGNvbG8DYmYxBHBvcwMxBHZ0aWQDQjMwMDlfM QRzZWMDc3I-/RV=2/RE=1483931691/RO=10/RU=http%3a%2f%2fwww.poli- tics.ox.ac.uk%2fmaterials%2fcentres%2fsocial-justice%2fworking-papers%2fSJ017_ Lister_MirageofSocialJustice.pdf/RK=0/RS=2PZpvJKXitnOfEmYXD0aPqo7NiQ- on December 3, 2016.

Marx, K. (2008). *Critique of the Gotha Program.* Rockville, MD: Wildside Press.

Mill, John Stewart. (1869). *On liberty* (4th ed.). London, UK: Longman, Roberts & Green, Bartleby.com, 1999. Retrived from http://www.bartleby.com/130/ on January 7, 2017.

Mises Institute. (2014). Biography quote of Murray Rothbard. Retrieved from https://mises. org/library/biography-quote-murray-rothbard on July 26, 2017.

Miller, D. (2005). Justice and boundaries. Speech presented Centre for the Study of Social Justice Conference. Nuffield College, Oxford. November 26, 2005.

National Association of Black Social Workers. (n.d.). Mission statement. Retrieved from http://nabsw.org/?page=MissionStatement on January 3, 2016.

National Association of Social Workers. (1999). *Code of ethics of the national association of social workers.* Washington, DC: Author. Retrieved from http://socialworkers.org/pubs/ code/code.asp on August 8, 2016.

Nielsen, K. (1979). Radical egalitarian justice: Justice as equality." *Social Theory and Practice,* 5(2), 209–226.

Nigeria Association of Social Workers. (2017). Law backing social work. Retrieved from http://www.nasow.org/law-backing-social-work/ on March 4, 2016.

Nozick, R. (1974). *Anarchy, state and utopia.* New York, NY: Basic Books.

Nussbaum, M. (1999). *Sex and social justice.* New York, NY: Oxford University Press.

Oyeshile, O. (2008). A critique of the maximin principle in Rawls' theory of justice. *Humanity & Social Sciences Journal, 3*(1), 65–69.

Rawls, J. (1971). *Theory of justice.* Harvard, MA: Harvard University Press.

Reisch, M. (2014). *Social policy and social justice.* Thousand Oaks, CA: Sage.

Rogers, T. D. (2004). Rawls's theory of justice from a utilitarian perspective. *Macalester Journal of Philosophy, 13*(1), article 5. Retrieved from http://digitalcommons.macalester.edu/cgi/viewcontent.cgi?article=1030&context=philo/ on January 3, 2017.

Tannenubaum, N., & Reisch, M. (2001). *From charitable volunteers to architects of social welfare: A brief history of social work.* Ann Arbor, MI: School of Social Work, University of Michigan.

United Nations. (n.d.). Universal Declaration of Human Rights. Retrieved from http://www.un.org/en/universal-declaration-human-rights/index.html on January 13, 2016.

World Bank. (2016, October 2). Poverty overview. Retrieved from http://www.worldbank.org/en/topic/poverty/overview on December 4, 2016.

World Health Organiation and UNICEF. (2015). Progress on sanitation and drinking water, 2015 update and MDG assessment. Retrieved from http://www.who.int/water_sanitation_health/monitoring/jmp-2015-update/en/ on December 4, 2016.

CHAPTER 4

Critical Thinking

The Key to Policy Practice

In his "Farewell Address" to the country in January 2017, President Barak Obama said,

> For too many of us, it's become safer to retreat into our own bubbles, whether in our neighborhoods or on college campuses, or places of worship, or especially our social media feeds, surrounded by people who look like us and share the same political outlook and never challenge our assumptions. . . . And increasingly, we become so secure in our bubbles that we start accepting only information, whether it's true or not, that fits our opinions, instead of basing our opinions on the evidence that is out there. But without some common baseline of facts, without a willingness to admit new information, and concede that your opponent might be making a fair point, and that science and reason matter, then we're going to keep talking past each other, and we'll make common ground and compromise impossible. (The White House, 2017)

President Obama succinctly challenged individuals to think critically while rejecting the common and growing practice of only seeking out and believing information that merely validates our positon. Relying on evidence that only confirms one's ideas and beliefs is a long-standing behavior. A number of research studies have explored such phenomena. One in particular, a 2011 research study explored whether individual desires are more powerful than personal beliefs (Bastardi, Uhlmann, & Ross, 2011). The study included couples who (a) expected to have children in the near future and (b) believed that home care was better than sending them to a daycare program. Half the participants expected to use out-of-home daycare, whereas the remaining half planned to provide in-home care (Bastardi et al., 2011, p. 731). The couples were given two studies; one concluded that in-home care is better than daycare, whereas the other report concluded that daycare is better than in-home care (Bastardi et al., 2011, p. 731). After reviewing the two contradictory reports, the research found that couples who believed that home care was better and planned to care for their children concluded that the study that found home care was best was more convincing. Conversely, couples who planned on using daycare reached the opposite conclusion based on the report that daycare, compared to home care, was a better option for children (Bastardi et al., 2011, p. 731). Ok, but what does this study and President Obama's comments have to do with critical thinking? The answer is quite clear: People are *biased* to interpret evidence in ways that are consistent with their personal desires while disregarding differing data. Daniel Levitin, PhD, professor of executive education at the University of California Berkley, writes that an oddity about people is that it is hard to let go of a personal conviction "even in the face of overwhelming evidence and scientific proof to the contrary" (Levitin, 2015, p. 205).

Questioning subjective opinions and accepting information that runs counter to long-held personal beliefs is difficult at best. People do not like to admit that they may be wrong and, as a result, look to create and maintain a personal comfort zone. Yet effective policy practice requires the social worker to consistently challenge personal as well as group and organizational beliefs, opinions, and positions in order to ensure the most effective policy recommendations are put forth. Seeking out and discerning valid and reliable data and information sources are central to this process. This practice is much more than "cutting and pasting" findings from a journal article, government report, or a website. A cornerstone in policy practice, in fact all of social work practice, is the ability to apply critical thinking (CT) skills.

THE NEED FOR CRITICAL THINKING

CT is an ongoing process of questioning, seeking answers, and drawing conclusions on a specific subject or issue. On the surface, this seems simple enough, but for a moment think back to the recent 2016 presidential election and conversations with friends and colleagues that may have evolved into debates. Typically, a politically directed conversation begins with some observations, some pointed and others less so. "Did you hear what so-and-so said? Do you believe that, how stupid was she/he?" The friend might respond, "Yes, and he/she was absolutely correct!" At that point, the line is drawn as the two persons begin their debate; voices may rise, they probably interrupt each other, and they often begin their counterpoints statements with, "Yes, but . . ." Not unexpectedly the friendly debate transforms into an argument where people begin thinking of comeback statements or responses, all the while not fully listening to the entirety of their friend's comments. And where are we when the debate ends? Probably at the same place when the initial conversation began. Debates such as these typically lack CT and are firmly rooted in and guided by one's own beliefs.

A recurring barrier to effective policy practice is the reliance on partisan debates. Positions based on individual or group biases, beliefs, and prejudices while dismissing others' points leads nowhere, and the issue at hand remains unsolved. There is little to be gained by one side making a claim that the other attempts to debunk. Partisan discussions are framed by everyone believing they are right and their opposition is just plain wrong. There is an absence of middle or common ground. Television's cable network and radio talk shows are filled with so-called news shows illustrating such interplay. Panel members throw out numbers or quote national polls to substantiate their positions; interestingly enough, few of the panelists question the accuracy of the information or if the data might be biased, for example, generated by a "conservative" or "liberal" think tank. Few views, if any, are ever changed, but the political combatants end their discussion with a self-satisfying belief that "I won." Such discussions or debates are closed-minded to counterintuitive ideas or positions. Unfortunately, such arguments typify the general approach to solving policy strategies and more often than not result in unproductive policies.

Avoiding this quagmire is difficult, though necessary. The first step rests with the social worker's willingness to risk developing a conclusion that may run counter to what she or he believes. This is the essence of CT—finding the best answer even if it is different from the individual or group's position. Effective issue analysis and policy development is firmly rooted in a critical thinking process.

CRITICAL THINKING DEFINED

Critical thinking is a foundational principle in higher education and, as noted by former Harvard University President Derek Bok (p. 67), a unique skill set developed by students throughout the baccalaureate studies. Bok, whose views of CT are widely shared by faculties among universities worldwide, goes on to say that the maturity of an individual's critical thinking throughout his or her academic experience is among the primary purposes of a liberal arts–based education (Bok, 2006, p. 67). Social work education also notes the importance of critical thinking in its Educational Policy and Accreditation Standards (EPAS). Specifically, EPAS competency number four notes that critical thinking underpins "practice-informed research" and "research informed practice" through the application of "principles of logic, scientific inquiry, and culturally informed and ethical approaches to building knowledge" (Commission on Accreditation, 2015, p. 8).

CT involves pursuing a variety of data and information points, determining if the information is reasonable, and how does the information inform and influence one's choices. Defined as "reasonable and reflective thinking focused on deciding what to believe or do" (Fisher, 2001, p. 7), CT thrives in an intellectual environment where a rational "disciplined process of actively and skillfully conceptualizing, applying, analyzing, synthesizing, and/or evaluating information gathered from, or generated by, observation, experience, reflection, reasoning, or communication, as a guide to belief and action" (Critical Thinking Community, n.d.).

Let's be clear on one point. Critical thinking is not just criticizing or debunking a position for the sake of being negative or rhetorical (see Box 4.1). It is not debasing other perspectives in an effort to strengthen one's own particular position. CT is neither an opinion nor an ideological stance, but it does create a roadmap, guided by sound evidence, that allows a person to arrive at an effective destination.

Box 4.1
CRITICAL THINKING

- "Critical thinking describes the process we use to uncover and check our assumptions" (Brookfield, 2006, p. 11).
- "self-directed, self-disciplined, self-monitored, and self-corrective thinking. It requires rigorous standards of excellence and mindful command of their use. It entails effective communication and problem solving abilities and a commitment to overcome our native egocentrism and sociocentrism" (Paul & Elder, 2007, p. 4).
- It is "deeper" than memorization and recall of factual information. When students think critically, they think deeply; they not only know the facts, but they take the additional step of going beyond the facts to do something with them. Critical thinking involves reflecting on the information received, moving away from "surface" memorization and toward deeper levels of learning (Cuseo, 2016).
- "the intellectually disciplined process of actively and skillfully conceptualizing, applying, analyzing, synthesizing, and/or evaluating information gathered from, or generated by, observation, experience, reflection, reasoning, or communication, as a guide to belief and action" (Scriven & Paul, 1987).
- Critical thinking calls for a persistent effort to examine any belief or supposed form of knowledge in the light of the evidence that supports it and the further conclusions to which it tends (Glaser, 1941).
- Critical thinking is identifying and evaluating evidence to guide decision making. Critical thinkers use in-depth analysis of evidence to make decisions and communicate his beliefs clearly and accurately (Critical Thinking Company, n.d.).
- "active, persistent, and careful consideration of any belief or supposed form of knowledge in the light of the grounds that support it and the further conclusions to which it tend" (Dewey, 1933, p. 118).
- "critical thinking occurs when students are analyzing, evaluating, interpreting, or synthesizing information and applying creative thought to form an argument, solve a problem, or reach a conclusion" (Great Schools Partnership, 2013).
- Critical thinking is deciding rationally what to or what not to believe (Norris, 1985).

WHAT CAN EFFECTIVE CRITICAL THINKING RESULT IN?

One of the most significant positive consequences of critical thinking is its potential to help individuals, groups, and institutions approach an array of instances, including social issues and people, in a new, more productive manner. CT helps discern fact from fiction while helping uncover bias and prejudice. Asking questions without clearly knowing their answers and probing through reasons for advocating certain positions helps identify falsehoods, deceptions, and half-truths.

There are numerous examples of falsehoods and deceptive statements in the political and policy-making worlds. All one needs to do is look at the most recent 2016 presidential race to find statements made by the Democratic and Republican nominees that were inaccurate in one form or another. Let's examine then Republican presidential candidate nominee Donald Trump's claim that the 2015 murder rate was the "highest it's been in 45 years" (Bump, 2016) and Democratic presidential nominee Hilary Clinton's assertion that "in the last seven years drug prices have doubled" (Kiely, 2016). One could accept both claims as correct and restate these comments to others; or, by applying CT to the claims, two very different pictures emerge on both statements. First, let's examine Trump's statement regarding a rising crime rate. A review of various Federal Bureau of Investigation reports shows that the murder rate in 2015 was 4.9 per 100,000 person compared to 7.9 persons in 1970, a 38% drop. Now let's look at Clinton's comments regarding a rise in drug costs. Data show that the cost for name-brand drugs had more than doubled but information also showed that more than 80% of *all* filled prescriptions were for generic drugs, which have seen a price drop of nearly 63% (Kiely, 2016). Through CT, we learn that Trump's assertion was a complete falsehood and that Clinton's comments were only partially true.

The CT process builds on the premise that no statement is accepted as true or factual simply because it is stated. Furthermore, CT is not an excuse for merely criticizing or demeaning others. The purpose of the CT process is to ensure that information is correct and firmly rooted in verifiable information from reputable and fair sources.

THE CRITICAL THINKING PROCESS

So just what are the characteristics of a sound critical thinker; what types of questions are asked to assess a specific situation? The skilled critical thinker, at a minimum, does the following:

- Asks essential, clearly framed questions that are precise and leave little room for subjective opinions
- Collects appropriate information and assesses the veracity of how it was gathered and synthesized

- Considers the conclusions to ensure they are well-reasoned and are directly related to and build on the gathered information
- Seeks out alternative explanations for the situation and again assesses the appropriateness of the information
- By comparing the various data and various viewpoints and differing explanations, determines which is the just and correct position while understanding their implications and practical consequences
- Is able to communicate well-defined solution(s) or position(s) to the matter at hand

The primary goal of CT is to create a pathway that leads to a rational, correct, and just way to resolve a specific problem. To that end, the CT process requires a thoughtful organization of an assortment of informational reports and data typically from a wide range of sources. A useful and important CT technique is to consider informational sources that generally disagree with each other such as conservative and liberal sources. The conflicting viewpoints force the social worker to consider the various points and reach a conclusion based on the merits of the argument and the validity of the data.

Critical thinking is an individual process; it is "self-directed, self-disciplined, self-monitored, and self-corrective" (Paul & Elder, 2007, p. 4). The key word is "self," which means the individual social worker must be fully aware that he or she is responsible for this process. No agency or organizational staff position is titled "CT Supervisor" or "CT Manager"; an agency does not have a separate "CT Room" or dedicated space for the social worker to visit. CT is the social worker's responsibility with the objective to build a rational and thoughtful process that distills facts from myth, truth from falsehoods, and opens the doors for clear, objective solutions to emerge.

Recognize Human Emotions

CT does not exclude emotions from entering the process; emotions are part of the human experience, and they neither can nor should be ignored. Being aware of and sensitive to the presence of human passions in everyday life situations is one thing; but it is another to ensure the influences of the human emotion or experience do not color or divert the CT process from a fair outcome.

Creative Thinking Is Helpful

Creative thinking is a by-product of successful CT. Imaginative reasoning is dynamic, vibrant, intuitive, and exciting. There are essentially *no rules of the game* when employing creative thought processes. Flexibility, brainstorming, visioning, and metaphorical relationships are common ingredients to stimulate curiosity, posing "what-if" statements to help foster differing perspectives. Creative thinking frees up the somewhat rigid critical thinking process by enabling a free flow of ideas and recognizing that some biases are impossible to disregard or subordinate.

Question One's Self

The social worker should question his or her individual positions, biases, and beliefs regarding any situation. Self-questioning and introspection are hallmarks of CT. An open-minded approach to thinking results in a robust and more in-depth understanding of the issue at hand. The social worker who adopts an open-minded approach is encouraged to understand differing positions and viewpoints, other beliefs, and rationales, which in turn allows the practitioner to consider alternatives and judge the veracity of the evidence. A close-minded approach is just the opposite with opponents' ideas, statements, positions, and proposals discounted as being invalid and scurrilous. Discounting different positions without attempting to appreciate their nuisances or the groundings on which they are built does little more than further solidify the "we–they" mentality.

Egocentric Reasoning

Individual beliefs and positions take shape for a variety of reasons, but the most common is egocentric thinking, which is best reflected by the following statements (Paul & Elder, 2007, p. 9).

- It is true because I believe it.
- It is true because we believe it.
- It is true because I want to believe it.
- It is true because I have always believed it.
- It is true because it is in my self-interest to believe it.

These statements do not consider critical thinking but rely on personal bias and one's own history. Take, for example, the experience shared by many—being told to eat a specific vegetable as a child. The author, as a child, really disliked cauliflower, but his mother said he had to eat it because "Eating cauliflower is good for you." One day he asked, "How do you know it is good for you?" His mother responded, "Because my mother, your grandmother, told me so." Applying the previously cited Paul and Elder statements to this experience results in the author concluding that eating cauliflower is good for the individual (see Table 4.1).

A policy that grows from egocentric thinking does little more than reinforce bias and prejudice. There is no room for self-questioning or reflective thinking nor is there

Table 4.1. WHY IS BROCCOLI GOOD FOR YOU? THE APPLICATION
OF EGOCENTRIC THINKING

Paul and Elder	Conclusion Reached as a Result of the Human Experience
It is true because I believe it.	I believe cauliflower is good for me.
It is true because we believe it.	My mother and grandmother believed cauliflower was good for us to eat; therefore, it is true.
It is true because I want to believe it.	I believe cauliflower is good for me because my mother and grandmother said it was and I want to believe them.
It is true because I have always believed it.	It is true because I have believed it for the better part of 60 years.
It is true because it is in my self-interest to believe it.	Eating cauliflower will help me live a longer, healthier life.

the desire to seek out additional information to verify an egocentric position. As a result, egocentric thinking hinders proactive change and maintains the status quo.

COMMON CRITICAL THINKING QUESTIONS

CT requires continual practice to develop exacting questions that yield a wide range of information. For a moment, consider how questions are framed with clients. The initial questions are general in nature, not overly complicated, but framed in a manner to gather an initial understanding of the situation. Over time, the social worker's questions become more complex and probe the situation in a deeper, more focused manner. The manner in which these questions are framed reflects a typology that includes lower to higher level skills (see Table 4.2). The questions essentially are creating and following a map to an unknown destination. The objective for each query is to find a piece to the puzzle that eventually results in a full, complete, and effective solution. At some point in the process the solution(s) may seem somewhat obvious. Although it may be tempting to say, "We have an answer," it is necessary to continue the process to its end. Why? New information may emerge that dramatically shifts the practitioner to a different answer.

At this point, it is fair to say, "OK, what are the questions that I should ask? Tell me specifically what I need to do and where I should begin." Asserting there is or promoting a specific order of exact questions to ask is disingenuous and of little use. Each individual social worker must develop his or her process and then develop unique queries that reflect him or her. Most social workers will agree that CT incorporates a wide range, an almost endless list of questions. Some examples

Table 4.2. EXAMPLES OF LOWER AND HIGHER LEVEL QUESTIONS IN THE CRITICAL THINKING PROCESS

Thinking Skills	Purpose	Sample Action Prompts	Example Questions
Lower Level			
Remembering	Memorize and recall facts	Recognize, list, describe, identify, retrieve, name	• What do we already know about . . . ? • What are the principles of . . . ? • How does . . . tie in with what we learned before?
Understanding	Interpret meaning	Describe, generalize explain, estimate, predict	• Summarize . . . or explain . . . • What will happen if . . . ? • What does . . . mean?
Higher Level			
Applying	Apply knowledge to new situations	Implement, carry out, use, apply, show, solve, hypothesize	• What would happen if . . . ? • What is a new example of . . . ? • How could . . . be used to . . . ? • What is the counterargument for . . . ? • Why is . . . important? • What is the difference between . . . and . . . ?
Analyzing	Break down or examine information	Compare, organize, deconstruct	• What are the implications of . . . ? • What are the implications of . . . ? • Explain why/explain how? • What is . . . analogous to? • How are . . . and . . . similar? • How does . . . effect . . . ? • Why is . . . happening? • What is the best . . . and why?
Evaluating	Judge or decide according to a set of criteria	Check, critique, judge, conclude, explain	• Do you agree or disagree with the statement . . . ? • What evidence is there to support your answer? • What are the strengths and weaknesses of . . . ? • What is the nature of . . . ? • What is the solution to the problem of . . . ?
Creating	Combine elements into a new pattern	Design, construct, plan, produce	• What do you think causes . . . ? Why? • What is another way to look at . . . ?

Source: King, A. (1995). "Inquiring Minds Really Do Want to Know: Using Questioning to Teach Critical Thinking," *Teaching of Psychology, 22*(1), p. 14.

include the following: When did it happen? Does it always happen the same way? Does it occur only as a result of . . . ? How would you explain what happened? Why did it happen? What might have happened if "X" occurred instead? What sources of information are available to review? What informational sources are accurate? What information should be discarded? What might happen if we decide to do "X"? What might happen if we decide not to do "X" What is likely to happen if we do "Y" versus "X"? How significant are the implications of this decision?

The most difficult questions, however, are those the practitioner asks himself or herself. Is the position the social worker advocating for built on a sound CT process? Has the social worker merely sought out only information and data sources that confirm or affirm her or his position? Honest and authentic self-reflection is essential to ensure that one's personal bias is not the driving force in the CT process. Every person has his or her own beliefs that are a result of a lifetime of experiences. Policy practitioners are professionally challenged to understand their individual beliefs and positions and how these impact their advocacy efforts. Additionally, policy practitioners must recognize there may be a multitude of other viewpoints, each with its own solution. And just as with the individual social work advocate, these diverse positions grow from individual experiences and those shared with others. Understanding how perspectives become solidified is a major component of the CT process (see Box 4.2).

Box 4.2

CRITICAL THINKING QUESTIONS TO UNDERSTANDING VIEWS, BIAS, AND POSITIONS OF SELF AND OTHERS

- How am I (they) looking at this situation; is there another way or are there multiple ways to explain the situation?
- Is there anything I (they) am taking for granted?
- What are my (their) thoughts and beliefs based on?
- Why do I (they) believe in this particular matter?
- What am I (they) actually focusing on?
- Is my (their) viewpoint the only reasonable perspective that makes sense? If so, how do I (they) know that?

- How do others consider the situation; why do they see the situation differently from me?
- Am I (they) having difficulty understanding the position(s) of others with whom I (they) disagree?
- How did I (they) reach my conclusions?
- Does it matter to me (them) personally what others may think of my (their) views?
- What should I study in order to understand other positions, beliefs, and perspectives that challenge or are different from my position?

CHALLENGES TO CRITICAL THINKING

Critical thinking is fraught with challenges. This is a process that must be continually practiced, or the necessary skills will remain underdeveloped and flawed. The individual must be able to risk his or her personal beliefs—"the idea that I may have been wrong all these years is not one I wish to deal with." Being intellectually independent can be a lonely existence.

Personal Values and Beliefs

A significant challenge to CT is to recognize when personal values and beliefs influence the collection and interpretation of evidence. One way to reduce or minimize one's bias is to adopt Rawls's (1971) "veil of ignorance," which attempts to remove external pressures and considerations from decision making. The most cited example of Rawls's veil of ignorance concerns the cutting of a cake for a group of people. One person must slice the cake and share the pieces with the group members; how will the cake be cut, and what are the specific instructions for cutting the slices? Rawls's thesis is that the cake will be cut as evenly as possible because no one knows who will get which piece. To ensure that the "slicer" gets his or her fair share, the pieces will be cut as equally as possible. If, on the other hand, the pieces of cake were uneven, then the larger slices may be taken when the slicer's turn comes, and he or she may be left with the smallest slice. The veil theoretically creates an environment that results in equal distribution. Unfortunately, the human condition does not allow one to fully and completely abdicate one's values and beliefs; a full and complete veil of ignorance is most difficult to achieve. No matter how systematic the decision-making process may be, the process itself does not exist in a valueless vacuum. Recognizing when one is disregarding evidence is paramount in critical thinking.

Power of Social Proof

A persuasive weapon of influence is social proof, whereby a person determines what is correct by figuring out what others think is truthful; the greater the number of people or groups that subscribe to a certain proposition, the greater the chances are the idea is correct (Cialdini, 2007, pp. 116–117). Or a social proof may depend on who is proposing or supporting a certain claim. Marketing uses social proof in its advertising on a consistent basis. Just look at television advertisements on any given day and you will see the following:

- A medical doctor wearing a white medical jacket with a stethoscope around her neck looks official and speaks with authority when promoting a specific pharmaceutical drug.

- Automobile advertisements using "real people, not actors" influence the viewer to "assume" the nonactors' reactions are real and not following a script.
- A celebrity speaking in a soft, almost mournful voice, promoting support for animal cruelty prevention programs, implies this famous person is concerned about the same issue as everyday people.

The term *social proof* suggests that an individual who is unsure what to believe or do will take cues from others; there is no examination or consideration of information and its accuracy; rather, the power of social proof rests with those who subscribe to a particular position.

Validity and Authenticity of Websites

The World Wide Web is young, yet it continues to grow and expand in ways that are virtually unfathomable. The Internet first became available free of charge to the

---

Activity Box 4.1

Do an internet search using the words "Abraham Lincoln, internet" and see what comes up? In particular, look for "Abraham Lincoln's Internet Wisdom". What you find is on numerious internet web sites; is the information accureate, correct? How do you know?

Retrieved from http://www.relatably.com/q/abraham-lincoln-believe-internet-quote on July 4, 2017.

public in 1991, whereas the term *Internet* was officially defined as a "global information system" in 1995 by the Federal Networking Council (The Networking and Information Technology Research Development Program, n.d.). It is impossible to know how many websites are on the World Wide Web (WWW) because no one group or organization is responsible for its oversight.

The basic axiom for the WWW is that just because it is on the Web does not mean it is accurate or truthful. The critical task for social workers is the ability to skillfully and thoughtfully access and apply appropriate reliable " . . . technology to multiple resources on any given topic" (Wardlow, n.d.).

The advantages of the digital age are easily distorted by the enticement of readily available "cut and paste" information for reports or studies. The ability to recognize a website's validity and reliability is key in today's digital age. There are numerous ways to access the validity of a website. Box 4.3 offers some simple and quick techniques to reduce the risks associated with Web-based sources.

Box 4.3
STEPS TO VALIDATE A WEBSITE'S AUTHENTICITY

1. **Look at the website's connection type.** A website that has an "https" tag (note the "s") is usually more secure—and therefore more trustworthy—than a site using the more common "http" (no "s") designation. But a site that uses an "https" connection can still be unreliable, so use other means to verify as well.
2. **Check the site's security status in your browser's address bar.** For most browsers, a "safe" website will display a padlock icon to the left of the website's URL.
3. **Other red flags.** Look for other red flags such as:
   - Multiple dashes or symbols in the domain name
   - Domain names that imitate actual businesses (e.g., "Amaz0n" or "NikeOutlet")
   - Domain extensions like ".biz" and ".info." These sites tend not to be credible.
   - ".com" and ".net" sites are the easiest domain extensions to obtain.
   - ".edu" (educational institute) or ".gov" (government) site
4. **Look for the website's "Contact" page.** A Contact page allows users to send questions, comments, and concerns to the Web page's owner. Call the provided number to verify the legitimacy of the website. The link to a Contact page is typically found at the bottom of the home page. It is a red flag if no Contact page is listed anywhere.
5. **Google transparency report**. This free aid detects safe and unsafe websites simply by typing in the URL. https://www.google.com/transparencyreport/safebrowsing/diagnostic/index.html

6. **Look at the domain.**
   - COM—This domain is intended for commercial entities (i.e., companies) but is open to any individual or entity.
   - EDU—Originally intended for all educational institutions. In the United States, this was restricted in 2001 to postsecondary institutions.
   - NET—Intended to hold only the computers of network providers; acts as "umbrella" that creates a portal to a set of smaller websites.
   - ORG—Originally intended for nonprofit organizations though it is open to any individual or entity.
   - INT—This domain is for organizations offices, and programs established by international treaties, or international databases.

   United States–Only Generic Domains
   - GOV—Intended for any kind of government, including federal, state, county, or local, office or agency.
   - MIL—This domain is used by the US military.

Country Code Top-Level Domains (These are nation/country specific)
   - .al—Albania
   - .au—Australia
   - .by—Belarus
   - .ch—Switzerland

For a complete listing as of January 3, 2017, see https://www.theguardian.com/news/datablog/2009/nov/24/internet-domain-names-worldwide

7. **Is it documented with footnotes or links?** Does the website cite credible sources within their work or point you to credible sources via URLs, such as a social work article with links to a source in *Social Work* or other major social work or social science journal?
   Be careful of sites like *Wikipedia*, which are collaboratively developed by users and not subjected to a blind peer review process. Any person can add or change information on these sites, and content may be full of misinformation. Wikipedia and other similar sites may be useful to read, but do not rely on these sites for expertise.
8. **What type of sites link to the website?** Is the website cited or linked to other websites? An indicator that a website is sound is if it is linked to or referenced by reputable organizations.
9. **What is the purpose of the website?** To sell a product; a personal hobby; a public service; further scholarship on a topic; provide general information on a topic; persuade the reader to adopt a particular point of view?
10. **Assess the quality of information**. When was it first published; is it regularly updated; when was its last posting; are other sources cited or linked; are the data the most current available?

11. **Beware of anonymous authors.** In general, reports and information with an author's name and affiliation are more reliable than works produced anonymously . . . *though this is not always the case.* If you do not know the author or his or her work, Google the name to check credentials.

12. **What type of sites link to the website you're evaluating?** Is the website being cited by others? An indicator that a website is sound is if it is linked to or referenced by other organizations.

    Go to either www.yahoo.com or www.google.com. In the search box, type "link:[name of your website]" with no space after the colon. An example using the United States–based Children's Defense Fund would look like: link:http://www.childrensdefense.org. The resulting search will contain websites that link to the site. Does it include reputable or well-known sites?

13. **Beware of bias.** There are scores of social policy–related websites, but many of them are run by groups that have a bias in favor of one political party or philosophy. A conservative website isn't likely to report objectively on a liberal politician, and vice versa. Look for nonpartisan sponsored websites; for example, the sponsoring group does not subscribe or endorse one political orthodoxy over another.

Sources: http://www.edb.utexas.edu/petrosino/Legacy_Cycle/mf_jm/Challenge%201/web-site%20reliable.pdf; http://journalism.about.com/od/reporting/a/Eight-Ways-To-Tell-If-A-Website-Is-Reliable.htm; http://www.svc.edu/library/docs/credible_websites.pdf; https://owl.english.purdue.edu/owl/resource/588/02/

Fake News

Bogus news stories are part of American history. Certainly one of the more famous shams was the 1938 Halloween radio broadcast of H. G. Wells's *War of the Worlds* that reported an alien invasion of the United States was taking place. Many of those in the listening audience did not realize that the transmission was fake, just a tale for Halloween. Rather, scores of people across the country assumed aliens were invading the nation—go to https://www.youtube.com/watch?v=OzC3Fg_rRJM to hear a replay of the actual broadcast.

Fake news continues to proliferate the American and worldwide landscape and in some instances resulted in violent consequences. In December 2016, for example, an armed gunman was arrested in a Washington, DC, pizzeria that was named in a fake news story as a business that was "harboring young children as sex slaves as part of a child-abuse ring led by Hillary Clinton . . . (he said to authorities) he was armed to help rescue children" (Kang & Goldman, 2015). And the 2016 US national presidential campaign cycle saw the proliferation of fake news and the difficulties to distinguish such stories from reality.

Box 4.4

EXAMPLES OF FAKE NEWS STORIES IN 2015 AND 2016

- A Fox News New York affiliate reported that the iPhone 5 was going to come with a holographic keyboard and projector.
- *The Boston Tribune*, a satire website that mimics an actual news publication, first reported that President Barak Obama's mother-in-law received a $160,000 pension for babysitting her granddaughters during Obama's time as president. Other news sites picked up and reported the story as fact.
- WTOE 5 News, a fantasy news website, first reported that Pope Francis endorsed Donald Trump. The fake news was picked up and reported by news outlets around the world.
- A number of conservative websites reported that President Obama signed Executive Order 13738, banning the Pledge of Allegiance in public schools. But there is no Executive Order 13738.
- A website, WhatDoesItMean.com, posted an article, "Top US Admiral Fired for Questioning Obama Purchase of Mansion in Dubai," that reported the Obama family has a vacation home in Dubai. But simply not true.
- Fake documents posted on a now deleted account that Hillary Clinton suffered from seizures and dementia in documents released by her longtime physician. Clinton's personal physician, however, countered to say the documents were fake.
- Fox News morning show Fox and Friends interviewer Brian Kilmeade began a segment titled, "Can people collecting food stamps in Colorado add marijuana to their shopping lists?" He answered his own question. "Right now," he declared, "the answer is yes!" But the answer is clearly "no" as SNAP benefits can only be used to purchase certain food items only from authorized sellers.

Given the multiplicity of purported news sites and the resending of "news" via social media, it is nearly impossible to know if a story is true or false when first reported. The retweeting and social media postings of false stories give them a life of their own to the point that some will always believe the ruse to be real, no matter the evidence that says otherwise. A few cautionary steps can be taken, however, when reading or hearing about a news item (see Box 4.4).

- Consider the source. Is it a fantasy or fake news site such as *National Report, World News Daily Report*, or *Stupid* (yes, that's its name!).
- Read the entire story, not just the headline.
- Check other news outlets to see what they are reporting on the item.

- Check the author. Do a search of the author's name to see what she or he has done in the past. If there is no author, then "buyer beware."
- The headline is unbelievable. A common ploy among fake news sites is creating a headline that seems outrageous, gets people angry, and is plain shocking. The headlines are written in a way to confirm a group's preconceived biases so that these individuals then pass the story on to others.
- Is the story an actual joke? The *Borowitz Report*, for example, appears in the *New Yorker Magazine* with the clear disclaimer, "Not the news" (Borowitz, 2017). Typical articles included "Putin to Sing at Trump Inauguration" (December 18, 2016) and Karaoke Machine Backs Out of Performing at Inauguration (January 15, 2017). Clearly, the columns are satire, but they frequently are picked up in the social media world as well as in mainline media.
- Confirm with fact checkers. Often there are news stories on issues we know little to nothing about. Verify sources whose primary responsibility is to authenticate information as well as the accuracy of a presentation. Such websites include FactCheck.org, Snopes.com, the *Washington Post* Fact Checker, and PolitiFact.com.

Information Overload

Equally challenging to effective CT is information overload. The ease of information accessibility can be overwhelming. For example, googling "social policy in Texas" resulted in 18.3 million identified sites, while the phrase "social policy in the United States" yielded 573 million possible sites (www.google.com). Many of these sites were repetitive, but even so, the ability to sort through various sites and discern good from bad information is a monumental task. In fact, most people only consider sites listed on the first couple of pages. Critical thinking requires disciplined analysis of the Web to ensure that every possible step is taken to find accurate information. One of the worst possible scenarios for a social worker is to advocate a position that is discovered to be based on faulty, inaccurate information. Such a result only reduces the chances of success while also calling into question the social worker's personal and professional credibility.

Information overload also mandates that the social worker determine when there is no need to collect additional data or information. There is no formula or mechanism to determine when enough evidence has been pieced together. A clear indicator that additional information is no longer needed is when patterns begin to emerge or information is repeating itself.

Immediacy Versus Thoughtful Assessment

As has been shown, proactive CT is a time-consuming process that requires the collection, distilling, and assessment of a variety of data points and information pieces.

A thoughtful and reflective process is essential in order for options or alternatives to emerge. This requires time, which often is not a luxury the practitioner has at her or his disposal. For example, a supervisor may ask the social worker to prepare a policy recommendation for review by the agency's board of directors the next day. Developing a proposal to achieve the greatest benefit for the greater good while helping those who are least advantaged requires time and simply cannot be rushed. Unfortunately, in today's world, time is a luxury and not viewed as a necessary condition for successful work. Social workers, in fact most people, are connected to their workplace 24/7; the written memo is virtually nonexistent, replaced by emails that can be sent from anywhere, any time of the day or night; turnaround time for reports has been shortened due to the expectation for quick information. Successful critical thinking, which takes time, is threatened by the absence of thoughtful process as the need for fast, rapid, and swift decisions becomes the primary work objective.

A FEW FINAL THOUGHTS

The willingness to change one's personal point of view or opinion is not easy. People just do not like to admit, "I was wrong" or "I don't know." Critical thinking is an important step that helps make personal change somewhat easier, but all people, including social workers, can be hard-headed in their views.

Yet for a social worker to be impactful in her or his practice, the practitioner must set aside personal beliefs and positions in order to find a best solution. Sometimes the result might be a long-held position the social worker holds; conversely, the resolution might be something the individual never would have considered. All too often people are far too wedded to and literally blinded by their beliefs to the detriment of finding out the best solution. In the political world, some individuals vote for a candidate from their own party, for example, Democrat, Green, Independent, Libertarian, or Republican; the idea of supporting the best individual, no matter the political party affiliation, is becoming less common.

Successful CT requires the social worker to recognize that he or she may not fully understand the situation or related information (see Activity Box 4.2). Similarly, critical thinking is best achieved by the individual's curiosity, creativity, and desire to seek out new, different, and more powerful solutions. Asking relevant questions; analyzing ideas; weighing out options against the facts; and asking for, listening to, and accepting feedback are important tools in the social worker's policy practice repertoire. The social worker is looking for proof, is able to adjust personal opinions when new facts emerge, and rejects incorrect and irrelevant information while suspending personal opinions and bias. Critical thinking is not a one-time occurrence but over time becomes part of the social worker's lifelong experience.

The bottom line is that CT, if done appropriately and honestly, will result in solutions that have the best opportunity to achieve the desired result that is firmly rooted in social justice (see Activity Box 4.1).

Activity Box 4.2

TRUTHS, DECEPTIONS, OR FALSEHOODS—WHAT DOES CRITICAL THINKING TELL YOU?

News Item or Statement	Initial Reaction: Agree, Disagree; Why?	Cite Three Sources That Confirm or Deny the Statement	Is This a Truth, a Falsehood, a Deceptions, or a Half-Truth?
In March 2016, Florida senator Marco Rubio said that the political and human-rights situation in Cuba had worsened since President Obama made his diplomatic opening to the island.			
It was reported on January 17, 2017, that the Congressional Budget Office predicts 18 million uninsured, higher premiums in first year after Obamacare repeal, and delay.			
A banana is a berry, and a strawberry is not a berry.			
Maine is the closest US state to Africa.			
Texas Senator Ted Cruz said during his bid for the Republican Party nomination for president that he would "end welfare benefits for those here illegally." The question to answer is: Are undocumented persons eligible for welfare benefits?			

In the early 2000s, a number of news organizations, including the BBC, ABC, CNN, and The Daily Mail, reported that the World Health Organization suggested that blond hair wasn't going to exist in the human population after 200 years. It had been determined that blond hair was a recessive gene that is being slowly usurped by the other hair colors. Due to this genetic takeover, the last natural blond would be born in Finland sometime over the next two centuries.			
During a television interview on January 8, 2010, former NYC Mayor Rudy Giuliani said, "We had no domestic attacks under Bush. We've had one under Obama."			
During the presidential campaign, Democratic Party nominee Hilary Clinton said more guns brought into New York and used in crimes come from Vermont, on a per capita basis, than any other state.			

On April 21, 2009, Minnesota Representative Michele Bachmann said, "Carbon dioxide is portrayed as harmful. But there isn't even one study that can be produced that shows that carbon dioxide is a harmful gas."			
In September, 2008, US Senator Joe Biden said, "When the stock market crashed, Franklin D. Roosevelt got on the television and didn't just talk about the, you know, the princes of greed."			

REFERENCES

Bastardi, A., Uhlmann, E., & Ross, L. (2011). Wishful thinking: Belief, desire, and the motivated evaluation of scientific evidence. *Psychological Science, 22*(6), 731–732.

Bok, D. (2006). *Our underachieving colleges, a candid look at how much students learn and why they should be learning more*. Princeton, NJ: Princeton University Press.

Borowitz, A. (2017). The Borowitz Report. Retrieved from http://www.newyorker.com/humor/borowitz-report on January 3, 2017.

Brookfield, S. (2006, reprint edition). *Developing critical thinkers, challenging adults to explore alternative ways of thinking and acting*. San Francisco, CA: Jossey-Bass.

Bump, P. (2016, December 7). Why does Trump keep saying that the murder rate is the highest in 45 years? *The Washington Post*. Retrieved from https://www.washingtonpost.com/news/the-fix/wp/2016/12/07/why-does-trump-keep-saying-that-the-murder-rate-increase-is-the-highest-in-45-years/?utm_term=.56b1ab9bca0c on December 24, 2016.

Cialdini, R. (2007). *Influence, the psychology of persuasion*. New York, NY: HarperCollins.

Commission on Accreditation, Commission on Educational Policy. (2015). *Educational policy accreditation standards*. Alexandria, VA: Council on Social Work Education.

Critical Thinking Community. (n.d.). Defining critical thinking. Retrieved from http://www.criticalthinking.org/pages/defining-critical-thinking/766 on November 18, 2015.

Cuseo, J. (2016). Questions that promote deeper thinking. Retrieved from http://oncourse-workshop.com/life-long-learning/questions-promote-deeper-thinking/ on December 10, 2016.

Dewey, J. (1933). *How we think: A restatement of the relation of reflective thinking to the educative process* (revised ed.), Boston, MA: D. C. Heath.

Fisher, A. (2001). *Critical thinking: An introduction.* New York, NY: Cambridge University Press.

Glaser, E. (1941). *An experiment in the development of critical thinking.* New York, NY: Columbia University.

Great Schools Partnership. (2013). The glossary of education reform. Definition of "critical thinking." Retrieved from http://edglossary.org/critical-thinking/ on December 28, 2016.

Kang, C., & Goldman, A. (2015, December 5). In Washington pizzeria attack, fake news brought real guns. *The Washington Post.* Retrieved from https://www.nytimes.com/2016/12/05/business/media/comet-ping-pong-pizza-shooting-fake-news-consequences.html?_r=0 on January 3, 2017.

Kiely, E. (2016, January 7). Clinton's misleading ad on drug prices. Retrieved from http://www.factcheck.org/2016/01/clintons-misleading-ad-on-drug-prices/ on December 24, 2016.

King, A. (1995). Inquiring minds really do want to know: Using questioning to teach critical thinking. *Teaching of Psychology, 22*(1), 13–16.

Levitin, D. (2015). *A field guide to lies, critical thinking in the information age.* New York, NY: Dutton House.

The Network Research and Information Technology Program. (n.d.). Definition of "internet." Retrieved from https://www.nitrd.gov/fnc/Internet_res.aspx on January 3, 2017.

Norris, S. P. (1985). Synthesis of research on critical thinking. *Educational Leadership, 42*(8), 40–45.

Paul, R., & Elder, L. (2007). *The miniature guide to critical thinking, concepts and tools* (4th ed.). Dillon Beach, CA: Foundation for Critical Thinking.

Scriven, M., & Paul, R. (1987). 8th Annual International Conference on Critical Thinking and Education Reform. Retrieved from http://www.criticalthinking.com/company on December 28, 2016.

Wardlow, L. (n.d.). Stronger student engagement. Retrieved from https://www.pearson.com/corporate/efficacy-and-research/schools-education-research/research-reports/teaching-in-a-digital-age/stronger-student-engagement.html on July 26, 2017.

The White House. (2017, January 10). President Obama's farewell address. Retrieved from https://www.whitehouse.gov/farewell on January 11, 2017.

CHAPTER 5

Contours of Analysis

"Analysis" is familiar to every person. Day in and day out, people make multiple decisions from the moment they wake up to the time they fall asleep at the end of the day. Analysis is the first step of each of these individual decision-making processes with each resulting in some sort of action. Some analysis is fast, quick, and easy, whereas other forms of scrutiny are laborious, requiring patience and time. Most daily analyses are subconsciously done and not even considered to be analysis:

- What is the weather today? What clothes should I wear?
- Should I eat this doughnut now, later, or maybe skip it today?
- Do I stop to fill up the car's gas tank now, or do I have enough to get around the remainder of the day?
- I really would like to get out of town for a long weekend, but should I go?
- What should I eat for dinner tonight?
- Can I afford to buy a new car, or should I keep repairing my used vehicle?

From one's home to the workplace to recreation, analysis is part of the daily human experience.

ISSUE AND POLICY ANALYSES

Issue analysis and policy analysis are far different and more complex compared to an individual's personal, everyday decision-making processes. Issue and policy analyses are formal, systematic, and disciplined exercises requiring the gathering of a variety of data, being able to discern "good" information from "bad," understanding the full consequences of the condition being addressed or attempting to be reconciled, and crafting a recommendation or series of options that target the issue within a social justice perspective. And just as important is communicating the analysis's findings in a clear, understandable manner.

Beginning Points for Issue and Policy Analyses

The first step in analysis is to understand the problem, issue, or policy that will be assessed. This understanding derives from an array of information; there is an art and science as to how it is collected and applied to a particular issue. First, all data should be as current as possible. The best-case scenario is that numerical references should have been collected within 2–3 years from the time of the analysis. Reports relying on 10- to 15-year-old data are likely to be outdated and not accurately reflect the current condition. Sometimes, however, the only available data are not up to date. In such cases, the analysis should clearly specify that (1) the data, while dated, are the most current available numbers and (2) the figures might not exactly reflect the present-day situation.

Second, finding reliable and valid data is critical when developing a neutral and unbiased study. Governmental sources, such as the Social Security Administration (https://www.ssa.gov/) and the US Census Bureau (http://www.census.gov/), are recognized as reliable unbiased sources.

A third source of easily accessible information is data reported on various websites. Such information should be viewed with caution until the site and its information are verified as legitimate (see Chapter 4, Box 4.3). A website's accuracy is easily verifiable: When was the page was last updated (typically this is found at the top or bottom of the page)? Are the sources for data clearly identified; are there organizations that link to the specific Web page? Use a search engine such as Google or Yahoo and type in "Link:[name of the website]" (i.e., "link:http://www.usa.edu"). The results will contain websites that link to the site; are these sites reputable and reliable?

A fourth information source includes reports issued by think tanks. A *think tank* is an independent organization that promotes its own unique intellectual independence that theoretically is free from external influences such as funding sources or outside pressure groups. Although some think tanks are nonpartisan, others reflect a political or philosophical ideology, that is, centrist, contractual, feminist, libertarian, and socialist (see Table 5.1). Understanding a think tank's particular leaning or philosophical foundations is easily determined by visiting the organizations Web page and, if available, click on the "about" link. An Internet search of a specific think tank will also provide additional information regarding the organization's ideological leanings. Accessing think tank reports and studies can provide unique and valuable insights and helps the social worker gain a broader view of a particular issue. At the same time, it is critical to understand a think tank's political or philosophical underpinnings to determine if and to what extent a report's findings are written in a manner that reflects a particular ideology.

A key point to remember with all think tanks and governmental agencies, as discussed in Chapter 4, is that it is virtually impossible to lay aside individual beliefs and values. Applying critical thinking principles is imperative when relying on any think tank or governmental report. The guideline "just because it is on the web

Table 5.1. EXAMPLES OF THINK TANKS AND THEIR POLITICAL LEANINGS

Name	Political Leaning	Stated Mission	Website
RAND Corporation	Nonpartisan	Focuses on the issues that matter most, such as health, education, national security, international affairs, law and business, the environment, and more. With a research staff consisting of some of the world's preeminent minds, RAND has been expanding the boundaries of human knowledge for more than 60 years.	www.rand.org
Pew Research Center	Nonpartisan	Independence, impartiality, open-mindedness, and professional integrity are indispensable to the mission and success of the Pew Research Center. To promote and preserve these values, the center's Code of Ethics includes the following policies: • Conflicts of interest • Prohibitions on electioneering • Integrity of research	www.pewresearch.org
Council on Foreign Relations	Nonpartisan	Resource for its members, government officials, business executives, journalists, educators and students, civic and religious leaders, and other interested citizens in order to help them better understand the world and the foreign policy choices facing the United States and other countries.	www.cfr.org
Heritage Foundation	Conservative	To formulate and promote conservative public policies based on the principles of free enterprise, limited government, individual freedom, traditional American values, and a strong national defense.	www.heritage.org
American Enterprise Institute	Conservative	To defend the principles and improve the institutions of American freedom and democratic capitalism—limited government, private enterprise, individual liberty and responsibility, vigilant and effective defense and foreign policies, political accountability, and open debate.	www.aei.org

Table 5.1. CONTINUED

Name	Political Leaning	Stated Mission	Website
American Foreign Policy Council	Conservative	To advance the security and prosperity of the United States by providing primary source information, as well as policy options, to persons and organizations who make or influence the national security and foreign policies of the United States; arranging meetings and facilitating dialogue between American statesmen and their counterparts in other countries; and fostering the acceptance and development of representative institutions and free market economies throughout the world in a manner consistent with the Constitution, the national interest, and the values of the United States.	www.afpc.org
Hoover Institute	Conservative and libertarian	This Institution supports the Constitution of the United States, its Bill of Rights, and its method of representative government. Both our social and economic systems are based on private enterprise from which spring initiative and ingenuity.	www.hoover.org
Freedom House	Conservative and libertarian	Freedom is possible only in democratic political environments where governments are accountable to their own people; the rule of law prevails; and freedoms of expression, association, and belief, as well as respect for the rights of minorities and women, are guaranteed.	www.freedomhouse.org
Philadelphia Society	Conservative and libertarian	To sponsor the interchange of ideas through discussion and writing, in the interest of deepening the intellectual foundation of a free and ordered society, and of broadening the understanding of its basic principles and traditions. In pursuit of this end, we shall examine a wide range of issues: economic, political, cultural, religious, and philosophic. We shall seek understanding, not conformity.	http://phillysoc.org/

(continued)

Table 5.1. CONTINUED

Name	Political Leaning	Stated Mission	Website
Cato Institute	Libertarian	To originate, disseminate, and increase understanding of public policies based on the principles of individual liberty, limited government, free markets, and peace. Our vision is to create free, open, and civil societies founded on libertarian principles.	www.cato.org
Black Feminist Think Tank	Feminist	A collective of intellectuals building and practicing radical Black feminism	https://www.facebook.com/The-Black-Feminist-Think-Tank-336038799936254/
Institute for Women's Policy Research	Feminist		http://www.iwpr.org/about
Competitive Enterprise Institute	Libertarian	Promotes libertarian ideals through analysis, education, coalition-building, advocacy, and regulation.	www.cei.org
Reason Foundation	Libertarian	Advancing a free society by developing, applying, and promoting libertarian principles, including individual liberty, free markets, and the rule of law.	www.reason.org
Center for American Progress	Liberal	To develop new policy ideas, critique the policy that stems from conservative values, challenge the media to cover the issues that truly matter, and shape the national debate.	www.americanprogress.org
Center on Budget and Policy Priorities	Liberal	Working at the federal and state levels on fiscal policy and public programs that affect low- and moderate-income families and individuals.	www.chpp.org
Human Rights Watch	Liberal	Dedicated to protecting the human rights of people around the world. We stand with victims and activists to prevent discrimination, to uphold political freedom, to protect people from inhumane conduct in wartime, and to bring offenders to justice. We investigate and expose human rights violations and	www.hrw.org

Table 5.1. CONTINUED

Name	Political Leaning	Stated Mission	Website
		hold abusers accountable. We challenge governments and those who hold power to end abusive practices and respect international human rights law. We enlist the public and the international community to support the cause of human rights for all.	
Brookings Institution	Centrist	Provide innovative and practical recommendations that advance three broad goals: strengthen American democracy; foster the economic and social welfare, security, and opportunity of all Americans; and secure a more open, safe, prosperous, and cooperative international system.	www.brookings.edu
Carnegie Endowment for International Peace	Centrist	To advance the cause of peace through analysis and development of fresh policy ideas and direct engagement and collaboration with decision makers in government, business, and civil society. Working together, our centers bring the inestimable benefit of multiple national viewpoints to bilateral, regional, and global issues.	www. carnegieendowment.org
Woodrow Wilson International Center for Scholars	Centrist	To commemorate the ideals and concerns of Woodrow Wilson by: providing a link between the world of ideas and the world of policy; and fostering research, study, discussion, and collaboration among a full spectrum of individuals concerned with policy and scholarship in national and world affairs.	www.wilsoncenter.org
Fabian Society	Socialist	Britain's oldest political think tank, founded in 1884, the Society is at the forefront of developing political ideas and public policy on the Left. The Society promotes: greater equality of power, wealth and opportunity; the value of collective action and public service; an accountable, tolerant and active democracy; citizenship, liberty, and human rights; sustainable development; and multilateral international cooperation.	http://www.fabians. org.uk/

(*continued*)

Table 5.1. CONTINUED

Name	Political Leaning	Stated Mission	Website
TASC (Think-tank for Action on Social Change)	Socialist	TASC is an independent, Irish progressive think tank whose core focus is economic equality and democratic accountability. Its mission is to produce policy analysis and present evidence-based proposals for the achievement of a more equal, flourishing society with accountable government and strong, responsible public engagement.	http://www.tasc.ie/

Sources: Black Feminist Think Tank, retrieved from https://www.facebook.com/The-Black-Feminist-Think-Tank-336038799936254/ on January 17, 2017; Fabian Society, retrieved from http://www.fabians.org.uk/ on January 18, 2017; Insidegov. Research Think Tanks, retrieved from http://think-tanks.insidegov.com/ on March 24, 2016; Institute for Women's Policy Research, retrieved from http://www.iwpr.org/about on January 17, 2017; TASC, retrieved from http://www.tasc.ie/ on January 17, 2017.

doesn't make it true" is also applicable to think tank and governmental reports. Typically, these reports provide specific recommendations, the reliability of which depends on the level of impartiality employed by the report's authors. This does not mean that a think tank or agency's report and recommendation(s) must be devoid of a political perspective; rather, the policy practitioner must be able to discern any preconceived notions, ideas, prejudices, and author(s)' biases that may be embedded in the report. The policy practitioner must consider the logic of the presentation, the validity and reliability of the report data, and the extent they support the final recommendations.

CRAFTING AN ANALYTIC FRAMEWORK

There are a variety of formats and templates available for a social worker to model when developing policy documents. *Policy alerts, policy memos,* and *policy briefs,* among others, are the more common forms of policy papers an advocate prepares in the workplace; the purposes, differences, and layouts of these specific presentations are discussed in Chapter 10. These various policy documents, while interrelated with each other, are direct offshoots of two larger analytic processes—*social issue* and *social policy analyses.* These two types of investigations provide the basis from which policy memos, briefs, and alerts are built.

Social issue analysis, which is also be referred to as *problem analysis,* explores a specific dilemma that impacts a large group of people and leads to a recommended organizational stand; *social policy analysis* focuses on an existing policy, its purpose, and strengths, and offers recommendations to strengthen or eliminate the policy. Both approaches are methodical in their applications, each requiring the framing of thoughtful, probing, rigorous, clear, and unambiguous questions. The specific queries need not be numerous nor complicated, but their objective is to gather specific information that results in well-thought-out remedies.

A social worker typically conducts *issue analysis* in his or her employing agency. An individual directly or indirectly related to the agency—a board member, the executive director, other staff, donors, or a community leader or group—raises a question about a social issue and the necessity to offer a new program targeting the unmet need. The initial discussions generally include the question, "Is this something we should be considering?" For example, an agency might ask if its mission includes adding direct mental health services for transgender youth. Prior to reaching a decision, the agency needs to fully understand the nature of the situation and, as a result, tasks one of the staff members to conduct a social issue analysis.

The second analytic method, *policy analysis*, examines an existing agency's policy to determine if the organization's program is achieving the policy's desired goal; identify what, if any, adjustments are required for the organization to be more effective in the agency's day-to-day work; or check whether the policy's usefulness has run its full course and it is time to redirect the organization's efforts.

In both cases, the final written report is typically considered an *intra-agency* document, a communication that remains internal to the organization's staff and board of directors. The report is focused, evidence-based, succinct, easily understood, and practical. The issue or policy analysis is not at all similar in format or style to an academic research or class paper. The agency-based report is generally short, void of academic jargon (i.e., discussing abstract research methods), and literally guides the reader from a clear beginning point to a series of recommendations or conclusions based on the report's findings. *Brevity in the final written report is an important guide.*

Both the issue analysis and policy analysis are not an end to themselves. Their shared purpose is to create a common beginning discussion point; the social worker's goal in writing the report is for the reader to understand the issue or policy in order to engage in a reasonable discussion that results in a formal decision. Content areas for issue and policy analyses share a number of common discussion points with slight differences (see Table 5.2).

An important note needs to be added. There are numerous policy and issue analytic models detailed in social policy textbooks and journal articles; each spells out a specific protocol for preparing policy specific documents (see Table 5.3). No single model or approach should be seen as the "best" approach to analysis. Rather, the social worker over time develops a unique style that fits his or her professional personality.

ISSUE ANALYSIS

A social problem is a *public issue* that shapes, changes, and affects the broader community in some form or fashion. It is defined as "a social condition (such as poverty) or a pattern of behavior (such as substance abuse) that harms some individuals or all people in a society and that a sufficient number of people believe warrants public

Table 5.2. FORMAT FOR SOCIAL ISSUE AND SOCIAL POLICY BRIEFS

Social Issue Brief	Number of Pages and Words	Social Policy Brief	Number of Pages and Words
Executive summary	• 1–1 ½ pages • <750 words	Executive summary	• 1–1 ½ pages • <750 words
Problem definition	• ½–1 page • 150–250 words	Social problem addressed	• ½–1 page • 150–250 words
		Policy description and policy goal(s)	• <2 pages • 800–1,000 words
People/communities impacted by the problem	• <2 pages • 800–1,000 words	Targeted population and program eligibility	• <2 pages • 800–1,000 words
Current programs sponsored by agency or other groups or organizations	• 1 page • 250–300 words	Types of benefits/ services provided	• 1 page • 250–300 words
Impact of current and past programs	• <2 pages • 800–1,000 words	Program outcomes	• <2 pages • 800–1,000 words
		Funding sources	• 1 page • 250–300 words
Summary	• <1 page • 250 words	Recommendation(s)	• As long as necessary; should be bulleted
Appendix	• As many as needed	Appendix	• As many as needed

concern and collective action to bring about change" (Kendall, 2007, p. 4). Social problems are complex and run the gamut of the human experience, including poverty, homelessness, cultural security, gender identify, sexism, ageism, racism, work and the economy, behavioral health, education, criminal justice, environment, and war and terror. And social work professionals, either directly or indirectly, deal with the effect of social problems on their clients.

An issue analysis model includes six areas: (1) executive summary/abstract; (2) problem definition; (3) people/communities impacted by the problem; (4) current/past programs, if any exist; (5) outcomes of the current/past programs; and (6) summary statement. In addition, the report may include an appendix of supporting documents (see Table 5.2). These content areas are not written in stone but may be modified per the organization's style preferences. Checking with one' supervisor or other staff will help the social work advocate determine the favored report style.

Table 5.3. SELECTED MODELS OF POLICY ANALYSIS

Author	Key Elements of the Model
Barusch, 2015, p. 70	1. Assess the fairness of the policy development process. 2. Describe the allocation rules embodied in the policy. 3. Determine the net effect of the policy on the vulnerable population. 4. Reach a conclusion regarding the policy's impact on social justice.
Chambers, 2000, p. 71	1. Goals and objectives 2. Forms of benefits or services delivered 3. Entitlement (eligibility) rules 4. Administrative or organizational structure for service delivery 5. Financing method 6. Interactions among the foregoing elements
DiNitto and Johnson, 2012, pp. 28–30	1. What is the problem defined? 2. What is the nature or cause of the problem? 3. What are the proposed policy alternatives, and what do they intend to accomplish? 4. To what extent will the proposed polices address the need? 5. What will the proposed policy cost? 6. What are the policy's unintended effects? 7. What recommendations might be made with regard to the proposed policy?
Dobelstein, 2002, p. 76	1. Identifying, understanding, or clarifying the problem 2. Identifying the location for policy decision 3. Specifying possible solutions (alternatives) 4. Estimating or predicting the impact (outcomes) of those solutions on different populations
Gilbert and Terrell, 2002, p. 60	1. What are the bases of social allocations? 2. What are the types of social provisions to be allocated? 3. What are the strategies for the delivery of these provisions? 4. What are the ways to finance these provisions?
Jansson, 2008, pp. 201–205	1. What is the social problem or issue? 2. What strategies can be identified to address the issue or problem? 3. What are the costs and benefits for each strategy? 4. Which policy will result in the most advantages for the most people? 5. How can support be garnered for this proposal? 6. What information is required by policy advocates to communicate support?

(continued)

Table 5.3. CONTINUED

Author	Key Elements of the Model
Popple and Leighninger, 2004, pp. 35–37	1. Delineation and overview of the policy under analysis
	2. Historical analysis
	3. Social analysis
	4. Economic analysis
	5. Political analysis
	6. Policy/program evaluation
	7. Current proposals for policy reform

Sources:

Barusch, A. S. (2015). *Foundations of social policy, social justice in human perspective* (5th ed.). Stanford, CA: Cengage Learning.

Chambers, D.E. (2000). *Social policy and social programs: A method for the practical public policy analyst* (3rd ed.). Boston, MA: Allyn & Bacon.

DiNitto, D., & Johnson, D. (2012). *Essentials of social welfare, politics and public policy.* Upper Saddle River, NJ: Pearson Education.

Dobelstein, A.W. (2002). *Social welfare: Policy and analysis* (3rd ed.). Pacific Grove, CA: Brooks/Cole; Gilbert, N., & Terrell, P. (2002). *Dimensions of social welfare policy* (5th ed.). Boston, MA: Allyn & Bacon.

Jansson, B. (2008). *Becoming an effective policy advocate* (5th ed.). Belmont, CA: Thomson Brooks/Cole.

Popple, P. R., & Leighninger, L. (2004). *The policy-based profession: An introduction to social welfare policy analysis for social workers* (3rd ed.). Boston, MA: Allyn & Bacon.

Executive Summary/Abstract

The issue analysis typically begins with an *Executive Summary,* also commonly called an *Abstract.* This short section includes 500–750 words and encapsulates the report's findings (see Box 5.1). The Executive Summary is one of the more important sections of the formal report and its significance cannot be overstated. Most decision makers do not have nor take the time to read lengthy documents; rather, they will read a summary statement and the recommendation or conclusion/summary sections. The bottom line for the social worker is to ensure that the Executive Summary is written in a compelling and convincing manner that succinctly identifies key findings with resulting recommendations.

Box 5.1

HELPFUL HINT

When typing a report, use a 12-point font and double spacing. Bold and italicize headings and subheadings to alert the reader that the report is transitioning from one section to another.

Problem Definition

The *Problem Definition* is a key foundation piece in an analysis; a poorly or inaccurate written description of the issue will immediately derail any change process. The definition identifies the issue in a simple, straightforward manner. It is forthright and exact in detail, neither verbose nor flamboyant. The specific problem is set forth in a matter-of-fact, unemotional, direct fashion.

Successful policy advocates find that the most effective problem description is one that is somewhat broad though instructive in helping the reader understand the problem. Also, the information reflects a neutral, nonpartisan position. The social worker's single objective in this section of the analysis is to outline the parameters of the issue while building the case for a series of recommendations.

People/Communities Impacted by the Problem

Once the problem is defined, the discussion sharpens its focus to identifying who is directly affected. Race, gender/gender identity, ethnicity, and age are common characteristics included in this section. Additionally, if appropriate, the assessment also specifies a specific locale (e.g., state, county, city, or neighborhood) that might be affected more so compared to others. The resulting data are assessed to determine if and to what extent there may be disproportionality and differences among and between groups and communities.

Numerical information is presented in a manner to show trends over time rather than basing figures on one point in time. Typically, data groupings or percentages should reflect a range of 5 or 10 years, that is, 2000–2005 or 2000–2010. Care must be taken when using an arbitrary cutoff because it might diminish critical information. For example, the average annual national unemployment for 2011–2015 was 7.2% compared to 6.8% for the preceding 5 years, 2006–2010 (Bureau of Labor, 2016). These two unemployment rates show little variance between the two periods. However, the 5-year percentages do not accurately reflect the 2008 global economic recession, which dramatically affected unemployment rates. The average unemployment rate for 2009 and 2010 was 9.5% or 32% higher than the 2011–2015 average and nearly 40% higher than the 2006–2010 rate (Bureau of Labor, 2016). The bottom line: Be cautious with data and be sure it fairly, clearly, and accurately reflects a situation.

Policy makers generally think of a social issue in terms of who is directly impacted by the problem. A significant point to remember is that all issues include *unintended* or *indirect consequences* on other people as well. For example, US high schools, as part of the national Common Core States Standard initiative, increased the number of required math and science courses; the reasoning for this change was to strengthen students' aptitude for math and science. An unintended consequence of this action, however, was an increase in the national high school dropout rate (Plunk, Tate,

Bierut, & Grucza, 2014). However, the impact of high school dropouts dramatically affects the broader community with research findings detailing that higher dropout rates correlate with increased crime. As a result, the simple change in a high school graduation requirement resulted in an unintended negative consequence for communities. Excluding discussion around unintended consequences results in an incomplete assessment of people and communities impacted by the social issue.

Current Program and Past Efforts

Following the *People/Communities Impacted by the Problem* section, the analysis shifts to a presentation of available *Current Program and Past Efforts* that addressed the issue. The discussion identifies agencies, organizations, or groups that sponsored the programs and their success in tackling the social problem. Program eligibility criteria are outlined as well as funding sources identified.

Impact of Current/Past Programs

A "lessons learned" discussion can be fruitful, but it does allow the decision makers to stray away from the so-called here and now and avoid often difficult and painful discussions. The format is a straightforward alphabetical listing of programs, the date the program began (and ended), and a short, two- to three-sentence description of the program. In some circumstances, the program list could easily take up multiple pages. In such cases, to keep the brief's narrative short, this discussion section could be illustrative of current and past programs while a complete list is included in the appendix.

Summary

As with any paper, a summary or concluding section draws attention to the salient or key points of the analysis. The section is brief, generally less than a page, and offers a "last chance" to have the final word on the issue (see Box 5.2). The summary also recommends a course of action, a solution to the issue, questions for further study, or next steps of what the agency might undertake.

Box 5.2

HELPFUL HINT

Always check and recheck spelling and grammar. A poorly written report reduces its potential impact.

There are three significant points to remember when writing a summary statement. First, do not simply repeat what was written in the brief. The summary begins with a concise overview of the findings followed with a recommended course of action. Second, stay away from sentimental or emotional appeals in an effort to solicit support for the report's findings. The social worker's goal is for the intended audience to use the report as a springboard for thoughtful, critical discussion on an issue; emotional pleadings are value laden, with facts and findings laid aside. Third, the recommendations must be based on the report's findings. Proposed "next steps" not clearly tied to the report raise an air of suspicion that the advocate is promoting his or her own agenda. Whether true or not, this often results in the readers disregarding or ignoring the report in its totality.

POLICY ANALYSIS

As previously reviewed, social issue analysis and policy analysis share similar formats, and, as a result, some content may overlap from one type of report to the other (see Table 5.2). As with issue analysis, a series of questions are asked and data are collected and synthesized, which helps build a well-thought-out, evidenced-based conclusion followed by clear, data-driven recommendations. As with all forms of policy analysis, the social worker should be mindful of his or her political ideology and biases and set these aside as much as possible to construct an objective view of the policy at hand.

Executive Summary/Abstract

The policy analysis begins with an *Executive Summary* also commonly referred to as an *Abstract*. This beginning section's format and content are similar to the introductory statement in social issue analysis, as previously discussed in this chapter. The Executive Summary typically is no more than 750 words or about one page, double-spaced. The Summary begins with an overview of the policy explaining its purpose/goal(s); describes the problem or issue being addressed; provides an overview of the targeted population; and bullets any recommendations.

Again, it is important to highlight the importance of the Executive Summary. It is common for those who make policy decisions to skim the analysis's narrative, though they will fully read the Executive Summary because it is concise and to the point.

Social Problem Addressed

All social policies address a specific issue. This section of the analysis outlines the parameters of the problem and highlights the "gap" that results from the problem and the desired state. The *gap statement* succinctly illustrates the breadth and depth of the problem to the intended audience and leaves only one conclusion for the reader to reach: A significant problem exists that requires our attention. These data should be robust and presented in such a manner that others will care about the problem and want to do something about the issue.

Consider the following gap statement regarding child poverty in the United States.

> In 2014, approximately 20 percent of school-age children were in families living in poverty. The percentage of school-age children living in poverty ranged across the United States from 12 percent in Maryland to 29 percent in Mississippi. (National Centre for Educational Statistics, 2016)

This statement clearly articulates that there are a large number of children nationwide living in poverty, although significant differences exist between the states, as illustrated by the 17% differential between Maryland and Mississippi. This may seem like a clear and a forthright statement, but is it? For example, look at the statement that 20% of school-age children live in poverty: How many school-age children are there—10 million, 20 million, or more or less? The statement references a subset of people, specifically children who live in families that are in poverty. Again, how many families are living in poverty—10 million, 20 million, maybe more or less? And what does 12% mean in Maryland compared to 29% in Mississippi? An important outcome of any statistical reference is for the reader to be able to fully appreciate and understand its meaning. In this case, how does one visualize 20%? What does 20% really mean; how large or small is it? What does it look like?

Let's examine an alternative gap statement that also focuses on children in poverty.

> Every fifth child (in the United States) is poor . . . and every fourth infant, toddler, and preschool child is poor. (Edelman, 2014, p. 2)

Most readers would find this latter statement easier to understand. We can visualize five children, and knowing one in each subgroup is poor presents a powerful portrayal of the dimensions of the problem. Merely stating the obvious, *There are poor children in the United States,* offers little new information. Percentages are helpful but remain vague and abstract. A strong gap statement is stated in a straightforward manner that is easy to understand, and, most important, conveys the magnitude of the issue in a direct manner.

The format and content in the problem statement begin with an overview of the issue. The statement briefly details its unique features on a national, statewide, or local/regional scale by relying on the most current available governmental and/or think tank data. As the problem statement takes on greater specificity, its focus narrows to the community the organization or agency's policy is targeting.

A danger when writing the problem statement is to include an overabundance of information. Too many tables, graphs, and statistics overshadow the message, and the reader becomes lost in a sea of numbers. Writing techniques such as including bulleted items and "informational boxes" are helpful techniques and tools to convey complicated information (see Chapter 10).

Policy Description, Goals, and Objectives

The third section of the analysis identifies the specific policy by its official title as well as any acronym(s) or other references. For example, the official title for the 1996 federal program that provides income assistance to low-income families is *Temporary Assistance to Needy Families*; its more common, though unofficial reference is *TANF*. This program replaced Aid to Families with Dependent Children (AFDC). Another example is the Patient Protection and Affordable Care Act (PPACA), also known as the Affordable Care Act (ACA), but commonly called "Obamacare." It is important for the report to include a policy's formal name as well as provide explicit references to all other titles in this section.

A brief, short, matter-of-fact statement describing the policy includes an overview of the policy, how it directly relates to the identified problem, and describes "the desired human condition or social environment expected to result from implementation of the policy" (Chapin, 2007, p. 135). The policy's goals and objectives are then listed in a straightforward presentation. A common format is to identify each goal followed by its specific objectives.

A *goal* is a broad plan that offers a clear view of what is to be accomplished by a specific program. The goal statement reflects a group or community's shared values and beliefs. A goal may seem to be idealistic and will require a herculean endeavor to be achieved, but its end result (i.e., a specific desired state) is worth the effort. For example, a goal of the US Department of Agriculture's Food and Nutrition Services Strategic Plan is to "Ensure that all of America's children have access to safe, nutritious, and balanced meals" (US Department of Agriculture, 2016). For a moment, consider the size and scope of a program that will "ensure" that "all" children will "have access to safe, nutritious, and balanced meals." This in and by itself is a massive undertaking, but most important is how will the public know if and when this goal is achieved?

Measuring the progress toward realizing a goal takes place through specific program objectives. An *objective* is precise, narrow in scope, concrete, measurable, and includes a time or designated date for completion of a specific activity to help achieve the goal. The objective is tied directly to the goal and is the vehicle to realize the goal's aspiration.

Writing a goal statement with supporting objectives is not as difficult as it may seem. A goal is a general statement of what needs to be accomplished or to be achieved; a goal is a desired state. An objective identifies a specific milestone with an exact timeline for achieving the specific activity or outcome. A useful technique when writing an objective is to ask: Who will do what when? For instance, course objectives are generally included in an academic course syllabus. The course objectives are generally introduced with the following statement: "Students who take this course will . . . or . . . By the end of the semester, the student will . . ." The "who" is the student; "will do what" is simply stated as "will"; and "when" is "by the end of the semester" or "take this course."

Targeted Population and Program Eligibility

All social policies are written with a specific, targeted population or client group in mind. Potential program participants are also referred to as *beneficiaries:* individuals whose lives will be changed because of the policy (Gilbert & Terrell, 2002, p. 66). Typically, we think of clients as *direct beneficiaries,* individuals who are immediately impacted by a policy and its resulting program. The direct beneficiary receives a specific advantage or benefit of some value. For example, a direct beneficiary of an elementary after-school program is a child in grades K–6; the direct beneficiary of a library card is able to check out books at the public library free of charge. The direct beneficiaries of the federally sponsored SNAP program are the individuals and families who are provided assistance to purchase food.

A second, less recognized population group includes the *indirect or unintended beneficiary.* These cohorts of people also should be considered in the analysis. An in-direct beneficiary is a person or group who is not directly participating in the specific activity but benefits from the other person's advantage. The parents or legal guardians of the child who is participating in the after-school program are indirect beneficiaries; they may have a sense of relief knowing their children are in a safe and secure place while not having to leave the child at home, unattended, while the adult is at work. An indirect beneficiary of the federal SNAP program is the farmer whose crops are purchased by and processed by food companies.

Specifying if a social policy is *universal* or *selective* is a second area to consider when assessing the targeted population and eligibility requirements. A universal policy benefits all people with no constraints placed on who is eligible to participate. In other words, all people are direct beneficiaries of the policy. A community's public parks are an outcome of a universal policy; there are no restrictions on who can use the park while park rules apply equally to all people.

A selective policy specifies formal eligibility criteria, which determine if an individual is qualified to participate in a specific program. Not all programs are available to all people. As a result, eligibility criteria screen people in as well as out of a program. A selective program operates under the premise that under no circumstance is a person entitled to a program's benefits; an individual simply does not have the right to claim a selective program's benefit.

A series of questions are asked to gain a full and complete understanding of a program's gatekeeping process. These include the following:

1. How are potential clients identified? Are they self-referred or referred by other agencies? Does the agency operate a formal outreach campaign?
2. Are there other population groups who could benefit from this program; if so, why are they excluded?
3. Are there similar programs elsewhere, either locally or in other states; if so, are the eligibility criteria similar; if not what are the differences and how would they impact this program?
4. Are there alternative or additional eligibility requirements that might be considered; would they engage more clients and/or reach out to a different population group?
5. Are there current eligibility requirements that should be modified or dropped; if so, why and how would such change(s) affect the program?

The types of eligibility criteria are endless and often reflect political leanings of the organizing group. They essentially establish cut-off points to eliminate and deny peoples' ability to benefit from the program. The more common forms of eligibility requirements include income level, age, race, gender identity, ethnicity, marital status, and employment status.

Political influences are commonly found in eligibility criteria: Are there specific behaviors a program participant must demonstrate in order to remain in the program that others in the community are not expected to complete; are time limitations imposed on a person's participation? For example, TANF, the federal program that provides financial assistance to the poor, requires the adult to work, and a person is limited to 5 years of TANF support over his or her lifetime.

Types of Benefits/Services Provided

Program services or benefits reflect a variety of shapes and forms. Generally, benefits are framed as either *in-kind* or *cash*. An in-kind benefit is described as a specific good or service; it cannot be traded for some other benefit, and there is little to no freedom of choice by the program participant as to what she or he may desire. The in-kind good or service is predesigned and offered in the same format to all clients. A meal and overnight stay provided by a homeless shelter is considered an in-kind good; clothing given away by an emergency organization following a hurricane is an in-kind good. An in-kind good is tangible; it generally can be seen and felt. Cash as a benefit allows for individual choice; it reflects the ultimate form of individual self-determination.

The cash or in-kind benefit models are also laced with political ideologies. Gilbert and Terrell (2002, p. 128) illustrate the conservative-progressive strain that exists with these two dichotomous benefit approaches: "Should needy families be provided a monthly income to cover their basic needs or should help be given as food and fuel, as clothing and shelter? Should children be guaranteed education in the basic public schools or should their families receive cash, or an equivalent voucher, providing them options in the educational marketplace?" Providing money directly to an individual in financial need reflects one of the social work profession's core principles, the right to self-determination (see National Association of Social Workers Code of Ethics, Section 1.02 Self-Determination). Yet there is a long-standing belief that a poor person is not trustworthy, especially with cash; this notion contends that the poor will use cash to buy drugs or alcohol in lieu of basic necessities (Blattman, 2014). This paternalistic view of people reflects a commonly held belief that "we" know what is in "their" best interests.

The cash and in-kind dichotomy can be expanded to include others forms of social provisions (Gilbert & Terrell, 2002, pp. 134–136). Such options include the following:

1. *Opportunities*—an action that results in a specific desired end while the benefit is available to a certain group of people.
    a. *Example:* Colleges and universities apply affirmative action principles in their admission processes to recruit underrepresented groups; special credit is given to military veterans in selected employment settings.
2. *Vouchers*—a document of some form that carries a monetary value to purchase a specific type of product. The individual has the ability to make certain choices.
    a. *Example*: Supplemental Nutrition Assistance Program (SNAP), formerly called food stamps, provides the individual a debit card or electronic benefit transfer (EBT). The card works similarly to a bank debit card and allows the individual to purchase certain food items or plants and seeds to grow food. The card cannot be used to purchase items such as clothes, alcohol, cigarettes, laundry detergent, toothpaste, soap, diapers, pet foods, household supplies, and vitamins.
3. *Services*—direct actions, such as individual counseling or case management, provided on behalf of the client. Such activities are nontransferable to others.
    a. *Example*: State-sponsored job training programs to assist individuals to develop skills and knowledge necessary to enter or re-enter the workforce and become economically self-sufficient. Programs vary by state with programs focused on specific population groups. New Mexico, for example, offers *on-the-job training* for veterans to develop their individual expertise in skilled occupations such as heating and air conditioning, welding, beverage/food services, landscaping, and auto mechanic (New Mexico Department of Veteran Services, n.d.).

The policy practitioner poses a number of questions when examining a program's specific services and benefits.

1. Do the program's services specifically address the issue? If so, how? If not, explain why.
2. Is there a public stigma associated with the program? Does the stigma discourage individuals from participating? How does the agency address the stigma in a proactive manner? What could the agency do differently to reduce the associated stigma while encouraging potential participants to enroll in the program?
3. Does the agency have enough resources to fully support the delivery of services?
4. What type of benefits/services are provided by other agencies to the same target group? Are these services duplicative with other organizations' services? If so, is the replication necessary?
5. Are there alternative benefits/services that might be provided? What would they require the agency to do differently, for example, hire additional staff, let go some of the current staff and hire people with a different skill set?

Funding Sources

Many sound program ideas are proposed but are never realized due to funding issues. All agency activities, no matter how small or how large, result in a financial cost to the agency. As with any expense, there must be an income stream to cover the cost. Otherwise, the agency will cease operations and close its doors.

Funding is derived from one or a combination of sources: public funds, private resources, or cash payment directly from clients. Public funding refers to local, state, or federal dollars that are allocated through an annual or biannual funding allocation. This might include a specific line item in a government's budget or through a grant in response to a public agency's *Request for Proposals (RFP)*.

Private funding includes funds generated through individual philanthropy or corporate, fundraising, and foundation grant awards. Nonprofit agencies also referred to as *nongovernmental organizations (NGOs)* rely on private funding sources as their primary revenue source. An NGO can apply for state and federal grants as well to support a new or ongoing activity. Funding is also available from insurance companies that reimburse for specific services, such as mental health counseling and health care.

Clients also pay for services in many programs. Program fees are frequently structured on a *sliding fee scale;* the actual cost of the service remains the same for all people, but an individual's cost is based on income. The higher the income, the more a person will pay.

The key for an organization's successful funding is threefold. First, revenue streams should be diverse; that is, it should not rely on one source for all or the majority of its funding. Second, an agency's core programs should be funded solely with permanent or *hard* dollars such as a state or county's annual allocation to the organization. Third, *soft money*, which consists of grant or private donations, should only be used to support a demonstration project and not be seen as a permanent revenue source for a core agency activity.

Policy-specific questions regarding funding include the following:

1. Is the funding adequate to provide the full range of benefits and services?
2. What would additional funding accomplish for the program; could more clients be served, could new and additional services be provided?
3. Is the funding secure and stable for the duration of the program?
4. Is the program funding based on one or multiple sources; what happens if one of the income sources becomes unavailable?
5. Does the agency redirect funds from one program area to another; if so, how does this impact the other programs?
6. Are there alternative funding strategies that could be employed to strengthen the program's benefits and services?

Program Outcomes

Program outcomes involve the gathering of empirical data to help the program staff assess its overall success in realizing program objectives. The collection of program outcome data is ongoing and systematic. The data, also referred to as *key performance indicators* (*KPIs*), are identified and monitored for each policy objective. KPIs are specific, identifiable indicators that are both monitored and measured over a period to determine the extent a policy's goal or objective is achieved. They are a quantifiable yardstick with the information generally reported as a percentage, rate, or ratio. For example, one of the federal Department of Veteran Affairs (VA) strategic goals is the elimination of "veteran homelessness by the end of FY 2015" (Department of Veterans Affairs, p. 23). The VA notes specific KPIs to measure the level of goal attainment: (1) identify the number of veterans placed in permanent housing; (2) identify the percent of veterans discharged from VA-funded residential treatment programs to permanent housing; (3) identify the percent of unsheltered veterans moved out of unsheltered status within 30 days of engagement; and (4) identify the number of homeless veterans on a single night (https://www.performance.gov).

Questions applied to assess the quality of program outcomes include the following:

1. To what extent have the outcomes been achieved; at this point in time, are the policy's goals realistic and attainable?
2. Are there any gaps in the outcomes?
3. Are the indicators specific?
4. Should other data be collected; if so, what KPI should be added?
5. How will one know when the policy's outcomes have been achieved?
6. How will one know that changes have occurred?

Recommendations

The conclusion of the policy analysis is a listing of recommendations or proposed next steps. A recommendation is specific and details practical steps to be taken that will result in a stronger outcome. Policy recommendations are the chief product of the policy analysis, and they incorporate three characteristics: conciseness, readability, and accuracy.

In the nonprofit world, there are two primary groups that will read a policy analysis: a board of directors and the organization's staff. An NGO's board of directors is the ultimate decision maker for the agency. These individuals are volunteers who lead other lives, including full-time jobs and family obligations, outside of the agency. As such, it is imperative to recognize they have little time to read and review page after page of data and detailed analysis. Similarly, an organization's staff is often burdened with agency work, and they too have little time to completely digest a full policy analysis.

In the governmental arena, there are two primary consumers of policy analysis reports: the elected official and her or his staff. As with an NGO's staff and board of directors, time is a luxury that few elected office holders or staff enjoy. Rarely do they read an entire bill or supporting analytic papers. As discussed in Chapter 7, legislators are inundated with thousands of proposals, and keeping up with each is virtually impossible.

For both the NGO and governmental policy analysis report, there is one simple guideline in the preparation of recommendations: Analyses are formatted in a clear, straightforward manner. This allows the reader to fully and quickly understand the recommendation in everyday language (see Box 5.3). Finally, each recommendation must be directly tied to the report's data and accurately reflect the analytic findings. This may seem obvious, but the decision makers will want to understand the evidence that supports the recommendations.

Generally it is best to keep the number of recommendations to no more than five, with three being an optimal number. A lengthy list of recommendations can be confusing while negatively affecting the decision makers and program staff. On the other hand, a shortened list of recommendations is not overwhelming and facilitates proactive changes. This does not mean the analysis avoids pointing out significant deficiencies, but how these are presented can impact a program's future.

An important social work strategy when writing a recommendation is to ensure it reflects a strengths-based perspective. A strengths-based proposal identifies and builds on the skills and abilities found in the program. Additionally, a strengths-based approach is positive and proactive while avoiding negative, derogatory, or paternalistic language or statements.

Finally, it is best to specify the recommendations in order of priority; that is, recommendation one is the most important matter to attend to, recommendation

---

Box 5.3

HELPFUL HINT

When you feel the report is complete and you are ready to submit it for formal review—*STOP*. Have a colleague read the report and ask him or her to give you honest feedback. Ask your coworker to be brutally honest and don't take the comments personally. Your goal is to ensure the report is clear and well written.

---

number two is the second most important, and so on. Prioritizing recommendations helps the decision makers understand what tasks need to be attended to first.

Questions to consider when preparing the recommendations:

1. Does the overall policy make sense?
2. What are the significant points of success?
3. Is the target population positively impacted by the program?
4. Does the evidence support continuation of the program, modifying the program, or expanding the program?
5. Are there similar programs elsewhere; if so, what are their results?
6. Given the analytic findings, what should the agency do?

SUMMARY THOUGHTS

Issue and policy analyses are essential activities in today's public and private social service agencies. Social workers in all positions, including management and administration as well as direct service lines, complete issue and policy analyses for their agencies (see Box 5.4). Sound assessment results in quality evidence that supports informed decision making. Issue analysis and social policy analysis facilitate the understanding of the nuances of issues that individuals, families, groups, and communities face each day.

Analyses conducted in a thoughtful, forthright manner, guided by the principles of critical thinking, will help decision makers in their policy-building processes. Crafting policy requires effective policy practice that provides information that is easily translatable into goals and objectives. The collection of relevant information through KPIs is the primary vehicle to ensure that quality services will be able to grow and evolve; assessment encourages introspection and the ability to change course if necessary.

Throughout issue analysis and social policy analysis, the social worker is guided by the overarching question: Is this fair and just? Are the eligibility criteria fair and just? Are the program benefits fair and just? Are the program participation requirements fair and just? At each step of the analytic process, the answer to these questions must be *yes*; otherwise the issue or policy is neither fair nor just.

Box 5.4

IMPORTANT DOS AND DON'TS IN WRITING REPORTS

Be Sure to	*Avoid If at All Possible*
1. Keep It simple with succinct statements.	1. Academic jargon and technical descriptions
2. Write in a way that engages the reader.	2. Small font size, e.g., anything less than 12 font size/pixel
3. Keep the report evidence based and focused.	3. Long-winded paragraphs
4. Write in the active voice.	4. Passive verb tenses
5. Use headings and subheadings.	5. Slang, clichés. or idioms (e.g., "This one should be a piece of cake") or qualifiers (e.g., really, hopefully, basically).
6. Use appropriate spacing.	
7. Facilitate readability through images, catchphrases, layout choices, and the provision of data as graphs or charts.	6. Out-of-date data and information
	7. Too much data because the information becomes confusing and blurs together
8. Write in the present tense.	
9. Check spelling and grammar, e.g., "then" or "than" or "that" instead of "who" (and visa versa).	8. Do not write out numbers; use numerals as numbers are easily seen and understood.
	9. Plagiarizing or claiming someone else's ideas or writing as your own; quote them and cite the source
10. Provide references at the end of the report.	
11. Have a coworker proofread the report when you are done.	10. Relying on "spell check"; although it is helpful, it is not foolproof
12. Verify ... verify ... verify ... and just to be sure, verify one more time.	11. Avoid BIG and SHORT words— always use the right word
	12. Stressing out over the writing

Quality programs and services can and do lead to positive life-changing moments for clients, help strengthen society, and ensure fairness and justice are part of the human condition. This is why social workers conduct issue and policy analyses; this is the heat of policy practice.

REFERENCES

Blattman, C. (2014, July 6). Why don't we trust the poor more to give them money? *The Dallas Morning News*. Retrieved from http://www.dallasnews.com/opinion/sunday-commentary/20140704-let-them-eat-cash.ece on March 13, 20116.

Bureau of Labor Statistics. (2016, June 7). Labor force statistics from the current population reports survey. Retrieved from http://data.bls.gov/timeseries/LNS14000000 on June 7, 2016.

Chapin, R. (2007). *Social policy for effective practice.* New York, NY: McGraw Hill.

Department of Veterans Affairs. (n.d.). Department of Veterans Affairs, FY2014–2020 strategic plan. Retrieved from https://www.va.gov/op3/docs/StrategicPlanning/VA2014-2020strategicPlan.pdf. March 19, 2016.

Edelman, M. W. (2014). *State of America's children, 2014.* Washington, DC: Children's Defense Fund.

Gilbert, N., & Terrell, P. (2002). *Dimensions of social welfare policy* (8th ed.). Upper Saddle River, NJ: Pearson Education.

Kendall, D. (2007) *Social problems in a diverse society* (4th ed.). Boston, MA: Pearson.

National Association of Social Workers. (n.d.). *Code of ethics of the national association of social workers.* Washington, DC: Author. Retrieved from http://socialworkers.org/pubs/code/code.asp on March 12, 2016.

New Mexico Department of Veteran Services. (n.d.). On the job training. Retrieved from http://www.dvs.state.nm.us/ojt.html on March 14, 2016.

Performance.gov. (n.d.). End veteran homelessness, performance indicators. Retrieved from https://www.performance.gov/content/end-veteran-homelessness?view=public#indi cators on March 26, 2016.

Plunk, A., Tate, W., Bierut, L., & Grucza, R. (2014). Intended and unintended effects of state-mandated high school science and mathematics course graduation requirements on educational attainment. *Educational Researcher, 43,* 230–241

United States Department of Agriculture. (2015, September 8). Definitions of food security. Retrieved from http://www.ers.usda.gov/topics/food-nutrition-assistance/food-security-in-the-us/definitions-of-food-security.aspx on March 18, 2016.

The Making of Social Policies

INTRODUCTION TO PART 2: THE MAKING OF SOCIAL POLICIES

Continuing with the metaphor of organizing a dinner party, Part 2 of the *Handbook* redirects our attention to where the things will take place: where the food will be prepared; how it will be available to the guests; how drinks will be served; and when the food will actually be served. The hosts look through their home and begin to picture what the party itself will look like and what needs to occur in order for the evening festivities to go smoothly.

Part 2 could easily be retitled "Policies are like sausages; it is better not to see them being made." The political process of policy and law development is often convoluted, complex, mind-boggling, unfathomable, frustrating, and nonsensical. Even with this very dismal backdrop, the social worker can be effective in helping effect proactive policy changes. The first ingredient necessary for successful policy practice, as discussed in Part 1, is the ability to critically think through problems and situations and propose solutions that are firmly rooted in evidence while reflecting fairness and justice. The second element in the recipe for success is the understanding of the systems where polices are developed, their differences, their commonalities, and ways to effectively traverse these political environments.

Social policy lives in either governmental or nongovernmental entities. Part 2 explores these, including the structures of federal, state, and local governments and those of nonprofit/nongovernmental agencies. Part 2 may seem similar to a political science 101 primer, which it is. A 2011 *Newsweek* report found that only 29% of Americans were unable to name the vice president, 44% were unable to define the Bill of Rights, and only 6% were able to locate Independence Day on a calendar (Romano, 2011). The Annenberg Public Policy Center of the University of Pennsylvania found similar results in a national survey of 1,416 adults (see Activity Box II.1):

- Just slightly more than a third of respondents (36%) could name all three branches of the US government.
- Just about the same number (35%) could not name a single one.

- Twenty-one percent of respondents incorrectly believed that a 5-4 Supreme Court decision is sent back to Congress for reconsideration.
- More than half of the respondents did not know which political party, Democrat or Republican, controlled the US House of Representatives or the US Senate. (Annenberg Public Policy Center, 2014)

QUESTIONS TO ACTIVITY BOX II.1

CITIZENSHIP TEST

The naturalization test, commonly called the "citizenship test," is comprised of 10 questions taken from a pool of 100 questions. The questions, which are open ended, are asked during the naturalization interview; 6 of the 10 questions must be answered correctly to pass the civics test. A copy of the 100 questions is available at https://www.uscis.gov/citizenship/learners/study-test/study-materials-civics-test.

Following are 25 questions from the pool of 100 questions. Take the test yourself; give 10 questions to other students to see how they would do on the "citizenship test." The questions are open ended, not multiple choice. The possible answers are listed following this section.

1. What is the supreme law of the land?
2. What is one right or freedom from the First Amendment?
3. What did the Declaration of Independence do?
4. What is the "rule of law"?
5. What stops one branch of government from becoming too powerful?
6. Who is in charge of the executive branch?
7. Who makes federal laws?
8. What are the two parts of the US Congress?
9. How many US Senators are there?
10. We elect a US Senator for how many years?
11. Who is one of your state's US Senators now?
12. We elect a US Representative for how many years?
13. In what month do we vote for President?
14. If both the President and the Vice President can no longer serve, who becomes President?
15. How many justices are on the Supreme Court?
16. What are two rights of everyone living in the United States?
17. How old do citizens have to be to vote for President?*
18. Who wrote the Declaration of Independence?
19. When was the Constitution written?
20. Name one war fought by the United States in the 1800s.
21. What did Susan B. Anthony do?
22. Who was President during World War I?

23. Before he was President, Eisenhower was a general. What war was he in?
24. Name <u>one</u> of the two longest rivers in the United States.
25. Why does the flag have 13 stripes?

Source: US Citizenship and Immigration Services. (n.d.). Study materials for the civics test. Retrieved from https://www.uscis.gov/citizenship/learners/study-test/study-materials-civics-test on January 28, 2017.

Part 2 is organized around governmental and agency-based policy protocols and procedures. The discussion begins with the federal government and works it way to locally based nonprofit agencies. The chapters will convey the idea that policy practice is very different in the governmental sectors as well as between governmental and nonprofit arenas. In fact, the social worker might find that policy practice in a local agency is far more successful compared to work with the federal government. A second important take-away from Part 2 is that policy practice is much more than lobbying for or against a specific bill but also critical is the rule-making process at the federal and state levels of government.

Chapter 6 examines the workings of the federal government, including the three branches of government. Particular attention is devoted to how a bill becomes law, the barriers a proposal must overcome, and ways to influence a member of Congress to support or oppose a particular position. Policy practice in these three distinct areas includes a number of different activities and strategies that a social worker undertakes. A number of policy skills are discussed, including meeting with an elected official; participating in a local town hall meeting; testifying before a congressional committee; emailing, writing, or calling an elected official; the role of congressional caucuses (including the Social Work Congressional Caucus) in policy advocacy; political action committees as a vehicle to garner elected officials and political party support; and the generally overlooked practice area of rule making, which is the process of developing the program regulations and services.

Chapter 7 explores the next level of public development by shifting our focus to state and local governmental structures. A significant point in Chapter 7 is the marked differences between the various state governmental structures as well as between local governments within each state. There is no one uniform or common political protocol among the states, counties, cities, and towns. As such, understanding the nuances of state and local government is even more critical for the social worker in policy practice. The successful policy practitioner never assumes that passage of a bill or advocacy mechanism in one state will work in another.

The final chapter in Part 2, Chapter 8, shifts attention from the public to the private sector. Nonprofit agencies, also known as NGOs, provide an array of social services; and social workers, who are the primary employees in these settings, are in a position to advocate for proactive agency-based social policies and program initiatives. A number of strategies are discussed to effect change, which can occur at a much quicker pace compared to the slow, complicated law- and rule-making processes of the federal and state governments.

ANSWERS TO ACTIVITY BOX II.1

1. • the Constitution
2. • speech
   • petition the government
   • religion
   • assembly
   • press
3. • announced our independence from Great Britain
   • declared our independence (from Great Britain)
   • said the United States is free from Great Britain
4. • Everyone must follow the law.
   • eaders must obey the law.
   • Government must obey the law.
   • No one is above the law.
5. • checks and balances
   • separation of powers
6. • the President
7. • Congress
   • Senate and House (of Representatives)
   • (US or national) legislature
8. • The Senate and the House (of Representatives)
9. • 100
10. • 6Check the web for the correct answer
11. • Check the web for the correct answer
12. •2
13. • November
14. • Speaker of the House
15. • 9
16. • freedom of expression
    • freedom of speech
    • freedom of assembly
    • freedom to petition the government
    • freedom of religion
    • the right to bear arms
17. • 18 years or older
18. • Thomas Jefferson
19. • 1787

20. • War of 1812
    • Mexican-American War
    • Civil War
    • Spanish-American War
21. • fought for women's rights
    • fought for civil rights
22. • Woodrow Wilson
23. • World War II
24. • Missouri River
    • Mississippi River
25. • because there were 13 original colonies
    • because the stripes represent the original colonies

REFERENCES

Annenberg Public Policy Center. (2014, September 17). Americans know surprisingly little about their government, survey finds. Retrieved from http://www.annenbergpublicpolicycenter.org/americans-know-surprisingly-little-about-their-government-survey-finds/ on December 9, 2016.

Romano, A. (2011, March 20). How ignorant are Americans. *Newsweek*. Retrieved from http://www.newsweek.com/how-ignorant-are-americans-66053 on December 9, 2016.

US Citizenship and Immigration Services. (n.d.). Study materials for the civics test. Retrieved from https://www.uscis.gov/citizenship/learners/study-test/study-materials-civics-test on January 28, 2017.

CHAPTER 6

Federal Government–Based Policy Development

A social policy enacted by a governmental legislative body, including the US Congress, state legislatures, and local councils and boards, is typically called a *public policy*. Influencing a legislative proposal or amending an existing law is possible, but successful policy practice requires a fair amount of expertise of overall governmental structures and their particular workings (Hoefer, 2014, pp. 265–266). The configurations of legislative processes, however, differ significantly between and among the federal government, states, local, and county municipalities. Policy practice in these settings can be frustrating, laborious, and time consuming, but satisfying once an idea becomes policy.

A social worker's policy practice can occur in a variety of ways in the federal government. The practitioner might be a federal employee working in one of the many different federal agencies such as the Social Security Administration or the Department of Health and Human Services. Or the social worker might work for a national nonprofit organization, such as the Children's Defense Fund or a national think tank (see Chapter 5, Table 5.1), whose work is to influence or lobby governmental agencies and/or elected officials around social issues. Or the social worker may be a volunteer with an organization or professional association and work on behalf of that group to affect a new or revised policy position. Or the social worker may be a staff person for an elected member of Congress or a Congressional Committee.

FEDERAL GOVERNMENT—STRUCTURE

The US federal government is organized around three separate entities, also referred to as *branches of government*: executive branch, legislative branch, and judicial branch. This form of government is a *system of checks and balances* that theoretically ensures that no single branch of government can violate the law. The President of the United States heads the *executive branch* of government. The *legislative branch* of government is the US Congress, which includes the House of Representatives and the Senate. The *judicial branch* of government is the federal court system. Each branch has specified duties, roles, and functions, which are all spelled out in the US Constitution.

Executive Branch

The President of the United States, who is the de facto head of state and Commander in Chief of the Armed Forces, leads the executive branch of the federal government. The executive branch is responsible for implementing and enforcing the laws written by Congress; the President nominates individuals to the US Congress to direct the various federal agencies, including the secretaries of the 15 Cabinet-level departments. Individuals can hold these positions until a new president assumes office, at which time nominees for these offices are submitted to the US Congress for approval. The President also nominates individuals to serve as federal judges, which are lifetime appointments. Approval of these appointments is the responsibility of the US Senate as well.

A key presidential power is the *executive order (EO)*, which is a specific directive issued by the President to federal agencies, department heads, or other federal employees; such orders do not require congressional approval. EOs are a common tool used by the majority of the US Presidents and, as noted by Hudak (2014), "Executive orders ruffle feathers over policy, increase partisanship, and provoke separation of powers issues." The EO can initiate new initiatives, expand existing programs and services, or rescind previous orders. Examples of executive orders include the following:

- In his first week as President in January, 2017, Donald Trump signed an executive order reinstating the Mexico City Policy, which required nongovernmental organizations to agree as a condition of receiving any federal funding that they "would neither perform nor actively promote abortion as a method of family planning in other nations."
- Following the September 11, 2011, terrorist attacks, President George W. Bush issued an executive order that combined over 40 federal law enforcement agencies into a new Cabinet-level agency, the Department of Homeland Security.
- In 1988, President Ronald Reagan issued an executive order that excluded abortions at all military hospitals except in cases of rape, incest, or when the mother's life is threatened. In 1993, President Clinton rescinded the Reagan order with another executive order.
- In 1965, President Lyndon B. Johnson signed Executive Order 11246, which barred discrimination in federal employment because of race, color, religion, sex, or national origin.

- Soon after the December 7, 1941, attack on Pearl Harbor, President Franklin D. Roosevelt issued an executive order that required the internment of more than 120,000 Japanese Americans, many of whom were US citizens.
- The 1863 executive order issued by President Abraham Lincoln, better known as the Emancipation Proclamation, stated "all persons held as slaves . . . shall be then, thenceforward, and forever free."

Legislative Branch

The legislative branch of government, more commonly referred to as the US Congress or simply Congress, includes two chambers, the House of Representatives and the Senate. The formal name for a two-chamber legislature is *bicameral*, though this term is rarely used in day-to-day work in the US Congress or by policy practitioners.

The US Senate is comprised of 100 senators, two elected from each state for a 6-year term of office. This structure reflects the idea that each senator is equal to the other with no state having greater power or authority over another due to any unique or different attributes such as population size or geographic location. The smallest state, Wyoming, and the largest state, California, each have two US Senators, even though California's population, in 2017, is 67 times larger than Wyoming. The Senate proposes and considers new laws, approves or rejects presidential nominations, provides advice and consent on international treaties, and serves as the high court for impeachment trials. In 2016, the US Senate included 17 Senate committees with 70 subcommittees (The White House, n.d.).

The US House of Representatives includes 435 elected individuals who serve a 2-year term of office. Although each state is equally represented in the US Senate, this is not the case for the House of Representatives. A state's population determines the number of representatives it is entitled to have in the US House of Representatives. As a beginning point, each state is automatically assigned one representative seat while the remaining 385 seats are apportioned to the states based on the population. Thirteen states, territories, and the District of Columbia are represented by only one person in the House of Representatives (see Figure 6.1). Conversely, elected members from three states—California, Texas, and New York—account for nearly 27% of the US House of Representatives (United States House of Representatives, n.d.). Every 10 years, following the decennial census of the United States, the representatives' seats are reallocated to the states based on their updated population count. For example, the number of representatives from New York declined from 45 in the 1930s to 27 in 2016, whereas the number from California increased from 11 to 53 (Encyclopedia Britannica and United States House of Representatives, n.d.).

All members of Congress have a minimum of two offices, one in Washington, DC, on Capitol Hill and the other office in the congressperson's home state. Senators have one or more offices in their home state with the actual number

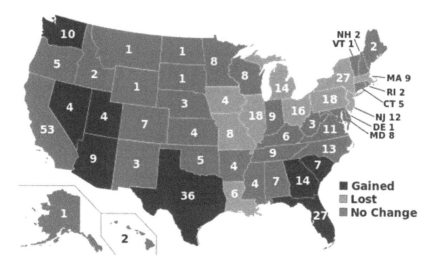

Figure 6.1.
Number of US House of Representatives congressional seats, seats gained, lost, or no change, by state following 2010 decennial census and reapportionment.
Source: Office of the Historian, United States House of Representatives, retrieved from http://history.house.gov/ on January 18, 2017.

impacted by the state's overall population and geographic size. For example, in 2016, Alabama Senators Johnny Isakson and David Purdue each maintained one office in Atlanta; Vermont Senators Patrick Leahy and Bernie Saunders each staffed two offices in their state; Texas Senators John Cornyn and Ted Cruz each had six offices in their home state (United States Senate, n.d.), and US Representative Niki Tsongas, one of seven social workers elected to Congress, maintains five district offices in Massachusetts (Congresswoman Niki Tsongas, n.d.).

The Washington, DC, office focuses on the political work of the elected official in Congress, whereas the local state-based office, also referred to as the *district office*, provides *constituent services*, which is also referred to as *casework*, not to be confused with the social work casework practice that is clinical in nature. District casework involves responding to constituent requests on a variety of matters though primarily seeking help in resolving bureaucratic snarls around benefits from federal programs such as Social Security or Veterans Affairs. District staff replies to mail, tracks local support or opposition on national issues, attends local events on behalf of the elected official, and generates a variety of communications, such as newsletters and email alerts, on behalf of the elected official to the local electorate and donors.

The number of staffers a house member or senator employs depends on a number of variables. A legislator's seniority, committee assignments, and leadership position in his or her chamber all add additional staff to a House or Senate office. Staff in the Senate and House members' offices normally include a *Legislative Director* (*LD*) and *Legislative Assistant* (*LA*). The LD's primary responsibility is to shape and

---

Box 6.1

POSSIBLE SOCIAL WORK INTERNSHIP

Meet with your program's Field Internship Office to discuss the possibility of conducting an internship in a political setting. This may include a US House of Representative or US Senator's national or district office, a state legislator's office, or a local city/county official office. These types of field placements are commonplace and provide a unique opportunity to experience policy practice in an up-close manner.

---

guide the representative or senator's legislative agenda. The LD's influence is extensive; often with the Chief of Staff, the LD identifies legislative priorities, advises the elected official to sponsor or co-sponsor a bill, and recommends how to vote on a bill. The LA monitors various pieces of legislation, often drafts, writes floor speeches, and meets with lobbyists and with local constituents. In addition to paid staff, the majority of congressional offices, both in Washington, DC, and in the local districts, hire volunteer interns (see Box 6.1).

Maintaining a strong relationship with a chief of staff, LD, and LA is critically important in policy practice. Just as important, the social worker should establish and maintain a strong relationship with the staff in the local district office. These local relationships can open doors to contacts in federal agencies as well as create opportunities to develop relationships with staff in the Washington, DC, office.

Judicial Branch

The purpose of the federal court system is to interpret the law, determine the constitutionality of the law, and apply it to individual cases; once the Supreme Court decides a case, the lower courts are required to apply the Supreme Court's interpretation to the facts of a particular case (The White House, n.d.).

A federal judge's position is for life, for example, no term limitation, and the individual can only be removed from office through an impeachment process conducted by the US Congress. The longest serving Supreme Court Justice was William O. Douglas, who served from 1935 to 1975, while the average term is approximately 16 years.

The US Supreme Court, which is the final arbitrator on all legal matters, is comprised of nine justices, including the Chief Justice and eight Associate Justices; in addition, the federal judicial system includes 94 district level trial courts and 13 courts of appeals (United States Courts, n.d.). As of January 25, 2017, there were 117 vacancies of various judgeships, including a vacancy on the US Supreme Court (United States Courts, n.d.).

History shows the federal court actions have dramatically shaped human rights and social justice issues in the United States. For example, the Supreme Court's 1896 decision *Plessy v. Ferguson* legalized *separate but equal* that in effect formalized segregation; this decision was eventually overturned with the Supreme Court's 1954 decision *Brown v. Board of Education*, which legally ended segregation (The Leadership Conference, 2016). More recently, in June 2016, the Supreme Court upheld Affirmative Action (Liptak, 2016) but at the same time stopped then President Barack Obama's immigration plan that would have protected up to 5 million undocumented immigrants from deportation (Liptak & Shear, 2016).

There are few tools available to an individual social worker or professional association to influence a court's decision. The primary advocacy mechanism used in the court system is the *amicus curiae*, a written legal brief typically filed during the appeals process. Those who file amicus curiae have no direct relationship to the case being heard. Amicus curiae literally means "friend of the court," and its purpose is to advocate with the court on points of the law that are in doubt or challenged. In general, an amici curiae focuses on issues concerned with the public interest such as social issues and civil rights. There are numerous rules regarding the brief, such as the petitioner must receive permission from the court to file the brief and the petitioner cannot be a litigant in the matter. In other words, an individual or association simply cannot file a brief—permission to file must be granted by the court.

The National Association of Social Workers (NASW) often files or joins with other groups in submitting amicus curiae to the courts. For example, NASW collaborated with a number of professional associations in filing two amicus curiae briefs supporting the Affordable Care Act mandate and Medicaid expansion (National Association of Social Workers, 2016); NASW also maintains an amicus brief database of the over 300 briefs NASW filed over the years. This database, however, is only available for review by the association's members and not the general public (see https://socialworkers.org/ldf/brief_bank/about.asp). The American Civil Liberties Union (ACLU) is one of the most consistent filers of briefs nationwide. The ACLU, for example, filed 149 friend of the court briefs in 2016 and slightly more than 2,000 briefs between 2000 and 2016 on a variety of topics (see Table 6.1).

The Supreme Court meets from October 1 through the following June or July. The justices' law clerks are responsible for the brunt of the work, including legal research and making recommendations to their justice they feel the Court should review. By custom, only four justices are required to agree if a case will be heard by the entire court.

During the oral argument phase of a case, each side is allotted 30 minutes to present its case, while the justices may interrupt at any time to ask any question they wish to pose. Following the oral argument, the justices meet in a closed session to decide the case with the chief justice assigning to one of the associate justices the responsibility to write the majority opinion as well as the dissenting opinion (if not a unanimous vote). It is common for individual justices to add their own written opinions on legal decision. The Supreme Court's final written decision can be explicitly detailed explaining the reasons that led to its conclusion; or a decision

Table 6.1. AMICUS CURIAE FILED BY THE AMERICAN CIVIL LIBERTIES UNION BY TOPIC, 2000–2017

	2017 As of 7/28/2017	2016	2011–2015	2006–2010	2002–2005	1997–2001	**TOTAL**
Capitol punishment	2	1	10	7	2	1	**23**
Criminal law reform	3	7	26	14	9	11	**70**
Disability rights	1	0	2	0	0	0	**3**
Free speech	4	2	77	49	13	10	**155**
HIV	0	0	3	17	29	0	**49**
Human rights	0	3	9	14	2	2	**30**
Immigrant rights	17	25	31	38	7	1	**119**
Juvenile justice	0	0	5	2	3	0	**10**
LGBT rights	7	30	361	26	28	0	**452**
Mass incarceration	3	1	39	132	24	13	**212**
National security	3	7	90	99	23	8	**230**
Prisoners' rights	1	2	18	16	2	3	**42**
Privacy and technology	3	7	60	12	16	13	**110**
Racial justice	3	6	33	30	1	1	**74**
Religious liberty	2	3	63	17	4	1	**90**
Reproductive freedom	1	41	159	5	7	1	**214**
Voting rights	1	13	16	17	2	2	**51**
Women's rights	3	2	71	43	12	0	**131**
TOTAL	**54**	**150**	**1073**	**538**	**184**	**67**	**2065**

Source: American Civil Liberties Union, Retrieved from https://www.aclu.org/search/amicus%20curia on July 28, 2017.

might be very short as was the case in the Supreme Court's rejection of President Obama's immigration plan in writing, "The judgment is affirmed by an equally divided court" (Liptak & Shear, 2016). The Supreme Court's decision is final and creates precedent for all legal hearings and future policies related to the matter.

FEDERAL GOVERNMENT—LEGISLATIVE PROCESS

All three branches of the federal government in one way or another are involved in formulating social welfare policy, but the primary arenas for a social worker's policy practice is with the legislative branch and federal agencies.

A popular Schoolhouse RockI video, *How a Bill Becomes Law*, offers a catchy, though simplistic presentation of a bill actually becoming a law (see https://www.youtube.com/watch?v=Otbml6WIQPo). Yet the classic video does highlight the key points in the legislative process.

A bill is introduced separately in the House, the Senate, or both chambers at the same time. A proposal traverses a series of steps while overcoming many barriers and hurdles to become a law (see Figure 6.2). The success rate of proposals becoming laws illustrates the difficulty of the legislative process. The US Congress introduced 96,023 different bills and resolutions from January 1999 through January 2015, of which only 3.5% (3,399) were passed by both chambers (see Table 6.2). For the same time period, no vote was taken on 79.884 (83.2%) of the bills or resolutions that were introduced, referred to committee, or reported by committee.

A proposed bill is assigned to a legislative committee once its formally filed by a legislator. The legislator who files a bill is known as the *sponsor*; other legislators may *cosponsor* a bill as well. The committee is responsible for reviewing and voting on the bill. Yet most proposed bills never have a hearing and, as a result, do not have a committee vote. In fact, about 8 out of 10 proposals "die" in committee (see Table 6.2).

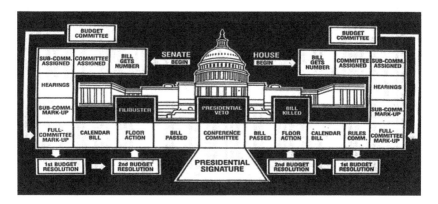

Figure 6.2.
How a bill becomes law, federal government.
Source: Edghill, M. (2013, September 20). AP U.S. government & politics—522, how a bill becomes law. Retrieved from http://edghillapgovt522.blogspot.com/search/label/Congress on May 12, 2016.

Table 6.2. PROPOSED US CONGRESSIONAL LEGISLATION STATUS, 1999–2017

Congressional Session	Date	Total Bills Introduced	Enacted Laws	Passed Resolutions	Voted Upon	Failed Legislation	Vetoed Bills	Other Legislation
115th*	1/3/17–7/28/2017	6,116	43	215	287	2	0	5,569
			1%	4%	5%	0%	0%	91%
114th	2015–2017	12,063	329	708	661	22	9	10,334
			3%	6%	5%	0%	0%	86%
113th	2013–2015	10,637	296	663	474	20	0	9,184
			3%	6%	4%	0%	0%	86%
112th	2011–2013	12,299	284	722	390	38	0	10,865
			2%	6%	3%	0%	0%	88%
111th	2009–2011	13,675	385	1,464	601	31	2	11,192
			3%	11%	4%	0%	0%	82%
110th	2007–2009	14,042	460	1,435	861	37	7	11,242
			3%	10%	6%	0%	0%	80%
109th	2005–2006	13,072	483	1,027	597	31	1	10,933
			4%	8%	5%	0%	0%	84%
108th	2003–2005	10,669	504	865	694	17	0	8,589
			5%	8%	7%	0%	0%	81%
107th	2001–2003	10,789	383	681	602	16	0	9,107
			4%	6%	6%	0%	0%	84%
106th	1999–2000	10,840	604	769	650	33	12	8,772
			6%	7%	6%	0%	0%	81%

*Note: Legislation for the 2017–2019 115th Congress is limited to January 1, 2016–July 28, 2017. For the most up-to-date information see https://www.govtrack.us/congress/bills/statistics.
Enacted laws: Enacted bills and joint resolutions (both bills and joint resolutions can be enacted as law).
Passed resolutions: Passed resolutions (for joint and concurrent resolutions, this means passed both chambers).
Got a vote: Bills and joint/concurrent resolutions that had a significant vote in one chamber.
Failed legislation: Bills and resolutions that failed a vote on passage or failed a significant vote such as cloture, passage under suspension, or resolving differences.
Vetoed bills (w/o override): Bills that were vetoed and the veto was not overridden by Congress.
Other legislation: Bills and resolutions that were introduced, referred to committee, or reported by committee but had no further action.

Source: Govtrak.us (nd). Statistics and historical comparison. Retrieved from https://www.govtrack.us/congress/bills/statistics on July 28, 2017.

This nonaction by Congress results in a proposal being reintroduced in multiple sessions. For example, the National Association of Social Workers has been the leading national organization pursuing the passage of the Dorothy I. Height and Whitney M. Young, Jr. Social Work Reinvestment Act, a proposal that would significantly enhance the social work profession. Yet the bill, which was originally introduced to Congress in 2007 (110th session) and reintroduced in the 111th, 112th, 113th, 114th and on March 1, 2017, in the 115th session, has yet to have had a committee vote. (For additional updated information, see http://www.socialworkreinvestment.org/.)

FEDERAL GOVERNMENT—INFLUENCING A MEMBER OF CONGRESS

There are multiple ways a social worker can influence a member of Congress. These range from meeting directly with an elected official in her or his home district to testifying before a congressional committee in Washington, DC. A *best practice model* for policy practice strongly encourages the social worker to employ multiple strategies when advocating a position with a member of Congress.

Meeting With the Elected Official

Only an elected member of the US House of Representative or the US Senate can introduce a bill to Congress; and the elected individual is the only person who is eligible to vote on a legislative proposal. Thus, the most critical component of policy practice is to identify a legislator who is sympathetic to the social worker's issue and convince that person to support, oppose, or introduce a bill.

The most effective strategy is meeting face-to-face with the legislator; this, however, generally only occurs if the policy practitioner has a prior personal or professional relationship with the individual or if someone known to the legislator initiates a meeting. Meetings are generally short, somewhere between 15 to 30 minutes. This results in the social worker's message being concise and compelling; info sheets, policy briefs, and policy memos are important handouts to leave with the legislator and his or her staff (see Chapters 9 and 10).

Town Hall Meeting

Most members of the US House of Representatives and the US Senate sponsor local constituent town hall meetings. These frequently occur on weekends or when the Congress is on a formal break. The town hall gatherings are open to the public and give individuals an opportunity to discuss issues or voice their concerns and preferences on any matter. A social worker can use the town hall meeting as a forum

---

Activity Box 6.1

ATTEND A CONGRESSIONAL TOWN HALL MEETING

Contact the local district office for either the local US Representative or US Senator and ask when a town hall meeting is planned. Attend the meeting and observe its protocols and in particular answer the follow questions:

- Are audience members encouraged to participate?
- Is the elected official in attendance; if so, does she or he seem interested in the comments?
- What do you feel have been the most effective questions and points raised? Why?
- What do you feel were the least effective questions and points raised? Why?

---

to express her or his thoughts on an issue; similarly, the social worker can organize others to speak as well to demonstrate to the elected official that there is significant local interest in the matter (see Activity Box 6.1).

A town hall may be *issue specific* or an *open forum*. The *issue-specific* town hall normally includes a panel of local "experts" each making a brief 5- to 10-minute presentation while the meeting itself is moderated by a community leader. The moderator need not be a supporter of the legislator but should be skilled in running a large group meeting as well as having some background on the town hall topic. Following the panel members' comments, the moderator opens the town hall to questions from the audience. The legislator generally sits off to the side so as not to distract attention from the panel but does offer concluding comments at the end of the town hall meeting.

The *open forum* town hall features the legislator as the primary speaker with time set aside for questions. The elected official or her or his chief of staff acts as the moderator in this format. Following the legislator's opening comments, people in the audience can ask any questions or raise any issue for the legislator to respond to.

Testify to a Congressional Committee

In general, it is very rare for an individual social worker to simply show up and testify before a congressional committee. Specific rules regarding a committee's meeting, who can testify, and what types of materials can be submitted are published by the specific committee on its website. The public announcement is made prior to a committee's meeting with instructions on how to request to testify or submit testimony to the committee (see Box 6.2).

Box 6.2

INSTRUCTIONS FOR SUBMITTING A REQUEST TO TESTIFY BEFORE US HOUSE OF REPRESENTATIVES COMMITTEE ON APPROPRIATIONS SUBCOMMITTEE ON LABOR, HEALTH AND HUMAN SERVICES, EDUCATION AND RELATED AGENCIES

House Committee on Appropriations Subcommittee on
Labor, Health and Human Services,
Education and Related Agencies
Instructions for Submitting a Request to Testify at Public Witnesses
Hearing & Testimony for the Record

The Public Witnesses Hearing will be held on Tuesday, March 25, 2014 at 10:00 A.M in Rayburn House Office Building: 2358-C.

DEADLINE TO SUBMIT REQUEST TO TESTIFY: FRIDAY, MARCH 7, 2014
If you would like to submit a request to testify please send an email with the subject line: "**Request to testify**" to **LH.Approp@mail.house.gov.** In the email please state who will be testifying, the subject of the testimony, and contact information. You may also submit this information via fax at 202-225-3509.

While the subcommittee will honor as many requests to testify as possible, capacity constraints prevent us from honoring every request.

We will only notify those requestors who have been selected to testify. All requesters will receive notice from the subcommittee as soon as possible.

Those selected to testify will receive further instructions at that time.

DEADLINE TO SUBMIT WRITTEN TESTIMONY FOR THE RECORD:
FRIDAY, MARCH 8, 2014
If you would like to submit written testimony for the record, please send your testimony via email to: LH.Approp@mail.house.gov with the subject line: "written testimony for the record." You may also submit this information via fax at 202-225-3509.

All written testimony must comply with the following requirements:

- Your testimony should not exceed five pages
- Type on standard 8.5 x 11-inch letter size paper
- Double-spaced type in 12-point font with 1-inch margins
- Clearly indicate your name, title, and institutional affiliation (if any) at the top of the first page
- Clearly state in the first paragraph the agency, program, and amount of funding involved in the request
- Do not include color or detailed photos; however, the use of charts and tables and the use of appropriate bold type and bullets is acceptable

Source: US House of Representatives Committee on Appropriations (March 25, 2014). Hearings, public and outside witness hearing, documents. Retrieved from http://appropriations.house.gov/calendar/eventsingle.aspx?EventID=371685 on June 25, 2016.

Rules regarding testimony, including who is able to appear before a committee, are very stringent. For the most part, the committee invites individuals to address the group; the speakers generally represent a professional association, such as the Council on Social Work Education, National Association of Social Workers, or the American Psychological Association, and are recognized experts on the issue. Others commonly invited to testify include individuals who have unique, personal experience with the issue or celebrities who have taken the matter on as a personal cause.

Email, Write, and Call the Elected Leader

Each member of Congress maintains a website; the Web portal to the US House of Representative's members' Web pages is http://www.house.gov/representatives/ and https://www.senate.gov/senators/contact/ for members of the US Senate. The members' individual pages include a "Contact" link that allows an email to be sent directly to the Washington, DC, office. The website also includes the addresses and phone numbers of the district and the Washington, DC, offices.

Both senators and representatives pay close attention to their mail and the volume of phone calls on various topics to gauge their constituency's interests. Conducting an email, letter writing, or phone call campaign (or combination of these communication techniques) is an effective strategy to raise an issue with a legislator and keep the matter on his or her "radar screen."

Nonconstituent Communication

The social worker who is not a constituent of the elected member of Congress faces a more daunting challenge in gaining the support of a representative or senator. The most obvious strategy is for the social worker to identify an individual or group who are constituents and work with them. A nonconstituent social worker can contact a NASW chapter office in the legislator's home state and seek help in identifying possible social workers to join the effort (see https://socialworkers.org/chapters/default.asp for contact information of the NASW chapters). A second approach a social worker might adopt is to identify one of the legislator's staff whose work portfolio includes the issue at hand and directly contact this person. A review of the individual congressional Web page lists staff members' contact information and in some instances their areas of responsibility.

Finally, if all else fails, a simple phone call to an elected person's office asking, "Who can I talk to concerning (the issue)?" will direct the social worker to the initial contact person. This "cold call" requires the social worker to be very convincing and, in particular, in a short amount of time show how the elected person's involvement fits and benefits his or her political agenda. No matter what the staff person says, the social worker should proactively but assertively ask, "Can we meet to discuss this?"

Congressional Caucuses

Members of the House and Senate have the opportunity to join one or more *caucuses*. A caucus is a formal structure in the US House of Representatives but not in the US Senate. However, senators are able to join a House-sponsored caucus. A caucus is political by nature, often supported by members of one political party; a caucus provides representatives and senators, who share a common interest on an issue or cause, a forum from which to pursue common legislative objectives. The number of congressional caucuses during the 114th Congress totaled 454 different groups (Committee on House Administration, 2016) while 228 caucuses were formally registered with the US House of Representatives Committee on House Administration at the onset of the 115th Congressional Session, which convened on January 4, 2017 (see Appendix 1). These groups reflect a variety of interests; some may seem frivolous while others are focus on critical issues. The importance of a caucus depends on the interests of the party, as each caucus, no matter how insignificant it may seem, has a political constituency that is important to the individual congressional members.

The US House of Representatives Committee on House Administration has oversight responsibility for all congressional caucuses. Any member of the US House of Representatives may organize a caucus and recruit other members of Congress to join. As an official congressional caucus, the group must register with the House Committee on House Administration; the Committee's website includes links to the caucuses for the current congressional session and a number of previous sessions (https://cha.house.gov/member-services/congressional-memberstaff-organizations). The Committee on House Administration updates the list throughout a congressional session and includes the names and contact information for the caucus's chair and cochair(s), and congressional staff who support the group.

Box 6.3
CONGRESSIONAL SOCIAL WORK CAUCUS*

---

*Check the Congressional Social Work Caucus web site for the most current, up-to-date contact information.

Contact information:
Congressional Social Work Caucus
2267 Rayburn HOB
Washington, DC 20515
Phone: (202) 225-2661
Fax: (202) 225-9817
Web address: http://socialworkcaucus-lee.house.gov/

Social work advocacy is the focal point of the Congressional Social Work Caucus (CSWC), which promotes the social work profession as well as advocates on issues of importance to the profession (see Box 6.3). The CSWC stated purpose is as follows:

> to create a platform on the Hill representing the interests of over 600,000 social workers throughout the United States who positively impact the lives of the elderly, the disadvantaged, children, veterans, or other individuals in need of guidance and direction in their lives. CSWC will work to foster interdisciplinary cooperation with relevant disciplines, and work with various stakeholders in local government and communities. The CSWC will also strive to expand congressional internship opportunities for social work students. The CSWC is committed to advancing and sustaining the social work profession's ability to continue to respond to our nation's most vulnerable populations. (Congressional Social Work Caucus, n.d.)

During the 114th Congressional session, January 2015 to January 2017, the CSWC totaled 62 members, most of whom were Democrats (see Box 6.4); membership for the 115th Congressional session was not posted at the time of the *Handbook*'s publication. Membership in the CSWC is open to any member of Congress; as with all congressional caucuses, an elected member learns about a caucus from his or her colleagues, membership associations, or from constituents in their districts (see Activity Box 6.2).

Activity Box 6.2

ADVOCATE TO YOUR US HOUSE OF REPRESENTATIVE AND US SENATORS TO JOIN THE SOCIAL WORK CONGRESSIONAL CAUCUS

Check the Social Work Congressional Caucus (SWCC) membership Web page (http://socialworkcaucus-lee.house.gov/membership) to see if your US House of Representative and US Senators are members of the SWCC. If they are, write and thank them for supporting the SWCC.

If the members are not CSWC members, create an advocacy plan to encourage them to join the Caucus. For example, contact the local NASW unit and the state chapter for assistance; work with your program's Student Association to launch a campaign to encourage the members' support for the CSWC. Consider using email, letter writing, and phone calls to the members' Washington, DC, and district offices; also, see if the officials are planning a town hall meeting; if so, plan to attend and ask them in the open forum to join the SWCC.

Box 6.4

CONGRESSIONAL SOCIAL WORK CAUCUS MEMBERSHIP, 114TH CONGRESSIONAL SESSION, JANUARY 2015–2017*

*The Social Work Caucus membership for the 2017–2019 Congressional Session was not posted at the time of the *Handbook*'s publication. Check the Caucus web site for membership updates and information: http://socialworkcaucus-lee.house.gov/.

Members	Members
Chairperson—Barbara Lee (D-CA)	Rep. Michael Honda (D-CA 17)
	Rep. Darrell Issa (R-CA 49)
Rep. Karen R. Bass (D-CA 37)	Rep. Sheila Jackson Lee (D-TX 18)
Rep. Madeleine Bordallo (Guam)	Rep. John Lewis (D-GA 5)
Rep. Ron Barber (D-AZ 2)	Rep. Dave Loebsack (D-IA 2)
Rep. Sanford D. Bishop Jr. (D-GA 2)	
Rep. Corrine Brown (D-FL 5)	Rep. Carolyn Maloney (D-NY 12)
	Rep. Betty McCollum (D-MN 4)
Rep. G. K. Butterfield, Jr. (D-NC 1)	Rep. Gregory W. Meeks (D-NY 5)
Rep. Lois Capps (D-CA 24)	Sen. Barbara Mikulski (D-MD)
Rep. Andre Carson (D-IN 7)	Rep. Jerrold Nadler (D-NY 8)
Rep. David N. Cicilline (D-RI 1)	
Rep. Yvette D. Clarke (D-NY 9)	Rep. Grace Napolitano (D-CA 38)
	Rep. Beto O'Rourke (D-TX 16)
Rep. Lacy Clay (D-MO 1)	Rep. Mark Pocan (D-WI 2)
Rep. Emanuel Cleaver, II (D-MO 5)	Rep. Donald M. Payne (NJ-10)
Rep. Steve Cohen (D-TN 9)	Rep. Jared Polis (D-CO 2)
Rep. Gerald "Gerry" Connolly (D-VA 11)	
Rep. John Conyers (D-MI 13)	Rep. Charles B. Rangel (D-NY13)
	Rep. Lucille Roybal-Allard (D-CA 40)
Rep. Elijah E. Cummings (D-MD 7)	Rep. Bobby L. Rush (D-IL1)
Rep. Danny K. Davis (D-IL 7)	Rep. Gregorio Sablan (D-NMI)
Rep. Susan A. Davis (D-CA 53)	Rep. Linda T. Sanchez (D-CA 38)
Rep. Rosa L. DeLauro (D-CT 3)	
Rep. Lloyd Doggett (D-TX 35)	Rep. Loretta Sanchez (D-CA 46)
	Rep. Jan Schakowsky (D-IL 9)
Rep. Keith Ellison (D-MN 5)	Rep. Robert C. "Bobby" Scott (D-VA 3)
Rep. Bill Foster (D-IL 11)	Rep. José E. Serrano (D-NY15)
Rep. Marcia L. Fudge (D-OH 11)	Rep. Krysten Sinema (D-AZ 9)
Rep. Raúl M. Grijalva (D-AZ 7)	
Rep. Luis V. Gutierrez (D-IL 4)	Sen. Debbie Stabenow (D-MI)
	Rep. Paul D. Tonko (D-NY 20)
Rep. Alcee Hastings (D-FL 20)	Rep. Niki Tsongas (D-MA5)
Sen. Heidi Heitkamp (D-ND)	Rep. Maxine Waters (D-CA 35)
Sen. Mazie K. Hirono (D-HI)	Rep. Joe Wilson (R-SC2)
Rep. Eleanor Holmes Norton (D-DC)	Rep. John Yarmuth (D-KY 3)
Rep. Rush Holt (D-NJ 12)	

Note: The Caucus membership will be updated following the convening of the new Congress in January, 2017. A current membership list can be found on the Caucus's Web page: http://socialworkcaucus-lee.house.gov/.

Source: Congressional Social Work Caucus. (n.d.). Membership. Retrieved from http://socialworkcaucus-lee.house.gov/membership on June 24, 2016.

A congressional caucus can be an excellent source of information as well as provide direction on policy matters. All US House of Representative caucuses are formally registered with the Committee on House Administration; the US Senate, on the other hand, does not have any formal caucuses. A listing of and contact information of the various caucuses is available through the Committee on House Administration website ((https://cha.house.gov/member-services/congressional-memberstaff-organizations).

Caucuses are an important tool for building a coalition of support on a particular policy matter. There are a number of caucuses, while not social work specific, that focus on interest areas shared by the social work profession (see Box 6.5). A caucus provides an important and established vehicle to raise an issue or concern. A social worker, for example, advocating for a veteran's issue during the 114th Congress, January 3, 2015–January 3, 2017, might have contacted one or more of the congressional caucuses that focus on veterans' affairs such as the Congressional Rural Veteran's Caucus, Congressional Hidden Heroes Caucus for Military and Veteran Caregivers, Congressional Veterans Jobs Caucus, Immigrant Service members and Veterans Caucus, Congressional Post-9/11 Veterans Caucus, or the Veterans Congressional Fellowship Caucus (see Appendix 1).

Box 6.5

EXAMPLES OF CONGRESSIONAL CAUCUSES THAT FOCUS ON AREAS OF SOCIAL WORK INTEREST, 115TH CONGRESSIONAL SESSION, CONVENED JANUARY 4, 2017

- Bipartisan Heroin Task Force
- Bipartisan Historically Black Colleges and Universities Caucus
- Bipartisan Taskforce for Combating Anti-Semitism
- California Public Higher Education Caucus
- Climate Solutions Caucus
- Congressional 21st Century Skills Caucus
- Congressional Access to Civil Legal Service Caucus
- Congressional Addiction, Treatment and Recovery Caucus
- Congressional Adult Literacy Caucus
- Congressional Air Force Caucus
- Congressional Home Health Caucus
- Congressional Homelessness Caucus
- Congressional Independent Colleges Caucus
- Congressional Labor and Working Families Caucus
- Congressional LGBT Equality Caucus
- Congressional Lung Cancer Caucus
- Congressional Lupus Caucus
- Congressional Military Family Caucus
- Congressional Military Mental Health Caucus

- Congressional Animal Protection Caucus
- Congressional Army Caucus
- Congressional Arthritis Caucus
- Congressional Assisting Caregivers Today Caucus
- Congressional Black Caucus
- Congressional Border Security Caucus
- Congressional Brain Injury Task Force
- Congressional Career and Technical Education Caucus
- Congressional Caucus for Women's Issues
- Congressional Caucus on International Exchange and Study
- Congressional Caucus on Maternity Care
- Congressional Caucus on the Deadliest Cancers
- Congressional Central America Caucus
- Congressional Chemistry Caucus
- Congressional Childhood Cancer Caucus
- Congressional Children's Health Care Caucus
- Congressional Coalition on Adoption
- Congressional Community College Caucus
- Congressional Cystic Fibrosis Caucus
- Congressional Dyslexia Caucus
- Congressional Green Schools Caucus
- Congressional Hearing Health Caucus
- Congressional Heart and Stroke Caucus
- Congressional Hispanic Caucus
- Congressional Hispanic Conference

- Congressional Military Sexual Assault Prevention Caucus
- Congressional Neuroscience Caucus
- Congressional New Americans Caucus
- Congressional Opportunity Action Group
- Congressional Out of Poverty Caucus
- Congressional Primary Care Caucus
- Congressional Privacy Caucus
- Congressional Public Health Caucus
- Congressional Public Transportation Caucus
- Congressional Research and Development (R&D) Caucus
- Congressional Skin Cancer Caucus
- Congressional Social Work Caucus
- Congressional US-Mexico Friendship Caucus
- Congressional Urban Caucus
- Congressional US-China Working Group
- Congressional Veterans Jobs Caucus
- Congressional Victims' Rights Caucus
- Congressional Youth Challenge Caucus
- House Rural Education Caucus
- Immigrant Service Members and Veterans Caucus
- Mental Health Caucus
- Northern Border Caucus
- Tuberculosis (TB) Elimination Caucus

Source: House Administration Committee (February, 2017). 115th Congressional member organizations (CMO). Retrieved from https://cha.house.gov/member-services/congressional-memberstaff-organizations on February 21, 2017

Not to be overlooked are the *congressional staff organizations* (*CSOs*), which are also regulated by the House Committee on House Administration. Although not as numerous as the congressional caucuses, the CSOs reflect the interests of members' staffs. Each CSO is sponsored by a House member, whereas congressional staff are responsible for their activities. During the 114th Congressional session, there were 31 CSOs (see Box 6.6). A CSO can become an ally in a policy practitioner's efforts to help garner the support of various members of Congress.

Box 6.6

CONGRESSIONAL STAFF ORGANIZATIONS (CSO), 114TH CONGRESSIONAL SESSION, JANUARY 3, 2015–JANUARY 3, 2017*

---

*The staff organizations for the 2017–2019 Congressional Session was not posted at the time of the Handbook's publication. Check the Staff Organization's web site for membership updates and information: https://cha.house.gov/member-services/congressional-memberstaff-organizations

- Armenian American Staff Association
- Black Republican Congressional Staff Association
- Capitol Hill Bible Study Staff Association
- Congressional African Staff Association (CASA)
- Congressional Asian Pacific American Staff Association (CAPASA)
- Congressional Black Associates
- Congressional Catholic Staff Association
- Congressional Hispanic Staff Association
- Congressional Jewish Staffers Association (CJSA)
- Congressional Legislative Assistants Staff Association (CLASA)
- Congressional Legislative Directors Association
- Muslim Staff Association
- Congressional South Asian-American Staff Association (CSAASA)
- Congressional Staff Association for Constitutional Studies
- Congressional Technology Staff Association (CTSA)
- Congressional Vegetarian Staff Association
- Congressional Yogi Association
- Faith on the Hill Staff Association (FHSA)
- Foreign Affairs Congressional Staff Association (FACSA)
- House Chiefs of Staff Association
- Italian American Staff Association
- Latter-day Saints Staff Association
- Lesbian, Gay, Bisexual and Transgender Congressional Staff Association (LGBT CSA)
- The Professional Administrative Managers (PAM)
- Public Relations, Event Planning and Protocol (PREP) Staff Association
- Republican Communications Association (RCA)
- Service Academy Graduate Staff Association
- Space Advocates Staff Association
- Western Chiefs of Staff Organization
- Women of Faith
- Working Mothers Staff Association

Source: House Administration Committee (September 28, 2016). 114th Congressional Member Organizations (CMO). Retrieved from https://cha.house.gov/member-services/congressional-memberstaff-organizations on February 21, 2017.

Political Action Committees and Governmental Relations Offices

Many national organizations staff a Governmental Relations' Office or political action committee (PAC). The purpose of both organizational units is the same: to influence legislators around matters that are important to a specific organization and the broader professional community.

A *Governmental Relations Office*, also referred to as an *Office of External Affairs*, represents an organization and advocates on its behalf with policy makers at the local, state, and federal levels; these offices generally are responsible for formulating and advancing the organization's legislative agenda. These offices are prohibited from making a fiscal donation to an elected official.

A PAC is an independent group, although they may have indirect ties with an organization, a political group, or a candidate himself or herself. A PAC collects money and uses it to support candidates or campaigns for or against a specific ballot initiative or legislation (Janda, Berry, & Goldman, 2008); a PAC may receive up to $5,000 from any individual, other PAC, or political party committee per calendar year, and PAC donations are not tax deductible. A PAC can give $5,000 to a candidate per election (primary, general, or special) and up to $15,000 annually to a national political party. Correspondingly, a PAC may receive up to $5,000 in donations from one individual, other PACs, or party committees each year. There are two types of PACs: (1) *separate segregated*—sponsored by an organization and can only solicit funds from its membership; and (2) *nonconnected*—not part of an association and can solicit funds from individuals or groups (Federal Election Commission, n.d.; see Box 6.7).

It is usual for a professional membership association to sponsor or align itself with a PAC that reflects the organization's mission and values. For example, the American Psychological Association, the American Medical Association, the American Nurses Association, and the National Association for Alcohol and Drug Abuse Counselors each has a PAC that advances its individual interests. Funding is derived from members, typically during the annual membership renewal or

---

Box 6.7

FEDERAL ELECTION COMMISSION AND POLITICAL ACTION COMMITTEES

The Federal Election Commission has regulatory oversight for all PACs; specific information regarding PACs can be found at the Commission's website: http://www.fec.gov/ans/answers_pac.shtml#pac.

activation process or through a specific fundraising drive. Typically, a volunteer membership committee governs the PAC, though a paid staff is commonplace for larger PACs.

The National Association of Social Workers sponsors a PAC, Political Action for Candidate Election (PACE), with funding coming directly from the NASW membership (see http://socialworkers.org/governance/cmtes/pace.asp). In addition, many NASW state chapters sponsor their own political action committees; funding comes from the national office of NASW as well as from additional donations by state members. The national PACE is governed by a volunteer board of directors and "endorses and financially contributes to candidates from any party who support NASW's policy agenda" (National Association of Social Workers, 2017). The national PACE limits its endorsements and potential contributions to individuals who are running for Congress or the Presidency, whereas the state-based NASW PACE endorses and provides financial support to individuals running for statewide office.

A social worker can approach a PAC or an organization's Governmental Relations Office as a resource to garner support for an issue. A PAC might view the particular matter as important to its mission; a candidate or elected official who supports a PAC's interest strengthens his or her position to receive its future political endorsement and possible funding. A Governmental Relation's Office, although not able to financially support a candidate or elected official, is in a position to notify its staff, association membership, and supporters of the politician's backing on the issue as well as to lobby directly on the issue itself.

FROM CONGRESSIONAL LAWS TO FEDERAL PROGRAMS

Once a bill passes both chambers of Congress and is signed into law by the president (or if Congress overrides a presidential veto), the new law is referred to a specific federal agency for implementation. The process of developing specific federal regulations and rules is the vehicle that creates, manages, and provides a program and its resulting services structure. The *rule-making process* occurs largely unnoticed in the offices of the government agencies rather than in the halls of Congress. There are more than 50 different federal regulatory agencies (see Table 6.3). Regulatory agencies are empowered to create and enforce rules (program regulations), which carry the full force of a law. Included in the law passed by Congress is the designation of a specific regulatory agency that is responsible for program oversight, including rule making.

In general, the federal regulatory system is guided by a basic principle that new or amended regulations cannot take effect until the public has had time to review and comment on the proposals. The federal rule-making process, which is governed by the Administration Procedures Act of 1946 (APA), establishes the procedures

Table 6.3. EXAMPLES OF FEDERAL REGULATORY AGENCIES, NAME AND PURPOSE

Federal Agency	Common Reference	Purpose
Bureau of Alcohol, Tobacco and Firearms	ATF	Protects communities from violent criminals, criminal organizations, the illegal use and trafficking of firearms, the illegal use and storage of explosives, acts of arson and bombings, acts of terrorism, and the illegal diversion of alcohol and tobacco products.
Consumer Product Safety Commission	CPSC	Enforces federal safety standards
Department of Veterans	VA	Oversees all veteran health and benefit programs
Drug Enforcement Administration	DEA	Enforces the controlled substances laws and regulations involving growing, manufacture, or distribution of controlled substances appearing in or destined for illicit drug traffic. The DEA also supports programs designed to reduce the availability of drugs.
Environmental Protection Agency	EPA	Establishes and enforces pollution standards
Equal Employment Opportunity Commission	EEOC	Administers and enforces Title VIII or the Civil Rights Act of 1964 (fair employment)
Federal Aviation Administration	FAA	Regulates and promotes air transportation safety, including airports and pilot licensing
Federal Communications Commission	FCC	Regulates interstate and foreign communication by radio, telephone, telegraph, and television
Federal Deposit Insurance Corporation	FDIC	Insures bank deposits, approves mergers, and audits banking practices
Federal Energy Regulatory Commission	FERC	Regulates the interstate transmission of natural gas, oil, electricity, natural gas, and hydro power projects
Federal Reserve System	FED	Regulates banking; manages the money supply
Federal Trade Commission	FTC	Ensures free and fair competition and protects consumers from unfair or deceptive practices
Food and Drug Administration	FDA	Administers federal food purity laws, drug testing and safety, and cosmetics
Interstate Commerce Commission	ICC	Enforces federal laws concerning transportation that crosses state lines
National Labor Relations Board	NLRB	Prevents or corrects unfair labor practices by either employers or unions
Nuclear Regulatory Commission	NRC	Llicenses and regulates nonmilitary nuclear facilities
Occupational Safety and Health Administration	OSHA	Develops and enforces federal standards and regulations ensuring working conditions
Securities and Exchange Commission	SEC	Administers federal laws concerning the buying and selling of securities

and specific program protocols necessary to implement the law. The federal rule-making process is described as:

> A Federal agency can begin the rulemaking process for any number of reasons, including: receiving a petition from an individual, interest group, or industry group; proactively reviewing its own regulations; or being ordered to by a court decision.
>
> The rulemaking process can start in a number of different places—including but not limited to—a request for information, asking for comments on a petition submitted to the agency, and the publication of a Notice of Proposed Rulemaking (NPRM).
>
> Most Executive branch agencies will accept comments via email or on Regulations. gov—and, with the launch of our new commenting feature, through FederalRegister. gov (where we send the comments to Regulations.gov on your behalf). As part of the rulemaking process, they will use Regulations.gov to manage the information within a docket. Some agencies will also add any comment they receive via email to that docket so that anyone interested can see the complete collection of public comments. (Federal Register, n.d.)

The rule-making process begins with the regulatory agency's development of "proposed rules" to govern a specific program. By law, the rule-making process requires that time be made available for public comments, which reflects the belief that the broader community has a right to be involved in the rule-making process. The APA mandates agencies must publish all proposed new regulations in the Federal Register (see https://www.federalregister.gov/) at least 30 days before they take effect, and they must provide a way for interested parties to comment, offer amendments, or to object to the regulation. The notice specifies how the public can submit comments or participate in public hearings on the proposed rule (see Appendix 2). In addition to its official website, the Federal Register also utilizes social media as a source for public input with a Facebook page (https:// www.facebook.com/FederalRegister) and a Twitter account (https://twitter.com/ FedRegister).

There are limited exceptions to the public comment period that allows a regulatory agency to bypass public input and immediately enforce the new or amended rules. This often occurs when Congress specifies an exact implementation date in its law or if the law is in response to an emergency. However, this is not always the case. A 2012 Government Accountability Office found that approximately 35% of major rules and 44% of nonmajor rules bypassed the public comment requirement between 2003 and 2010 (US Government Accountability Office, 2012). The same report also found that federal agencies often did not respond to public comments as well. The report stated:

> For example, in one of the 26 rules, an agency defined a pre-existing condition to implement the Patient Protection and Affordable Care Act and sought public comment. The agency received 4,627 comments, but has not published a response to them. When agencies do not respond to comments requested, the public does not know whether the

agency considered their comments, or if it intends to change the rule. As the courts have recognized, the opportunity to comment is meaningless unless the agency responds to significant points raised by the public. (US Government Accountability Office, 2012)

The public comment period in the rule-making process offers the social worker an important opportunity to impact directly the structure and delivery of a federal program. The public comment period uses multiple forms of communication though statements sent via email are the quickest way to submit recommendations. It is important to remember a call for public comments will result in thousands of emails and other forms of communication. Expecting an immediate response or even one within a short time period is unrealistic. And, as reported in by the Government Accounting Office, regulatory agencies do have a record of not responding to submitted comments (US Government Accountability Office, 2012). An important guide for effective policy practice is to *consistently and persistently* communicate with the office responsible for the specific rule-making process.

Working with a large governmental organization is, in general, slow and tedious and requires a resolute, methodological approach by the practitioner. The federal employee can become an important ally in a policy change effort. Having contacts within an organization opens the doors to important opportunities. Determining who is the best person or office to contact and meet on a particular issue can be a daunting task, but it is certainly achievable and well worth the investment in time and energy.

A VALUABLE RESOURCE FOR SOCIAL WORK STUDENTS

The Washington, DC-based Congressional Research Institute for Social Work and Policy (CRISP) was created in 2012 as an independent, nonpartisan 501(c)4 with its mission to expand " the participation of social workers in federal legislative and policy processes" (Congressional Institute for Social Work and Policy). CRISP envisions itself as a "bridge" between researchers and various federal agencies. CRISP also helps secures legislative internship positions for students and helping build a strong base of social workers who are able to work in and influence public policy, in particular at the federal level. The CRISP web site provides a portal to a variety of interesting related political blogs and web sites through a specific link, Morning Coffee News & Blogs (see http://crispinc.org/morning-coffee-news-blogs/).

Social work students with an interest in policy practice will find a number of opportunities available through CRISP including, among others, an Ambassador Program, which is an 8-month policy and leadership development program, and a Student Advocacy Day on Capitol Hill in Washington, DC.

A FEW FINAL THOUGHTS

It should be quite apparent that initiating and creating policy change at the federal level is sluggish and laborious with hurdle after hurdle to overcome. Although a group may have a good idea, such as the National Association of Social Worker's Social Work Reinvestment Act (National Association of Social Workers), the chances of getting a congressional committee, let alone the entire House or Senate, to vote on the bill is minuscule. Although the odds of finding a quick remedy to a policy issue are small, it is important to meet continually and advocate persistently to elected members of Congress or their staffs.

The key people to identify for policy-specific matters are the staff in local district offices and the legislative director/legislative assistants in the Washington, DC, offices. These individuals can directly help with a policy matter or direct the practitioner to the appropriate federal office.

Congressional caucuses aligned with specific issues offer unique opportunities to work with a group of legislators who have publically expressed their particular interests in this policy area. Successful caucus work begins (1) by identifying the caucus chair and key staff person(s) for the caucus; and (2) determining if any of the caucus members represent the social worker's congressional district (the social worker then becomes a "constituent"). Coalition building with social work groups, such as state chapters and local units of NASW, in the caucus members' congressional districts begins to build a wide, caucus member–specific constituency base from which to advocate for an issue.

Social work policy advocacy can be most impactful during the rule-making process. Policy practice has long ignored this crucial segment in federal program development while focusing attention on the congressional legislative process. Through rule making it is possible to have pieces added to a program that were not specified in the legislation while working to ensure that program requirements and protocols are fair, just, and address the social issue effectively.

Working with federal-based social policy or issues that require congressional attention is a slow and tedious process. Persistent, consistent, and well-thought-out work can lead to proactive, justice-based change. The frustration with federal legislative politics is that most proposals will not be quickly attended to nor acted upon. And it is highly probable that change may never occur. Even against all odds, the social worker engaged in policy practice continues her/his efforts. Why? Because change is possible.

REFERENCES

Committee on House Administration. (2016, June 6). Congressional member and staff organizations, 114th CMO. United States House of Representatives. Retrieved from https://

cha.house.gov/member-services/congressional-memberstaff-organizations on June 24, 2016.

Congressional Institute for Social Work and Policy (2017). Crips mission. Retrieved from http://crispinc.org/sample-page/ on July 4, 2017.

Congressional Social Work Caucus. (n.d.). Purpose, mission, and goals, mission statement. Retrieved from http://socialworkcaucus-lee.house.gov/about-me/purpose-mission-goals on January 26, 2017.

Congresswoman Niki Tsongas. (n.d.). Congresswoman Niki Tsongas. Retrieved from https://tsongas.house.gov/#dialog on May 12, 2016.

Encyclopedia Britannica. (n.d.). House of Representatives, United States government. Retrieved from http://www.britannica.com/topic/House-of-Representatives-United-States-government on May 18, 2016.

Federal Election Commission. (n.d.). Quick answers to PAC questions. Retrieved from http://www.fec.gov/ans/answers_pac.shtml#pac on June 1, 2016.

Federal Register. (n.d.). Federal rulemaking process. Retrieved from https://www.federalregister.gov/reader-aids/recent-updates/2014/07/new-submit-a-formal-comment-feature on January 20, 2017.

Hoefer, R. (2014). State and local policy advocacy. In M. Reisch, M. (ed)., *Social policy and social justice* (pp. 259–280). Thousand Oaks, CA: Sage.

Hudak, J. (2014, January 14). Obama's executive orders; a reality check. Brookings. Retrieved from http://www.brookings.edu/blogs/fixgov/posts/2014/01/30-state-of-the-union-obama-executive-orders-hudak on June 2, 2016.

Janda, K., Berry, J., & Goldman, J. (2008). *The challenge of democracy: American government in a global world* (10th ed.). Boston, MA: Cengage Learning.

The Leadership Conference. (2016). The Supreme Court and civil rights. Retrieved from http://www.civilrights.org/resources/civilrights101/supremecourt.html on June 24, 2016.

Liptak, A. (2016, June 23). Supreme Court upholds affirmative action program at the university of texas. *The New York Times*. Retrieved from http://www.nytimes.com/2016/06/24/us/politics/supreme-court-affirmative-action-university-of-texas.html on June 24, 2016.

Liptak, A., & Shear, M. (2016, June 23). Supreme Court ties blocks Obama's immigration plan. *The New York Times*. Retrieved from http://www.nytimes.com/2016/06/24/us/supreme-court-immigration-obama-dapa.html on June 24, 2016.

National Association of Social Workers. (2016). NASW legal briefs. Retrieved from https://www.socialworkers.org/advocacy/healthcarereform/legalbriefs.asp on June 24, 2016.

National Association of Social Workers. (2017). Advocacy. Retrieved from http://socialworkers.org/pace/default.asp on January 24, 2017.

National Association of Social Workers. (n.d). Social work reinvestment act. Retrieved from http://www.socialworkreinvestment.org/ on June 24, 2016.

United States Courts. (2017, January 25). Judicial vacancies. Retrieved from http://www.uscourts.gov/about-federal-courts rom http://www.uscourts.gov/judges-judgeships/judicial-vacancies on January 25, 2017.

United States House of Representatives. (n.d.). Directory of representatives, 114th Congress, 2nd session. Retrieved from http://www.house.gov/representatives/ on May 18, 2016.

United States Senate. (n.d.). Senators of the 114th Congress. Retrieved from http://www.senate.gov/senators/contact/ on June 18, 2016.

US Government Accountability Office. (2012). Federal rulemaking: Agencies could take additional steps to respond to public comments. GAO 13-21. Washington, DC: Author.

The White House. (n.d.). The judicial branch. Retrieved from https://www.whitehouse.gov/1600/judicial-branch on May 18, 2016.

The White House (n.d.). The legislative branch. Retrieved from https://www.whitehouse.gov/1600/legislative-branch on May 18, 2016.

CHAPTER 7

State and Local Government–Based Policy Development

Former Speaker of the US House of Representatives Tip O'Neil famously said, "All politics is local" (O'Neil & Hymel, 1994). O'Neil was referencing his personal experience as a politican that local issues are the ones constituents feel, understand, and, most important, expect to be resolved as quicly as possible. Many national and global social issues are hard to comprehend or fully appreciate. It is difficult, for example, to fully grasp the prediction that by "2025, 1.8 billion people will be living in countries or regions with absolute water scarcity, and two-thirds of the world population could live under water stress conditions" (United Nations, 2014). Yet in 2014, 2015, and 2016, the residents of Flint, Michigan; Hoosick Falls, New York; and North Bennington, Vermont, fully recognized the magnitude of a water crisis when local water supplies were discovered to be contaiminated with life-thretaneing chemicals, including lead and perfluorooctanoic acid (PFOA). A human issue on other continents, halfway around the world, had become a real-life, hands-on local issue for the citizens of Flint, Hoosick Falls, and North Bennington.

State and local governments are front and center in the daily lives of all people. Issues faced on a daily basis in state and local governments across the United States are broad and far reaching:

- Creating long-lasting, good-paying employment opportunities
- Providing assistance to people during times of unexpected disasters such as hurricanes, earthquakes, or fires
- Ensuring that neighborhoods are safe from crime
- Supporting critical social services such as mental health, substance abuse, and child welfare
- Providing a vibrant, modern transportation infrastructure
- Offering affordable and safe housing
- Making sure that public schools offer a quality education

Box 7.1
THE UNFUNDED MANDATE

A common shared dislike among state governments toward the federal government is the passage of a bill that is a "unfunded mandate." An unfunded mandate is when Congress passes a bill that requires the states to implement a program, though the federal government does not provide financial support for the policy. According to the National Governors' Association, "Federal action increasingly has relied on states to carry out policy initiatives without providing necessary funding to pay for these programs. State governments cannot function as full partners in our federal system if the federal government requires states to devote their limited resources toward complying with unfunded federal mandates" (National Governors Association, 2015).

People fully expect their governor, state representatives, the local mayor and city council members, and county government officials to effectively confront and resolve these and the plethora of other social issues in their communities.

A significant portion of social work policy practice takes place within state and local governments. State and local policy practice shares some similar approaches, but the unique character of states and local governments requires the social worker to employ diverse policy practice strategies (see Box 7.1).

STATE GOVERNMENT STRUCTURES

State governmental structures are comparable with the federal government: There is a head of state, a legislative branch, and a judiciary. All 50 states have a governor while 49 states have a two-chamber legislature; Nebraska is the lone state with a one-chamber legislature. In 25 states, the legislature is simply called the *Legislature* or the *State Legislature*; in 19 states, the legislature is recognized as the *General Assembly*. The state legislatures in Massachusetts and New Hampshire are formally referred to as the *General Court* while the legislatures in North Dakota and Oregon are called the *Legislative Assembly*.

The US Constitution identifies the authority of the federal government and specifies what states cannot do (United States Senate, see Constitution, Section X), but the 10th Amendment to the US Constitution reads:

> The powers not delegated to the United States by the Constitution, nor prohibited by it to the States, are reserved to the States respectively, or to the people. (Bill of Rights Institute, 2016)

Because of this stipulation in the US Constitution, each state has its own constitution, which in turn spells out its responsibilities and obligations to its citizens. Although there is significant diversity in both content and sizes among the 50 different state constitutions, there are basic responsibilities common among the states (see Table 7.1).

Table 7.1. EXAMPLES OF POWERS OF FEDERAL, STATE, AND LOCAL GOVERNMENTS

Exclusive Powers of Federal Government	Exclusive Powers of State Government	Powers Shared by Federal and State Governments	Services Provided by Local Government
Print money (bills and coins)	Establish local governments	Establish courts	Education
Declare war	Issue licenses (e.g., driver, marriage, hunting, fishing)	Create and collect taxes	Fire
Establish an army and navy	Regulate interstate commerce	Build highways	Police
Enter into treaties with foreign governments	Conduct elections	Borrow money	Human services
Regulate commerce between states and international trade	Ratify amendments to the US Constitution	Make and enforce laws	Public works (construction and maintenance of all county-owned or county-operated assets and services like sewers, solid waste and storm water management)
Establish post office and issue postage	Provide for public health and public safety	Charter banks and corporations	Urban planning/zoning
Make laws necessary to enforce the Constitution	Exercise powers neither delegated to the national government nor prohibited from the states by the US Constitution	Spend money for the betterment of the general welfare of residents	Economic development
	Establish a state constitution (e.g., set legal drinking and smoking ages)	Transportation	Parks and recreation

Source: Fairfax County Virginia. (n.d.). Explaining federal, state and local government responsibilities in Virginia. Retrieved from http://www.silooo.com/file/explaining-federal-state-and-local-government.aspx on May 16, 2016.

Differences among state governance processes begin with their individual constitutions. Although the constitutions differ in structure, they do identify common responsibilities that affect peoples' lives on a daily basis in a personal manner:

- Rules regarding marriage and distribution/maintenance of birth and death certificates
- Developing and implementing public school policies
- Procedures and regulations (e.g., minimum age to obtain a driver's license)
- Laws regarding theft, rape, and murder
- Creation of safety measures such as police, fire, and roads

The average length of a state constitution is 26,000 words compared to about 8,700 words for the US Constitution (Ballotpedia, n.d.a.). Alabama has the longest state constitution with over 172,000 words and 770 amendments. Vermont, on the other hand, has the shortest state constitution with 8,295 words (USLegal, 2016). It is commonplace for states not to just amend their constitutions but replace the entire document; 30 states have replaced their governing documents at least one time, whereas Georgia and Louisiana have totally rewritten their constitutions on nine separate occasions.

The typical state legislature includes two chambers: a lower house and upper house. States refer to the lower house in different ways, including the *Assembly, General Assembly, State Assembly, House of Delegates,* or *House of Representatives;* the upper house is commonly called the *Senate.* Following the November 2016 general election, there were 7,346 state representatives (Ballotpedia, n.d.b.) with the chambers ranging in size from 49 (Nebraska) to 424 (New Hampshire) total members (National Conference of State Legislatures, February 15, 2016).

The National Governors Association reported that as of January 2017, Republicans held 33 governorships, 16 for Democrats, and 1 Independent; when accounting for US territories and commonwealths, the numbers changed to 35, 17, and 3, respectively (National Governors Association, 2017). Republicans controlled 67 state senate and house chambers, whereas Democrats were the majority in 31 chambers. Since 2000, the Republican Party has controlled the state legislative chambers the majority of the time, though it is interesting to note there was a significant upswing in the number of split legislative chambers, one being Democrat and the other Republican (see Table 7.2). Only future elections will tell if this is a one-time occurrence and a reflection of the 2017 national election or if this a new trend in state electoral politics.

Nebraska is the only state with one legislative chamber, also known as a *unicameral* legislature, and, as a result, it is considered nonpartisan. As a nonpartisan legislature, the role of political parties is minimized in the legislature and the election of state officials. For example, a candidate's political party is not listed on the election ballot in Nebraska; the two candidates who obtain the most votes in a primary election face each other in the general election. In other states, each party

Table 7.2. PARTISAN COMPOSITION OF STATE
LEGISLATURES, OVER TIME

Year	Republican	Democrat	Split Control
2017	25	5	19
2016	30	12	7
2015	30	11	8
2014	27	19	3
2013	26	19	4
2012	27	15	7
2011	25	16	8
2010	14	27	7
2009	14	27	7
2008	14	27	7
2006	16	23	10
2004	20	19	10
2002	21	16	12
2000	18	16	15
1998	17	20	12
1886	17	20	12
1994	15	22	12
1992	7	26	16
1990	6	29	14
1988	8	29	12
1986	9	27	13
1984	10	28	11
1982	10	34	5
1980	15	28	6

Notes.: The historic table shows the party control as of January in each year except
for 2014 and 2015.
Prior to 2008, data are avilable only for even-numbered years.

Source.: National Conference State Legislatures (2017). State partisan composition. Retrieved from http://www.ncsl.org/research/about-state-legislatures/
partisan-composition.aspx#2016 on January 27, 2016.

selects a winner in the primary, and the winners of each party run against each
other in the general election.

States do not share a common time period or length of time for their legislatures to be *in session*. A state's constitution specifies a legislature meeting date
and the duration of its session. In 2016, state legislatures in 46 states met annually, whereas four—Montana, Nevada, North Dakota, and Texas—convened
every 2 years (National Conference of State Legislatures, 2016). A legislature's
time in formal session also varies from state to state. For example in 2016, the
Arkansas state legislature met for 27 days; the California legislature met for

240 days; the Massachusetts legislature met for 207 days; and the Indiana legislature met for 65 days (Andrews, 2016); and Montana, Nevada, North Dakota, and Texas did not meet as their legislatures convene in only odd-numbered years (see Table 7.3).

Table 7.3. STATE LEGISLATIVE SESSION DATES, 2016

State	Start Date	House Bill Intro Deadline	Senate Bill Intro Deadline	Sine Die Adjournment (approx.)	Special Sessions/ Governors' Actions/Other Deadlines
Alabama	02/07/17	None	26th legislative day	05/31/17	
Alaska	01/17/17	02/20/17	02/20/17	04/16/17	
Arizona	01/09/17	02/10/17	01/30/16	04/22/17	
Arkansas	04/13/16	04/27/16	04/27/16	05/09/16	
California	01/04/16	02/19/16	02/19/16	08/31/16	
Colorado	01/13/16	02/03/16	01/29/16	05/11/16	
Connecticut	02/03/16	02/05/16	02/05/16	05/04/16	
Delaware	01/12/16	None	None	06/30/16	
Florida	01/12/16	01/12/16	01/12/16	03/11/16	
Georgia	01/11/16	02/29/16	02/29/16	03/24/16	
Hawaii	01/20/16	01/27/16	01/27/16	05/05/16	
Idaho	01/11/16	01/29/16	01/22/16	03/25/16	
Illinois	01/13/16	02/11/16	02/19/16	05/31/16	01/09/17 lame duck session 11/15/16–12/01/16 veto session
Indiana	01/05/16	01/12/16	01/08/16	03/10/16	
Iowa	01/11/16	01/22/16	01/22/16	04/29/16	
Kansas	01/11/16	02/10/16	02/10/16	05/02/16	
Kentucky	01/05/16	02/29/16	03/02/16	04/15/16	
Louisiana	03/14/16	04/05/16	04/05/16	06/06/16	
Maine	01/06/16	None	None	04/16/16	
Maryland	01/13/16	02/12/16	02/05/16	04/11/16	
Massachusetts	01/06/16	None	None	07/31/16	08/01/16–12/31/16 informal session
Michigan	01/13/16	None	None	12/31/16	

Table 7.3. CONTINUED

State	Start Date	House Bill Intro Deadline	Senate Bill Intro Deadline	Sine Die Adjournment (approx.)	Special Sessions/ Governors' Actions/Other Deadlines
Minnesota	03/08/16	None	None	05/23/16	
Mississippi	01/05/16	02/08/16	02/08/16	04/21/16	
Missouri	01/06/16	03/07/16	03/07/16	05/13/16	
Montana	No regular session in even-numbered years				
Nebraska	01/06/16	N/A	01/20/16	04/20/16	
Nevada	No regular session in even-numbered years				10/10/16–10/15/16 special session re: stadium
New Hampshire	01/06/16	01/06/16	None	06/01/16	
New Jersey	01/12/16	None	None	12/31/16	
New Mexico	01/19/16	02/03/16	02/03/16	02/18/16	09/30/16–10/06/16 special session re: budget
New York	01/06/16	None	None	06/17/16	
North Carolina	04/25/16	05/10/16	05/10/16	07/01/16	12/21/16 special session re: HB2
North Dakota	No regular session in even-numbered years				
Ohio	01/05/16	None	None	12/31/16	
Oklahoma	02/01/16	02/01/16	02/01/16	05/27/16	
Oregon	02/01/16	01/19/16	01/19/16	03/03/16	

(*continued*)

Table 7.3. CONTINUED

State	Start Date	House Bill Intro Deadline	Senate Bill Intro Deadline	Sine Die Adjournment (approx.)	Special Sessions/ Governors' Actions/Other Deadlines
Pennsylvania	01/05/16	None	None	11/30/16	11/16/16—last day of regular session 11/30/16—official sine die
Rhode Island	01/05/16	02/23/16	02/11/16	06/18/16	
South Carolina	01/12/16	04/15/16	05/01/16	06/02/16	
South Dakota	01/12/16	02/04/16	02/04/16	03/29/16	
Tennessee	01/12/16	01/25/16	01/25/16	04/22/16	
Texas	No regular session in even-numbered years				
Utah	01/25/16	02/04/16	02/04/16	03/10/16	11/16/16 special session re: road funding
Vermont	01/05/16	03/11/16	None	05/06/16	
Virginia	01/13/16	01/22/16	01/22/16	03/11/16	
Washington	01/11/16	None	None	03/10/16	
West Virginia	01/13/16	None	None	03/12/16	
Wisconsin	01/12/16	None	None	03/15/16	
Wyoming	02/08/16	02/12/16	02/12/16	03/04/16ss	

Source: Multistate Associates Incorporated. 2016 State Legislative Session Dates. Retrieved from https://www.multistate.com/state-resources/legislative-session-deadlines on January 27, 2017.

Legislative calendars and specific dates for introducing legislation are subject to change each year. The easiest way to monitor a session's dates is to log onto a state legislature's website. These websites provide a wealth of information, but most important, the website is a direct portal to the entire legislature. Web information typically includes links to the individual members' websites; listing and bill status of current legislation; the roll of standing and special committees with members identified and meeting schedules posted; a bill search engine; and maps of the capitol and legislative offices.

Bills introduced in state legislatures follow a similar review path as those considered by the US Congress. A measure can be introduced in either one or both chambers, except Nebraska, which has only one chamber, but only by an elected official of the state legislature; it is assigned to a committee for potential hearings and review; and a vote is required to move the bill to the full chamber for consideration. Once a measure is passed by one chamber, the proposed measure is referred to the other body for consideration. Finally, a bill, once it becomes law, is assigned to a state agency for specific rule making; this process, too, is similar to the federal government rule-making process. Figure 7.1a–c illustrates the legislative processes for three states—Oklahoma, Kansas, and North Carolina. Although there are differences, in general, the procedures are similar among the states.

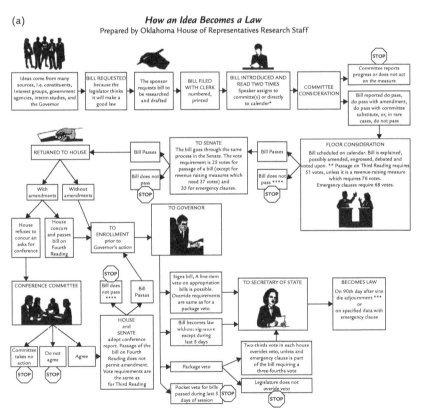

Figure 7.1a.
How a bill becomes law, state examples: Oklahoma.

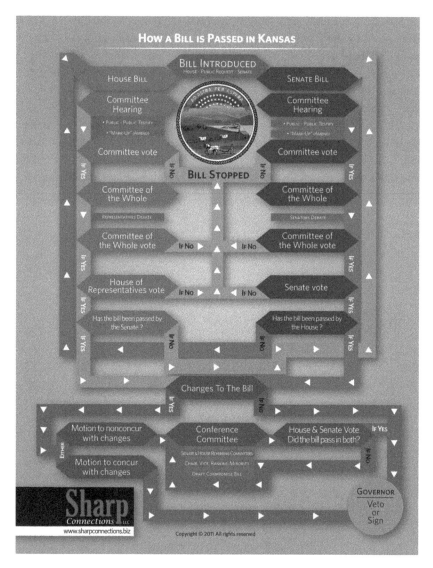

Figure 7.1b.
How a bill becomes law, state examples: Kansas.

Senate and House Committees

A legislature's work is completed through various committees in both chambers. House and Senate members are appointed to standing committees in each chamber generally by the elected leader of the House or Senate. A *standing committee* is essentially permenant and continues to meet in each legislative session; a standing committee is considered more important than others, such as a *select committee*—a temporary group appointed to study a particular matter and usually does not draft

(c)   HOW AN IDEA BECOMES A LAW

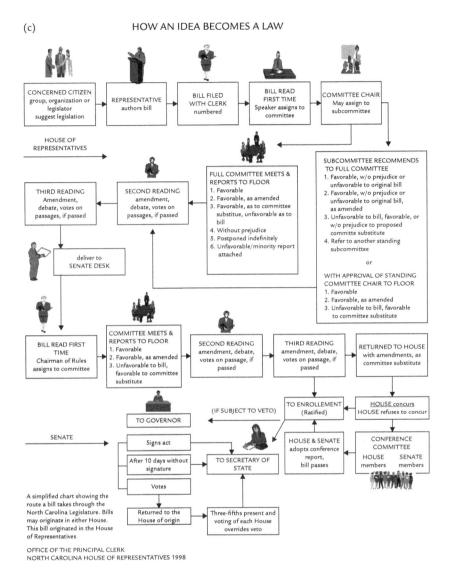

Figure 7.1c.
How a bill becomes law, state examples: North Carolina.

legislation—or a *joint committee*—similar to a select committee but its members
come from both legislative chambers. Members with seniority or political influence
generally are appointed to the more important standing committees, such as the
Appropriations or Budget committees, which are responsible for state expenditures
and program funding.

The House or Senate Committee offers excellent opportunities to influence the
direction of a proposed legislative bill. Every measure, unless it is an emergency
piece of legislation, is required to have a public hearing and debate prior to a vote.
Known as *sunshine laws*, these state-specific regulations ensure and protect the

public's right to access all governmental records and meetings (Ballotpedia, n.d.c.). State-based sunshine laws, while worded differently, include common themes. The Pennsylvania Sunshine Law is typical of the state-specific regulations as it specifies, among other items:

- An agency, for example, the House or Senate, is required to publish a notice of its first regular meeting at least three days in advance.
- The agency is required to publish a schedule of its remaining regular meetings.
- Any special meetings and rescheduled meetings outside of the previously published schedule require 24 hours' notice.
- Public notice is not required for an emergency meeting or conference (Lefkowitz, 2016).

Once a bill is filed by a legislator, it is assigned to a specific committee for the hearing process to begin (see Figure 7.1a–c). As with bills proposed in the US Congress, a proposal in a state legislature must overcome significant hurdles throughout the entire process. The state-based legislative process is difficult and complicated and, as with policy practice at the federal level, patience and persistence are required.

As discussed in the previous chapter, the majority of proposed bills fail at the federal level; this, too, is the fate for proposed measues in state legislatures across the United States. Minnesota's legislature, in 2015, considered 4,605 proposals, of which 77 (2%) were eventually enacted (Minnesota Legislative Reference Library, n.d.); legislators in Texas during its 2015 legislative session filed 6,276 bills, of which 1,322 (21%) were ultimately passed (Texas Star Alliance, 2015). In summing up the work of the 2015 Texas legislative session, Mekelburg (2015) wrote:

> Lawmakers will tell you the legislative process is not designed for passing bills. In fact, some insist it is exactly the opposite. The sheer number of bills filed each session does not bode well, as lawmakers struggle to get their voices—and bills—to be heard, and some see their bills die repeatedly.

Committee Process

A bill once introduced by a legislator is assigned to a committee whose responsibility is to consider the proposal and decide if the bill should be reviewed by the full legislative chamber. The committee's responsibility is to debate the merits of bills under consideration, review reports prepared by staff and other groups, and hear testimony from interested parties. Once a bill is scheduled for review by the committee chair, the bill's author, for example, the legislator who introduced the bill, is usually the first to speak and introduces the bill to the committee. The public then has the opportunity to voice support for or opposition to a bill.

Working with a legislative committee involves a four-prong strategy: (1) public testimony, (2) committee staff relationships, (3) identifying potential allies, and (4) engaging legislators.

Public Testimony

Note that Chapter 9 details the specifics and nuances in testifying before a legislative committee. Committee action is the most important phase of the legislative process; a proposal simply cannot become law without agreement by a committee and a majority vote of each chamber.

The committee chair is a key person in this process as she or he decides if and when a proposal will be reviewed by the committee. All proposed bills are referred to an appropriate committee for review, but there are no regulations or statutes mandating it must reviewed by a committee.

A bill scheduled by a committee chair for review must include time for testimony and public input. Specific rules regarding public testimony are published on a state house's or committee's Web page. To address a committee, an individual must first register with the committee, typically at the time of the hearing. A growing number of state houses allow individuals to register electronically with kiosks located in the state capitol, though a number of states require the person to fill out a request form at the time of the hearing and submit the paperwork to the committee staff person. The electronic or paper registration forms allow an individual to register his or her support or opposition to the bill under consideration while not requiring the person to testify before the committee; the social worker can also speak on a bill for informational purposes without indicating support or opposition.

In general, an individual's comments to the committee are time limited, most often 3 minutes or less, with committee members asking questions following the individual's comments. The legislature committee's website generally lists time limits for testimony. It is common for committee members not to ask any questions. A lack of questions should not be interpreted as a sign of disinterest on the legislators' part; legislators often want to end the hearing to move on to other committee, house, or senate business.

It is highly advisable to provide a written copy of the testimony to the committee; Chapter 9 details best practices for preparing written testimony as well as how to present comments to a legislative committee.

Committee Staff Relationships

Individuals who either work for a specific legislator or are retained by the committee itself staff every committee. Some staff members are paid professionals, whereas others are volunteers such as college interns. A committee's staff is responsible for the legislative group's work and, as a result, holds a very powerful position in the legislative process. Committee staff prepares the members' briefing and work packets, provides legislative briefs or bill analyses, conducts research on a bill and the issue it addresses, ensures that key people will be available to testify, and, in general, keeps the committee meeting process moving in a timely manner. Most important, staff members review all legislation that is referred to the committee and recommend to the committee chair if a bill should be considered. The high volume of legislation a committee reviews requires a screening process to determine which bills are heard and those that *die in committee*. Legislators rely heavily on their staff—for policy research, to help constituents, to keep the legislative process running, and administrative support, among other jobs. An important point to remember is that *legislators trust information from their staff more than from any other source.*

Policy practice includes proactively building strong relationships with a committee's staff. Over time, a positive policy practitioner–staff relationship can open legislative pathways that otherwise might be closed. Relationship building with a committee's staff is no different from creating positive relationships with client systems. Key attributes that foster positive, strong relationships include respectful and serious dialogs, treating the individual with dignity while not being judgmental.

Each social worker has her or his own way of building strong relationships with clients; there are no "to do" or "not to do" lists or required steps. Social workers understand from their practice that the most effective means in relationship building is by asking open-ended questions while showing interest in the person. Typical questions asked of a committee staff person include the following:

- Can you tell me how best to prepare to testify before the committee?
- What do members look for in a testimony?
- Are there specific protocols, especially unwritten, rules that I should be aware of?
- Do you have ideas you can share with me that can help lead to an informative testimony?
- Does the committee prefer a specific format for written testimony?
- Whom should I follow up with after the testimony?

The key, and most important question a social worker can ask a committee staff person is "What can I do to help you with this issue?" This query demonstrates the openness to form a positive, proactive, helpful partnership.

Potential Allies

There are groups of people who support or oppose just about every issue that a state legislature addresses. Some are formal groups, which are part of an existing organization or agency; they may be multi- or single-issue groups. Some groups organize around a specific issue with the sole purpose to support or defeat a proposed bill.

Examples of single-issue groups are the National Rifle Association (lobbies for laws that minimize restrictions on firearm use and ownership—https://home.nra.org/) and Emily's List (support for Democratic, female, pro-choice candidates—http://www.emilyslist.org/). Examples of multi-issue advocacy groups include the People for the American Way (advocate for the values and institutions that sustain a diverse democratic society— http://www.pfaw.org/) and the American Conservative Union (advance the goals and principles of conservativism—http://www.conservative.org).

Knowing what groups support a particular position and being able to unite these groups in a common effort is an important technique for the policy practitioner. Successful policy practice understands that strength is shown through numbers. Intergroup collaboration expands resources, broadens lobbying strategies, and increases the possibilities for a bill's passage or defeat. Building a collaborative group requires the social worker to either use her or his network or create a new circle of concerned people and organizations. Identifying potential supports and getting them to commit to an advocacy effort is an important first step in building a powerful collaboration (see Box 7.2). Potential allies include the following:

- Any legislator(s) who already favors the proposal or issue
- Actual or potential beneficiaries of the policy
- People who work in NGOs or other organizations that provide services targeting the issue
- Recognized "experts" in the field
- Community and business leaders who understand and can speak directly about the issue
- Celebrities who are sympathetic to the issue and can speak convincingly about the proposal
- Professional or other organizations concerned with the issue or with the population affected
- Be careful not to write off people with whom you may disagree on other issues

---

Box 7.2

POSSIBLE COLABORTORS MIGHT NOT BE WHO WE THINK THEY MIGHT BE

Do not to write off a person, group, or organization because you may disagree with them on other issues. Policy practitioners often find that persons who opposed social work issues in the past may in fact support other social issue initiatives and become allies. Positive ties and relationships built during an advocacy campaign can result in future alliances, or, at a minimum, others will be more willing to listen to the social worker's perspectives about issues on which there is disagreement.

In addition to individuals and other social service agencies and organizations, state-specific *political action committees* (PACs) and *Governmental Relations* (GR) offices are also potential collaborators. A PAC endorsed individual is more inclined to support an organization's stand; similarly, an agency's GR office may have strong relationships with a House or Senate member's office. A state PAC and agency GR office often have long-standing relationships with elected officials and staff members; a policy practitioner can take advantage of these relationships by partnering with existing PACs or GR offices. Joining an existing or forming a new collaboration with established PACs and GR offices lends instant credibility to the social worker. An elected official or staff person will often think, "If this person is a friend of x PAC or y GR office, then this person's ideas must be legitimate and worth listening to." In addition, a PAC or GR office may add the policy practitioner's issue to its ongoing legislative agenda, which in turn broadens the political base supporting or opposing the social worker's issue.

Engaging Legislators

Finding an elected House or Senate member to champion a bill's passage or defeat is a critical piece in policy practice. A bill, which is already introduced in a House or Senate chamber, includes a sponsor and possibly a number of cosponsors. Meeting with these individuals and/or their staff is a vital step to mapping out a legislative strategy. When meeting with an elected person and/or the staff, the social worker's goals should be clear, specific, and involve something the lawmaker can specifically do. Providing the legislator with a copy of the proposed bill, a fact sheet, or info sheet is an important task for the social worker; be sure enough copies of handouts are available for the staff as well (see Activity Box 7.1). Discussion detailing these and other handouts is reviewed in Chapter 10.

An equally important, and often underutilized, strategy by the policy practitioner is to build a relationships with elected social workers in the House or Senate as well as those who work on committee or office staffs. The common bond of being social workers creates a unique opportunity for the policy practitioner to engage with a professional colleague who understands the issue from the profession's perspective. Again, working with the elected social worker's staff to help craft a policy practice strategy is essential, as the elected individual will have little time to think through and develop alternative or compromise policy positions (see Box 7.3).

State-Based Rule-Making Process

The policy practitioner's work does not end with the passage of a bill but continues with the rule-making process (see Box 7.4). The final social services' program is a direct result of rule making and, as such, this process is where a program's specifics are detailed

---

Activity Box 7.1

MEET WITH A STATE LEGISLATOR

Meet with a local state legislator to gain his or her insights on successful advocacy techniques.

1. From your perspective, what are effective advocacy efforts; similarly, what are ineffective approaches?
2. What has the greatest and least influence on you: emails, letter writing, telephone calls, personal visits to the district office, personal visits to the capitol office, or meetings when the legislature is out of session? Please discuss the pros and cons of each communication technique.
3. How do you decide to introduce or cosponsor a bill? How should advocates approach you when they would like you to sponsor or cosponsor a bill?
4. What do you consider to be the most pressing human services issue for the community and the state? What are your ideas on how best to approach the issue?

Invite the local state representative to a class.

1. As a class, prepare an advocacy presentation on a social service issue that is pertinent to the community.
2. Ask the legislator the same questions as above.

---

and codified. State-based rule making is similar to the process employed by the federal government (see Chapter 6). A state generally employs three components in the process: (1) notification of intent to initiate rule making; (2) publication of rule changes or new rules; and (3) opportunity for the public to provide formal input prior to the adoption of final rule. Box 7.5 illustrates the State of Washington's rule-making process, which is similar to those in all states. One of the more comprehensive rule-making

---

Box 7.3

TODAY'S OPPONENT MAY BE TOMORROW'S ALLY

Regardless of how a legislator votes on a particular bill, the social worker should *always* maintain contact and good relations with the legislator and her or his staff. Burning bridges is never a good outcome in policy practice. The general rule of thumb: Today's opponent may be tomorrow's ally.

Box 7.4
SIGNIFICANE OF KEY WORDS IN RULE MAKING

Must is used to denote a *required* action.

Should denotes a recommended, not required, action.

May is used for purely discretionary actions.

I/you refers to the person preparing the notice or performing the referenced task or activity.

We/us refers to colleagues in the Department of State's Division of Administrative Rules.

Source: https://www.dos.ny.gov/info/rulemakingmanual.html#using

---

Box 7.5
RULE-MAKING PROCESS, STATE OF WASHINGTON

---

1. NOTIFICATION OF INTENT TO DO RULE MAKING

The department notifies stakeholders about the intent to adopt a new rule, amend, or repeal an existing rule through appropriate ListServs, postings on the agency's website, and by filing the appropriate forms with the Office of the Code Reviser. The notification includes the following:

- A brief description of the subject, including the associated Washington Administrative Code (WAC) chapters or WAC numbers
- Reasons why rules on this subject may be needed and what they might accomplish
- How interested parties can participate in the rule-making activities

2. PROPOSITION OF RULE CHANGES AND OPPORTUNITY TO PROVIDE FORMAL INPUT

The department provides stakeholders and interested parties the opportunity to submit formal comments on proposed rules before the department makes a final decision to adopt rules.

The department holds a scheduled public rule-making hearing. An individual may provide comments either by attending the public hearing, submitting written comments using the agency's online rules comment site at Policy Review, or by mailing or faxing the comments to the department by the specified deadline.

The deadline and process for how to express objections in writing of the use of the expedited rule-making process. . . . is typically 45 days after the date the rule form is filed.

3. ADOPTION OF FINAL RULE

At the conclusion of the public comment period, the department must consider all formal comments received and must file the adopted rule language with the Office of the Code Reviser.

Typically, stakeholders are required to comply with the adopted rule 31 days after the department adopts the rule language. There are exceptions; the effective date of the adopted rule may be specified as something other than 31 days.

A concise explanatory statement that documents the formal comments that were received and the department's responses are sent to stakeholders, anyone who submitted comments, and anyone who asks for it.

Source: http://www.doh.wa.gov/AboutUs/RuleMaking/WhatisRuleMaking

---

publications is issued by the New York Department of State (2012), *Rule Making in New York Manual.* The manual includes a number of chapters with information on topics such as pre-proposal rule review; how to propose a rule; how to withdraw or revise a proposal; how to adopt a rule; how to adopt an emergency rule; and how rules are "sunsetted," the formal process to determine if a rule is maintained, modified, or ended (see Chapter 12).

The state-based rule-making process provides the social worker with an important opportunity to influence the actual structure of a state-level program. It is at this point of the process that specific program procedures, protocols, and program designs are crafted. The policy practitioner's advocacy shifts from passing or amending a proposed bill to specifying explicit recommendations to the agency. The social work policy practitioner can easily learn about her or his own state's rule-making process by simply conducting a Web search with a phrase such as "Rule Making in (name of state)" or "Proposed Rule Making in (name of state)."

No matter the state, there is a common guideline that all policy practitioners should remember: Building strong working relationships with agency staff is essential in this process. A social worker considered a valuable resource by rule-making staff has a far better chance of success compared to the individual who is viewed as an obnoxious harsh critic or a "policy bully."

LOCAL GOVERNMENTAL STRUCTURES

Each level of government—federal, state, and local—provides a specific set of services and safety nets to its constituents. These systems of prescribed responsibilities are set forth in the federal and various states' constitutions as well as in local city, town, or county charters, constitutions, ordinances, or statutes. All states are broken into subdivisions that include *counties* (called parishes in Louisiana and boroughs in

Alaska) and *cities* or *townships*. Each of these governing subdivisions has its own set of governing rules, agencies, and elected officials.

Local government—city, town, and county—is closest to the public and it is here that individuals, groups, and communities have their most frequent governmental contact. According to the US Census Bureau, in 2012 there were 89,004 local governments in the United States, including the following:

- 3,031 counties
- 64 parishes
- 19,522 municipalities (e.g., cities, towns, boroughs, and villages)
- 16,364 townships
- 37,203 special districts (i.e., single service or group of services such as fire protection and water supply, historic preservation, and mosquito abatement)
- 2,884 independent school districts (United States Census Bureau, 2016)

The social worker can correctly infer that a consequence of the sheer number of local[1] governments is the lack of one preferred model of administration to oversee the development and implementation of social policies. The absence of a uniform national state and regional governance model requires the practitioner to develop an understanding of a local community's history while delving into its current political landscape. Awareness of a community's past and present offers insight into its values and beliefs.

County Governance

County government is found in all states except Massachusetts and Rhode Island, whereas counties in Louisiana are called *parishes* and in Alaska they are *boroughs*. Not surprisingly, the name of the county governance board varies from state to state with titles such as Board of Supervisors, County Board of Councilors, Board of County Commissioners, Board of Freeholders, Select Board, or Commissioners Court; this elected group serves as the executive branch of county government.

It is correct to assume that counties are an arm of state government and carry out many services mandated by the state and federal governments. County government is generally responsible for building and maintaining roads; developing recreational facilities; running local county airports; constructing and operating jails; managing a judicial system; maintaining public records; collecting property taxes; issuing vehicle registration and transfers; and registering voters. Counties also provide law enforcement, conduct elections, and provide certain health and social services.

---

1. Local government, unless specified, includes or is referencing city, town, village, county, and borough.

It is common for a county board to have advisory boards and commissions on a variety of issues. Local citizens volunteer to serve on these groups and, as a result, are able to influence a proposed policy initiative or the development of *area social services.* Local commissions focus on an assortment of topics ranging from airport and agricultural oversight to health and human services matters. Such commissions include Youth Services Board (Chesterfield County, VA), Adult Aging Commission (Sacramento, CA), Center for Health Care Services (Bexar County, TX), Mental Health Board (Clay County, MO), Disabilities and Special Needs Board (Charleston County, SC), Alcohol, Drug Addiction and Mental Health Services Board (Summit County, OH), and the Human Rights Commission (Snohomish County, WA).

An individual or group may also speak before the county commissioners during a board's regular scheduled meeting. Regulations regarding individual and group presentation are outlined on the board's Web page. In general, commissioners or board members are the only individuals allowed to place an item on the board's agenda. As a result, to have an item placed on an agenda, the policy practitioner should identify a county commissioner who is most likely to support or be sympathetic to an issue and ask him or her to bring the matter to the full board. An alternative approach is for the policy practitioner to work with board staff to see if they can help get the item placed on an agenda. Or the social worker can contact a commissioner with whom the policy practitioner has an established relationship. Also, the policy practitioner, if a resident of the county, can contact his or her commissioner as a "constituent." If the social worker is not a resident of the county, then finding a local resident who supports a particular issue is important because this individual can serve as the conduit between the social worker and the commissioner.

Commission or board meetings are open to the public and include a "public hearing" section on the agenda. Rules governing public testimony at a county board meeting are similar to those for a legislative committee. An individual addressing the board must first complete a registration card prior to the hearing; there is often a time limit for an individual's comments; and it is best to have prepared written testimony for the board.

Most boards meet on a weekly basis though their work is generally completed in committees that meet between formal board meetings. The committee meetings are often not publicized or open to the public and, as a result, a board's recommendations only become known during the formal weekly meeting.

Cities and Townships

The two most common models of local government include *Council-Manager* and *Mayor-Council.* Authority and power in the Council-Manager model rests with the council itself; it oversees the administration of the city, creates policies, develops the budget and authorizes expenditures; appoints a professional city manager to carry out day-to-day administrative operations; and the mayor is generally selected by the Council from its members (National League of Cities, 2016). According to the National League of Cities (2016), more than half of all cities in the United States use the Council-Manager model.

In the *Mayor-Council* model, the mayor is elected by the public. The mayor, the highest ranking official in a city and official leader of the local government, is a regular member of the city council and serves as its presiding officer. The mayor also oversees a city's departments such as the police, fire, housing, social services, and transportation departments. The mayor's position is generally a full-time salaried job. In this governing model, the mayor is the most powerful member of the council with the duties and related powers specified in the city charter or constitution. This model, according to the National League of Cities (2016b), is more common in older, larger cities (see Table 7.4). The mayor often decides what is placed on the agenda for council review. The mayor, who is the highest-ranking official in a city, is the official leader of the local government, a regular member of the city council, and serves as its presiding officer. The mayor also oversees a city's departments such as the police, fire, housing, social services, and transportation departments.

Members of a local city council are generally called *council member, alderman, selectman, freeholder, trustee,* or *commissioner*; the number of persons who serve on a local council range from 5 to 51 individuals with no national standard nor formula that identifies the number of individuals a council member represents (National League of Cities, 2016a).

The local council serves as the city's legislative branch of government. The council members are elected by the city's residents; the council's primary task is to decide which services are provided and how to pay for them (National League of Cities, 2016a). A city council develops laws, monitors the operation and performance of city agencies, makes land use decisions, and is responsible for approving the city's budget.

Similar to county government, local city councils establish a variety of boards and commissions as a mechanism for residents to participate in a city's governance process. City boards/commissions mimic the county boards/commissions focusing on a wide range of issues such as Native American Commission (Fargo, ND), Sustainable Energy (San Diego, CA), Human Rights Commission (Rockville, MD), Commission on Latino and Hispanic Affairs (Bloomington, IN), and Human Service Advisory Committee (Kirkland, WA).

City council meetings provide opportunities for public comment. The protocols are typically listed on a city council's Web page. As with testifying before a county board or a state legislative committee, comments are time limited, generally 3–5 minutes in length. Some councils include stringent guidelines for public comments. For example, Berkley (CA) City Council's *Guidelines for Public Comment, Written Communications, and Council Meeting Order* state:

Up to ten (10) speakers may speak for two minutes. If there are more than ten persons interested in speaking, the Presiding Officer may limit the public comment for all speakers to one minute per speaker. Speakers are permitted to yield their time to one other speaker, however no one speaker shall have more than four minutes. (City of Berkeley, 2016)

Table 7.4. THE FORM OF GOVERNMENT IN THE 30 MOST POPULOUS US CITIES

Rank	City Name	State	Form of Government
1	New York	NY	Mayor-Council
2	Los Angeles	CA	Mayor-Council
3	Chicago	IL	Mayor-Council
4	Houston	TX	Mayor-Council
5	Philadelphia	PA	Mayor-Council
6	Phoenix	AZ	Council-Manager
7	San Antonio	TX	Council-Manager
8	San Diego	CA	Mayor-Council
9	Dallas	TX	Council-Manager
10	San Jose	CA	Council-Manager
11	Indianapolis	IN	Mayor-Council
12	Jacksonville	FL	Mayor-Council
13	San Francisco	CA	Mayor-Council
14	Austin	TX	Council-Manager
15	Columbus	OH	Mayor-Council
16	Fort Worth	TX	Council-Manager
17	Louisville-Jefferson County	KY	Mayor-Council
18	Charlotte	NC	Council-Manager
19	Detroit	MI	Mayor-Council
20	El Paso	TX	Council-Manager
21	Memphis	TN	Mayor-Council
22	Nashville-Davidson	TN	Mayor-Council
23	Baltimore	MD	Mayor-Council
24	Boston	MA	Mayor-Council
25	Seattle	WA	Mayor-Council
26	Washington	DC	Mayor-Council
27	Denver	CO	Mayor-Council
28	Milwaukee	WI	Mayor-Council
29	Portland	OR	Commission
30	Las Vegas	NV	Council-Manager

Source: National League of Cities (2013). Forms of Muncipal Governments. Retrieved from http://www.nlc.org/build-skills-and-networks/resources/cities-101/city-structures/forms-of-municipal-government on May 12, 2016.

Town Meeting

It is common for a local community to host a *town meeting* as a forum for citizen input. Typically, a forum's focus is on a specific issue (e.g., homelessness or after-school programs) and is sponsored by a local governing group such as a city council or school board. Town meetings run by a governmental entity are typically fact finding; that is, they seek residents' ideas and reactions to a particular issue.

Nonprofit agencies as well as groups and associations also sponsor town meetings. Such gatherings are a strategy to gather local support for a particular issue while broadening collaboration with potential partners.

There are also town meetings in which local residents of a community come together to vote on a number of local issues, including budget as well as policy issues. Traditionally found throughout the New England states, town meetings provide a unique opportunity for a policy practitioner to affect a local issue. Meetings are organized as an open forum to encourage participants to ask questions or state their views on a matter; voting occurs on a variety of items, ranging from purchasing a firetruck to donating money to a local nonprofit group. The chair of the town meeting is a *moderator* whose role is to ensure the assembly is run fairly, that all views are heard, and that the process moves along as planned.

Town Meeting Day in Vermont typifies this form of local, grassroots governance. Held annually on the first Tuesday of March per the state's constitution, the meeting addresses articles (e.g., topics), which are prepared by the local Select Board and announced by a *town meeting warning* that is published "at least 30 days before the meeting" (Markowitz, 2003, p. 3). Vermont law provides Town Meeting Day as a holiday for state government employees while allowing any worker in the state the right to take unpaid leave from work to attend his or her annual town meeting (Markowitz, 2003, p. 5). Town Meeting Day allows residents over age 18, and on the voting role, to discuss and vote on the business of their town; any issue is open to debate (Markowitz, 2003, p. 3).

A FEW FINAL THOUGHTS

State and local political work is much more personal compared to the workings of the federal government, and this is even more prononuced in city and town government. There are approximtely 700,000 people in a US House of Representatives Congressional District; a state house member in Wyoming represents approximately 9,394 persons (Ballotpedia, n.d.d.), 63,850 in Oregon (Oregon State Legislature), 167,500 people in Texas (Texas House of Representatives, n.d.), and 8,797 residents in Maine (Maine House of Representatives, 2014). And the number of residents a local city council or Select Board member represents is even smaller. For example, according to the formal decennial census in 2010, the total population for Dover, Vermont, was 1,124 (City-Data.com, 2016) with each member of the Dover five-person Select Board representing approximately 225 individuals. It is highly probable that residents of Dover, Vermont, see their elected officials on a weekly if not a daily basis in neighborhood stores or in community gatherings while residents in Oregon might only see their state representative on television.

There are numerous ways a social worker can influence policy at the state or local levels of government.

- Testifying before a legislative committee provides direct access to decision makers.
- Organizing a broad-based collaborative demonstrates breadth and depth of support for the policy practitioner's position.
- Always being on the lookout for new potential allies is vital to strengthening an advocacy group's influence.
- Volunteering to serve on the various citizen committees, councils, and commissions in local government provides the social worker the opportunity to help craft new proposals.

Yes, Tip O'Neil was right: All politics is local. An individual social worker, who is locally based and connected to his or her community, has a unique opportunity to impact social policies in a place that can offer results in a meaningful manner. Although the social worker continues to build strong local relationships with elected officials, their staffs, those who can influence the political process, and with local people (e.g., constituents), working on the message to ensure that it is clear and understandable is a constant professional task. Just as important is for the social worker to remember to examine the recommended strategy through the core question that permeates all social work policy practice: Is this fair and just?

REFERENCES

Andrews, A. (2016, June 14). 2016 Legislative session calendar. Denver, CO: National Conference on State Legislatures.

Ballotpedia. (n.d.a.). State constitutions. Retrieved from https://ballotpedia.org/State_constitution on May 20, 2016.

Ballotpedia. (n.d.b.). State legislatures. Retrieved from https://ballotpedia.org/State_representatives#New_Hampshire on January 27, 2017.

Ballotpedia. (n.d.c.). State sunshine laws. Retrieved from https://ballotpedia.org/State_sunshine_laws on May 20, 2016.

Ballotpedia. (n.d.d.). Wyoming house of representatives. Retrieved from https://ballotpedia.org/Wyoming_House_of_Representatives on May 20, 2016.

Bill of Rights Institute. (2016). Bill of Rights of the United States of America (1791). Retrieved from http://billofrightsinstitute.org/founding-documents/bill-of-rights/ on May 20, 2016.

City-Data.com. (2016). Dover, Vermont. Retrieved from http://www.city-data.com/city/Dover-Vermont.html on May 20, 2016.

City of Berkeley. (2016). Guidelines for public comment, written communications, and council meeting order. Retrieved from http://www.ci.berkeley.ca.us/ContentDisplay. aspx?id=21090#PUBLIC_COMMENT on May 29, 2016.

Lefkowitz, D. (2016). The sunshine law. Retrieved from http: //r.search.yahoo.com/_ ylt=AwrBT.N2THlXjjMAdGRXNyoA;_ylu=X3oDMTEyb29zOWx1BGNvbG8DYm YxBHBvcwMxBHZ0aWQDQjE4NzlfMQRzZWMDc3I-/RV=2/RE=1467596022/ RO=10/RU=http%3a%2f%2fwww.dced.state.pa.us%2fpublic%2foor%2fSunshineLaw. pdf/RK=0/RS=ZXsHWUtM0ItR7pogU5heB80V2ac- on May 18, 2016.

Maine House of Representatives (2014, December 3). Representatives. Retrieved from http:// legislature.maine.gov/house/reps.htm on May 20, 2016.

Markowitz, D. (2003). Town meeting day, a Vermont tradition. Montpelier, VT: Office of the Secretary of State.

Mekelburg, M. (2015, June 2). What actually passed the Texas legislature. *Houston Chronicle.* Retrieved from http://www.chron.com/news/politics/article/What-actually-passed-the-Texas-legislature-6301754.php on May 20, 2016.

Minnesota Legislative Reference Library. (n.d.). Number of bills introduced and laws passed in the Minnesota legislature, 1849–present. Retrieved from https://www.leg.state.mn.us/ lrl/histleg/bills on May 20, 2016.

National Conference of State Legislatures. (2016). Annual versus biennial legislative sessions. Retrieved from http://www.ncsl.org/research/about-state-legislatures/annual-versus-biennial-legislative-sessions.aspx on May 18, 2016.

National Conference of State Legislatures. (2016, February 15). Sizes of state legislatures. Retrieved from http://www.ncsl.org/research/about-state-legislatures/sizes-of-legislatures.aspx on May 20, 2016.

National Governors Association. (2015). Principles for state-federal relations. Retrieved from https://www.nga.org/cms/home/federal-relations/nga-policy-positions/page-ec-policies/col2-content/main-content-list/principles-for-state-federal-rel.html on December 4, 2016.

National Governors Association. (2017). Current governors. Retrieved from https://www. nga.org/cms/governors/bios on January 27, 2017.

National League of Cities. (2016). Forms of municipal governments. Retrieved http://www. nlc.org/build-skills-and-networks/resources/cities-101/city-structures/forms-of-municipal-government from on May 17, 2016.

O'Neil, T., & Hymel, G. (1994). All politics is local and other rules of the game. Holbrook, MA: Bob Adams, Inc.

Oregon State Legislature. (n.d.). House of representatives. Retrieved from https://www.ore-gonlegislature.gov/house on May 20, 2016.

Texas House of Representatives. (n.d). How a bill becomes law. Retrieved from http://www. house.state.tx.us/about%2Dus/bill/ on May 20, 2016.

Texas Star Alliance. (2015, June 16). Summary of the 84th Texas legislative session. Retrieved from http://www.texasstaralliance.com/summary-of-the-84th-texas-legislative-session/ on May 20, 2016.

United Nations. (2014). Water scarcity. Retrieved from http://www.unwater.org/publica-tions/publications-detail/en/c/204294 on June 30, 2016.

United States Census Bureau. (2016, May 19). Census bureau reports there are 89,004 local governments in the United States. Retrieved from https://www.census.gov/news-room/releases/archives/governments/cb12-161.html on May 21, 2016.

United States Senate. (n.d.). Constitution of the United States. Retrieved from http://www. senate.gov/civics/constitution_item/constitution.htm on May 20, 2016.

USLegal. (2016). Vermont constitution. Retrieved from http://system.uslegal.com/state-constitutions/vermont-constitution/ on May 20, 2016.

CHAPTER 8

Agency-Based Policy Development

S ocial workers are familiar and closely involved with nonprofit social services, also referred to as *nongovernmental organizations* (*NGOs*) in the international community. According to the US Department of Labor *Occupational Handbook*, more than half of the social workers nationwide in 2014 worked in nongovernmental agencies, including individual and family services, health care, nursing homes, and residential facilities (Department of Labor, Work Environment, 2015). And the same Department of Labor report notes that employment opportunities for social workers in the nonprofit arena will, by 2024, continue to grow by as much as 19% (Department of Labor, Job Outlook, 2015).

And just who are these nonprofit agencies where social workers find their jobs? According to the Urban Institute in 2013, there were approximately 1.41 million nonprofit organizations registered with the federal government Internal Revenue Service (IRS). From 2002 to 2012, the number of IRS registered nonprofit organizations rose from 1.32 million to 1.44 million, an 8.6% increase (McKeever, 2015). Nonprofit agencies reflect a broad spectrum of interests, including art, health, education, and advocacy groups; labor unions; and business and professional associations (McKeever, 2015). Religious and faith-based associations as well as informal groups that generate less than $5,000 in annual revenue are not required to register with the IRS. A non-IRS-registered group is formally referred to as an *unincorporated* nonprofit and is not tracked in any formal numerical count of nonprofit organizations. As a result, it is impossible to identify the exact number of nonprofit agencies, groups, or organizations in the United States.

Nonprofit groups that most social workers are engaged with are commonly referred to as *501(c)(3)*; the numerical designation 501(c)(3) reflects the IRS tax code status for a *charitable organization*. The IRS code severely restricts a 501(c)(3)'s ability to directly engage in the politics (see Box 8.1). The Code specifically notes that a registered nonprofit "may not attempt to influence legislation as a substantial part of its activities and it may not participate in any campaign activity for or against political candidates" (Internal Revenue Service, 2017). The IRS code does

---

Box 8.1

THE POLICY PRACTITIONER AND THE NONPROFIT AGENCY

The IRS tax code limits the political work and activities of a 501(c)(3) organization. Any individual affiliated with the organization (e.g., volunteer or paid employee) is bound by the IRS rules. Advocating for a particular position, publically supporting a proposed bill, or endorsing/not endorsing a political candidate violates the tax code. A social worker should first understand the nonprofit's policy regarding advocacy activities—the adage *Act now and ask for forgiveness later* simply will not work and may potentially cost the social worker her or his job as well as jeopardizing the agency's 501(c)(3) status. A social worker, on his or her own personal time, may engage in advocacy work, but at no time can or should the social worker reference his or her employment with the nonprofit agency. To be safe, the social work advocate should clearly state, "These are my own personal views and do not represent any group or association with which I am affiliated."

---

not prohibit a nonprofit employee from "educating" others on a proposed or existing policy; a social worker may discuss in a public forum or with a legislator the possible effect a proposed bill may have on people or a community; a nonprofit employee cannot simply state in any forum, "I oppose this bill." Specific "educating" techniques are detailed in Chapter 9.

It is incorrect to assume that any nonprofit agency is a 501(c)(3). In fact, the IRS provides 29 different tax-exempt statuses to 501(c) groups (see Box 8.2). Additionally, the IRS identifies six alternative classifications for other 501 groups, including the following:

> **Advocacy groups**—These organizations are formed to influence the legislation or government policies on particular issues.
>
> **Membership organizations**—They benefit a certain group of people who join the organization with membership often based on a certain set of characteristics. Examples include National Association of Social Workers, veterans groups, and trade associations.
>
> **Social and recreational clubs**—The primary activity of such groups is providing recreation facilities and platforms for its members. Charitable activities may also be undertaken but not as a priority. Examples include college social/academic fraternities and sororities; country clubs; amateur hunting, fishing, tennis, swimming, and other sport clubs; dinner clubs that provide a meeting place, a library, and dining room for members; hobby clubs; and homeowners or community associations whose primary function is to own and maintain recreational areas and facilities.

Auxiliary organizations—These organizations are set as a subsidiary or as a support organization to a parent organization. The parent organization may be a "for-profit" or a "not-for-profit" organization in this case.

Employee benefit funds—These are organizations that may or may not be supported by the employer of the organization but are established with the prime objective to formulate plans and raise funds for employee benefits (NPO Central, 2017).

Box 8.2

IRS-DESIGNATED 501(C) AND OTHER TAX-EXEMPT ORGANIZATIONS

- **501(c)(1)**—Corporations Organized Under Act of Congress (including Federal Credit Unions)
- **501(c)(2)**—Title-holding Corporation for Exempt Organization
- **501(c)(3)**—Religious, Educational, Charitable, Scientific, Literary, Testing for Public Safety, to Foster National or International Amateur Sports Competition, or Prevention of Cruelty to Children or Animals Organizations
- **501(c)(4)**—Civic Leagues, Social Welfare Organizations, and Local **Associations of Employees**
- **501(c)(5)**—Labor, Agricultural and Horticultural Organizations
- **501(c)(6)**—Business Leagues, Chambers of Commerce, Real Estate Boards
- **501(c)(7)**—Social and Recreational Clubs
- **501(c)(8)**—Fraternal Beneficiary Societies and Associations
- **501(c)(9)**—Voluntary Employee Beneficiary Associations
- **501(c)(10)**—Domestic Fraternal Societies and Associations
- **501(c)(11)**—Teachers' Retirement Fund Associations
- **501(c)(12)**—Benevolent Life Insurance Associations, Mutual Ditch or Irrigation Companies, Mutual or Cooperative Telephone Companies, etc.
- **501(c)(13)**—Cemetery Companies
- **501(c)(14)**—State-Chartered Credit Unions, Mutual Reserve Funds
- **501(c)(15)**—Mutual Insurance Companies or Associations
- **501(c)(16)**—Cooperative Organizations to Finance Crop Operations
- **501(c)(17)**—Supplemental Unemployment Benefit Trusts
- **501(c)(18)**—Employee Funded Pension Trust (created before June 25, 1959)
- **501(c)(19)**—Post or Organization of Past or Present Members of the Armed Forces
- **501(c)(20)**—Group Legal Services Plan Organizations

- **501(c)(21)**—Black Lung Benefit Trusts
- **501(c)(22)**—Withdrawal Liability Payment Fund
- **501(c)(23)**—Veterans Organization
- **501(c)(24)**—Section 4049 ERISA Trusts
- **501(c)(25)**—Title Holding Corporations or Trusts with Multiple Parents
- **501(c)(26)**—State-Sponsored Organization Providing Health Coverage for High-Risk Individuals
- **501(c)(27)**—State-Sponsored Workers' Compensation Reinsurance Organization
- **501(c)(28)**—National Railroad Retirement Investment Trust
- **501(c)(29)**—Qualified Nonprofit Health Insurance Issuers

Other Tax-Exempt Organizations

501(d)—Apostolic organizations with the purpose of operating a religious community where the members live a communal life following the tenets and teachings of the organization. The organization's property is owned by each of the individuals in the community, but, upon leaving, a member cannot withdraw any of the community's assets. The organization's income goes into a community treasury that is used to pay for the organization's operating expenses and supporting members and their families.

501(e)—Cooperative hospital service organizations that are organized to provide services for multiple tax-exempt hospitals.

501(f)—Cooperative service organizations of educational organizations that invest assets contributed by each of the organization's members.

501(j)—Amateur sports organizations that either conduct national or international sporting competitions or develop amateur athletes for national or international sporting competitions.

501(k)—Day care centers may qualify as tax-exempt under Section 501(k). The day care center must provide child care away from their homes. At least 85% of the children served must be cared for while their parent or guardian is either employed, seeking employment, or a full-time student. Most of the day care center's funding must come from fees received for day care services. The day care center must also provide child care services to the general public. The tax exemption for certain day care centers was part of the Deficit Reduction Act of 1984.

501(n)—Charitable risk pools that pool insurable risks of its members, which are tax-exempt charities.

Source: Department of the Treasury, Internal Revenue Service (January 2017). Tax-exempt status for your organization. Publication 557. 67-68. Retrieved from www.irs.gov/pub/irs-pdf/p557.pdf on February 7, 2017.

Box 8.3

501 (C)(3): NONPROFIT ORGANIZATION DEFINITION

Nonprofit organizations are commonly called "a 501." This comes from its designation based on the IRS Code, Section 501(c)(3), that allows for federal tax exemption of nonprofit organizations, specifically those considered public charities, private foundations, or private operating foundations. The organization is regulated and administered by the US Department of Treasury through the Internal Revenue Service. There are other 501(c) organizations, indicated by categories 501(c)(1)–501(c)(29); see Box 8.2.

Each year, 501(c)(3) nonprofit organizations generate a significant amount of money for their work. In 2013, they accounted for just over three quarters of the total nonprofit sector's revenue and expenses, $1.73 trillion and $1.62 trillion, respectively, and more than three fifths of nonprofit assets, $3.22 trillion. In 2014, total private giving from individuals, foundations, and businesses to 501(c)(3) programs amounted to $358.38 billion, an increase of just over 5% from 2013. Nationwide, 25.3% of US adults volunteered an estimated 8.7 million hours with nonprofits in 2014 with the cash equivalent of these hours totaling approximately $179.2 billion (McKeever, 2015). Just how big are these figures? The US auto industry, a leading business enterprise in the country, reported a combined new and used auto sales of nearly $1.1 trillion in 2014 (Eisenstein, 2014) nearly $600 million below the nonprofit income for the similar time period.

From a social work perspective, the majority of the profession's nonprofit experience is with 501(c)(3) agencies that offer a broad range of individual, family, group, and community services (see Box 8.3). These NGOs fall into two categories: (1) a local agency that is a member of a state or national association; or (2) a local agency that is independent and holds no state or national affiliations. Examples of affiliated NGOs include Planned Parenthood and Mental Health America. Planned Parenthood's national offices are located in New York City and Washington, DC, while in 2016, 59 locally based member agencies operated more than 650 health centers nationwide (Planned Parenthood, n.d.). The national office for Mental Health America is located in Alexandria, Virginia, with over 200 associate chapters providing services in 41 states in 2016 (Mental Health America, n.d.).

Independent, nonaffiliated NGOs are locally organized agencies/associations with no direct relationship to or sponsorship by a state group or national membership association. Examples of independent, nonaffiliated NGOs include the Arlington (Texas) Life Shelter, which provides emergency shelter for men, women, and children; Breaking Free, a nonprofit program in St. Paul, Minnesota, that works with women involved in abusive situations, exploitation, and prostitution/sex trafficking; Lambert House, a Seattle, Washington–based center for GLBTQ youth that empowers young people through the development of leadership, social, and life skills; and the Waikiki Community Center, located in Honolulu, Hawaii, which offers multigenerational services for individuals and families in need.

NGO ORGANIZATIONAL STRUCTURE

Nonprofit agencies structures typically includes a *board of directors, administration, professional staff,* and *volunteers* (see Figure 8.1). Some NGOs include an *advisory board* in lieu of or in support of a board of directors.

The nonprofit agency structure reflects a pyramid organizational model "that centralizes authority in one leader . . . recognizes two business operations, business and social work." (Vrouvas, 2016). In this model, the agency's designated leader is the *Executive Director* (ED), who in some settings is referred to as the *Chief Executive Officer* (CEO). The ED is directly responsible for all of the agency's activities such as direct services to clients, the agency's day-to-day administrative functions that support the direct services, and representing the agency to the broader community, including other social service agencies/networks and funding entities, and program donors. The administration may include midlevel unit managers who coordinate specific services as well as supervise professional staff (see Table 8.1). A typical 501(c)(3) agency also includes support staff whose role is to provide technical backing, ongoing training programs, human resources support, finance and accounting services, and clerical assistance, among others. Finally, nonprofit agencies have a long history in and a reliance on recruiting, training, and maintaining a volunteer pool. Volunteer tasks are very specific with a focus on assisting the professional staff and support staff.

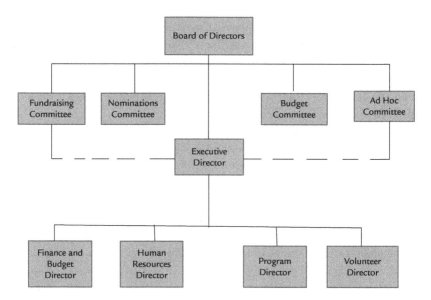

Figure 8.1.
Example of nonprofit agency flow chart, pyramid model.

Table 8.1. KEY ROLES IN A NONPROFIT ORGANIZATION

Board of directors	The board is comprised of individuals from the community. Individuals reflect a variety of backgrounds, though all have expressed an interest and commitment to the organization's mission and/or targeted clients. It is common for a board to include a client as well. Board members are largely inspired to serve the community and gain personal satisfaction in their individual and collective efforts. Board members typically are not paid or receive any financial compensation for their work on behalf of the NGO. The board is directly responsible for the agency's work and establishes the NGO's policies. The board's work is specified in the NGO's by-laws and other related governance documents.
Board chair	The chair of the board of directors is second in importance to the agency. The board chair may also be titled board president. The chair coordinates the work of the board (e.g., oversees board meetings and board committees) and is in continual communication with the NGO's executive director. The board chair often represents the NGO to external groups and organizations; additionally, the chair typically appoints individuals to board committees. The board chair is generally elected by the board of directors.
Board committees	A board of directors generally carries out its responsibilities through committees. Some committees are ongoing or standing (e.g., budget), while others are temporary ad-hoc committees established to focus on a specific item for the agency.
Executive director	The NGO is led by a paid staff person who is hired by the board of directors. The executive director is directly responsible to the board and is accountable for the day-to-day work by the NGO.
Professional staff	The professional staff includes midlevel management supervisors and the individuals who provide the direct services to the clients. The staff may work with the board of directors on some board committees as well as on professional staff committees.
Volunteers	Volunteers are key individuals in most NGOs. They are unpaid workers who support the professional staff and/or the operations of the agency. The volunteers supplement the staff, primarily in providing service to clients.

Source: McNamara, C. (2016). Basic overview of nonprofit organizations. Retrieved from http://managementhelp. org/organizations/nonprofits.htm on May 15, 2016.

Agency Programs and Services
Mission, Goals, and Objectives

An agency's programs are directly tied to the organization's stated mission and its supporting goals and objectives. The mission statement, goals, and objectives are essentially *directional documents*, which outline an agency's specific purpose while aligning its resulting services and activities with each other. One school of thought is that the mission, goals, and objectives are written as broadly as possible to allow for flexibility in programming and the ability for the agency to be nimble in its larger environment and responsive by quickly adding new initiatives. Conversely, mission, goals, and objective statements that use specific, targeted language result in clearly focused programs. Some believe that a tightly knit set of governing documents constrains an agency's ability to implement new programs quickly and respond to an immediate situation or funding opportunity. Both of these approaches have their own merits and limitations. Some foundations and governmental funding proposals expect specific and exact goals and objectives, whereas others prefer the specificity be detailed in program descriptions and their outcome statements. The bottom line is that every nonprofit program must include a mission statement with related goals and objectives.

Agency Activities

A 501(c)(3)'s funding, staff, and resources are organized around specific programs. From an administrative perspective, resources are allocated in a manner and with the expectation that each program activity is successful. A common practice among nonprofit agencies is to identify core or essential programs and, as a result, ensure the maximum amounts of resources are allocated to these activities. When new initiatives are adopted, they are done so as auxiliary or demonstration programs. Over time, the success of the noncore programs may result in them becoming part of an agency's principal activities.

Categorizing programs as essential and nonessential can be a double-edged sword. Classifying service provides a rationale for resource distribution, which is especially important during periods of financial exigency. Conversely, organizing and distinguishing programs based on their relationship to a nonprofit agency's mission can negatively influence a staff's morale ("I am not seen as an important employee nor valued by this agency") as well as program funders ("The agency does not appreciate this specific program, which is important to me").

Board of Directors

While the CEO is responsible for the day-to-day work of an agency, the organization's board of directors is ultimately accountable for the conduct of the entire agency. The National Council of Nonprofits (2016) writes that

> Board members are the fiduciaries who steer the organization towards a sustainable future by adopting sound, ethical, and legal governance and financial management policies, as well as making sure the nonprofit has adequate resources to advance its mission.

An engaged board of directors helps an agency in its strategic planning, program monitoring and evaluation, public relations, and promotions/fundraising. Active board members, while not interfering with the day-to-day work of the ED or the professional staff, have a three-fold responsibility, including the following:

1. Reviewing the use of all agency assets, including facility, people, and good will; and provide oversight for all activities that advance the nonprofit's effectiveness and sustainability
2. Ensuring that overarching board decisions are made in the best interest of the NGO and not in the board members; individual or collective self-interest
3. Certifying that the nonprofit follows all laws and protocols based on ethical, evidenced-based practices; that the NGO follows its stated corporate purposes; and that all programs and services advance the agency's mission (National Council of Nonprofits, 2016).

Generally, there are two types of board of directors—*advisory board* and *participating board* (see Table 8.2). An advisory board provides guidance and feedback while the agency's ED is responsible for developing policy while maintaining and building new program initiatives. An advisory board meets far less frequently, generally once every 6 months. On the other hand, a participatory board is actively engaged and more involved with the NGO. It provides direction for the ED, who, in turn, must secure the board's approval for new initiatives or changes to existing programs.

There is no prescription for the number of persons who serve on a board. The board for a small agency, staffed by fewer than 25 persons, will include approximately

---

Activity Box 8.1
WHO'S ON THAT BOARD?

Identify a local nonprofit agency of particular interest. Go to their website and identify their board of directors. Answer the following questions based on what you are able learn from the website.

- Does the board follow a *Participatory* or *Advisory* model?
- What are the board's committees, if any?
- How engaged is the board with the NGO's work?
- Do the board members possess skill sets that directly help the NGO accomplish its mission?
- To what extent are the board members known or recognized as leaders or significant individuals in the broader community?
- Do you feel this is a successful board? If so, why? If not, why not?

Table 8.2. BOARD RESPONSIBILITY MATRIX

Board Responsibility Matrix		
Participatory Board		**Advisory Board**
The board acts to GOVERN the organization		The board acts to SUPPORT the organization
Objectives		
Represent the community's interests within the organization.		Represent the organization's interests in the community.
Processes for Action		
The board acts as a body.		Board members act as individuals or through committees.
Responsibilities		
• Determine mission and purpose. • *Legal*: Ensure compliance with federal, state and local regulations and fulfillment of contractual obligations. • *Financial*: Safeguard assets from misuse, waste, and embezzlement. • *Staff*: Select and monitor staff and evaluate their performance. • *Planning*: Determine strategies and overall priorities. • *Programs*: Determine the organization's program priorities, monitor implementation, and conduct evaluations to measure impact. • *Efficiency and impact*: Ensure a realistic budget that maximizes resources.		• Fundraising: Develop fundraising strategy; ensure adequate resources by raising funds and assisting staffing in raising funds. • *Public relations and community contacts*: Act as ambassadors to the community on behalf of the organization and its clients. • *Volunteer recruitment and volunteering*. • *Act as individual advisors*: advise staff in areas of expertise; act as sounding board for executive director and other executive staff. • *Lend names, personal credibility, and reputation* to the organization for use in brochures, grant proposals, and other formats.

Source: The Support Center for Nonprofit Management, *Workshop for effective non-profit boards of directors*. San Francisco, CA. See http://cnmsocal.org/.

10 to 15 persons. The board of directors for a large agency, with a staff in excess of 75 persons, may total as many 35 persons. A board that is too small may be overworked and not have the necessary expertise; conversely, a board that is too large may not be able to engage all the board members actively, which may result in them

losing interest in the agency (The Bridgespan Group, n.d.). No matter the size of the board, it is essential for the individual volunteers to feel their time, effort, and work are valued and important to the NGO (see Activity Box 8.1).

Boards typically operate within one of two governance models: an open model and a closed, top-down model. An *open model* program reflects a partnership between the NGO's board of directors, the executive director, and the staff. While the board is ultimately responsible for approving a program initiative, its beginnings can come from any source. Clients, volunteers, professional staff, the ED, or board members see and experience things from different perspectives. Embracing the diversity of understanding a particular service or issue easily leads to strengthening an existing program or advocating for a new, different initiative. The open model for program development builds on the premise that all persons engaged in the NGO are important members of its community and their individual insight is valued.

A *closed, top-down governance model* does not encourage staff, clients, and volunteers to make suggestions nor are they provided input opportunities. All decisions rest with the board of directors or the ED; program initiatives begin with the board, the ED, or a funding source. The staff's responsibility is to implement the board's directives in a professional, competent, ethical manner.

Finally, a successful board is one whose members offer a range of expertise to help the NGO realize its mission. Some agencies look for widely known and respected persons to serve on the board; the idea behind this approach is the board's makeup provides the agency with important credibility to the broader community. This approach better suits an *Advisory Board* model as the agency is essentially using the individual's reputation to gain an advantage in the broader community. The *Participatory Board* model recruits individuals whose expertise and skills sets are critical for an agency to achieve its mission, goals, and objectives. Over time, the desired skill sets for a board may change to reflect NGOs new initiatives. For example, an agency may begin a multiyear fundraising campaign to build a new facility; board members who are known among major foundations or are experienced in fundraising are an important asset.

INFLUENCING A BOARD OF DIRECTORS AND PROGRAM ACTIVITIES

A common saying understood by social workers is that *change is not easy.* Resistance is a common denominator in all change-oriented activities. The degree of personal emotional pain can be incredibly severe and debilitating even while understanding a new course of action will result in a positive, more productive outcome. Changing behavior patterns is literally moving from the *known* to the *unknown*. The *unknown* is filled with *fears* and *what ifs*, whereas there is comfort in the *known*, no matter how negative the situation might be. Boards of directors are no different from social work clients. EDs and policy practitioners alike find that it is difficult to convince a board that a change is necessary. No matter the issue or the agency, advocacy to change a course of action or to adopt a new program is a difficult sale.

Staff Influence of Own Agency

A common practice among EDs is to assign a staff person or appoint a staff committee to review a community issue or assess a current organizational policy. The individual or committee's work results in an *Issue Brief* or a *Policy Brief* (see Chapter 5). The brief provides the ED material necessary to make a recommendation or an "*information-only*" report to the board of directors. The individual staff person, the committee as a whole, or the committee's chair may be invited to join the board of directors for the ED's presentation. The individual responsible for compiling the report is often asked to present the findings to the board and answer any questions that may arise.

Protocols regarding a verbal presentation to a board differ from agency to agency, but there are some common features for all board presentations.

1. The board will generally hear the entire report before asking questions. In some instances, the board chair might ask for clarification of a statement while the report is given, but generally boards allow the entire report to be presented before asking any questions or making a point.
2. While the board meeting tends to be formal, for example, following some form of parliamentary rules of order, there is a general feeling of "welcome" to the staff member. The board sees the social work employee as an ally and someone who strongly believes in the agency's mission.
3. If the ED makes the presentation, she or he will typically answer the questions or respond to comments. At times, the ED will ask the key staff person to respond to a board member's comment or question.
4. Typical questions for an *Issue Brief* include the following:
   a. What is the scope of the issue, and who is directly impacted?
   b. Are other social services in the community agencies dealing with this issue?
   c. How successful are the current efforts?
   d. Are other cities/communities impacted by this or a similar issue?
   e. What have they done regarding this issue?
   f. How successful have their efforts been?
   g. Does the NGO currently have the resources (e.g., professional staff and funding) to address the issue?
   h. Is the issue in line with the NGO's mission, goals, and objectives?
   i. How will the proposed program response be sustained down the road, for example, in 5 years?

5. Typical questions for a *Policy Analysis Brief* include the following:
   a. How do you know the recommended changes will make a positive difference?
   b. Will the proposed policy changes cost the agency any additional resources (e.g., new staff or extra funding)?
   c. If additional resources are required, will they come from other program areas and, if so, what will the impact be on that program?
   d. How will the proposed program changes be sustained down the road, for example, in 5 years?

Influencing an Agency as an Outside Advocate Social Worker

Often times, a social worker will work with organizations, other than their own agency, on an issue. This may involve encouraging an NGO to adopt a new program or modify an existing one. A nonemployee can engage with an organization generally in one of three ways:

- An agency or group contracts with another NGO to conduct a study on a specific topic.
- An agency or group directly contracts with a social worker, often through private practice, to conduct a study on a specific topic.
- The social worker may be part of an external group that is seeking to remedy a local problem.

The process of influencing the agency is significantly different from attempting to engage a change effort in one's own agency. The social worker, whose agency is contracted to carry out the work, often does not know or has had minimal experience with any of the board members, the ED, or the agency itself. The lack of a strong relationship between the social worker and the board or ED typically results in a slow, cautious approach to the policy practitioner's work. This tentative approach is understandable, but over time, this should remedy itself as the board and ED engage and build a relationship with the social worker. The "caution" shown by a board and/or ED is demonstrated in a number of ways:

- Board members may ask few or no questions during initial meetings.
- The board chair merely thanks the advocate for "sharing" the information with the board and excuses the social worker from the meeting.
- Board members may pose questions that challenge the social worker's research methods and/or findings.
- Some board members may flatly reject the conclusions reached in the report, disagreeing with the logic that connects the research findings with the report's recommendations.

As an outside advocate, the social worker can address and reduce the natural credibility issues. First, the policy practitioner must work to establish a positive, working relationship with the agency's professional staff and/or the ED. Their endorsement of the outside advocate expertise to the board is essential for any recommendations to be seriously considered. At the outset of the work, the social worker should engage the staff and ED and maintain consistent contact and communication with them throughout the process. The policy practitioner who keeps them apprised of the work as well as asking for their comments, suggestions, and reactions is building an open, proactive, inclusive approach.

Second, the social work advocate must demonstrate respect and understanding of the agency's traditions, its governance structure, and the roles of the ED, staff, and board members. The social worker should determine with the ED if it is possible for the advocate to attend multiple staff and board meetings to keep the groups updated on the practitioner's work and answer questions they may have. Prior to attending either of these meetings, the social worker will find it beneficial to consult with the ED as often as possible to learn and understand the stakeholders' possible concerns; how the board meetings are run; and if there are specific procedures or a meeting etiquette that is followed. Asking the ED for help and listening closely to what she or he says is critical; attending multiple staff and board meetings allows the social worker to develop a more accurate picture of the board's operation while allowing them to become familiar with the social worker.

PRESENTING FINDINGS

A detailed discussion on presenting testimony or a report to a board is presented in Chapter 9, whereas Chapter 10 proposes a number of policy practice strategies and techniques that augment a presentation.

No matter the situation, the goal of any presentation is that it be clear, easily understood, and made in a simple, straightforward manner. There are five basic points to consider when making a presentation to a board:

1. How much time is allotted for the presentation—5 minutes, 10 minutes? Does this include a questions and answers (Q&A) period or is a Q&A in addition to the actual presentation?
2. Does the board expect copies of the actual presentation? Does each board member receive a complete copy of the final report? Can an abstract of the full report be provided to the board members while a complete copy is given to the ED and the board's chair and/or executive committee?
3. What type of equipment, if any, is available for a visual presentation: a computer with overhead projection, a Smartboard, or a white dry erase board?
4. Will the social worker make the presentation standing at a podium, sitting at a table facing the board, or sitting at the board's table? Is a microphone needed;

if so, is it stationary or a lavaliere mike (e.g., one that clips to the speaker's clothing)?

5. What is the role of the ED when a staff member or social worker consultant is making a presentation?

Meeting With the Executive Director

Presenting a report to the ED is far less formal than a board meeting. The ED and social worker's meeting is a more open, free flowing, back-and-forth conversation. At a minimum, the social worker always shares with the ED a written update at each meeting; the final report is provided to the ED in advance of the board presentation. The social worker should ensure that there is enough lead time for the ED to review the report and, if necessary, meet with the policy practitioner prior to the formal board presentation. Again, this approach reinforces an open, transparent inclusive model that strengthens the relationship between the ED and the policy practitioner.

The social worker who does not engage an ED throughout the process, does not provide both verbal and written updates, yet does give the CEO a copy of the final report prior to a board meeting will undoubtedly find his or her report receiving a negative reaction by the ED and the board. An ED simply needs time to read the report, reflect on its findings, and consider the recommendations in order to effectively engage with the board. Again, the objective for an outside advocate is to enlist the direct support of the ED and agency staff; consistent engagement with them throughout the work is a simple and obvious technique to garner their respect and support.

Board Presentation

Reporting to a board is not an easy task, even for the most experienced advocate. The social worker should expect to be nervous and possibly feel a sense of intimidation, given the uncertainty surrounding how the report will be received. Three key pieces create the foundation for a successful presentation:

1. *Preparation.* A well-thought-out presentation is strong, concise, and provides information in a persuasive manner so that the board is able to make an informed decision. It is not a time for rambling, disjointed, and ill-conceived thoughts. The successful presentation is delivered in a confident, smooth manner, one that is neither overbearing nor paternalistic.

   A useful preparation technique is to role-play the presentation multiple times to gain comfort with the presentation as well as being prepared for the unforeseen. For example, what happens if the equipment for a PowerPoint presentation does not work (yes, this happens quite frequently!). The unprepared practitioner will easily become flustered, but the individual who has role-played the presentation multiple times will easily move past any unintended disruptions.

Preparation also includes the social worker thinking through what questions might be asked and develops exact, concise answers. Friends and colleagues can role play the board and ask questions. Board members are strongly influenced by the policy practitioner's communication abilities and the confidence the social worker demonstrates in the presentation.

2. *Expectations.* The social worker must keep in mind the original intent of the study; what were the board of directors and the ED's expectations at the project's beginnings and did these change over time? As early as possible in the work, the social worker should learn what, if any, reservations the board or ED might have regarding the issue; doing so beforehand allows the social worker to be able to address the concerns in the final report and presentation.

3. *Clear messaging.* The final presentation to the board should begin with the report's essential message—*what* and *why now.* This is a simple, concise statement followed with the central findings. The presentation ends with specific recommendations of next steps or what programs and services the board might consider implementing.

Generally, the final board report includes a PowerPoint presentation. Chapter 10 includes a discussion of successful versus poor PowerPoint presentations. There are, however, two basic rules for the social worker to follow when making a PowerPoint presentation:

- Each PowerPoint slide should be limited in the words used or length of statements; in other words, do not clutter the slide.
- The social worker should never read the slide word for word and then look at the board to see if they have any questions. Board members can read the slide while the policy practitioner uses the slide as a jumping-off point to deepen or expand the discussion.

THE BOARD DECIDES; NOW WHAT?

Once a board makes a decision, it becomes the ED's responsibility to ensure their mandate is implemented. As with bills passed by any governmental body, a board's action requires an agency to apply its own rule-making process. An ongoing agency staff committee might have this responsibility, or the ED may assign the initiative to a specific program manager to articulate a program specifics. There are neither formal rules posting periods nor mandated "public" hearings in a NGO's rule-making process. An agency's procedures are much less formal and far less complicated compared to governmental rule making.

A social worker can influence this process by working directly with his or her colleagues. Similarly, the outside advocate, who built a relationship with staff during the report preparation period, can offer to assist with the program's development and implementation as well as be available to answer any questions.

A FEW FINAL THOUGHTS

Local nonprofit agencies often face the challenge of adding new programs or modifying existing services in order to remain a viable organization in the community. Individual donors, foundations, and other funding sources prefer to invest their funds in organizations with a successful record of accomplishment. As a result, the local NGO is more open to amending a current policy or implementing a new program initiative. Anecdotal experiences of social workers indicate that change efforts are easier to accomplish in a local, nonprofit agency compared to policy practice efforts in a local, state, or national governmental setting. Whereas local agencies have their own unique and shared bureaucratic idiosyncrasies, the NGO is generally easier to navigate with decisions made by a local board and not requiring the approval of a number of offices in Washington, DC, or in a state capitol. In other words, results are realized much faster in a local, nonaffiliated NGO compared to a federal government bill proposal with its need to traverse a long political vetting process followed by prolonged rule-making procedures.

There are policy practice strategies and professional skills that help increase the possibility of success in NGO initiatives (see Activity Box 8.2). First, demonstrating

---

Activity Box 8.2

INTERVIEW AN NGO SOCIAL WORKER AROUND THE EXTENT OF THEIR POLICY PRACTICE

Identify a social worker who works in a local NGO, possibly an individual in the same agency that you examined in Activity Box 8.1. Interview the social worker to learn about his or her own agency-specific policy practice. Some jumping-off questions might include the following:

- Have you helped develop a new policy or amend a policy in your agency? If so, can you tell me what led to this effort and what was the outcome?
- Have you made a presentation to the board? What was it like? What would you do differently?
- What do you feel makes for a good versus a bad board presentation?
- Do you feel that social workers in other agencies are encouraged to engage in agency-based policy practice?
- What would be your agency's response if you wanted to testify before a local (e.g., city council) or state legislative committee? Would you be encouraged to do so? Are there specific rules your agency has in place for such public statements?

respect for the NGO, its mission and procedures, the board, ED, staff, and clients is paramount for the social worker. Doing otherwise will result in a very high probability that the practitioner's report will be ignored.

Second, the policy practitioner's written reports should clearly show that the proposal will help the NGO achieve its mission while minimizing potential conflicts with other organizations. It is worth remembering that every nonprofit agency is part of a community's broader human services' network. EDs work long and hard on enhancing their relationships with other CEOs as well as working to enhance the agency's public image. Positive interagency relations increase the possibilities for future collaborations with the NGO viewed as a good partner.

Third, the social worker's report and recommendations should propose a "win-win" scenario for the NGO. Backing a board of directors or an ED into a corner might result in a temporary, short-term victory, but the long-term negative consequences will be significant for the social worker and his or her future advocacy efforts. A report's recommendations and proposed course of action are always written in positive, strengths-based language; the proactive approach will be seen as forward moving. A vital theme in any report to a board and/or an ED is that the proposed changes will strengthen the agency's programs and services while enhancing the organization's place in the broader community.

Working with a local NGO, either as an internal staff member or as an external consultant, provides the policy practitioner with the opportunity to realize proactive changes in human service programs and services. Policy practice at the national and even the state levels of governmental can be frustratingly slow. Local NGO-focused policy practice, on the other hand, can result in important, positive, and significant services and programs that answer the social worker's basic policy practice question in the affirmative: Is this fair and just?

REFERENCES

The Bridgespan Group. (n.d.). How should a nonprofit board of directors be structured. Retrieved from http://www.bridgespan.org/Publications-and-Tools/Nonprofit-Boards/Nonprofit-Boards-101/Nonprofit-Board-Structure.aspx#.V2ltAjUYFjU on May 15, 2016.

Department of Labor. (2015, December 17). Occupational outlook handbook: Job outlook. Retrieved from https://www.bls.gov/ooh/community-and-social-service/social-workers.htm#tab-6 on January 30, 2017.

Eisenstein, P. (2014, December 19). U.S. auto industry generates record $1.1 trillion in 2014 sales. The Detroit Bureau. Retrieved from http://www.thedetroitbureau.com/2014/12/u-s-auto-industry-generates-record-1-1-trillion-in-2014-sales/ on January 30, 2017.

Internal Revenue Service. (2017, January 26). Exemption requirements—501(c)(3) organizations. Retrieved from https://www.irs.gov/charities-non-profits/charitable-organizations/exemption-requirements-section-501-c-3-organizations on February 3, 2017.

McKeever, B. (2015, October 29). The nonprofit sector in brief 2015: Public charities, giving, and volunteering. The Urban Institute. Retrieved from http://www.urban.org/research/publication/nonprofit-sector-brief-2015-public-charities-giving-and-volunteering on January 30, 2017.

McNamara, C. (2016). Basic overview of nonprofit organizations. Retrieved from http://managementhelp.org/organizations/nonprofits.htm on May 15, 2016.

Mental Health America. (n.d.). About us. Retrieved from http://www.nmha.org/about-us on March 19, 2016.

National Council of Nonprofits. (2016). Board roles and responsibilities. Retrieved from https://www.councilofnonprofits.org/tools-resources/board-roles-and-responsibilities on May 16, 2016.

NPO Central. (2017). Types of nonprofit organizations. Retrieved from http://www.startnonprofitorganization.com/types-of-non-profit-organizations on February 2, 2017.

Planned Parenthood. (n.d.). Who we are. Retrieved from https://www.plannedparenthood.org/about-us/who-we-are on March 19, 2016.

Vrouvas, M. (2016). Organizational structure of a social service organization. *Houston Chronicle*. Retrieved from http://smallbusiness.chron.com/organizational-structure-social-service-organization-18124.html on May 15, 2016.

Impacting the Policy-Making Process

INTRODUCTION GUIDE TO PART 3: IMPACTING THE POLICY-MAKING PROCESS

Continuing with the dinner metaphor, as we begin Part 3, planning is complete and the food preparations and final arrangements will soon be underway. By the end of Part 3, the dinner table will be set and the party will be ready to begin.

Parts 3 identifies and focuses on key skills and strategies frequently used in policy practice. In effect, the overall purpose of Part 3 is to shift the reader's attention to the actual "doing" of policy practice. We begin with Chapter 9 examining specific practice skills that explore the nuances of testifying or making a presentation to a legislative committee; the components necessary for a clear, well-focused written testimony before a governmental body; steps taken in organizing specific advocacy activities, including a public forum, social work day at the legislature, and voter registration projects; and electoral politics as a means for social workers to identify and work for candidates who are supportive of social work issues.

Chapter 10 redirects the reader's attention to the role that social media and other tools for effective communication play in supporting the activities identified in Chapter 9. Technology continues to evolve at a rapid pace; it is hard to believe that email only first became available to the public in the early 1990s, Facebook was launched in 2004, and three Stanford University graduate students launched Snapchat, which was originally named Picaboo, in 2011. There are "virtual rooms" of every shape and form that a policy practitioner can access for a policy practice initiative. These platforms offer immediate and, in many instances, real-time communications. Yet the chapter emphasizes that policy practitioners neither can nor should remain complacent using only those virtual rooms with which they are familiar. Social media is constantly evolving with new platforms emerging almost on a daily basis. Within 10 years, the social media world will be vastly different from today. The key, however, is to understand and to harness the power of this technology, no matter the platform, in policy practice efforts.

Other topics examined in Chapter 10 include PowerPoint presentations, the "30-second elevator speech," giving a speech or presentation to a group of people other than a legislative committee, and examining newspaper opinion editorials (also known as "op-eds") and the "letters to the editor" section as a form of public education and endorsement of an issue.

Part 3 of the *Handbook* is where the fun begins in policy practice. Now the reader is at a point in her or his course of study to hone individual practice policy skills. But, as with every facet of policy practice and as these policy skills are developed, the social worker must keep in mind the simple, guiding question: Is this fair and just?

CHAPTER 9

Policy Practice Strategies, Tactics, and Techniques

The previous chapters examined the context that social workers find themselves in when working to effect change in social policy. The *Handbook*'s attention now shifts to the *doing* of policy practice. From the specific—testifying or making a presentation to a committee or in a public forum—to broader tactics such as using social media as a strategy. All of these are important and necessary tools in a policy practitioner's repertoire of skills, but supporting all of these tactics are the fundamental core abilities common among all social workers.

RELATIONSHIP BUILDING IN POLICY PRACTICE

A unique facet of social work is the professional's ability to work with diverse peoples and issues in a variety of settings. The ongoing enrichment and development of one's knowledge and skills through continuing education is necessary for effective practice. But recognizing and understanding the generic and flexible qualities of core social work skills allows the individual professional to crisscross multiple practice settings at any one time. Social workers quickly discover that policy practice skills are similar to those used in other areas of professional practice, in particular clinical practice with individuals, families, and groups:

- the ability to establish positive, trusting worker–client relationships;
- capability to communicate, verbally and in writing, clearly and succinctly;
- showing respect for others;
- engaging in active listening (clarifying, paraphrasing, summarizing, reframing, nonverbal attending);

- being aware of the external environment and its effect on the situation; and
- the ongoing awareness of the professional use of self.

Relationship building is a cornerstone for effective social work practice. Traditional helping models view the client–worker relationship as the necessary ingredient that leads to authentic, personal change (Bein, 2008; Edwards & Bess, 1998). The principle that a strong relationship results in proactive change is equally applicable in policy practice. A policy practitioner who is not viewed as trustworthy, honest, fair, open-minded, and respectful faces a near insurmountable hurdle in gaining the support of others.

A clearly written issue or policy brief that reflects the tenants of critical thinking will, in all probability, be disregarded if the social worker has a poor, ineffective relationship with those who will be making a decision on an issue. The responsibility of relationship building rests with the social worker, not the elected official, a CEO, or a board of directors.

A policy advocate must be able to connect with people—in particular, those who hold or subscribe to different positions. A positive relationship is easy to form and sustain with those who agree with the social worker. Constructing positive relationships with individuals who philosophically and politically disagree with the policy practitioner is an entirely different matter. Often times differences result in intense arguments fraught with emotions that escalate into unmovable "we–they" situations. "We can disagree without being disagreeable" is a simple guideline for the social worker to rely upon in building and strengthening relationships in the policy arena.

Advocating a position to a legislative committee or a board of directors without any prior person-to-person groundwork with legislators, their staff, or with boards of directors and CEOs is a recipe for failure. So where and how does the social worker begin?

There are some simple but obvious steps a social worker can take to begin and enhance relationships with policy makers. Table 9.1 identifies some common "dos and "don'ts" when meeting with a member of the US Congress, though these guides are applicable to any elected official, CEO, board of directors, other professionals, or advocates. These are essentially strategies in relationship building. In addition, the following list includes time-tested tips the author honed in his policy practice.

- Listen with your ears and your heart—pay attention to what's being said and how it is being said.
- Focus on the person; give the individual your undivided attention.
- Look directly at the person you are talking with, not over her shoulder or around the room.
- Really believe that the person you are talking to is smart.
- Do not patronizes others.
- Be aware of your body language as well as that of the person(s) you are engaging.

- Try to get the other person/people to do the majority of the talking.
- Remember—you and the policy maker share something in common: wanting to do good.
- Treat everyone nicely.
- Stay away from trendy sayings such as "My bad" or "That's sick" (which means, "That's pretty amazing").

Social workers understand that a positive relationship between the professional and client is essential in any change effort. Although this is often difficult in a clinical setting, it is even more challenging in policy practice due to the often contentious

Table 9.1. THE CAPITOL VISITS, WHAT TO DO AND NOT DO

The Dos	The Don'ts
• Be professional, courteous, positive, direct, clear, concise, factual, credible, and specific.	• Don't give inaccurate information or purposely lie.
• Do your homework.	• Don't be rude to a legislator and/or his or her aide.
• Always follow up with information you have promised.	• Don't make moral judgments based on a vote or an issue.
• Follow up a visit or telephone call to a legislator with an offer to be of assistance in the future.	• Don't waste a legislator's or aide's time.
• Use correct forms of address.	• Don't send a form letter.
• Follow the KISS rule: Keep fact sheets, letters, and testimony short.	• Don't fail to find out where a bill you are being asked about is in the legislative process.
• Be sure to include how you can be reached on all fact sheets and letters.	• Don't publicly or privately complain about a legislator or a member of his or her staff.
• Stay in contact with your legislator—it is the key to establishing a relationship of mutual trust.	• Never start or carry rumors.
• Treat members of the legislature as friends and as intelligent citizens.	• Don't hold grudges.
• Attend legislative hearings, committee meetings, budget mark-up sessions, and floor votes on your issues, if appropriate.	• Don't be argumentative or abrasive.
	• Don't interrupt a legislator when he or she is obviously busy.
• Always, always be truthful.	• Don't cover more than one subject, if at all possible, during a visit unless asked.
• Be reasonable, and realize that everyone thinks his or her issue is the most important one being considered.	• Don't write a letter longer than one page, if possible.
• Thank legislators for meeting with you and for their consideration, even if your comments are not well received.	• Don't blame legislators for all the things that go wrong in government.
• Treat members of the legislature as you would like to be treated. Use common sense.	• Don't be offended if he or she forgets your name or who you are, even if it is just 5 minutes after your visit.

Source: Joe Gagen. (n.d.). AAFP leader forum, legislative communications handouts. Retrieved from http://www. aafp.org/dam/AAFP/documents/events/alf_ncsc/alf_handouts/legislative-communications-handout.pdf   on April 22, 2016.

political nature of the process. Even so, it is incumbent that the social worker should always be fully aware of the need to focus on establishing and maintaining positive relationships.

WHO DOES THE POLICY PRACTITIONER REPRESENT?

A social worker simply cannot undertake an advocacy project without understanding the employing agency's protocols regarding such activities. Most social service organizations have explicit rules and/or guidelines in place that regulate an employee's participation in legislative advocacy matters. In particular, nonprofit 501(c)(3) agencies have very stringent rules relating to public advocacy; it is commonplace that NGO staff are not allowed to engage in any form of political activity. Some agencies, on the other hand, encourage their staff to be active in the community. The bottom line is that the social worker needs to be fully aware of her or his agency's policies related to policy practice and advocacy work.

A widespread practice among agencies is that the social worker must request and be granted permission before offering any written or oral testimony to a legislative group. Writing a letter on agency stationary that supports or opposes a specific issue, sending a politically directed email from an agency's network, visiting an elected official, or posting an item on social media that references the employee's connection to their workplace *all require* approval from the practitioner's employer.

Although such prohibitions are commonplace, the social worker can still engage in political matters. The social worker can use his or her vacation time to meet with a legislator or a governmental committee; a practitioner can write letters on his or her private stationary or send emails from a personal network. When agency bans are in place, the policy practitioner must distance himself or herself from the employer in all forms of communication; this is easily achieved with a simple statement, "I am Johnny/Jane Social Worker and have been working on children's issues for the past 15 years." Even so, a common question to the social worker from a legislator in response to this statement might be, "Where do you work?" The policy practitioner must answer the question in a forthright way but frame the response in a manner that distances and clearly separates his or her comments from the workplace: "I work for the Children's Safety Sake Agency but today I am here representing myself and not the organization."

Larger NGOs often include a Governmental Relations (GR) office or a governmental specialist as part of the agency's infrastructure. The GR office or legislative specialist is an extremely important resource. These internal agency specialists can aid in the preparation of written and oral presentations, help revise written comments, and review other materials that might be distributed in public forums. Similarly, it is common for a GR staff person to accompany the social worker to a legislative hearing and offer advice prior to the policy practitioner's testimony.

The bottom line is that the social worker needs to check with the employing agency to see what, if any, regulations are in place regarding political engagement. "If it's a good idea, go ahead and do it. It's much easier to apologize than it is to get permission simply is not acceptable in agency work, especially as it relates to political social work" (Lewis, n.d.).

TESTIMONY—SPEAKING TO A LEGISLATIVE OR GOVERNANCE COMMITTEE

One of the most common and basic policy practice techniques is speaking before a legislative or governance committee.[1] Commonly referred to as *testifying*, this portion of a committee's process allows the public to present their ideas and opinions on a particular issue or proposed legislative measure. Testimony can be verbal, written, or both, and its sole purpose is to influence the committee's final decision (see Box 9.2). No matter who is addressing a legislative committee, each witness is considered an "expert" whose role is to help the committee understand the issue from his or her perspective. All written comments and verbal presentations become part of the committee's permanent official record and may be used by committee members and/or their staffs in future work.

Most state and federal governmental websites often include a link to a "How to testify before a legislative committee" page with clear instructions on public testimony (see Washington State Legislature; Montana 64th Session; Eugene; City of Rockford; City of Columbus). Some governmental websites are less directive with minimal or no guidance (see Gainesville, Georgia; City of Rocky Mount). Even so, there are general steps that strengthen the social worker's testimony in all forms of public presentations.

1. *Pre-Hearing.* As with committees of the US House of Representatives and the US Senate, state and local legislative committees are required to formally "post" or announce a scheduled hearing according to the particular legislature's rules. These public meetings are also referred to as a *hearing* or *public comment period*. In Texas, for example, notice of public hearings must be at least 5 calendar days in advance during a regular session and 24 hours in advance during a special session (House Research Organization, 2015). The announcement includes the date, time, location, and purpose of the meeting (see Table 9.2). The announcements are posted on a committee's Web page as well as on the committee's physical bulletin board or in a space designated by the legislative body.

---

1. Legislators refers to elected federal, state, and local officials.

Table 9.2. NOTICE OF PUBLIC HEARING

House of Representatives
Notice of Public Hearing

COMMITTEE: Juvenile Justice & Family Issues
TIME & DATE: 10:00 AM, Monday, November 21, 2016
PLACE: JHR 140 CHAIR: Rep. Harold V. Dutton, Jr.

The committee will meet jointly with the House Committee on Human Services to consider the following charge:

Study and evaluate the practice of youth being recruited into human trafficking. Specifically, evaluate the scope of the pipeline of potential victims from foster care, including methods and means used to lure youth into trafficking. Evaluate the types of services that are available to support children and youth in the conservatorship of DFPS who are victims of human trafficking. Make necessary recommendations to assist DFPS in identifying, recovering, serving, or caring for children and youth who are victims of human trafficking prior to placement in foster care.

Invited and public testimony will be taken.

NOTICE OF ASSISTANCE AT PUBLIC MEETINGS
Persons with disabilities who plan to attend this meeting and who may need assistance, such as sign language, are requested to contact Stacey Nicchio at (512) 463-0850, 72 hours prior to the meeting so that appropriate arrangements can be made.

Prior to the actual public meeting, the policy practitioner should meet with the committee's Legislative Director (LD) or Legislative Aide (LA). The meeting's purpose is to develop a contact, for example, relationship building, with a key individual who works with the committee, which can be extremely useful as the legislative process unfolds. A second purpose of this meeting is to learn what specific information the committee members are seeking; how hearings are organized; and whether there are unique protocols the chair may employ. For example, does the committee expect a written copy of the testimony and, if so, how many copies should the social worker provide; is the witness lineup predetermined and, if so, when is the policy practitioner scheduled to speak; and does the LD or LA have any insight as to what types of presentation formats the committee prefers.

2. *Attend a Committee Hearing.* Attending at least one of the committee's hearings prior to the session is useful for the social worker to become acquainted with the committee and its protocols. Observing a committee at work and its procedures, as well as becoming familiar with the physical layout of the meeting room itself, provides familiarity with the hearing process. There is a great deal to take

in when observing a committee hearing, but the social worker will find the following areas extremely beneficial:

- How does the chairperson runs the meeting, formally or informally?
- What does the committee process itself look like; do committee members come and go or are they in attendance throughout?
- Where do the staff sit?
- To what extent do members interact with each other; do they whisper to each other while individuals are testifying?
- How do committee members ask questions—challenging, friendly, or somewhat aloof?
- How is the room set up for the hearing; does the witnesses stand at a podium or sit at a table?
- Where are the members in relation to the lectern or speaker's table—a few feet or yards away?
- How many people does the meeting room hold—25 or less, 50 to 100 or more?
- What looks like a good seat for the social worker that provides easy access to the speaker's lectern?
- Is there a clock nearby to keep track of time?

And just as important—what is the proximity of the bathrooms in relation to the meeting room? Hearings can sometimes drag on for hours on end before one is called to testify, and knowing the location of any facilities can be helpful.

No matter how experienced the social worker may be in speaking before a legislative committee, the policy practitioner will always have some level of nervousness. Being acquainted with a hearing's process and its physical surroundings reduces ambiguity, which in turn helps lessen the anxiety. There are enough unknowns in a public hearing, but reducing "external noise" increases the policy practitioners' self-confidence.

3. *The Testimony Itself.* The written testimony is a short paper, four or fewer double-spaced pages, using 12-point font, that advances a persuasive argument in a concise, clearly organized fashion. The testimony is not a 20-page academic paper filled with a lengthy analysis or a literature review. The testimony is written from the perspective that most legislators are not very familiar with the policy issue. The writing is succinct and direct, formal in style, avoids long flowing statements, and is free of professional jargon and acronyms.

The basic format for written testimony includes (1) cover page; (2) brief introductory paragraph; (3) a summary paragraph stating the social worker's opinion on the issue; (4) facts to support opinion; (5) alternatives or options, if appropriate; and (6) summary and thank you.

a. *Cover Page.* The cover page identifies the speaker by name; her/his organization and contact information, e.g., physical mail address and phone number(s), and email address; the bill's name and associated number; the committee's name; and, last, the date of the hearing (see Box 9.1). This cover page information is not read to the committee.

Box 9.1

EXAMPLE OF COVER PAGE FOR LEGISLATIVE TESTIMONY

Testimony Presented to (Governmental Unit, e.g., House, Senate, City Council Select Board) Regarding HB/SB or Bill (Number and Name) or Issue if non-bill

Prepared by

(Speaker's Name)

Official Title (if representing a group or organization)

Mailing Address

Phone Number(s)

Email address

Date

---

b. *Brief Introductory Paragraph.* The written testimony begins with a brief introductory paragraph. "*Chairman/woman/person* _____, *members of the committee. My name is* _____ *and I live at (provide home address) and today I am here representing (name the organization or group). I am here to support/ oppose/neutral HBxxx.*"

c. *Summary Paragraph Stating the Social Worker's Opinion.* This section provides an abstract of the rational that outlines the reasoning behind the policy practitioner's recommendation. In general, the paragraph is three to five sentences long.

d. *Facts to Support Position.* This is the data driven section of the written testimony. Relevant numbers and statistics are cited, most often in a bulleted format or in pie charts or bar graphs. A word of caution is to avoid the over using statistics. It is appropriate to provide more detailed statistical information in an appendix.

e. *Alternatives or Options, If Appropriate.* A policy practitioner who is opposing a specific proposal should also provide one or two alternatives for the committee to consider. It is best to identify a preference for one option and outline why this alternative is the best solution to the problem. Again, the social worker's task is two-fold: to get the committee to oppose a bill while substituting a more preferable option in its place.

4. *Summary and Thank You.* The concluding written statement is similar to the opening comments with a summary statement supporting or opposing the proposed legislation. The social worker also recognizes the committee by thanking them for their time and noting that he or she is willing to answer any questions.

"Chairman/woman/person _____, *members of the committee, in conclusion, I strongly urge the committee to (support or oppose) HB/SB/City Council proposal (number and name). I appreciate the opportunity meet with you today. I may be reached as follows (presenter's contact information, which is the same as listed on testimony's cover sheet) and in the meantime would be happy to answer any of your questions."*

Box 9.2

EXAMPLE OF TESTIMONY

Chairman Dutton, Chairman Raymond, and members of the committee, thank you for the opportunity to testify before you today.

My name is Dixie Hairston and I work for CHILDREN AT RISK on our anti–child sex trafficking initiatives in North Texas. CHILDREN AT RISK is a nonprofit organization dedicated to improving the lives of children through public policy and advocacy.

As you may know, Texas is considered to be a hub for human trafficking activity in all its various forms. Our state generates the second highest number of calls to the National Human Trafficking Hotline, **the most common calls involve sex trafficking cases where children are caught in the commercial sex trade.**[1]

Even though this may be bad news, Texas is a leader in anti-trafficking policy and was one of the first states to pass human trafficking legislation in the United States. Still, gaps exist.

Unfortunately, victims of child sex trafficking are often some of the most vulnerable children in our communities. Traffickers prey upon these youth by providing them with food, shelter, attention and affection; filling a void often left as a result of childhood abuse and neglect. This highly manipulative recruitment strategy often makes children involved in the CPS system at higher risk for being sex trafficked.

The National Center for Missing and Exploited Children reported that 1 out of every 5 children reported to them as runaways in 2015 were likely victims of sex trafficking. Furthermore, they report that almost 74% of those children were in the care of child social services or foster care when they went missing.[2]

Last session, several bills were passed that allowed for easier prosecution of those who purchase sex from children, provided better resources for child victims and extended the Texas Human Trafficking Prevention Task Force. Legislation was also passed that created a Child Sex Trafficking Prevention Unit in the Governor's Criminal Justice Division to specifically address sex trafficking of children in our state.[4] Additionally, the omnibus bill, HB 10, requires key agencies, including DFPS, to designate an authorized individual to improve both internal and external responses to human trafficking and promote a more coordinated statewide effort.

Last December, in a lawsuit brought against officials of the State of Texas by a class of former foster children, Federal Judge Janis Jack held that Texas

Child Protective Services has violated the constitutional rights of the children in its care. These rights include the right to be free from an unreasonable risk of harm and protection from psychological and physical abuse. In short, foster children have a constitutional right to personal security and reasonably safe living conditions. The 260-page judgment is heartbreaking to read, but it is especially pertinent to child trafficking.

While CHILDREN AT RISK supports Texas DFPS and recognizes the *extremely* challenging circumstances caseworkers in our state face every day, the current system does not keep children in government custody reasonably safe from harm.

Inadequate resources for screening, identification and subsequent placement in appropriate, therapeutic environments for children entering or returning to the CPS system after being sex trafficked all contribute to the likelihood these children will suffer from acute and lifelong effects caused by commercial sexual exploitation.[5]

Worse still, placing these now-brutalized victims in standard CPS placements without regard to the unique and complex trauma associated with sex trafficking prevents the child from being stabilized and puts the them at further risk of re-victimization, strengthening of trauma bonds they have with their trafficker and higher risk of running away again.[6]

High caseload burdens among caseworkers and children aging out of the system in placements hundreds of miles away from their support network have created large holes in the DFPS safety net and contributes to the pipeline that directly connects the foster care system and the multi-million-dollar illegal sex industry that commercially exploits thousands of children each year.[7]

But there are some very encouraging updates coming out of the newly formed Child Sex Trafficking Unit within the Governor's Office.

They have been working closely with DFPS and other stakeholders to identify gaps, promote best practices and build the capacity of our state to eradicate child sexual exploitation.

Their immediate priority is to develop and enhance trauma-informed services and support for survivors of child sex trafficking so that they can heal and thrive. They will achieve this by working to create a continuum of care for victims in each region from immediate recovery to long-term restoration.

While they are working to build up regional systems, they are also working to fill common gaps statewide. Their office will be facilitating a grant application process for best and promising practices in providing services to victims of child sex trafficking.

In addition to initiatives like this, our recommendations for the committee include:

- Designated caseworkers that are specifically assigned to children who are at high risk of being exploited or trafficked or who are returning to the system after being trafficked.

- These case workers should have a low caseload burden and have specialized training on highly traumatized children.
- A comprehensive plan for children who age-out of foster care that will help prevent them from having to resort to prostitution in order to meet their needs for food and shelter.
- Strengthened coordination within and between different state agencies in screening, identification and placement procedures for children returning to the foster care system as victims of sexual abuse or child sex trafficking.
  - *Last session, HB 1217 made assessing for trafficking when a child returns to care a requirement. However, Judge Jack's verdict states that this documentation is often not flagged or monitored closely due to high caseworker turnover.*
- Finally, more resources need to be directed to creating a network of safe, appropriate and therapeutic housing for children that have been trafficked or sexually abused.
  - This should also include increased access to trauma-focused, evidence-based mental health services and rehabilitative services.

Thank you for your time today and please feel free to ask any follow-up questions.

References:

[1] National Human Trafficking Resource Center. Retrieved from https://traffickingresource-center.org/states

[2] National Center for Missing and Exploited Children. (2016). Child Sex Trafficking. Retrieved from http://www.missingkids.com/1in5

[3] CHILDREN AT RISK. (2015). 84th Texas Legislature Report on Legislation Impacting Children. Retrieved from http://173.45.238.175/content/wp-content/uploads/2015/08/84th-comprehensive-summary-final.pdf

[4] CHILDREN AT RISK. (2015). 84th Texas Legislature Report on Legislation Impacting Children. Retrieved from http://173.45.238.175/content/wp-content/uploads/2015/08/84th-comprehensive-summary-final.pdf

[5] Shared Hope International. National Report on Missing and Exploited Children. Retrieved from http://sharedhope.org/wp-content/uploads/2012/09/SHI_National_Report_on_DMST_2009.pdf

[6] US Department of Health and Human Services Administration for Children, Youth and Families. (2015). Guidance to States and Services on Addressing Human Trafficking of Children and Youth in the United States. Retrieved from http://www.acf.hhs.gov/cb/resource/human-trafficking-guidance

[7] US District Court Southern District of Texas, Corpus Christi Division. (2015). Memorandum Opinion and Verdict of the Court.

Note: This testimony was presented to the Texas House of Representatives Juvenile Justice & Family Issues per the public hearing notice in Table 9.2.

Source: Dixie Hairston, Public Policy Coordinator and Mandi Sheridan Kimball, Director, Public Policy and Government Affair, Children At-Risk, Houston, TX. Received February 16, 2017.

5. *Questions and Answers.* Questions are generally asked when an individual concludes her or his presentation. It is common for committee members not to make any observations or ask questions, especially if there are a number of witnesses scheduled to speak before a committee. The social worker should not feel disappointed nor interpret that the committee is disinterested in the practitioner's comments if no questions are asked.

   When a question is asked, an unwritten rule for committees is to answer the question through the committee chair and then respond to the person who asked the question: "*Chairman/woman/person* _____, *Senator/Representative* _____, *you ask an interesting question and I believe . . .*" A committee member may ask any question she or he wishes; some are focused while others may sound like rambling statements. It is appropriate for the policy practitioner to ask for clarification if he or she is unsure what the committee member is asking. No matter the question, the policy practitioner's response should be concise and accurate. Under no circumstances should the social worker guess or make up an answer. *A fundamental and basic rule when giving public testimony is not to answer a question unless one is sure of the answer.* A social worker's reasonable response if unsure of an answer might be, "*I do not have the information readily at hand but I will get this to your office, and the chairman/woman/person's office, tomorrow by (identify a specific time).*" It is imperative that the policy practitioner provide the information by or, preferably, prior to the stated date and time; this only reinforces the social worker's credibility and trustworthiness with the committee.

6. *The Presenter's Copy of the Testimony.* The presenter's personal comments should be typed in a large font, such as 16–20 points, which is easier to read and allows one to keep track of the talk while looking back and forth between the panel members and the written comments. The social worker reads the statement slowly but not in a monotone manner; throughout the entire presentation, the policy practitioner looks at each committee member as often as possible. Some podiums include a digital timer or a series of lights, that is, green (continue talking), yellow (2 minute or less to speak), or red (time is up). The practitioner can place a watch or use a timer on a smartphone to keep track of time directly on the podium and within direct eyesight if there is no built-in clock on the podium. Remember—looking at one's wristwatch sends a message that the policy practitioner is nervous as well as unaware of time and not in control of the situation. Simply looking down at the podium in a quick glance at a watch or smartphone is casually done and most often goes unnoticed.

7. *The Social Worker's Turn to Testify.* When called to testify, the policy practitioner should hand copies of the testimony to committee staff person as he or she approaches the podium; the social worker should clarify how and when to distribute written materials during the meeting with the staff person prior to the scheduled testimony.

   There are two schools of thought regarding verbal and written testimony. One believes that the written document mirrors word for word the testimony given by the social worker. This approach allows committee members to read the testimony as it is being delivered and make notes on the document. An alternative model is the social worker's statement is an abstract of the much longer written testimony, which allows the social worker to highlight key points. Both options are appropriate with neither choice being stronger or more suitable over the other.

8. *Extra Copies of Formal Testimony.* Finally, it is useful for the social worker to have additional copies of her or his testimony for non–committee members who are attending the committee hearing. Print and broadcast media, aides from other legislators' offices, and representatives of organizations and advocacy groups, as well as interested individuals often will ask for a copy of the presentation.

Group Testimony

Some committees allow for group testimony, which permits any number of persons as a group to address the committee. In general, the group will identify two to four individuals to speak on behalf of the group while other group members stand behind the speakers. The initial speaker acts as the group's convener, provides a succinct, 30-second summary statement of the group's position, and then introduces the first speaker. Each speaker begins in a similar manner.

> *Chairman/woman/person* _____, *members of the committee. My name is* _____ *and I live at (provide home address) and today I am here with these persons who stand behind me to support/oppose/neutral HBxxx.*

Each speaker's comments are brief and, most important, different, highlighting one or two points. Once a person's comments are concluded, she or he introduces the next speaker.

> *Chairman/woman/person* _____, *members of the committee, at this time I would like to introduce* _____.

The last speaker ends the statement by reintroducing the group's convener, who offers a summary statement and ends by stating:

> *Chairman/woman/person* _____, *members of the committee, we appreciate the opportunity meet with you today and are happy to answer any of your questions.*

To Confront or Not

Some advocates strongly believe that aggressive confrontation is the most successful technique to create change. Although there are times when assertive protests are an appropriate option, policy practice with a legislative issue typically suggests avoiding such conflicts. The policy practitioner must understand the consequences of carrying out a demonstration of any form in a legislative committee room. At a minimum, the protesters will be asked to remain quiet; in some instances, the group will be forcibly removed from the chamber and possibly arrested. A short-term gain might be the publicity that results from such actions; the incident may make the evening television news, be reported in social media, or be a story in the next day's newspaper. Yet the social worker will need to weigh this temporary public visibility against the long-term consequences of working with the legislative group it has aggressively confronted to find a positive outcome.

The policy practitioner's primary goal is to gain the committee's support for a particular stand on an issue. Confrontation creates a hostile relationship, which is difficult to overcome. On the other hand, the social worker can help build a working relationship where solutions are possible by simply being respectful of the committee and its process. Accusing committee members of causing a particular problem or trying to "shout them down" does little more than alienate them from the social worker's cause while reducing the chances of finding a resolution to the issue. The policy practitioner, as well as others who may speak as part of the social worker's group, should resist the temptation to scold, intimidate, blame, or insult the committee members or other witnesses. It is useful for the social worker, prior to the hearing, to meet with supporters and encourage them to refrain from overt demonstrations such as cheering, clapping, and/ or jeering.

Professionalism

At all times a social worker should carry himself or herself in a manner that best represents the social work profession. Sections 5.01(b) and (c) of the National Association of Social Workers Code of Ethics states, "Social workers should uphold and advance the values, ethics, knowledge, and mission of the profession. Social workers should protect, enhance, and improve the integrity of the profession" and "Social workers should contribute time and professional expertise to activities that promote respect for the value, integrity, and competence of the social work profession" (National Association of Social Workers, 2016). Professionalism addresses the content of the message (based on rigorous research and critical thinking) and the manner in which the testimony is presented.

There are many negative misconceptions of the social work profession, which influence how others perceive a policy practitioner's message. Public testimony before a legislative committee is an important opportunity to challenge these preconceived stereotypes while enhancing the social work profession's stature.

When observing a committee hearing, look closely at speakers from other professions: What they are wearing (t-shirts with a printed slogan or a formal outfit)? Do they use professional terminology or speak in everyday language? How do they address the committee (are they formal or folksy)? Are their statements devoid of words and phrases such as "umm" or "ahh" or "you know"? Watching professionals from other disciplines address a legislative hearing is an excellent way to identify and mimic others' successful presentations.

Testimony—The Day of the Presentation

Arriving at the hearing room well in advance of a scheduled committee meeting is wise. Appearing before a legislative committee can be a somewhat unnerving experience, and the pre-testimony period should not add any unnecessary tension to the day. Simple things such as finding a parking space can be difficult and walking to the building, especially during inclement weather, adds to the unease of the moment. Also, a committee's hearing room may have changed, and finding the new location is unexpected news. Arriving early also allows the social worker to meet with other colleagues as well as to make a brief visit with the committee's staff person: "Just stopping by to say 'hi' and I will see you in a bit. Hope all is well."

A major reason to arrive early is to find an aisle seat in close proximity to the podium. When called to testify, the social worker wants the easiest route to the lectern; having to climb over people from a middle seat in a row of 10 to 20 seats is not especially easy, knowing that other people, including the committee's members, are watching the social worker come up to the lectern.

Testimony—The Session Itself

As the hearing progresses, the policy practitioner should listen closely to the comments of other witnesses. Their observations may be similar to the social worker; rather than repeating what has already been said, which legislators generally do not appreciate, the policy practitioner should revise, as necessary, her or his verbal testimony by putting a different spin on the points or respond to questions that the legislators posed to other speakers. In other words, the social worker should be flexible and willing to modify his or her comments at the last moment.

Some final points about the hearing itself.

1. When in the meeting room, turn off, or at least mute, cellphones. There is nothing more bothersome and a sign of disrespect for the committee than having a cell phone go off with a jingle or song in the middle of a hearing or when social worker is actually testifying.
2. The lectern's microphone should be about 6 inches away from the speaker. Speaking too close into a microphone makes the voice overbearing and loud; and people are not able to hear the speaker if the individual is too far away from the microphone.

3. Be mindful of the time. Have a watch on the lectern or a running stopwatch in order to monitor the time. It is common for the committee chair to interrupt a speaker if he or she runs over the allotted time. To say the least, it is embarrassing for a witness to be told to stop speaking. If this occurs, under no circumstances should the policy practitioner say, "But I haven't finished my comments." Rather, a more appropriate response is, *"Chairman/person _____, I apologize for running over my time; I have provided the committee a copy of my testimony for your consideration. Again, thank you for your time and I would be happy to answer any questions at this time."*

4. Remember to avoid professional jargon; the best testimony uses common, everyday language.

5. The social worker should plan to spend the entire day at the committee hearing. It is common for hearings not to begin on time, take breaks during the day, and continue into the evening hours.

6. It is appropriate to bring a light snack into a meeting room; this can be very helpful if a meeting runs for 3 hours or longer.

7. People should not clap, cheer, or jeer others' testimony. This slows down the committee's process while displaying disrespect for the committee members and other witness.

Testimony—Supporters in the Room

It is common for supporters of the social worker's position to also attend the committee hearing. Although most will not speak, they should complete a witness card, either an electronic or a paper version, expressing their support or opposition to the matter at hand.

Legislators like to know the level of support or opposition for a proposed initiative. Some advocacy groups wear brightly colored t-shirts emblazoned with a snappy catchphrase, a motto, or the agency's name. The committee members sit facing the audience, and it is easy to take notice of people if they stand out from the commonly worn dark suits. Other groups wear colored ribbons for a cause pined to their lapels or jackets. For example, the yellow ribbon symbolizes support for the military; pink ribbons are connected to breast cancer issues; and green ribbons demonstrate support for environmental affairs. In lieu of a ribbon, a group might wear the same colored flower. When the social worker, who also is wearing a colored flower or ribbon, addresses the committee, he or she should reference that supporters of the issue are wearing same colored symbolizing their support: *"Chairperson ____ and committee members. You might note that I am wearing a yellow rose on my lapel. This flower symbolizes my support, as well as those here today attending this hearing, for HB/SB_____."* When making such a statement, committee members, who might be looking down at their notes or engaged in a sidebar conversation with a colleague, will look up to see who is actually in the room. The social worker, as well as supporters of the issue, should wear the same colored flower or symbol in all follow-up contacts with legislators and/or their staffs. The flower, ribbon, or symbol begins to take on a life of its own and nonverbally reminds people of the issue it reflects.

Meeting rooms differ in size and set-up. The committee members sit in the front of the room while their staffs generally sit behind them or off to the side. The witness's lectern or table is directly in front of the committee chair; witnesses and observers sit behind the witness area. The number of audience seats available ranges from 10 to 100 or more; the typical meeting room on average holds about 50 seats for the public.

If the social worker is bringing a group of people to the hearing, it is best to arrive well before the hearing and claim the front-row seats; this is the prime location because legislators and their staff members can easily see those in the first few rows. Conversely, those sitting in the back of the room are less recognizable to the committee members.

An excellent organizing strategy is for the policy practitioner's colleagues and supporters to sit in the first few seats on both sides of a row and in as many rows as possible; this forces others, especially persons or groups who oppose the group's position, to the middle seats. Otherwise, when called to testify, the policy practitioner must climb over a number of people, which is very awkward. It is commonplace for someone who is trying to move out of a middle seat to drop his or her notes or trip over someone's foot!

A final note: One can leave one's chair during a hearing, but if the person plans to return to the hearing, it is best to leave a jacket or some item on the seat to signal that it is occupied. Otherwise, someone else can claim the chair.

Testimony—Follow-Up Work

The post-hearing phase begins as soon as the individual or group has finished their testimony. This post-meeting effort is just as important as the testimony itself. First, the policy practitioner must provide any promised follow-up information to the committee. If, for example, the social worker stated during the testimony, "I will get you this information tomorrow by 1:00 p.m.," then, no matter what, this must occur. Ensuring the promised information is received prior to the specified time enhances the social worker's credibility. Conversely, being late with or not following up with the information lessens the practitioner's reliability in the eyes of the legislators and their staff.

The day following the hearing (preferably the first thing in the morning), the policy practitioner contacts her or his primary committee staff contact person. The purpose of this communication is to thank the staffer for their help while asking what they might suggest the social worker should do next. For instance, are there some committee members the social worker should contact, or is there additional information the staff person feels will be helpful to the committee?

The next series of contacts is with the legislators themselves. These should be phone calls to their offices as well as emailing the legislator directly. Electronic messages should be personalized and not sent as a blast or group message. Again, the purpose is to thank the legislator and ask if he or she would like any additional information.

The policy practitioner also organizes others to contact the committee members' offices as well as their own representatives. The number of phone calls and email messages on a specific issue helps a legislator gauge the level of support or opposition to an issue. Minimal or no communication implies a lack of concern or support, while a constant, persistent stream of emails and phone calls indicates significant external interest.

Shortly after the initial office emails and phone calls are completed, the policy practitioner initiates a letter-writing campaign to the committee members. A *form letter* is a pretyped communication and only requires an individual's signature; form letters are quickly distributed to supporters and mailed. Although the form letter is easy to organize, its impact is minimal as legislators and their staffs generally disregard them. The clear assumption is that it takes little effort to send a form letter; all one needs to do is sign one's name while an organization mails the form letter.

A sound letter-writing campaign involves handwritten letters; typewritten letters are just as good if the language differs from letter to letter. The message is short (see Box 9.3) with three to four paragraphs, about 150 to 175 words in total, and no more than one page in length.

Following the letter-writing effort, the next phase of advocacy begins with office visits to committee members and their staff. These face-to-face visits remind the legislators and staff that the policy issue is important to a group of constituents. The request is simple—*"I hope the committee will vote to (support/oppose) the legislation. Is there any information that I can provide to help (legislator's name) decision on this matter?"*

When visiting a legislator or their staff, the advocate leaves a one-page info-sheet or dashboard handout that provides additional information on the issue (see Chapter 10). If the policy practitioner visits a legislative office five different times, he or she should leave five different info-sheets. The same holds true for other supporters of the issue when they visit legislators.

Box 9.3

LETTER TEMPLATE FOR AN ELECTED OFFICIAL

Date

The Honorable (fill in the name of state representative)
77 South High Street
Columbus, OH 43215-6111

or

The Honorable (fill in the name of your state senator)
Statehouse, Senate Building
Columbus, OH 43215

Dear Senator _____ or Representative _____:

Identify oneself, a constituent, a social worker; specify the bill and its number and if you support or oppose the legislation.

I am writing you today as one of your constituents to strongly urge you to support HB xxxx. I am a professional social worker and every day I see the impact that the lack of affordable housing has in our community and throughout the state. My sense is that most if not all people in Ohio believe that children should be able to grow up in permanent homes in safe communities. SBxxxx will help us realize this dream.

The next statement should be as specific as possible, asking the legislator to do something.

I ask that you support SBxxxx to insure that funding becomes available to low-income families so they too can move into affordable housing. Your support, and that of your colleagues in the Senate, is in fact an investment in Ohio's future.

Thank the legislator for their time, interest, and support.

Thank you very much for your time and efforts to increase affordable housing in our state. Please feel free to call on me if I can be of any assistance.

Sincerely,
Name
Contact information

ORGANIZING A TOWN HALL MEETING

The objective of a *town hall meeting* is to broaden the understanding of an issue and increase local attention to the issue. The town hall meeting is an open assembly for the public to participate in a discussion on a specific topic. Some meetings present new proposals, whereas others are open forums focused on an emerging issue. A significant outcome of a well-run town hall meeting is the collection of feedback and ideas from the broader community.

   A town hall meeting general lasts no longer than 2 hours. Although the meeting itself might seem short, the preparation for a successful town hall requires a great deal of legwork on the part of the policy practitioner.

1. *Formats*: There are three basic town hall meeting formats: Briefing Panel, Media Roundtable, and a Policy Panel.
    a. *Briefing Panel*—Consists of three to four individuals and a moderator. The panel discussion and presentations generally last for 45 minutes to 1 hour followed by a question and answer (Q&A) period with the audience.
    b. *Media Roundtable*—This format targets local media representatives who make up the audience. The goal is for the media to do follow-up stories on the issue. The panel remains the same size, whereas the audience is small and limited to local media members.
    c. *Policy Panel*—This format allows the public to testify to a panel of community leaders, agency executives, or governmental officials. This format encourages the public to describe their experiences and urge the panelists to adopt certain positions. Following this type of meeting, the panelists meet to discuss what they learned and identify possible next steps.
2. *Planning Committee.* An organizing committee of 10 to 12 persons helps oversee the overall meeting, organize its agenda, recruit individuals to attend the meeting, and assist with the town hall itself. The committee includes key persons who belong to possible or existing collaborative agencies, organizations, or groups; media representatives; and highly visible and respected individuals from the local community. A prime role for the committee is to help raise awareness of the issue and provide credibility for the event.
3. *Finding a Location and Date.* A town hall briefing or policy panel is held in a large space while the media roundtable can take place in a conference room. For the larger venue, the planning committee should identify a central location with adequate free parking, if possible. State office buildings, hospitals, colleges, schools, community centers, and libraries are excellent venues and may be reserved at little or no cost. Planning committee members often have inroads to venue sights and can help secure the space. The date and time of the town hall are just as important as the accessibility of the building. It is important to avoid scheduling a meeting that conflicts with other community events. A good practice is to review local community calendars to see what events are set, their scheduled beginning and ending times, and their locations. Except for emergencies, a town hall should always avoid all religious or governmental

holidays. In general, holding a town hall meeting on a weekday evening is less likely to result in scheduling conflicts for speakers and guests, and it increases the chances that desired meeting space will be available.

4. *Panel Members.* Panel members should be experts on the topic, trusted and well-respected individuals, or individuals whose personal stories help others understand the issue. Strong panels include persons with a broad range of experience such as academicians, elected officials, community leaders, and other professional social workers or individuals in human services. The broader the experiences and backgrounds of the panel members, the easier it is to increase the audience's understanding of the topic.

5. *Moderator.* The town hall moderator plays one of the most important roles in the meeting. This individual facilitates the entire meeting, ensures the agenda is followed, fields questions from the audience, asks her or his own questions, and makes sure the meeting ends on a positive note. Preferably, the moderator should have some understanding of the topic, but the key is for this person to be skilled and adept in running a large, open meeting. The individual should be a strong communicator and feel comfortable speaking in front of people. It is common for an academician or news reporter to moderate a town hall. A media person who moderates a town hall will ensure there is some radio, television, or newsprint coverage; at the same time, it is important to recognize that competitor media groups will, in all probability, not cover the meeting.

6. *Promoting the Town Hall Meeting.* Drawing media attention to an issue is important in building public awareness of the issue. Simply inviting a reporter to a town hall rarely succeeds. The media needs to understand why this is an important news item and how their coverage will help the community. Reporters often have specific "beats" that they cover such as health, politics, crime, lifestyle, and neighborhood issues. Reporters whose focal areas closely align with the town hall issue are more inclined to attend the meeting. Similarly, media who previously reported a story or news about the policy practitioner's agency may be inclined to attend the town hall as well. Finally, planning committee members may have useful media contacts, and they should reach out to and invite these individuals to the event.

The town hall meeting date, time, and location should be added to all available community events calendars as quickly as possible. Typically, it is free to advertise on such calendars, and the various public announcements help reduce the possibility of other groups scheduling an event for the same time. Published schedules of events are generally available in newspapers, announced on local radio stations, and posted on organizational websites, as well as other online media blogs such as MySpace and Facebook. Similarly, posting flyers, posters, and banners throughout the community, especially in the targeted neighborhood(s), is an economical way to reach a large audience. Community bulletin boards are available in a variety of locations such as schools, community centers, post office lobbies, supermarkets, libraries, hospitals, and coffee houses.

7. *Setting Up the Event.* The meeting itself requires a group of volunteers who are responsible for the venue's setup. Typical tasks include staffing a sign-in table,

arranging the meeting room, making sure the podium or table for the panel members is set up properly, and ensuring the equipment and sound system work. Volunteers in the event set-up also handle requests from the media; greet and seat members of the audience and panelists; record comments and questions from the audience; and handle any other unexpected logistical matters.

8. *Materials to Distribute at the Town Hall.* As people arrive for the meeting, they should sign in at a registration table. There are two different sign-in sheets, one for the public and a second for media representatives (see Tables 9.3 and 9.4).

Table 9.3. EXAMPLE OF TOWN HALL MEETING PUBLIC SIGN-IN SHEET

Town Hall Meeting Public Sign-In Sheet
(location)
(Date)

	Name	Address	Email address	Phone number	Would you like to join our Facebook page?		Would you like to be added to the mailing list?	
1					Yes	No	Yes	No
2					Yes	No	Yes	No
3					Yes	No	Yes	No
4					Yes	No	Yes	No
5					Yes	No	Yes	No
6					Yes	No	Yes	No
7					Yes	No	Yes	No
8					Yes	No	Yes	No
9					Yes	No	Yes	No
10					Yes	No	Yes	No
11					Yes	No	Yes	No
12					Yes	No	Yes	No
13					Yes	No	Yes	No
14					Yes	No	Yes	No
15					Yes	No	Yes	No
16					Yes	No	Yes	No
17					Yes	No	Yes	No
18					Yes	No	Yes	No
19					Yes	No	Yes	No
20					Yes	No	Yes	No

Table 9.4. EXAMPLE OF TOWN HALL MEETING MEDIA SIGN-IN SHEET

Town Hall Meeting Media Sign-In Sheet
(location)
(Date)

	Name	Organization	Email address	Phone number	Would you like to join our Facebook page?		Would you like to be added to the mailing list?	
1					Yes	No	Yes	No
2					Yes	No	Yes	No
3					Yes	No	Yes	No
4					Yes	No	Yes	No
5					Yes	No	Yes	No
6					Yes	No	Yes	No
7					Yes	No	Yes	No
8					Yes	No	Yes	No
9					Yes	No	Yes	No
10					Yes	No	Yes	No
11					Yes	No	Yes	No
12					Yes	No	Yes	No
13					Yes	No	Yes	No
14					Yes	No	Yes	No
15					Yes	No	Yes	No
16					Yes	No	Yes	No
17					Yes	No	Yes	No
18					Yes	No	Yes	No
19					Yes	No	Yes	No
20					Yes	No	Yes	No

The sign-in sheet includes space for a person's name, address, and additional contact information (email and phone number); the sign-in sheet also provides an opportunity to add participants to various list-serves, Facebook pages, and newsletters. This database is an invaluable tool that provides the policy practitioner a list of potential allies to help advocate on the issue; it is a source of potential supporters and volunteers and can help identify people who might be interested in appearing before city councils or speaking at legislative hearings.

Collaborative partners can distribute their own information packets to the registrants. It is a good idea to offer space free of charge to organizations and groups to sponsor their own information table. Allowing other groups to set up information tables also increases participation in the town hall meeting itself.

9. *The Town Hall Meeting.* The meeting should begin on time. It is frustrating for those persons who arrive prior to the announced start time to wait for the session to begin 30 minutes late. Starting and ending a meeting as announced demonstrates respect for the audience while conveying a message that the sponsoring group is well organized.

A planning committee representative begins the town hall with a brief welcome and introducing key individuals, such as area elected officials, local "celebrities," agency(s) executive directors, and the town hall moderator. This should take no more than 5 minutes. The moderator comments begin with a brief overview of the meeting's purpose, its agenda, and reviews nuts-and-bolts items such as turning off cellphones, location of bathrooms, and if and when a break will occur. The moderator calls on each panelist to speak, generally for 5–7 minutes per person. A technique to help keep the speakers aware of the time is to have a volunteer off to the side or seated directly in front of the panel, who holds up a piece of paper noting the time left written in large, easily read words, for example, "3 MINUTES, 2 MINUTES, 1 MINUTE." Panel members are told prior to the session beginning where the timekeeper will be seated.

The Question and Answer (Q&A) period, which generally lasts 30–45 minutes, begins once the panelists have concluded their individual presentations. There are two types of Q&A formats: (1) audience members come up to a microphone to ask their questions, and (2) audience members write their questions on a 3x5 card that the moderator then reads to the panel. The 3x5 card format allows the moderator to control the flow of the meeting; there are no 5- to 10-minute "speeches" from the audience, which is common in the open-microphone format; the moderator is able to combine similarly written questions into one query; and, finally, the planning committee has all the written questions to review after the meeting. The moderator should also be prepared with some questions to ask if the audience is small or only a few 3x5 cards have been submitted.

The moderator ends the town hall by thanking the panelist and the audience and reintroduces the planning committee representative to make the closing comments.

10. *Town Hall Participant Evaluation Form.* During the Q&A portion of the meeting, volunteers discreetly distribute an evaluation form (see Table 9.5) to the audience. The moderator will ask the audience participants to

Table 9.5. EXAMPLE OF TOWN HALL MEETING EVALUATION

(Town Hall Meeting Name)

Your comments and feedback are important. Please complete and leave this evaluation at the registration table. Thank you for your participation and help today!

1. *Overall Program:* ☐ Excellent ☐ Good ☐ Fair ☐ Poor
   Comments: _____
   _____

2. *Panelist Presentations:* ☐ Excellent ☐ Good ☐ Fair ☐ Poor
   Comments: _____
   _____

3. *Moderator:* ☐ Excellent ☐ Good ☐ Fair ☐ Poor
   Comments: _____
   _____

4. Was the program presentation beneficial to you? ☐ Yes ☐ No
   Comments: _____
   _____

5. Did you receive the information you expected? ☐ Yes ☐ No
   Comments: _____
   _____

6. What did you find most helpful?
   Comments: _____
   _____

7. *Meeting Site:* ☐ Excellent ☐ Good ☐ Fair ☐ Poor
   Comments: _____
   _____

8. What would like to see happen next?
   _____
   _____
   _____

9. *Additional Comments:*
   _____
   _____
   _____

complete the evaluation and leave it at the sign-in table. The evaluation typically is a one-page form that helps the planning committee determine what worked well in the meeting; the evaluation form is action research, not a tool to gather data for an in-depth research study for journal publication. Most important, the evaluation should include an *open-ended question* asking the individual to suggest steps they feel should be taken. Such a question often yields excellent recommendations while sending a message to the audience participants that their ideas and views are wanted and valued.

11. *Post–Town Hall Debriefing Session.* The planning committee meets soon after the town hall meeting concludes, usually within a week following the town hall meeting. The purpose is to review participant evaluation and feedback comments and discuss if the meeting's goals were achieved. The debriefing's primary objective is to develop an action plan, including developing possible policy recommendations, information dissemination, and media outreach.

A town hall meeting provides an excellent springboard for the policy practitioner to expand public support for an issue, helps broaden and strengthen a collaborative effort among agencies and advocacy groups, and helps to solidify an action plan. Although the meeting itself is short in duration, the pre- and post-planning efforts require time and patience.

ADVOCACY DAY AT THE (LEGISLATURE, CITY HALL, COUNTY BOARD . . .)

An advocacy day is an excellent activity that mobilizes supporters around a specific issue. Participants can be in the hundreds or as small as a dozen or fewer persons. This lobbying event can be organized by existing organizations or by ad hoc groups. For example, a number of state chapters of the National Association of Social Workers, such as Arizona, Texas, Virginia, West Virginia, and Nevada, sponsor advocacy days at their respective state legislatures. Some states hold multiple advocacy days each year, whereas other state legislative days occur every other year.

An advocacy day brings together the persons to advocate on one or more issues before a legislative body. These are empowering activities for a policy practice initiative as individuals, in a coordinated effort, are able to state their case to a number of legislators within a truncated time. Box 9.4 illustrates two state NASW chapter legislative days' agendas. The more common format includes an overview of the day, discussion on the policy practice issue(s),and,

Box 9.4

EXAMPLES OF AGENDAS FOR SOCIAL WORK LEGISLATIVE DAYS

**Example 1: Arizona Agenda Social Work Day at
the Legislature 2015 events.
February 10, 18, 26, 2015
Agenda***

*The agenda for the event is as follows, and it is subject to change.

NOTE: Optional Early sign in at **8:00 am** is for participants that would like to come early to view a committee hearing and to sign up for the "Request to Speak System" early in the day. If you do not want to view a committee hearing, you can arrive by **10:00 am** to sign in, with the Social Work Day program beginning at **10:30 am**. You will have the opportunity to view a committee hearing in the afternoon if you choose this option.

8:00 AM–10:00 AM—*Optional early sign* in at the Arizona Capitol Museum/Historic Senate Chambers for SW day the attendance sheet for those interested in attending a committee hearing.

Senate Committee Meetings
9:00 AM Federalism, Mandates and Fiscal Responsibility
9:00 AM Rural Affairs and Environment

House Committee Meetings
No morning committees scheduled; 9:00 AM Caucus
10:00 AM –10:30 AM—*Sign in* for SW Day at the Arizona Capitol Museum/Historic Senate Chambers attendance sheet and registration at the request to speak system.
10:30 AM –11:00 AM —*Program begins*; focus on our priorities, fact sheets.
11:00 AM–11:30 AM—*Advocacy Activities*
11:45 AM—*Group Photo*—in Front of Historic Capitol
12:15 PM–1:25 PM—*Lunch and Speakers* at the Rose Garden
1:30 PM—*Introduction in the Galleries* of the SW Day student participants at the Senate and House Floor Galleries
2:00 PM—*Debrief:* SW Day participants meet at the lawn to debrief and option to attend committees.

Senate Committee Meetings

2:00 PM Water & Energy

House of Representatives Committee Meetings
2:00 PM Banking & Financial Services
2:00 PM Health

2:00 PM Transportation & Infastructure
2:30 PM—Certificate Distribution and Dismissal

Source: Arizona Chapter of the National Association of Social Workers. (n.d.). Retrieved from http://www.naswaz.com/?page=SWDay2015&hhSearchTerms=%22social+and+work+and +day+and+legislature%22 on June 2, 2016.

Example 2: North Carolina Advocacy Day
March 25, 2015 Agenda

Advocacy 101: How and what do I talk to my legislators about? Why is it important for social workers to be here? Hear from legislators, MSW lobby-ists and social work advocates.

Advocacy 101 Session 1
7:45 am—Registration Opens
8:15 am—Session begins
9:30 am—Session Concludes Participants are encouraged to schedule a meeting with their legislators anytime after 9:40 am

Advocacy 101 Session 2
9:45 am—Registration Opens
10:15 am—Session begins
11:30 am—Session Concludes
Participants are encouraged to schedule a meeting with their legislators any-time after 11:40 am

Source: National Association of Social Workers North Carolina Chapter (nd). NASW-NC Advocacy Day. Retrieved from http://www.naswnc.org/?page=292 on June 2, 2016.

in some instances, brief workshops on lobbying tips. The Texas NASW chap-ter, for example, prepared a webinar on the legislative day and posted it on the chapter's website prior to the actual legislative day (see http://www.naswtx. org/events/EventDetails.aspx?id=532740).

Bringing together dozens, and in many instances hundreds, of volunteers to lobby a legislative group requires a great deal of hands-on coordination. A general session starts the day with the group typically reconvening at the end of the day to share their results. Each volunteer completes a *Meeting Report* that summarizes his or her individual visits, outcomes, and possible next steps or follow-up (see Box 9.5). This form is essential to continue developing a successful legislative strategy.

Box 9.5

LEGISLATOR MEETING SUMMARY REPORT

Legislator Meeting Report Form

Date: _____

Name of Legislator: _____

District Represents: _____

Office Number: _____

Office Phone: _____

Contact with the Legislator

☐ Met personally with the legislator only

☐ Met personally with legislator and legislative staff

☐ Met personally with legislative staff

☐ Did not meet with anyone, left information

If the meeting included legislative staff, identify staff member(s).

Name: _____

Title/Position: _____

Contact Information: _____

(Attach copy of business card if available)

Did anyone else attend the meeting with you? Please list their names and associations they represent.

Issues Discussed

_____

_____

_____

☐ Supportive   ☐ Opposed   ☐ Not Sure

☐ Wants additional info

Provide additional comments on the back of this form.

Your Name: _____

E-mail/Phone_____

Agency/Organization:_____

City, State: _____

ELECTORAL POLITICS

Working with elected officials who support a social worker's issues is much easier than working with an individual who opposes the practitioner's efforts. In fact, it is common for a policy practitioner's efforts to focus on stopping a proposed bill rather than enhancing existing services. But why should social workers engage in electoral politics, in particular, volunteering in a candidate's election campaign? The answer is simple and obvious: If the candidate wins the election, she or he will be more inclined to listen to supporters, especially individuals who worked in the election. The goal of campaign work, also known as *electoral politics,* is to work for and help elect candidates to public office whose beliefs and philosophies reflect and support the social work profession's ideals. Electoral politics includes two components: *working in a candidate's campaign* and *running for office.*

Working in a Candidate's Campaign

Every candidate for any elected office, be it a local city council seat or for the office of President of the United States, needs volunteers and staff to help with the campaign. Volunteers help with a range of activities such as stuffing envelopes, staffing a phone bank, and distributing yard signs. The campaign itself is coordinated by a group of individuals, which most often includes the following positions:

- *Campaign Manager*—overall coordinator and manager of the campaign; must work well under pressure and possess excellent supervision and problem-solving skills
- *Treasurer*—legally responsible for finances; submits campaign financial reports to appropriate public agencies
- *Steering Committee*—high-profile individuals who are respected in the broader community; they do not necessarily do day-to-day work; there name lends important credibility to the campaign
- *Campaign Committee*—experienced individuals who work closely with the campaign manager to help out the electoral strategy
- *Volunteer Coordinator*—second in importance to the campaign manager; ensures there are a sufficient number of volunteers for all facets of the operation
- *Scheduler*—responsible for screening requests for meetings and event appearances; works closely with the campaign manager
- *Fund Raiser*—works closely with the treasurer to ensure that necessary dollars are available to implement the campaign's work

The skill set of a social worker easily meets the demands of the majority of these campaign leadership positions as well as the ongoing volunteer tasks. For example, a campaign manager and volunteer coordinator need to be experienced in working with people, able to build effective relationships, and have the ability to keep sight of the desired outcome; similarly, social workers are experts in communication and, as a result, can be very effective phone bank volunteers.

So what is the initial step for the policy practitioner in electoral politics? Policy practice introduces the social worker to a number of politically inclined individuals, some of whom already hold elective positions while others are considering a run for office. Policy practice helps the social worker identify individuals who understand and support the profession's values. A social worker may support a number of candidates but because of limited time can only work in one campaign.

Once deciding on the candidate to support, the social worker contacts the candidate directly, the campaign manager, or the volunteer coordinator and simply says, "What can I do to help the campaign?" Best practice dictates that the social worker should be a consistent volunteer, an individual the campaign team can count on. A typical fall election cycle begins around Labor Day in September with the election held approximately 9 weeks later on the first Tuesday in November.

A social worker can help the campaign immensely by recruiting other social workers to join the electoral team. A proactive strategy is for a group of social workers to commit one night each week for the duration of the fall election to staff the campaign office. The social workers might wear t-shirts or large buttons with a statement such as "Social Workers for _____"; this positive engagement promotes the profession while letting the campaign staff and the candidate know that social workers are part of the electoral team.

A social worker can host a house party or gathering for social work colleagues to meet the candidate. The gathering creates a unique opportunity for the nominee to learn about the concerns of the profession while also potentially broadening the campaign's volunteer pool as well as receiving possible donations.

A very important electoral task is the *Get Out the Vote* (GOTV) operation, which often makes the difference between success and defeat on election day. A GOTV campaign identifies potential supporters and works to make sure they actually vote. Developing a database of potential supporters through a phone bank and neighborhood door-to-door campaign is among the most cost-effective and beneficial activities to a campaign. If the volunteer learns an individual is supportive of the candidate, the voter's name and contact information are recorded; the individual is also asked if he or she would like to put up a yard sign. A basic rule in phone bank and door-to-door campaigns is *Never Argue With The Voter*; if the voter does not support the candidate, simply say "Thank you" and hang up the phone or go to the next door. If the person being visited or called is not home or does not answer the phone, a door hanger or phone message should be left saying something to the effect of "I stopped by (or called) on behalf of ____(candidate's name) but you weren't home. I hope that I can meet you sometime soon to discuss the issues that are important to you."

About one week prior to the actual Election Day, the GOTV campaign shifts into full gear with a *voter blitz*. The blitz utilizes the database developed through the door-to-door and phone bank efforts; volunteers call each supporter to remind them to vote on Election Day; door-to-door literature drops also are the final direct

Table 9.6. PRE-ELECTION VOTING DAY OPTIONS, JANUARY 2016

State	In-Person	By Mail			
		No Excuse Absentee	Absentee, Excuse Required	All Mail Voting	Permanent Absentee Status
Alabama			•		
Alaska	•	•		(a)	
Arizona	•	•		(a)	•
Arkansas	•		•	(a)	
California	•	•		(a)	•
Colorado				•	
Connecticut			•		
Delaware			•		
D.C.	•	•			•
Florida	•	•		(a)	
Georgia	•	•			
Hawaii	•	•		(a)	•
Idaho	(b)	•		(a)	
Illinois	•	•			
Indiana	(b)		•		
Iowa	(b)	•			
Kansas	•	•		(a)	
Kentucky			•		
Louisiana	•		•		
Maine	(b)	•			
Maryland	•	•		(a)	
Massachusetts	(c)		•		
Michigan			•		
Minnesota	(b)	•		(a)	•
Mississippi			•		
Missouri			•	(a)	
Montana	(b)	•		(a)	•
Nebraska	•	•		(a)	
Nevada	•	•		(a)	
New Hampshire			•		

Table 9.6. CONTINUED

State	In-Person	By Mail			
		No Excuse Absentee	Absentee, Excuse Required	All Mail Voting	Permanent Absentee Status
New Jersey	(b)	•		(a)	•
New Mexico	•	•		(a)	
New York			•		
North Carolina	•	•			
North Dakota	•	•		(a)	
Ohio	(b)	•			
Oklahoma	(b)	•			
Oregon				•	
Pennsylvania			•		
Rhode Island			•		
South Carolina			•		
South Dakota	(b)	•			
Tennessee	•		•		
Texas	•		•		
Utah	•	•			•
Vermont	(b)	•			
Virginia			•		
Washington				•	
West Virginia	•		•		
Wisconsin	(b)	•			
Wyoming	(b)	•			
TOTAL	**34 states + DC**	**27 states + DC**	**20 states**	**3 states**	**7 states + DC**

Source: National Conference of State Legislatures, January 2016. Retrieved from http://www.ncsl.org/research/elections-and-campaigns/absentee-and-early-voting.aspx on April 18, 2016.

(a) Certain elections may be held entirely by mail. The circumstances under which all-mail elections are permitted vary from state to state.

(b) Although these states do not have Early Voting in the traditional sense, within a certain period of time before an election they do allow a voter to apply in person for an absentee ballot (without an excuse) and cast that ballot in one trip to an election official's office. This is often known as "in-person absentee" voting.

(c) Massachusetts has Early Voting only during even-year November elections, beginning in 2016. Currently it does not permit Early Voting in primaries or municipal elections.

mail piece to reinforce the candidate's message and remind people to vote. With the growing accessibility and use of social media, texting, Tweets, and emails are now common reminder tactics employed by campaigns.

A well-honed GOTV effort also develops strategies to make sure supporters take advantage of early voting, absentee voting, and mail voting. Most states employ one of these alternative pre-election voting methods (see Table 9.6). Reaching out to residents of nursing homes, self-assisted care, and other residential facilities leads to an often-untapped voter base.

A last GOTV consideration is making sure that potential voters have transportation to the polls on Election Day. Campaigns use volunteer drivers to take people to the polls; obviously, the driver should be able to carry on a conversation with a stranger—a basic social work skill—concerning the candidate. Also, the candidate's campaign literature is available in the car to be given to the voter on the way to the polling location.

Running for Office

The idea of a social worker running for and winning an elective local, state, or national office is not unheard of and is becoming more common with each election cycle. For a moment, consider the knowledge, skills, and experiences a social worker brings to the political arena. Social workers understand the complexities of social issues and the negative consequences for people and their communities if left unattended; social workers are remarkably skilled in communication and relationship building; social workers understand and appreciate the value of difference and diversity; and social workers are adept at building coalitions among diverse groups. All of these create a unique springboard for a social worker to enter the world of electoral politics.

The social worker policy practitioner who runs for a political office ensures that her or his ideas are presented to the electorate throughout a campaign. And, if elected, the social worker is in a position to translate her or his philosophies into legislation. It is not unheard of for social workers to run for various local, state, and national offices and win. Many of these individuals go on to have long careers in politics. Social worker and Senator Barbara A. Mikulski (D-MD) was initially elected to the US Senate in 1986 and in March 2012 became the longest serving woman in the history of the US Congress[2]; among her many committee assignments, Mikulski was the senior member of the Senate's Health, Education, Labor, and Pensions Committee, which had oversight for education, labor, health care and services for seniors, long-term care, and women's health (Mikilski, n.d.). Social worker and Texas State Representative Elliott Naishtat was first elected to the Texas House of

---

2. Senator Mikulski retired from the US Senate in 2017.

Representatives in 1990 and had been re-elected 13 times prior to his retirement in 2017; his background as a social worker helped him as a member of the Human Services Committee and Vice Chair of the Public Health Committee (Texas House of Representatives, n.d.). The National Association of Social Workers compiles a list of social workers holding local and state elected office (see Appendix 3).

Merely wanting to run for an office and actually doing it are two very different things. Any candidate for public office must first take a personal inventory—is there time to conduct a campaign, is the candidate's family/partner supportive, does the person have the drive to win, and what is the individual's fundraising ability? Political parties as well as private consulting firms offer workshops on how to launch and run a campaign; anyone interested in running for an office should attend such training opportunities. The best training ground, however, is to have worked as a volunteer or staff person in someone else's electoral bid. Direct experiences such as these are invaluable when running for an elective office.

A social worker who is considering running for elective office should contact other social workers who have traveled down this same path. These individuals can share their experiences, observations, "dos and don'ts," and what it means to hold an elected position. The individual should not be shy about contacting others for help; if one is hesitant in doing so, then he or she probably should not be running for a public office.

Finally, a social worker should contact his or her state's NASW PACE Committee or other social work groups that are politically inclined to see what insight or guidance they can give related to any endorsement process as well as fundraising ideas.

VOTER REGISTRATION CAMPAIGN

Voter registration programs have a long history in the United States as a mechanism to recruit supporters for candidates and issues. Historically and currently, there have been and continue to be scores of voter registration programs all with the similar objective: to register individuals to vote.

- On August 26, 1920, the 19th Amendment to the US Constitution was ratified "enfranchising all American women and declaring for the first time that they, like men, deserve all the rights and responsibilities of citizenship." On Election Day in 1920, millions of American women exercised their right to vote for the first time (History, n.d.).
- The National Congress of American Indians, first organized in 1944, focuses on four areas, including: Get-Out-The-Vote and registration efforts; election and voter protection awareness and advocacy; voter and candidate education; and tribal access to data (National Congress of American Indians, 2001–2006).
- In 1964, a voter registration drive called the Mississippi Summer Project, whose purpose was to register African Americans while expanding their

voting throughout the South, played a pivotal in the Civil Rights movement (Foner & Garraty, 1991). The historic summer effort was "comprised of black Mississippians and more than 1,000 out-of-state, predominately white volunteers, (who) faced constant abuse and harassment . . . (by) the Ku Klux Klan, police and . . . state and local authorities" and led to the murders of three volunteers, New Yorkers Michael Schwerner and Andrew Goodman, and a local Afro-American, James Chaney (Foner & Garraty, 1991).

- VotoLatino, organized in 2004, uses voter registration as a key ongoing program to empower the Latino community across the United States (VotoLatino, 2015).

Voter registration projects are an important strategy for reaching out and empowering underrepresented groups of people to be actively engaged in the political process. Unfortunately, organizing and implementing a registration project is not easy and is fraught with challenges. Historically, barriers were built to deny people the right to vote, and such roadblocks continue well into the 21st century. Accusations that states are working to limit voting rights are common among national and state organizations. The National Association of Colored Persons (NAACP) notes that there are numerous obstacles to voting "among them the implementation of mandatory identification and 'purge' programs by states, the failure of designated registration entities to carry out their responsibilities, and the use of voter suppression tactics" (NAACP Legal Defense and Educational Fund, n.d.). The League of Women Voters writes, "many states have developed laws, rules or procedures that limit access to the ballot box" (League of Women Voters, n.d.). The American Civil Liberties Union argues that persons with disabilities face significant barriers to voter registration opportunities (Minzer & Smith, 2015).

There is no single law that creates a standard, uniform procedure for voter registration. The 2002 Help America Vote Act established minimum standards for voting systems by mandating states to improve their election procedures, including modernizing their voting machines and strengthening registration processes. The actual implementation of the 2002 law was left to the individual state's discretion and, as a result, each state has its own rules and regulations governing voter registration.

The first step in a registration campaign is to review a particular jurisdiction's rules. There is a specific office or a department in every state responsible for its elections. Not unexpectedly, these offices' names differ from state to state. For example, among the more common titles are the Department of Elections (Delaware), Elections Division (Arkansas), State Board of Elections (Kentucky), Office of Elections (Hawaii), and State Election Board (Oklahoma). Complete understanding of a state's registration regulations is crucial to ensure that those who are registered are done so legally. The American Association of University Women (AAUW) stresses it is important to know the answers to the following questions before conducting a registration project:

- How long before the election do voters need to be registered to be eligible to vote? (Remember that there are primary and general elections, each with different voter registration deadlines.)
- What is the age requirement for volunteers registering people to vote?
- Do voters need to declare a party affiliation?
- What are the rules for people who have been convicted of a felony?
- How must registration forms be submitted to election officials?
- What is the required length of residency prior to an individual registering to vote?
- Are college students eligible to register to vote in the locality and state where they are enrolled?
- Is there a required training for volunteers to be able to register voters? (AAUW, n.d.)

An individual can register to vote when applying for a driver's license, and a growing number of local governments offer online registration sites. An important objective for a voter registration campaign is to develop a database of potential supporters for an upcoming election. The social worker's follow-up communications with these new registered voters are designed to (1) get them to vote and (2) support their issue and/or candidate(s).

There are two typical approaches to voter registration other than through driver's license registration and local government online websites: *outdoor canvassing* or *staffing a table/booth*. In both methods, individuals complete the necessary registration form, are offered election and polling place information, and provided information on the advocacy issue or preferred candidate. Most important, every attempt is made to get the new registrant's name and contact information for follow-up purposes. No matter what, never argue with the person; if he or she says "No, I am not giving you my name," be pleasant and say, "Thank you" but still attempt to register the person.

Outdoor canvassing involves volunteers, typically in small groups of two to three persons, going door to door in neighborhoods or stopping people in a mall or on a major street and asking them to register. The canvassing can be especially productive in places where there are large gatherings of people, including festivals or special events. Permission is generally required from an event's organizer or from local officials to carry out the canvassing; again, state and local rules need to be checked.

A booth or table set up for a local event, at a faith-based service/activity, or in front of a store is a common method to register individuals. The volunteers should be outgoing and able to engage strangers in conversation in a positive, friendly manner. Staffing a voter registration booth or canvassing a community involves the same skills:

- *Eye Contact.* Looking directly at a person is vital for engaging and establishing credibility with the individual.

- *Assuming Support.* Be self-assured and assume the individual will register.
- *Body Language.* The volunteers should not sit behind the table but be out in front of it. The volunteers should be outgoing, happy, and enthusiastic. The volunteers should approach people because passers-by will rarely approach a table on their own.
- *Accuracy.* At a minimum, they need to check each registration card to ensure it is legible, complete, and accurate. Follow County Election Officials' rules (Project HOME).

It is commonplace for individuals to be apprehensive about and resistant to registering. Social workers certainly are familiar with the dynamics of resistance, which is a common phenomenon in all helping relationships. Box 9.6 offers common roadblock questions or statements that indicate a hesitance toward registering. The suggested responses reflect an understanding of the individual's feelings while not being domineering or forceful. Rather, the key to success is to frame comments in a gentle, respectful, but persuasive manner.

Finally, a voter registration effort can gain legitimacy from a local official governmental proclamation. These documents are generally issued by a local government office (i.e., mayor, city council, state representatives) or county select board. Having a local mayor declare a certain week as "Voter Registration Week" adds valuable publicity to the effort. Guidelines and procedures on obtaining a proclamation are listed on the government's website; search phrases include "City Proclamation Guidelines," "Requests for a Proclamation," "Proclamation Requests," "Mayoral Proclamations," or "Ceremonial Documents."

Box 9.6

VOTER REGISTRATION RAPS AND TIPS, COMMON RESPONSES

VOTER REGISTRATION RAPS AND TIPS

VOTER REGISTRATION COMMON RESPONSES

Excuse : I'm in a hurry.
Response : "No problem. We'll get this done in 20 seconds. What's your last name?"

Excuse : I don't want Jury Duty.
Response : "Actually, juries are not only selected by voter rolls anymore. They use drivers' license, tax forms, and many other sources. What's your last name?"

Excuse : My vote doesn't count.
Response : "I hear you. A lot of times it's difficult to see how one vote makes a difference. That's why we're part of a campaign to get 5,000 folks to the polls. You and I both know that 5,000 votes count. So, what's your last name?"

Excuse : Politicians are all liars. They don't care about us.
Response : "I know what you mean. Many politicians seem to care more about the wealthy than they do about you and me. That's why I'm out here registering voters, so that we make them listen to regular folks like us. What's your last name?"

Excuse : I don't do politics.
Response : "You know there are a lot of us who are frustrated with politics. That's why we're talking about the issues affecting our daily lives: things like access to affordable health care, decent living wages, quality education. Forget about the politics; I know we both want to have our voices heard on these issues. So, what's your last name?"

Excuse : I'm cool.
Response : "I know: that's why you're registering to vote. What's your last name?"

Excuse : I'm not a resident.
Response : "Do you live here now? You actually only have to have lived in Pennsylvania for 30 days prior to the election."

Excuse : I'm not from Philadelphia." *or* "I'm from out of town." *or* "I'm not from here.
Response : "Do you live in Pennsylvania? This form is Pennsylvania State-wide."

Excuse : I never have voted, never will.
Response : "You know, I never used to register voters before, but this year is the year to start. It's never too late to get your voice heard on the issues that concern you the most. So, how do you spell your last name, then?"

Excuse : I'll take care of it later.
Response : "Here, I'll just get you done real quick. It'll take 20 seconds and I'll save you the postage. What's your last name?"

Excuse : I don't want to give you my information.

Response : Your information will not be shared or sold for any purposes. Plus the election is completely confidential and your voting information is protected by law.

Excuse : I don't have time.

Response : I know you are really busy. Filling out this form only takes a couple of minutes, and I can make sure it gets turned in for you. You can save time by registering with me today.

Excuse : I can't register to vote.

Response : May I ask why not? I am trained on eligibility for voting and may be able to help you.

Please return all forms and pledge cards to 1515 Fairmount Ave. Call 215-232-7272, ext. 3042 or ext. 3061 if you have questions or problems. *Updated: 2/19/16*

Source: Vote for Holmes Coalition (February 19, 2016). Voter registration raps and tips. Retrieved from https://projecthome.org/posts/2016/02/voter-registration-materials-2016 on June 3, 2016.

A FEW FINAL THOUGHTS

Policy practice takes many forms and takes place in a variety of settings. From working in campaigns, testifying to a legislative committee, to canvassing a neighborhood to register persons to vote, the social worker's role and tasks are varied and different. Testifying before a committee can be nerve racking but exciting and certainly fruitful; helping persons to register to vote reflects one of social work's core beliefs of empowerment; running for elective office exposes oneself to full public scrutiny. Suffice to say, policy practice is not easy.

The actual skills, techniques, and employed policy practice strategies are not foreign to a social worker. Social work education and resulting practice provides the individual practitioner the opportunity to hone her or his talents in such a manner that is equally applicable in both clinical and macro settings. Social work indeed is a unique profession that can make an incredible difference in the lives of people, groups, and communities.

REFERENCES

AAUW. (n.d.). How to organize a voter registration drive. Retrieved from http://www.aauw. org/resource/organize-a-voter-registration-drive/ on April 10, 2016.

Bein, A. (2008). *The Zen of helping: Spiritual principles for mindful and open-hearted practice.* Hoboken, NJ: John Wiley & Sons, Inc.

City of Columbus, Ohio. (2016). Rules for speaking at Columbus city council. Retrieved from https://columbus.gov/council/toolkit/rules-for-speaking-at-city-council/ on March 12, 2016.

City of Rockford, Illinois. (December 30, 2015). Wards and alderman. Retrieved from http://www.rockfordil.gov/wards-and-aldermen.aspx on March 12, 2016.

City of Rocky Mount, North Carolina. (2016). Agendas. Retrieved from http://rockymountnc.gov/government/mayor____city_council/agendas/ on March 12, 2016.

Edwards, J. K., & Bess, J. M. (1998). Developing effectiveness in the therapeutic use of self. *Clinical Social Work Journal, 26*(1), 89–105.

Eugene. (n.d.). Public participation. Retrieved from http://www.eugene-or.gov/524/Public-Participation on March 12, 2016.

Foner, E., & Garraty, J. A. (1991). The reader's companion to American history. Retrieved from Freedom Summer at http://www.history.com/topics/black-history/freedom-summer on April 18, 2016.

Gainesville, Georgia. (2016). Council meetings. Retrieved from http://www.gainesville.org/council-meeting on March 12, 2016.

Help America Vote Act of 2002. 107th Congress Public Law 252. 2002. Retrieved from https://www.gpo.gov/fdsys/pkg/PLAW-107publ252/html/PLAW-107publ252.htm on April 28, 2016.

History. (n.d.). The fight for women's suffrage. Retrieved from http://www.history.com/topics/womens-history/the-fight-for-womens-suffrage on April 16, 2016.

House Research Organization. (2015, March 4). House committee procedures: 84th legislative session. Texas House of Representatives. Retrieved from www.hro.house.state.tx.us/pdf/focus/compro84.pdf on February 10, 2017.

League of Women Voters. (n.d.). New barriers to voting: eroding the right to vote. Retrieved from http://library.lwv.org/content/new-barriers-voting-eroding-right-vote on April 14, 2016.

Lewis, J. J. (n.d.). Grace Hopper quotes. About women's history. Retrieved from http://womenshistory.about.com/od/quotes/a/grace_hopper.htm on June 12, 2016.

Minzer, S., & Smith, E. (2015). Access denied: barriers to online voter registration for citizens with disabilities. New York, NY: American Civil Liberties Union.

Montana 64th Session. (2015, June 11). Testifying before a committee. Retrieved from http://www.leg.mt.gov/css/About-the-Legislature/Lawmaking-Process/testify.asp on March 12, 2016.

NAACP Legal Defense and Educational Fund. (n.d.). Barriers to voting. Retrieved from http://www.naacpldf.org/case-issue/barriers-voting on April 16, 2016.

National Association of Social Workers. (2016). Code of ethics of the National Association of Social Workers. Retrieved from http://socialworkers.org/pubs/code/code.asp on April 10. 2016.

National Congress of American Indians (2001 2016). Native vote. Retrieved from http://www.ncai.org/initiatives/native-vote April 16, 2016.

Project HOME. (2016). Who we are. Retrieved from https://projecthome.org/about on June 3, 2016.

Senator Barbara A. Mikulski. (n.d.). Biography and principles. Retrieved from https://www.mikulski.senate.gov/about-barbara/biography on June 10, 2016.

Texas House of Representatives. (n.d.). Biography. Retrieved from http://www.house.state.tx.us/members/member-page/?district=49 on June 10, 2016.

VotoLatino. (2015). What we do. Retrieved from http://votolatino.org/what-we-do/#our-work on April 18, 2016.

Washington State Legislature. (n.d.). How to testify in committee. Retrieved from http://leg.wa.gov/legislature/Pages/Testify.aspx on March 12, 2016.

CHAPTER 10

Social Media, Info Sheets, and Other Tools for Effective Communication

Discussion in previous chapters examined techniques for writing issue analyses, policy briefs, and preparing and delivering written testimony; also examined were methods for presenting findings or making recommendations to an NGO board of directors and/or legislative committees.

Social workers recognize and fully appreciate that communication is an art and a science. The art involves the piecing together of words and crafting sentences that clearly express concepts and ideas in an understandable manner; the science is relying on tested communication techniques that provide the pathway for recognizing the message's full intent. There are two important sayings that underlie the art and science of communication:

- "How it is said is just as important as what is said."
- "Words are important."

Messages, presentations, and handouts must be clear, crisp, and to the point. The era of long-winded presentations or 20-page research papers in the world of policy practice is over. Today, messages are framed in a direct manner with communications and responses expected to be nearly instantaneous, in a 24/7 global-wide contact mode. Taking advantage of the immense possibilities of digital technologies while linking them with time-tested policy practice communication tools affords the policy practitioner an opportunity to advocate for and craft justice-based social policies and services.

SOCIAL MEDIA

Social media is a powerful tool for building online communities that quickly and easily shares information with the public. The Pew Research Center reports that by 2015, 65% of American adults were actively using social networking sites (Perrin, 2015). The research also found that seniors, individuals over age 65, are not as technologically challenged as the myth purports, with 35% of those 65 and older using social media in 2015, compared with just 2% in 2005 (Perrin, 2015). Facebook, Twitter, Pinterest, YouTube, Instagram, Reddit, Google+, and blogging are among the various social media platforms that have and continue to demonstrate their power in organizing constituencies and diverse groups around social issues. We might think of these platforms as "virtual rooms" that offer unobstructed avenues for communication, coordination, and mobilization. Roane (2014) writes that there are

> thousands of possible of rooms in which to communicate . . .. [These rooms have] morphed into a mansion where myriad activities take place . . . a shopping mall, a banking center, a rotisserie league in fantasy baseball, a medical library, a classroom, a poker table, a convention, a fashion runway, a business forum, a matchmaking service, a photography studio and the therapist coach. (p. 71)

Technologies and related apps continue to evolve with new platforms becoming available on a daily basis with each site having its own rules and etiquette though they share a number of common customs (see Box 10.1 and Figure 10.1). The social work precept, the professional use-of-self, equally applies in the social media world as well as in day-to-day worker–client interactions. The policy practitioner who uses social media as a communication and an organizing tool must be fully attentive to a virtual room's particular boundaries and be able to recognize acceptable and unacceptable behaviors. The policy practitioner as the facilitator of a room sets its tone through her or his messages as well as models "best practices" for the community.

The power of social media as an information source and organizing tool is in its infancy stage as social advocates are continuing to learn how to harness the everchanging possibilities of digital technology. One thing is certain, however: Social media has enormous potential to create and sustain change as it has metamorphosed from being an entertainment tool into a global arena for political movements.

On the fun side, social media created the *flash mob*, where individuals met at a preordained location and time to perform an unusual, often humorous, and pointless act (Goldschmidt, 2011; Wasik, 2011). However, its influence on local, national, or global matters rests with its ability to report and monitor human events

Box 10.1

SAMPLING OF SHARED CUSTOMS AND ETIQUETTE FOR SOCIAL MEDIA

- Become familiar with the tutorials that provide information for each platform.
- Don't upload or write anything that you wouldn't want revealed in front of your favorite grandparent.
- Be aware that postings are checked by potential employers and others.
- Don't write in CAPS because this comes across as shouting.
- Before sending or posting any message, reread it to be sure it should be sent.
- Check who you are sending a message to. Did you hit "reply all" when you meant to only reply to the sender and not the group?
- Keep it brief, most of the time.
- When we count words (to create a brief message), we may be discounting our message.
- Take personal responsibility for the content that you publish on blogs, wikis, or any other public forum.
- Don't use ethnic slurs, personal insults, obscenity, or engage in any online conduct that would not be acceptable at work.
- Respond to all comments as quickly as you can.
- Know the art of the hashtag. 1 hashtag is fine. 10 hashtags are not.
- Don't *Like* your own post.
- Don't post or tag photos of fans, customers, or employees without permission.

Source: Roane, S. (2014). How to work a room. New York, NY: HarperCollinss; James, G. (2014, May 1). 13 social media rules to live by. Retrieved from http://www.inc.com/geoffrey-james/ 13-social-media-rules-to-live-by.html on February 3, 2017; Lee, K. (2015, March 2). The 29 most common social media rules: Which ones are real? Which ones are breakable? Buffer. Received from https://blog.bufferapp.com/social-media-rules-etiquette on February 3, 2017.

instantaneously in all corners of the world. Horrific events, which at one time had no visual evidence to document incidents, are now no longer cloaked in a shroud of secrecy. The world watched the Arab Spring in December 2010 unfold on both television and through social media outlets. A study of the impact of Facebook and Twitter on the Arab Spring noted that nine out of ten Egyptians and Tunisians used Facebook to raise awareness within their countries as well as around the world in the ongoing civil movements to help organize activists (Mourtada & Salem, 2011, p. 6). In the United States, a series of social media posts in July 2016 involving the deaths of African Americans shot by police officers in Minnesota and Louisiana, which followed similar shootings in other US cities "stoked outrage around the country" and led to violent protests in numerous cities across the United States. In

Figure 10.1.
Day without immigrants.
Source: Retrieved from Facebook.com on February 16, 2017.

February 2017, social media, in particular Facebook (see Table 10.1), became the national organizing vehicle for a "Day Without Immigrants" (Ngo, 2017), which was a " boycott, a response to President Trump's pledges to crack down on those in the country illegally, use 'extreme vetting' and build a wall along the Mexican border" (Stein, 2017). The boycott called "for immigrants not to attend work, open their businesses, spend money or even send their children to school" (Stein, 2017). Word was spread through various social media platforms and, as a result, thousands of businesses quickly joined the national protest to show their opposition to the Trump Administration's executive order for immigration.

Social media continues to evolve as new virtual rooms update "live" transmissions, such as Facebook Live and Periscope, which allow individuals to interact with and be part of an event in real time. For policy practice, the possibilities of live postings are endless from streaming speeches and rallies to interviews with legislators and key informants. Live streaming of events will enhance immediate, up-to-date communications with the public and further engage a constituency even if they are not physically present at an event.

Table 10.1. DOS AND DON'TS OF SOCIAL MEDIA

Content	Suggestions	Potential Pitfalls	URLs
Short status updates	Post informative, interesting, or engaging updates, e.g., I am presenting a poster at conference X, come and say hi!" "Has anyone got experience with technique Y?"	Avoid boring or too personal updates (e.g., "I just had a sandwich"), gossip, personal attacks, or excessive negative feelings. Be aware of the sensitive nature of posting about unpublished data, proposals, reviews, collaborators, students, etc.	http://www.twitter.com www.facebook.com
Longer text	Informative: current research, new papers, conference reports. Discussion: Opinion pieces, reflections, and creative writing	Shorter texts (500–700) words are more likely to be read in full. Use images, hyperlinks, or multimedia to make text more engaging. Avoid jargon.	http://www.wordpress.com http://www.blogger.com http://www.tumblr.com https://plus.google.com/
Photos	Snapshots from live research, lab/field trips. Data that might not be published otherwise. Use tags or hashtags to contribute to existing image pools and make images accessible.	Avoid using pictures protected under copyright or without appropriate creator attribution, photos of people without having their permission, images you might want to use in a publication.	http://www.flickr.com http://www.pinterest.com http://www.instagram.com http://www.facebook.com
Video	Short clips taken with camera or smartphone Interviews, techniques, lectures and talks	Make use of captions to provide additional information. Think about appropriate length (shorter might reach more people). Avoid using copyrighted music.	http://www.youtube.com http://www.vimeo.com http://www.vine.co
Links	Use link shorteners to save space and track clicks.	Avoid posting links without any or with a vague description.	http://www.twitter.com http://www.reddit.com https://plus.google.com/ http://www.facebook.com
Audio	Soundbites of field trips, events. Longer audio pieces, e.g., interviews, recordings of talks or podcasts	For longer pieces, pay attention to microphone quality and acoustics of the surroundings.	http://www.audioboo.com

Table 10.1. CONTINUED

Content	Suggestions	Potential Pitfalls	URLs
Publications and CV items	Invest time to create a professional online presence and keep it up to date.	Before uploading full-text versions or preprints, carefully check publisher conditions.	http://www.academia.edu http://www.researchgate.net http://www.linkedin.com

Source: Osterrieder, A. (2013, July 11). The value and use of social media as communication tool in the plant sciences. Biomed Central. Retrieved from http://plantmethods.biomedcentral.com/articles/10.1186/1746-4811-9-26 on May 18, 2016.

As a policy practice tool, social media is much more than posting a picture, an article, or a link to a particular website. A well-organized social media campaign engages its constituency in a back-and-forth dialogue with interactions multidirectional between the policy practitioner and constituents and the constituents with each other. A constant open forum built on a broad-based, integrated social media model fosters a sense of identity, connection, and ownership, all of which help strengthen and support a change effort.

A cautionary note needs to be discussed before moving any deeper into the role of social media and policy practice. A common error in today's social media world is the mixing of personal communications with work-related messages. It is common to read postings that share private information, such as eating a sandwich at a certain restaurant or checking into a hotel. Such messages, while appropriate for personally directed media postings, *are neither suitable nor applicable* for a work-related site. Conversely, posting a link to a policy-specific news article and asking for comments on a personal page does not engage followers with the issue (see Table 10.1). Sharing personal information is fraught with potential pitfalls that in the end can hurt the policy practitioner's efforts. The most effective way to ensure there is a clear distinction between work and personal communiqués is to maintain separate, work-only and personal accounts on the various platforms.

An organized policy practice cause should have a *Digital Coordinator,* who is responsible for coordinating the social media campaign, including screening of potential messages and monitoring all postings. The policy practitioner cannot undertake such a task given her or his overall coordination of the issue campaign. The social worker does maintain direct and consistent contact with the Digital Coordinator to ensure that upcoming events, new info sheets, and dashboards are posted in a timely manner. The social worker should also maintain a constant presence in the virtual rooms by posting her or his comments or responding to comments/suggestions made by others. At a minimum, the policy practitioner should post at least once a day, although it is better to comment a minimum of three times each day, typically in the morning, noontime, and late afternoon. Multiple postings send a clear message to a constituency that the social worker is actively engaged in the campaign. On the other hand, the public might interpret a lack of postings to mean the policy practitioner is neither working nor involved with the particular issue.

Numerous digital platforms and social media venues are available free of charge to support ongoing communications between individuals, groups, and organizations. A robust social media approach utilizes a variety of different platforms, with one serving as the hub or central communication base. An effective social media campaign recognizes that the majority of individuals, groups, or organizations are not sophisticated in all social media platforms. Thus, a well-thought-out strategy incorporates a number of different virtual rooms to ensure the information is shared as quickly as possible to a broad audience. A primary platform, which is the most commonly used room among the constituency, serves as the hub that links with other platforms to ensure people can access information through a virtual room with which they are familiar and access. There is no one preferred hub to all policy practice social media campaigns. A hub should always reflect the level of use by the targeted audience (see Figure 10.2).

Understanding a constituency's preferences for social media venues increases the prospect of reaching a broader audience. The initial questions asked when organizing a social media campaign include, Who is the targeted audience, What are their preferred social media platforms, How often do they participate in social media (i.e., once a day, once and hour, etc.), and Do they have different preferred times to

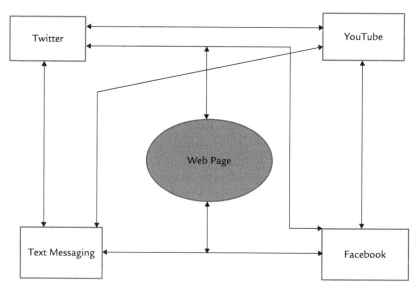

Figure 10.2.
A generic model for a social media campaign.

be on social media? For example, younger persons, ages 14–17, favor in descending order YouTube, Facebook, and SnapChat. Research shows that adults between the ages of 35 and 54, prefer Facebook, YouTube, and Twitter. In 2014, Facebook and YouTube were the two most accessed platforms, more than double the use of other sites such as Twitter, Instagram, Google+, Snapchat, Vine, WhatsApp, Reddit, Pinterest, and Tumblr (Bennett, 2014). In addition to these platforms, texting is a widely used digital communication method; Fox (2011) found that nearly one third of adults prefer to receive a text message than to be called on their mobile phone. The data suggest that to reach a broad, diverse spectrum of people, the minimum core social media pieces for the policy practitioner to utilize include texting, Facebook, and Twitter (see Figure 10.2). But it is important to remember that the popularity of these virtual rooms may lessen over time and as new more advanced venues become available.

1. *Texting.* Email facilitates quick and easy messaging, but research shows that most email messages are not read (Jordan, 2013). *SMS* (Short Message Service), more commonly called *texting,* is a short message, up to 160 characters, though longer messages are automatically split into several parts (Triggs, 2013). According to the Pew Research Center, in 2011, 73% of adult cell phone owners texted while 95% of young adults, ages 18–29, send or receive an average of 87.7 text messages each day; conversely, adults between the ages of 50 and 64 send or receive approximately 11 messages each day (Smith, 2011). In other words, cell phones with their texting capabilities have become a staple and an acceptable means for social interaction (Hyman, 2014), though younger users show a greater likelihood of texting compared to older individuals.

2. *Facebook.* A Facebook page built around the specific policy issue provides a focal point to share information with interested people, collaborative partners, and supporters. Posting information on Facebook related to legislative hearings, a lobby day, policy briefs, and other information is accessible to the public. A typical informational posting for any event includes its date, time, location, when people should arrive to fill up the meeting room, what to wear, and where to park. As soon as possible following the event, pictures are posted with messages from the policy practitioner and event participants.

   Setting up a Facebook page is simple (see https://www.facebook.com/pages/create.php). The first step is to select a category for the group. Of the six categories, the *Cause or Community* group is best suited for policy practice issues. Once basic information for the initial setup is completed (i.e., description of issue, links to partner groups, and upload possible pictures), the page is ready to be open to the group. An important and useful characteristic of Facebook is its posting options, which include plain text status, photos with captions, links with captions, videos with captions, an event page, and a location check-in. The location check-in allows for real-time posting, whereas the other tools create opportunities to build a robust up-to-date communication tool.

3. *Twitter.* Twitter is an extremely mobile-friendly technology that allows the social worker to communicate with large groups instantaneously at the same time. According to Twitter, in June 2016, there were 313,000,000 active monthly users with 83% using mobile phones, and 1 billion unique visits monthly to sites with embedded Tweets (Twitter, 2016). The global community, however, dominates its use, with Twitter reporting that 79% of all accounts are outside the United States (Twitter, 2016). These data show that Twitter use in the Unitd States, in 2016, was in its infancy stage but as with other digital technologies, its usage will grow as more people become familiar with its possibilities.

Twitter is probably best known for its use of "hashtags," # and "@" for username. The # symbol indexes words and phrases and allows people to follow a conversation or topic, while the @ sign is used for mentioning or replying to other users. Hashtagged words that become widespread become *Trending Topics*, which are popular at a particular moment in time, rather than topics that were widely shared for a previous period. Trending Topics helps the individual discern the most up-to-the-minute emerging topics of discussion on Twitter.

Signing up for a Twitter account is easy and free of charge. The Web link https:// twitter.com/ provides easy access to the sign-up page. For advocacy purposes, the social worker creates a policy issue–specific Twitter account for others "to follow" and learn of updates and matters related to the issue. The policy practitioner encourages issue supporters, including individuals, groups, and organizations, to create a Twitter account and "follow" the social worker's issue-specific Twitter account. To "follow" someone is an unpretentious three-step process (see Box 10.2). New users will find Twitter to be a simple platform to use while allowing messages and updates to be shared quickly, nearly in real time.

Searching the Web with a phrase such as *best techniques to communicate with Twitter* results in millions of different websites. Some sites identify as few as seven tips (Foley, 2015), 12 tips (Blakley, 2012; Walter, 2016), 31 tips (Krogue, 2013), and as many as 50 tips (Urban, 2014). At a minimum, a good tweet begins with a catchy headline or title, uses shortened links, uses hashtags, and is fewer than 140 characters. The tweet should avoid abbreviations, slang, and professional jargon because some readers may not be familiar with them, resulting in vague and misunderstood messages.

Utilized correctly, social media becomes the glue that holds a group of people together around an issue. Additionally, social media recruits new supporters to join a campaign. Names collected on sign-in sheets from public meetings and members of collaborative groups and organizations are the initial consumer base in the social media strategy. These individuals should be encouraged to *invite* their family and friends to sign up on the various platforms; additionally, supporters are encouraged to repost the various messages, postings, and tweets. The more active and broader the communication, the greater the potential becomes to expand the issue's support base, which in turn results in stronger political leveraging.

Box 10.2

TWITTER—HOW TO FOLLOW SOMEONE ON TWITTER

Step 1: Tap the **Search** icon on the main menu at the top of the Twitter app. Enter the name of the person you want to follow and then tap that person's name on the list of search results to load the person's profile page.

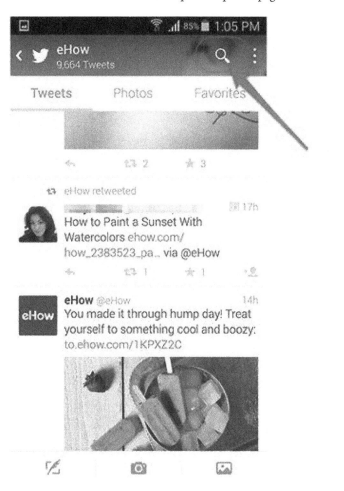

Step 2: Tap the **Follow** button on the profile page to begin following that person.

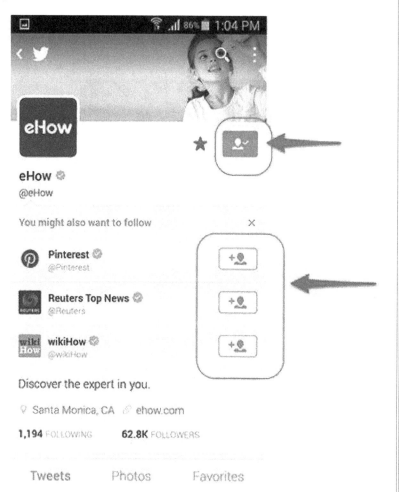

Step 3: After you tap the Follow button, it turns blue and a checkmark appears, indicating that you are now following the account. The Twitter app displays a list of related accounts you may also want to follow. Tap the **Follow** icon next to any of these suggested accounts to begin following them.

Source: Tennyson, A. (March 31, 2015). How to follow someone on twitter. Teachwlla. Retrieved from

https://www.techwalla.com/articles/how-to-follow-someone-on-twitter on February 3, 2017.

INFO SHEETS

An info sheet is a brief, generally one-page handout that provides specific information on an issue (see Figure 10.3). The purpose of an info sheet, also referred to as a *fact sheet*, is to encourage the reader to take action on a specific topic (Health Advocacy Tool Box, n.d.). This document provides a brief overview of an issue while providing key information in an easily understood format. Typically, an info sheet includes numbers, tables, and charts each augmented with brief written statements.

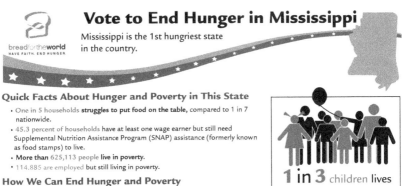

Figure 10.3.
Example of Info Sheet.
Source: Bread for the World. (2016, February 24). Hunger and poverty state fact sheets. Retrieved from http://www.bread.org/library/hunger-and-poverty-state-fact-sheets-2016 on May 12, 2016.

The key challenge in designing an effective info sheet is balancing the key data with the written statements. Too much data can be confusing, whereas too little does not shed light on the problem; furthermore, an overly wordy info sheet is difficult to review quickly. A key point for an effective info sheet is that *it should take no more than 30 seconds to read.* Some key pieces for a useful info sheet include the following:

- It should be easy to read at a glance, with at least 12- to 14-point font.
- Title of info sheet is prominent.
- Include contact information.
- Key information is highlighted and the first item presented on the info sheet.
- Information is self-contained; do not refer to other fact sheets or previous documents.
- Use bullets when possible.
- Leave a lot of white space.
- Bold key words and use text boxes and graphics to emphasize significant points.
- Simple graphs and charts provide key information with just a glance. Pie charts are the easiest to understand.
- Use color throughout to highlight different points (Center for Rural Health; Health Advocacy Tool Box; Suess, 2011–2016).

Info sheet data must be up to date and from reputable sources. Cutting and pasting Web-sourced information may result in misinformation; the accuracy of a Web source data must be 100% reliable (see Chapter 4, Box 4.2). When it comes to pulling together data and statements from various sources, the policy practitioner must always *verify, verify, verify* (Community Tool Box, 2016).

Each time a social worker visits a legislator or his or her staff, the social worker should leave an info sheet; if visiting the same legislator or staff on multiple occasions, the social worker should provide different info sheets to broaden understanding of the issue. When using multiple fact sheets on a specific issue, it can be easy to confuse which info sheets were left at which office. One way to diffuse this problem is to build a multiweek info-sheet strategy, with one fact sheet distributed the entire first week and a different info sheet disseminated each succeeding week. As info sheets are developed, they should be published in or linked to the various virtual rooms.

POLICY MEMOS AND BRIEFS

A *policy memo* or *policy brief* is a short presentation that offers information and recommendations on a particular social policy or issue to a legislator, a legislative committee, and related staffs. The memo or brief differs from an info sheet in that the former is a short written analysis, whereas the info sheet includes graphics that reflect the policy practitioner's position. The Woodrow Wilson School of Public and International Affairs (2014) notes that a policy memo "must be well-organized, clearly written and succinct, with a logical connection between the background information, evidence and conclusions/recommendation." The memo is not a lengthy research report, but a summation of findings and recommendations. The memo is written in a manner that is both specific and concise (hence the name "brief") and is devoid of dramatic presentations, jargon, clichés, and emotional language. A brief is written in a manner that is opposite to a college term paper. The most important information and any recommendations are provided first, whereas in a term paper, the case is developed first followed by the recommendations or conclusion.

Luciana Herman (2012) of the John F. Kennedy School of Public Policy identifies six sections that are included in a policy brief.

- BLUF Statement—*Bottom Line Up Front*
  - State the problem in terms specific to the policy maker.
  - Explain why a policy change is necessary.
  - Briefly detail the problem with a focus on the issue, not its background.
- Explain the Pros and Cons of the Issue
  - Review the current policy(s).
  - Explain why change is necessary.
- Explain the Recommendation(s)
  - Lay out an argument for why this option(s) is better.
- Implementation or Next Steps
  - Identify how and when to implement the findings; identify significant risks or obstacles.
- Conclusion
  - Return to the big picture of the issue; what is the goal of the recommendation(s); what will happen if the policy recommendation is or is not implemented.
- Annexes
  - Although not necessary, graphs, charts, tables, or other related data can be appended to the brief.

Box 10.3 presents a policy memo prepared by social work policy practitioners at the Houston, Texas–based Children At-Risk policy advocacy organization. The memo was provided to a Texas legislative committee that was considering legislative options on human trafficking (see Chapter 9, Tables 9.2 and 9.4).

Box 10.3

POLICY MEMO PRESENTED TO THE TEXAS LEGISLATURE

CHILDREN AT RISK SUPPORTS ACTIONS TO
Combat Child Sex Trafficking Among Youth in the Foster Care System

The National Center for Missing and Exploited Children reported that one out of every five children reported to them as runaways in 2015 were likely victims of sex trafficking. Furthermore, they report that almost 75% of those children were in the care of child social services or foster care when they went missing.[1]

CHILDREN AT RISK supports Texas DFPS and recognizes the extremely challenging circumstances caseworkers in our state face every day. However, the current system does not keep children in government custody reasonably safe from harm. This is especially true for children at-risk for, or who have already become victims, of sex trafficking. Though DFPS is to be commended for progress made, the agency still faces inadequate resources for screening, identification and subsequent placement in appropriate, therapeutic environments for children entering or returning to the CPS system after being sex trafficked—all of which contribute to the higher likelihood these children will suffer from acute and lifelong effects caused by sex trafficking. Additionally, high caseload burdens among caseworkers and children aging out of the system in placements hundreds of miles away from their support networks have created large holes in the DFPS safety net and contributes to the pipeline that directly connects the foster care system and the multi-million dollar illegal sex industry that commercially exploits thousands of children each year.[2]

Background. Texas is considered to be a hub for human trafficking activity in all its various forms. Our state generates the second highest number of calls to the National Human Trafficking Hotline. The most common calls involve sex trafficking cases where children are caught in the commercial sex trade.[3] Texas is a leader in anti-trafficking policy and was one of the first states to pass human trafficking legislation in the U.S. Since 2003, when that first bill was passed, we have come a long way in understanding this heinous crime.

1. National Center for Missing and Exploited Children. (2016). Child sex trafficking. Retrieved from http://www.missingkids.com/1in5
2. US District Court Southern District of Texas, Corpus Christi Division. (2015). Memorandum opinion and verdict of the Court.
3. National Human Trafficking Resource Center. Retrieved from https://traffickingresourcecenter.org/states

Last session, several bills were passed that allowed for easier prosecution of those who purchase sex from children, provided better resources for child victims and extended the Texas Human Trafficking Prevention Task Force.[4] Legislation was also passed that created a Child Sex Trafficking Prevention Unit in the Governor's Criminal Justice Division to specifically address sex trafficking of children in our state.[5] Unfortunately, victims of child sex trafficking are often some of the most vulnerable children in our communities. Traffickers prey upon these youth by providing them with food, shelter, attention and affection; filling a void often left as a result of childhood abuse and neglect. This highly manipulative recruitment strategy often makes children involved in the CPS system at a higher risk for being sex trafficked.

Last December, in a lawsuit brought against officials of the State of Texas by a class of former foster children, Federal Judge Janis Jack of the U.S. District Court of the Southern District of Texas, Corpus Christi Division held that Texas Child Protective Services has violated the constitutional rights of the children in its care. These rights arise because state custody of a child creates a "special relationship" that triggers substantive due process protections which include the right to be free from an unreasonable risk of harm and protection from psychological and physical abuse. In short, foster children have a constitutional right to personal security and reasonably safe living conditions. The 260-page judgment is heartbreaking to read, and is especially pertinent to child trafficking.

However, there are some very encouraging updates coming out of the newly formed Child Sex Trafficking Unit within the Governor's Office. They have been working closely with DFPS and other stakeholders to identify gaps, promote best practices and build the capacity of our state to eradicate child sexual exploitation. Their Immediate priority is to develop and enhance trauma-informed services and support for survivors of child sex trafficking so that they can heal and thrive. They will achieve this by working to create a continuum of care for victims in each region from immediate recovery to long-term restoration. While they are working to build up regional systems, they are also working to fill common gaps statewide. Their office will be facilitating a grant application process for best and promising practices in providing serv ices to victims of child sex trafficking.

---

4. CHILDREN AT RISK. (2015). 84th Texas Legislature Report on Legislation Impacting Children. Retrieved from http://173.45.238.175/content/wp-content/uploads/2015/08/84th-comprehensive-summary-final.pdf

5. CHILDREN AT RISK. (2015). 84th Texas Legislature Report on Legislation Impacting Children. Retrieved from http://173.45.238.175/content/wp-content/uploads/2015/08/84th-comprehensive-summary-final.pdf

Policy recommendations include:

- Strengthened coordination within and between different state agencies in screening, identification and placement procedures for children returning to the foster care system as victims of child sex trafficking. This is important because sexualized children placed with nonsexualized children creates an opportunity for abuse and childhood sexual abuse strongly correlates with later trafficking/commercial sex.
  - *Last session, HB 1217 made assessing for trafficking when a child returns to care a requirement. However, Judge Jack's verdict states that this documentation is often not flagged or monitored closely due to high caseworker turnover.*
- More resources directed to creating a network of safe, appropriate and therapeutic housing for children that have been trafficked.
  - *This should also include increased access to trauma-focused, evidence-based mental health services and rehabilitative services.*
- Designated caseworkers that are specifically assigned to children who are at high risk or are returning to the system after being trafficked.
- These case workers should have a low caseload burden and have specialized training on highly traumatized children. A comprehensive plan for children who age-out of foster care will help prevent them from having to resort to prostitution in order to meet their needs for food and shelter.

For questions or comments, please contact: Mandi Sheridan Kimball, Director, Public Policy and Government Affairs, 713.869.7740 or mkimball@childrenatrisk.org, Jamey Caruthers, Senior Staff Attorney, 713.869.7740 or jcaruthers@childrenatrisk.org, or

Dixie Hairston, Public Policy Coordinator, 214-599-0072 or dhairston@childrenatrisk.org www.childrenatrisk.org

Source: Mandi Sheridan Kimball, director, Public Policy and Government Affairs, Children At-Risk, Houston, Texas. Received February 16, 2017.

DASHBOARD INDICATORS

The driver of a car often glances at the auto's dashboard to quickly get important information: how fast the car is going, whether the engine is overheating, how much gas is there, and so on. *Key Performance Indicators (KPIs)* are similar to an auto's dashboard; information is easily understood with a simple cursorily review. This is a visual presentation of the issue, rather than bullet-listed statements, one after the other, as is done with an info sheet.

The dashboard is a purely metric presentation that graphically details and measures a specific issue. The National Conference of Nonprofits (2016) writes that in the current era of visualization, dashboard presentations are an effective technique to communicate critical information with staff, donors, and the broader community (see Figure 10.4).

The dashboard itself should follow the "3 Cs": colorful, catchy, and clear. Using speedometers, gauge charts, and other creative formats draws attention to the graph

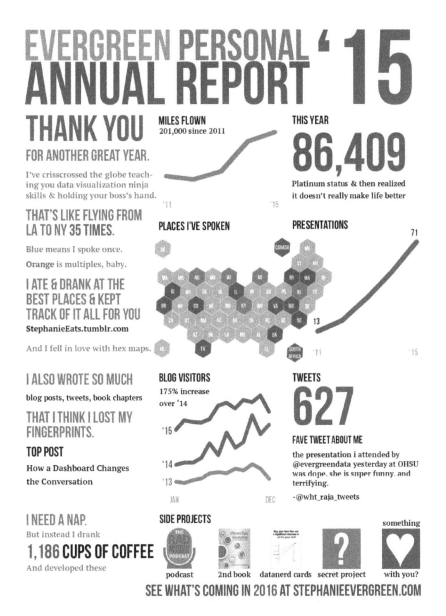

Figure 10.4a.
Example of dashboard handout: an organizational annual report.

Figure 10.4b.
Example of dashboard handout: a city-based social issue.

while being very easy to understand (see Figure 10.4). Completed dashboards are posted and frequently updated on the organization's main Web page; it is a good idea to keep the initial dashboards posted for baseline comparison purposes as data are updated. Dashboard update alerts are posted in or linked to the various virtual rooms in order for supporters to also have the most current available information at their disposal. Finally, the dashboards can be organized into an effective, one-page

Indiana Health Dashboard

Source: Indianaindicaators (2017). Retrieved from
indianaindicators.org/StateDashboard.aspx on February 17, 2017.

Mental Health & Mental Disorders

Inadequate Social Support: Adults (%) 18 and older without social or emotional support

Gauge scale from left to right: 30 to 9

Indiana	
19.1	
U.S.	Goal
19.6	N/A

Alzheimer's Disease Mortality: Alzheimer's disease deaths per 100,000 population (age-adjusted)

Gauge scale from left to right: 75 to 0

Indiana	
29.4	
U.S.	Goal
N/A	N/A

Figure 10.4c.
Example of dashboard handout: a state-based social issue.

info sheet that is given to legislators, legislative staffs, agency board of directors, and other interested parties.

POWERPOINT PRESENTATIONS

The PowerPoint, while widely used in board of directors' meetings, public meetings, town hall meetings, and in classrooms, is one of the least understood presentation formats. Repeatedly, PowerPoint presentations include too many slides and are overburdened with words. It is common for a presenter, whose allotted time for a presentation is drawing to an end, to say, "We are about out of time, let me skip over these next slides." The audience sits in silence as the presenter quickly clicks through the remaining slides without saying a word. Another familiar mistake that PowerPoint presenters make is to read each slide word for word while ignoring the fact that people in the audience are able to read the slide as well.

In a PowerPoint presentation the author attended, a colleague leaned over during the talk and said, "This session should have been titled Death by PowerPoint!" Approximately 15 minutes was assigned to the presenter whose PowerPoint contained over 60 slides, and each slide was written in a 10-point font, with the words quickly flying in and out the slides, fading, turning, and spinning sideways. The presenter stood facing the screen and reading each slide while occasionally glancing at the audience; he spoke to the slides and not to the audience. Yes, this presentation was indeed *Death by PowerPoint.*

A PowerPoint is a tool that augments the speaker's comments. All too often, speakers make the PowerPoint the focal point of the talk, which results in dozens of slides packaged into a presentation. A guiding principle when developing a PowerPoint presentation is, What happens if the electricity goes out; will I still be able to get my message across? If the answer is *yes*, then the policy practitioner has developed an effective media presentation; if the answer is *no*, then the social worker needs to get back to the drawing board and rethink the PowerPoint.

The amount of time set aside for a presentation and the complexity of the issue dictate the number of slides for a talk. There are no specific prescriptions to determine how many slides are appropriate for a certain amount of time. However, on average, a presenter should spend no more than 2 minutes reviewing the content on one slide. If 15 minutes is allotted for a presentation, then simple mathematics suggests approximately seven slides is appropriate.

Whereas seven slides might seem suitable for a 15-minute PowerPoint presentation, the social worker might consider reducing the number of slides to four or five. The fewer number of slides helps ensure the presentation is not rushed, that no slides are skipped over at the end of the talk, and that time is available for questions and answers. Limiting the number of slides available sharpens the presentation focus while not overloading the audience with too much information.

The initial slide includes the presentation's title and the social worker's contact information. Note that the introductory slide is not counted as one of the content slides. The social worker begins the actual presentation with a crisp 30-second purpose statement: "For the next 15 minutes we will be examining . . . My hope is that after this presentation you will . . ." This brief introduction informs the audience of the talk's purpose and the social worker's expectations.

The slides are simply designed, with each page including a title with the specific information as it relates to the title. The fewer the words, the better; long sentences or paragraphs are hard to read. Best practice calls for bulleted words, phrases, or short statements of seven or fewer words with no more than four bulleted points per slide. Remember, the PowerPoint supports and augments the policy practitioner's comments (see Box 10.4).

Selecting background and word colors is critical. If possible, the social worker should visit the room prior to the presentation to determine the optimal color scheme. Background and text or graphic colors need to contrast with each other in

Box 10.4

SOME BASIC RULES FOR EFFECTIVE POWERPOINT PAGE

- Bullets should line up on the left. It is easier for the eye to follow from left to right.
- Bullets should not be on the right-hand side of the screen. It is harder to read when they are lined up on the right.
- Backgrounds are important for the aesthetics of a PowerPoint page. They should never overpower the words or information that is displayed.
- When you are trying to portray a message when using clip art or images, always make sure they do not distract from the information.
- Fonts and backgrounds should complement each other and be easy to read. The background color and font color should be distinctively different.
- The font color should stand out on the chosen background color. It should be easy for the audience to view.
- When using graphics, one good graphic will do better than several poor ones.
- If someone could question why you are using a graphic, don't use it.
- Graphics should relate to the information you are trying to portray.
- When making lists on your Powerpoint, remember the rule of four. Four items on the page is easier for the mind to remember.
- Stay away from gimmicky fonts. Keep type sizes consistent.
- DON'T USE ALL CAPS!
- Avoid text overload.
- When too much information is on the screen, your audience will begin to lose interest in your blah blah blah blah blah blah blah!
- Vary font for emphasis or to group words together. Use visually simple fonts for a visually stimulating appearance.

Source: Patrick, L. (May 9, 2013). Bad/good PowerPoint slides. Slide Share. Retrieved from http://www.slideshare.net/Lynnylu/presentation1-20887067 on February 3, 2017.

order for the audience to easily read the slide (see Box 10.5 and Box 10.6). The best contrast combinations are a dark background with light text and graphics or a light background with dark text and graphics (Think Outside the Slide, 2005–2016). Black-and-white text is easily read by most people; blue text with a yellow background, or visa versa, is visible to the majority of people while taking into account various forms of visual color impairments (Dutton, 1999–2010).

Selecting the font size is a straightforward process. The key consideration is to ensure those in the back row are able to read the slide. A 24-point font might work best for one presentation, whereas a 48-point font is necessary for the same

Box 10.5

SUGGESTED COLOR SCHEMES FOR POWERPOINT PRESENTATIONS

1. ***Dark Background with Light Text and Graphics***
   Background—a dark blue (navy shade) or dark purple
   Text and Graphics—white or yellow
   Accent Colors—red, lime green, camel orange, light blue

   The dark blue or dark purple background gives good emotional feelings as the predominant color on the screen, and the yellow and white text and graphics have good contrast with the background. The accent colors should be used to highlight a word or portion of a graphic, not overused or they will become annoying.

2. ***Light Background with Dark Text and Graphics***
   Background—warm beige
   Text and Graphics—dark blue, black, dark purple
   Accent Colors—dark green, burgundy

   The beige background combines the emotional impact of brown and white without gaining too much of the negative effect of these colors such as boring and staid. The dark text and graphic colors provide enough contrast to make the item stand out on the screen. The accent colors again are for emphasis and should not be overused.

3. *Color Combinations to Avoid* Some colors should not be used together for a variety of reasons.

   Red and Green—these two colors clash with each other and are very hard to read. Also, people who have color deficiency will have trouble figuring out what you are trying to say on the slide.

   Orange and Blue—another pair that causes a disturbing effect on readers as the colors seem to vibrate against one another.

   Red and Blue—these two colors just do not have enough contrast to be seen well when used together. This combination also seems to suffer a further loss of contrast when projected on a screen.

4. **Background Graphics or Patterns** Many presenters want to make their slides more visually appealing by having a graphic or pattern as the background of the slide. This should be used with caution. Many times, the graphic or pattern has areas where the background color changes shade from dark to light or from light to dark. This means that the background is not actually one uniform shade, and it makes picking a contrasting text and graphic color very difficult. It is common that the text is visible on the first few words of a line but then disappear into the background for the rest of the line because of a change in the background. One effect for graphics or logos is to use an embossing effect where the graphic looks like it is slightly raised in the background, but the effect is very subtle and does not cause large changes in background color shade.

Source: Think Outside the Slide (2005–2016). Choosing colors for your presentation slide. Retrieved from http://www.thinkoutsidetheslide.com/choosing-colors-for-your-presentation-slides/.

Box 10.6

EXAMPLE OF GOOD AND BAD POWERPOINT SLIDES

BAD POWERPOINT SLIDE

INTRODUCTION

Motor Car, any self-propelled vehicle with more than two wheels and a passenger compartment, capable of being steered by the operator for use on roads. The term is used more specifically to denote any such vehicle designed to carry a maximum of seven people.

The primary components of a car are the power plant, the power transmission, the running gear, and the control system. These constitute the chassis, on which the body is mounted. The power plant includes the engine and its fuel, the carburettor, ignition, lubrication, and cooling systems, and the starter motor.

GOOD POWERPOINT SLIDE

1. Reframe the Issue

presentation that is in a larger room. In other words, the room's size influences the font's size. But what if the policy practitioner does not have an opportunity to visit the presentation room beforehand? Clearly, it is best to err on the side of large fonts, 24 to 30 point. Similarly, font should never be less than 18 point.

There is an excellent saying that is often disregarded by PowerPoint users: *A picture is worth a thousand words.* A picture conveys a powerful message while allowing the social worker to build on the visual emotions. Finding the right picture takes time but, if done correctly, it becomes a potent, emotional visualization that conveys a critical message.

It is also worth remembering that neither the presenter nor any room furnishings should *block the screen!* The audience needs to be able to view the screen completely; the bottom or sides of the slide should not be cut off with shadows from the podium or silhouettes of people. In a similar manner, the speaker should not stand directly in front of the screen; she or he can walk back and forth on the stage but should never stop in a place that blocks or cuts off any portion of the screen.

One last point regarding a PowerPoint presentation: Approach each PowerPoint presentation believing that in all likelihood something will go wrong. Although practicing the actual PowerPoint multiple times is important and helps leads to a smooth, coherent presentation, it is advisable to have a backup presentation, such as handouts, in case of any unforeseen crises. Sometimes the room may not have a screen, the electricity may be out, someone forgot to bring a computer or a projector, or the room is too bright for a PowerPoint (no shades on the windows). The presentation can be just as effective with printed handouts.

THE PUBLIC SPEECH

A speech or public presentation is an important tool in the policy practitioner's skill box. The social worker may speak to small groups of 8–15 persons such as a legislative committee or a board of directors; the practitioner may also speak to larger groups numbering 25–50 persons such as a group of volunteers; also, the social worker may have the opportunity to present to thousands of persons at a conference or a rally. No matter the setting, the size of the audience, or how experienced or inexperienced one is in *speechifying*, talking in front of others is a nerve-racking experience. Yes, there are speakers who look comfortable and relaxed when in front of a group; they simply have learned how to handle their anxiety and use it to strengthen their presentation.

There are some key points to recognize when giving a speech. First, the audience wants the practitioner to succeed. In fact, the audience will feel sympathy for the speaker who stumbles over or mispronounces a word (University of Pittsburg, 2008). So don't worry about misspeaking, just be yourself and "go with the flow." Second, as one's talk progresses, his or her anxiety begins to diminish. Why? The speaker is becoming more familiar with his or her present state; is adjusting to the podium or table where she or he is seated or standing; and, most important, is able to gauge the audience's reaction to his or her comments.

Although anxiety is inevitable for most talks, some commonsense techniques will help build a positive, effective speech.

1. *Know the Audience.* A preliminary understanding of the meeting and its audience helps shapes the social worker's comments. Questions to ask include the following: Who is attending? How many people are expected? What is the goal of the program? and Who else is on the program? If speaking to another organization or assembly, the policy practitioner can get a sense of the audience by visiting the sponsoring group's website or reviewing its online newsletters.

2. *Audience Members Are Smart People.* People asked to give a speech or talk are seen as "experts" and invited as such. Although the social worker may have something of interest to share with the audience, under no circumstances should the practitioner speak in a patronizing, paternalistic, or demeaning manner. The policy practitioner's objective at the conclusion of a talk is for audience members to ask, "How can I become involved or help?" Respecting others as equals is a major step to realizing this objective.

3. *Prepare the Speech Beforehand.* This might seem like common sense, but it is common for people to get up in front of a group without any written notes or having thought through a fully prepared speech. This often results in a rambling, disjointed presentation; it is especially difficult for this person to know when to end as the words just keep coming, and coming, and coming. Some presenters use a small card or one sheet of paper to write down key points they wish to touch on; others write out the complete talk and read the speech verbatim from the paper. The bottom line is that *the policy practitioner must be prepared and know exactly what he or she wants to say.*

4. *Practice, Practice, Practice.* The more one practices the speech, the more comfortable he or she will become with the message (University of Pittsburg, 2008). The words, unique phrases, sentences, and paragraphs literally become imprinted in one's memory, thus allowing the individual to frequently look at audience without losing one's place in the talk.

   All speakers feel that their talk will be spot on, written, and perfectly formatted. This is normal and part of everyone's ego. A policy practitioner is advised to role-play or have a "dry run" with the speech. Having a colleague or small group listen to the social worker give the talk is an important part of the practice phase. Those in the audience must be free to give honest and open feedback to the social worker; and the practitioner must trust and respect those offering comments and not be upset with their suggestions. Listen to and reflect on the feedback, as it is generally correct.

5. *Speak Slowly.* An outgrowth of anxiety is to speak fast; the more nervous one is, the quicker the cadence. Taking a deep breath, or a series of deep breaths, helps relax an individual prior to talking; consciously being aware of one's tempo

and pace is important as well. The goal is to translate the anxiety into positive energy. Engaged speakers, individuals who show a passion and excitement for their topic, are in all probability shifting their anxiety into a positive force.

6. *Act Confident.* Many speakers begin their comments by admitting their nervousness; while this may seem like an honest, transparent comment, in reality this diminishes the talk while also making the audience somewhat uncomfortable (University of Pittsburg, 2008). A speaker who comes across as a confident, avid expert gains the audience's support.

7. *Wear Comfortable Clothes.* Comedian Billy Chrystal famously said during one of his Saturday Night Live skits, "It's better to look good than to feel good" (Fernando's Hideaway, n.d.). Yet a speaker who wears comfortable, familiar clothing will feel more confident about himself or herself in the moment and, as a result, the speech will be delivered in a more assured and assertive manner.

8. *Arrive Early.* Arriving early to give a talk helps in a number of ways. The social worker can quickly scan the room and see how it is laid out, where a clock is located to monitor time during the talk, and where the speaker will be standing or sitting. Again, familiarity with the space reduces unnecessary concern. A second, and just as important benefit to arriving early is the social worker can introduce himself or herself to audience members as they arrive. Greeting and meeting attendees helps build a speaker–audience relationship.

Toastmasters International (2016), an internally recognized organization in communication and leadership development, identifies five tips for delivering a successful speech.

- *Be prepared.* The audience is giving their time and consideration; the speaker needs to rehearse enough to raise his or her confidence to leave a good impression.
- *Start strong.* The speech begins with a powerful opening that grabs the audience's attention. This can be a joke, fact or statistic, or a compelling story.
- *Be conversational.* Avoid reading your speech word for word. Referring to notes or points from an outline helps the speech be more free-flowing and delivered in a conversational tone.
- *Speak with passion.* The speaker who believes in what she or he is saying is in a position to keep your audience's attention. Show the passion in the talk.
- *Be patient.* Mistakes during the presentation itself can lead to frustration. Every speaker makes mistakes; it is not easy, but experience and practice sharpen one's speaking skills.

Observing other speakers in terms of their delivery and style is a useful way to hone one's own techniques. Watching and listening to people speak on various television shows, during conferences, or in any forum helps identify what skills work better than others.

One last cautionary note: *Be sure your cell phone is off!* One of the more embarrassing moments a speaker faces is if his or her cell phone rings during the talk.

The speaker looks surprised, fumbles in her or his pocket to find the phone, apologizes while shutting the phone off, and then says something like "Now where was I?" Where are you? You are in front of a group, speaking to them. So make sure you give the audience your undivided attention by shutting off your cell phone.

Once a speech is over, the social worker often is excited, fueled by adrenaline, and ready to get going. Harnessing the post-speech enthusiasm is just as important as reducing the pre-talk anxiety. If done correctly, the practitioner's passion and commitment are contagious to the group, and now they may be willing to take the next steps in the change process.

THE 30-SECOND ELEVATOR SPEECH

The so-called *30-second elevator speech* is a brief statement that conveys the essence of a critical message in a brief period of time. The elevator speech is based on a chance but brief encounter with a significant person. The challenge put forth in an elevator speech is: "How would you explain a particular issue in a way that gains the other's person's interest on the same issue if fate placed you in an elevator with a key leader and you only had the time it takes to get from the top of the building to the bottom?"

The author has had many such encounters: sitting next to a member of the US House of Representative on an airplane for a 3-hour trip; bumping into a US Senator while he was playing with his dog on Capitol Hill in Washington, DC; and multiple unexpected encounters such as meeting a county judge while on a run in a park. The author had a real-life elevator meeting with Democratic Party presidential candidate John Edwards in the fall of 2007; Edwards was at a hotel for a fundraising event while the author was attending a professional social work meeting in the same hotel. Recognizing the unique opportunity, the author quickly moved into his elevator speech on student loan forgiveness for social workers, an issue that was being discussed nationwide:

> Hi, Senator Edwards, I hope your day is going well. My name is Ira Colby; I am a social worker, the current president of the Council on Social Work Education, and dean of the University of Houston Graduate College of Social Work. You probably know social workers are employed in difficult jobs across the country and have low salaries. Yet they amassed incredible debts while going to college for their undergraduate and graduate degrees. I hope you will support a federal loan forgiveness program for social workers, similar to the one in place for medical students.

Senator Edwards said he would like additional information and provided the author his business card while writing down his chief-of-staff's contact information. This brief encounter took place in less than 30 seconds, and three floors later Edwards walked off the elevator, waved goodbye, and said, "Thank you." Did the elevator speech work? If success is determined by the enactment of a bill, then the answer is no; if success is measured by Edwards asking for additional information, then the speech worked. There is no way of measuring the overall effect of this brief encounter because Edwards's presidential aspirations ended a few months later, and shortly thereafter a personal scandal ended his political career.

The elevator speech is preplanned, rehearsed, and can be shared with appropriate people during unexpected encounters. The goal is to convince another person, generally a stranger, that the issue is important and his or her support would be most helpful. The desired outcome is that the person's interest is piqued and the person asks the policy practitioner for more information.

There are five key components to an elevator speech: (1) introduce yourself; (2) provide job title and work affiliation, if appropriate; (3) make a succinct statement describing the problem; (4) offer a proposed solution, if appropriate; and (5) thank the person for his or her potential help. The number of words and/or sentences used in an elevator speech is impossible to determine; each person speaks with a difference cadence, and some people talk fast while others speak very slowly. The important ingredient in the message is that it speaks concisely to one issue in a clear, understandable manner.

OP-EDS AND LETTERS TO THE EDITOR
Op-Eds

An op-ed, short for *opinion editorial*, is a short essay published in a newspaper opposite the editorial page. Op-eds are written by syndicated writers, experts in a given subject area, or the newspaper's readers. The op-ed presents the author's ideas or opinion on a timely subject and is an excellent tool to raise awareness and persuade others on a particular topic (see Box 10.7 and Appendix 4).

A well-written op-ed is not objective because it clearly sets forth an opinion. The typical op-ed is written in an informal, conversational style. The goal is to engage the reader by using every day, conversational language, which helps the reader fully understand the author's position. Using short paragraphs is pretty much the norm, and the op-ed is generally around 700 words. Newspapers publish op-ed submission guidelines on their website as well as in the hard copy of the paper itself (see Appendix 5).

The op-ed editor for *The New York Times* wrote a succinct set of guidelines for composing an op-ed:

> Most pieces we publish are between 400 and 1200 words. They can be longer when they arrive, but not so long that they're traumatizing. Submissions that are reacting to news of the world are of great value to us, especially if they arrive very quickly. Write in your own voice. If you're funny, be funny. Don't write the way you think important people write, or the way you think important pieces should sound. And it's best to focus very specifically on something; if you write about the general problem of prisons in the United States, the odds are that it will seem too familiar. But if you are a prisoner in California and you have just gone on a hunger strike and you want to tell us about it—now, that we would like to read. We are normal humans (relatively speaking). We like to read conversational English that pulls us along. That means that if an article is written with lots of jargon, we probably won't like it. (Hall, 2013)

Box 10.7
EXAMPLE OF OP-ED WRITTEN BY A SOCIAL WORKER

My husband died by suicide. Here's what happened during my awkward call with the NRA.

By Jennifer Stuber
Washington Post, April 8, 2016

Jennifer Stuber is an associate professor of public policy at the University of Washington, where she co-founded the organization Forefront: Innovations in Suicide Prevention.

It wasn't the hardest phone call I've ever made, but it was certainly awkward. I was cold-calling the National Rifle Association. Because the NRA is well-known for offering gun safety training, I wanted to know whether the organization had ideas on how to reduce the number of firearm suicides. Half of all suicides in the United States are by firearm, and roughly two-thirds of all firearm deaths are suicides. Given the NRA's opposition to virtually all gun regulation, I knew this was a touchy area.

A far harder call was the one I received from a Seattle police officer a few years earlier. The officer told me that my husband had ended his struggle with anxiety and depression with a single bullet. Suddenly, I was a 38-year-old widow and a single parent of two young children. I was left wondering how this had happened and whether it could have been prevented. I was deeply angry at myself, at my husband, at a treatment system that failed him and at a society that made it easy to buy a pistol. I wasn't the best person to try to start a conversation with the NRA. No wonder it took me a few years to make the call.

But I learned a couple of surprising things from that call and the many follow-up meetings with a local NRA lobbyist and the executive director of the Second Amendment Foundation.

First, they were not just willing to talk but also willing to listen. There was a simple reason for their openness: They are no more immune from the pain of suicide than anyone else. Every year in the United States, about 750,000 of us experience a sudden disruption in our lives due to the suicide of a loved one or close friend. With such high rates of suicide, nearly all of us will be touched by the suicide of someone we know at some point in our lives. Gun rights advocates are no exception.

Second, I learned why the NRA had never focused its gun safety programs on suicide prevention. Like most of our society, it had bought into the myth that if someone wants to kill him or herself, there's nothing you can do about it. But the opposite is true: Suicide is our nation's most preventable cause of death when the right resources and services are in place.

Once we got past that misconception, the NRA and Second Amendment Foundation became active participants in a year-long conversation about reducing the number of suicides by firearm in Washington state. With the leadership of state Rep. Tina Orwall (D), we formed a working group that included gun rights advocates, public-health experts and individuals who have been affected by suicide.

One of the most effective ways to prevent suicides is to make it harder for a person considering suicide to access "lethal means." Some people have the impulse to use a firearm to end their lives. Others may choose a less violent ending, such as a drug overdose. Our working group concentrated on limiting access to both of these lethal means. We were encouraged by studies showing that even temporary impediments to obtaining lethal means may save the life of an at-risk person. In some cases, all that's needed is enough time for the most serious feelings of pain and hopelessness to subside.

Last week, I was on another call, with the office of Washington Gov. Jay Inslee (D). This time, the news was good—he would sign a new law designed to reduce the number of suicides by firearm and overdose in Washington. This law, passed March 31, is the first nationwide to bring together gun advocates and the firearm industry with suicide prevention advocates. It is supported by the NRA, the Second Amendment Foundation and many others interested in injury prevention and mental health. There was strong backing by legislators on both sides of the political aisle, including one who is an avid hunter and who shared that this law would change the way he stores firearms in his home.

The law calls for developing suicide prevention messages and training for gun dealers, shooting ranges, gun shows, pharmacies and drugstores. Participation by gun stores and ranges will be voluntary, and work will be done to create incentives for the industry to participate. The legislation also begins a new program to pair suicide prevention and gun safety education with the distribution of storage devices and medication disposal kits. It updates firearm safety pamphlets and the state's hunter safety course to incorporate suicide awareness and prevention.

Over the past decade, suicide prevention has become recognized as one of our greatest public-health challenges. The new law in Washington state is a big step forward. But this bipartisan legislation can also mark the beginning of a different way of talking about gun violence in America. For too long, we've allowed the debate over legal rights to dominate the conversation. It's time to give equal emphasis to what we have in common, including the grief we all feel over suicide.

Source: Stuber, J. My husband died by suicide. Here's what happened during my awkward call with the NRA. Washington Post. April 8, 2016. Retrieved from https://www.washington-post.com/opinions/i-made-an-awkward-call-to-the-nra-and-found-that-we-had-common-ground/2016/04/07/4214bed2-fb67-11e5-886f-a037dba38301_story.html?utm_term=.de12f17bd4d6 on December 2, 2016.

The format of an op-ed is simple and straightforward. The lead paragraph's goal is to grab the reader's attention so the reader will want to read the entire piece. The following paragraphs build the case with compelling numbers, facts, and illustrative anecdotes. The final paragraph tells the reader what the author wants the reader to do, with the final sentence of the op-ed being a compelling statement (see Appendix 4).

Letter to the Editor

The *Letter to the Editor* is a shorter version of an op-ed that provides an opportunity for an individual to write a succinct statement on one specific issue. In general, a letter to the editor responds to an opinion expressed by the newspaper's editorial board; offers a rejoinder to an op-ed; or is a reaction to a news story printed in a recent edition of the paper. Letters are brief, approximately 150 to 175 words in length, and as a result, they must be brief. The letter should cite the article, editorial, op-ed, or issue in the first sentence: "Dear editor, The recent article 'Homeless in Town' (April 6, 2015) was a very important reminder . . ."

Every newspaper includes guidelines on submitting a letter. As with op-ed submissions, the information is available on the newspaper's website as well as in each edition of the paper, generally on the same page where letters are printed (see Appendix 5).

A FEW FINAL THOUGHTS

This chapter presented an overview of key techniques and strategies employed in policy practice. As with all realms of social work practice, methods and approaches in the policy world are always changing. Technologies and virtual rooms are constantly being refined with new rooms added or older ones renovated or discarded. Although texting and Tweeting are commonplace in 2017, they probably will be obsolete by the year 2025, if not sooner; a different more impactful visual presentation tool will replace PowerPoint.

The Web provides links to numerous sources to construct creative dashboards with a number of these sites offering free templates. Many sites with additional subscription fees allow members to download more advanced software packages. One last piece of advice to consider when building a dashboard for a policy practice matter: Keep the key, important data in the middle of the page with less important data off to the sides. Remember, an automobile's key dashboard information is straight ahead of the driver's eyes, while secondary or minor details are generally smaller and off to the side on the dashboard's periphery.

The ability to speak to small and large groups and the ability to convey a crisp and engaging message to a legislator, board member, or volunteer are fundamental policy practice skills. Paying close attention to speakers, how they present, and what works helps the social worker sharpen his or her public speaking skills.

Finally, the policy practitioner must be willing to grow and change as a professional. Social workers, in fact all professionals, become comfortable with their individual skills and processes over time. Effective policy practice requires the social worker to update and be familiar with as many facets as possible of the technological world, the ever-changing political environments, and continued professional self-development regarding policy practice theory, techniques, and strategies. The ability to change one's techniques, to discard outdated modalities, and to continue to seek out more effective communication tools is a hallmark of a proactive social worker, one whose goal is help foster a successful strategy in the policy arena. As the author attests, policy practice in 1975 was very different from its counterpart in 2000 and, similarly, policy practice in 2016. And, most assuredly, policy practice will be far different in the year 2025.

REFERENCES

Bennett, S. (2014, October 21). The 13 most popular social networks (by age groups). *SocialTimes*. Retrieved from http://www.adweek.com/socialtimes/popular-social-networks-age/502497 on May 19, 2016.

Blakley, J. (2012, July 18). 12 tips for effective # marketing. *Postano*. Retrieved from http://www.postano.com/blog/12-tips-for-effective-twitter-hashtag-marketing on May 19, 2016.

Center for Rural Health. (2002–2016). Communication tools: Fact sheets. University of North Dakota School of Medicine & Health Sciences. Retrieved from https://ruralhealth.und.edu/communication/factsheets on May 12, 2016.

Community Tool Box. (2016). Section 15. Creating fact sheets on local issues. Retrieved from http://ctb.ku.edu/en/table-of-contents/participation/promoting-interest/fact-sheets/main on May 12, 2016.

Dutton, F. (1999–2010). Websites for the colorblind. Colors for the Blind. Retrieved from http://www.toledo-bend.com/colorblind/CBwebsites.asp on April 12, 2016.

Fernando's Hideaway. (n.d.). Retrieved from http://snltranscripts.jt.org/84/84dfernando.phtml on April 28, 2016.

Foley, K. (2015, December 9). #TweetTip: 7 steps for writing effective twitter add copy. Twitter. Retrieved from https://blog.twitter.com/2015/tweettip-7-tips-for-writing-effective-twitter-ads-copy on May 19, 2016.

Fox, Z. (2011, September 19). 31% of U.S. adults prefer to be reached by text message (study). Mashable. Retrieved from http://mashable.com/2011/09/19/31-of-u-s-adults-prefer-to-be-reached-by-text-message-study/#_Jbk4WxBZqq9 on May 22, 2016.

Goldschmidt, K. (2011) Adolescents texting and twittering: The flash mob phenomena. *Journal of Pediatric Nursing, 26,* 167–169.

Hall, T. (2013, October 13). The op-ed and you. *The New York Times*. Retrieved from http://www.nytimes.com/2013/10/14/opinion/op-ed-and-you.html?_r=0 on May 22, 2016.

Health Advocacy Tool Box. (n.d.). Fact sheets and action alters. Retrieved from http://www.cthealthpolicy.org/toolbox/tools/fact_sheets.htm on May 12, 2016.

Herman, L. (2012). Policy memos. Harvard Kennedy School, John F. Kennedy School of Government. Retrieved from http://shorensteincenter.org/wp-content/uploads/2012/07/HO_Herman_Policy-Memos_9_24_12.pdf on February 7, 2017.

Hyman, I. (2014, January 26). Cell phones are changing social interaction. *Psychology Today*. Retrieved from https://www.psychologytoday.com/blog/mental-mishaps/201401/cell-phones-are-changing-social-interaction on May 18, 2016.

James, G. (2014, May 1). 13 social media rules to live by. Inc. Retrieved from http://www.inc.com/geoffrey-james/13-social-media-rules-to-live-by.html on February 3, 2017.

Jordan, J. (2013, October 8). 48% of emails are opened on mobile; gmail opens down 20% since tabs. Litmus. Retrieved from https://litmus.com/blog/48-of-emails-are-opened-on-mobile-gmail-opens-down-20-since-tabs on May 20, 2016.

Krogue, K. (2013, August 30). 31 Twitter tips: How to use twitter tools and twitter best practices for business. *Entrepreneurs*. Retrieved from http://www.forbes.com/sites/kenkrogue/2013/08/30/31-twitter-tips-how-to-use-twitter-tools-and-twitter-best-practices-for-business/#4227ce8b2432 on May 19, 2016.

Mourtada, R., & Salem, F. (May 2011). Civil movements: The impact of Facebook and Twitter. *Arab Social Media Report, 1*(2). Retrieved from www.mbrsg.ae/...4cd7-9104-b8f1f405cab3/...in-the-Arab.aspx on February 3, 2017.

National Conference of Nonprofits. (2016). Dashboards for nonprofits. Retrieved from https://www.councilofnonprofits.org/tools-resources/dashboards-nonprofits?__qca=P0-720561649-1468278961633&_hjIncludedInSample=1&has_js=1&_ga=GA1.2.1209013987.1468278961&__unam=6da976a-155dc3ef525-7963532c-2 on May 22, 2016.

Ngo, N. (2017, February 15). El burrito mercado, others closed today for "day without immigrants'" strike. Twin Cities Pioneer Press.com. Retrieved from http://www.twincities.com/2017/02/14/minneapolis-st-paul-restaurants-close-for-day-without-immigrants-strike/ on February 16, 2017.

Osterrieder, A. (2013, July 11). The value and use of social media as communication tool in the plant sciences. Biomed Central. Retrieved from http://plantmethods.biomedcentral.com/articles/10.1186/1746-4811-9-26 on May 18, 2016.

Patrick, L. (2013, May 9). Bad/good PowerPoint slides. Slide Share. Retrieved from http://www.slideshare.net/Lynnylu/presentation1-20887067 on February 3, 2017.

Perrin, A. (2015, October 8). Social media usage: 2005–2015. Pew Research Center. Retrieved from http://www.pewinternet.org/2015/10/08/social-networking-usage-2005-2015/ on February 4, 3017.

Roane, S. (2014). *How to work a room*. New York, NY: HarperCollins.

Smith, A. (2011, September 19). How Americans use text messaging. Pew Research Center. Retrieved from http://www.pewinternet.org/2011/09/19/how-americans-use-text-messaging/ on May 18, 2016.

Stein, P. (2017, February 15). Immigrant workers plan strike Thursday as part of "Day Without Immigrants" protest. *Washington Post*. Retrieved from https://www.washingtonpost.com/news/local/wp/2017/02/15/immigrant-workers-plan-strike-thursday-as-part-of-day-without-immigrants-protest/?utm_term=.d9f52d02296d on February 16, 2017.

Suess, E. (2011–2016). How to write a fact sheet. Small Business Bonfire. Retrieved from http://www.smallbusinessbonfire.com/how-to-write-a-fact-sheet/ on May 12, 2016.

Tennyson, A. (2015, March 31). How to follow someone on twitter. Teachwlla. Retrieved from https://www.techwalla.com/articles/how-to-follow-someone-on-twitter on February 3, 2017.

Think Outside the Slide. (2005–2016). Choosing colors for your presentation slide. Retrieved from http://www.thinkoutsidetheslide.com/choosing-colors-for-your-presentation-slides/ on June 3, 2016.

Triggs, R. (2013, October 13). Who uses sms and how does it work. Retrieved from http://www.androidauthority.com/what-is-sms-280988/ on May 18, 2016.

Twitter. (2016). Twitter usage, company facts. Retrieved from https://about.twitter.com/company on May 22, 2016.

University of Pittsburg. (2008, August 12). Speaking in the disciplines. Retrieved from http://www.speaking.pitt.edu/student/public-speaking/speechanxiety.html on February 12, 2016.

Urban, D. (2014, April 21). 50 Tweetable twitter tips you wish you knew years ago. Hubspot. Retrieved from http://blog.hubspot.com/marketing/twitter-tips-list#sm.001lprz2a11n8dvat0m1rjj5567fk on May 19, 2016.

Walter, E. (2016). 12 most effective ways to engage on Twitter. Open Forum. Retrieved from https://www.americanexpress.com/us/small-business/openforum/articles/12-most-effective-ways-to-engage-on-twitter/ on May 19, 2016.

Wasik, B. (2011, December 16). #Riot: Self-organized, hyper-networked revolts—Coming to a city near you. *Wired Magazine*. Retrieved from www.wired.com/magazine/2011/12/ff_riots/ on May 18, 2016.

Woodrow Wilson School of Public and International Affairs. (2014, October 28). Policy memo writing tips. Retrieved from http://wws.princeton.edu/admissions/wws-blog/item/policy-memo-writing-tips on January 12, 2017.

Not the End but the Beginning

INTRODUCTION TO PART 4: NOT THE END BUT THE BEGINNING

The author's first involvement in policy practice occurred when he was about 8 years old. A neighbor decided to run for an open city council seat on a platform that challenged a major national corporation whose home offices were in the community; the neighbor had worked at the company for many years but felt it was taking advantage of the local community. He based his campaign on wanting to do something about what he termed "bad corporate behavior." The author canvassed a number of neighborhoods on behalf of his neighbor, going door-to-door passing out leaflets and other informational items. Election day arrived, and the neighbor easily won the council seat. At the postelection party, the newly elected city council representative called the author to the stage, lifted him up, and said, "This is my number-one campaign staffer!" A few weeks later, the national company, his employer, transferred him to another state; he either had to quit his job so he could stay on city council or give up his seat and move elsewhere. He moved. At a very young age, the author was introduced to the nasty, cutthroat side of politics. Not discouraged, over the ensuing years, the author continued to volunteer in political campaigns. He worked in phone banks, went door-to-door canvassing, helped raise money for candidates, and even managed an individual's race for a state house seat. In addition to the political campaign work, the author testified on many occasions to state and local legislative committees while working with national social work associations to advance the profession's agenda. The common denominator in all of these volunteer efforts was the author's support of individuals and ballot initiatives he felt reflected the same ideals and beliefs around fairness and justice.

Policy practice begins differently for each person. For some, the pathway starts in a manner similar to the author; they are not really sure what they are doing but are driven by the belief that what they are doing is right. For others, policy practice and advocacy starts in an educational program. They enroll in a social work program with the goal of moving into some form of clinical work; yet somewhere along the course of their studies they are introduced to social policy and its direct impact on our everyday work. Policy practice then becomes part of their clinical skills repertoire. How we begin our journey in policy practice and the political world is not important; it is essential, however, that each social worker incorporates policy practice into his or her everyday social work activities.

Chapter 11 includes a glossary of policy-related words and phrases. As has been shown throughout the *Handbook*, the policy world has its own unique language and jargon. Knowing and understanding the meaning of a particular word or phrase within a given context is important; their meanings change from one setting to another. The glossary is by no means the last and final word. It does, however, provide what the author considers to be key phrases and terms that policy practitioners use.

Finally, the *Handbook's* last chapter encourages the reader to look to the future, to tomorrow, and what we, as social workers and as global citizens, can and should do to help realize a fair and just world for all people. In reality, the final chapter of this book is neither written nor finalized. The "last chapter" will be authored by current social work students who, after their graduation, will and work to create just and fair policies and services for all people.

The dinner metaphor has slowly evolved throughout the *Handbook*. Now, the doorbell is ringing or someone is knocking on the door. Let the party begins! We are ready to engage in policy practice.

CHAPTER 11

Glossary of Policy Practice–Related Terms

Social policy and policy practice rely on a own set of unique words and phrases. Throughout the *Handbook*, references when to use or stay away from "professional jargon" or "acronyms" are made. Whereas the policy practitioner will use her or his own discretion when or when not to use such wording, it is imperative that the social worker be familiar with the common words and phrases that are part of the social policy world.

Why do words matter? Why can't we just say what we want?

First, words are powerful in and by themselves (Olmstead, 2013). Words, if used correctly, can inspire, motivate, encourage, and make people feel good about themselves and others. Yet a wrong word or phrase can water down or even eliminate a group's enthusiasm, lower their expectations, and be very hurtful. A 1930s British politician, Pearl Strachen Hurd, noted the power of words when writing, "Handle them carefully, for words have more power than atom bombs" (Judythemorgan, 2014). Hurd's characterization offers an important reminder for the social worker: Understand a word and both its implied and inferred meaning. For example, some consider the term *illegal immigrant* as pejorative, while for others view this as an accurate description of a person's nonlegal status in the United States. In 2013, the Associated Press dropped the use of the term *illegal immigrant* from its style guide, noting:

> Our goal always is to use the most precise and accurate words so that the meaning is clear to any reader anywhere . . .. (the) AP will also avoid sweeping labels like "undocumented" or "unauthorized" used by some in the news media who avoid the term "illegal immigrant." (Planas, 2013)

Jeffery Toobin, a lawyer and senior legal analyst for CNN, wrote a commentary in *The New Yorker* magazine, "Should I use the term Illegal Immigrant?" (Toobin,

2015). He was responding to criticism for comments he made in a previous article focusing on the US immigration policy in which he referred to a mother and father as illegal immigrants. Toobin (August 5, 2015) concluded, "It's clearly wrong to call someone 'an illegal' . . . A person, as a person" and the phrase "illegal immigrant" was "toxic."

Second, words often carry multiple meanings. As such, a word can mean something different to different people at different times. Words are not static because their meanings change over time while often times reflecting cultural differences. Understanding a word or phrase and how it is used in a particular situation can easily impact the tone of a conversation. For example,

- Would you want to be called "awful?" It depends; on one hand, you could be seen as "inspirational" or some might see you as being "unpleasant."
- Someone comes up and whispers in your ear, "The person sitting next to you washes their clothes in barf?" Would you get up and move? Well, you probably would not need to because "barf" is a laundry detergent. *Barf* in Farsi means "snow" or "white."
- Someone just told me you are "sick." I am confused—are you "ill" or did you do a "good thing" or something "amazing"? Similarly, you were just called "bad"; well, what did you do "wrong," or are you "discouraged," or did you do something that was "incredible" or "outstanding?"
- You are attending a social work conference reception and someone offers you a glass of "pee." Would you drink it? Probably not if the meeting is in the United States, but if the meeting is in Ghana, you would not have any issue. "Pee Cola" is a popular soft drink produced in Ghana.
- You are out with a colleague and you say, "I see you use a 'Lumia'; how do you like it?" While a "Lumia" is an android mobile device, you better be careful because "Lumia" translates in Spanish slang to "prostitute."

Third, a single word creates an impression and feeling that will remain with others, either virtually or in person. The saying "a picture is worth a 1,000 words" can aptly be changed to "a single word is worth a 1,000 pictures." That is to say, one particular, exact word can create a powerful, long-lasting mental picture. Following the December 2012 murder of 26 innocent people at Sandy Hook (CT) Elementary School, many newspapers used a single word as their front-page headline to convey the magnitude of this horror (Moos, 2012).

- Connecticut Post—*Shattered*
- The Kentucky Enquirer—*AGONY*
- The Day—UNTHINKABLE
- The Kansas City Star—*Horrific*
- The News Leader—*HORRIFYING*
- The Citizen's Voice—*Why?*

- Green Bay Press Gazette—*Tragedy*
- The Anniston Star—*SENSELESS*
- San Francisco Chronicle—*Unspeakable*
- The Journal News—*UNIMAGINABLE*
- The Morning Call—*OVERWHELMING*
- The Pantagraph—*HEARTBREAK*
- Herald Times Reporter—*ATROCITY*
- Standard Speaker—*SLAUGHTER*
- Times Herald Record—*MASSACRE*

Finally, words are the vehicle that makes people human. They allow us to talk with others, to share our feelings, ideas, concerns, and beliefs; words connect people with people. Words help us express in a way that an image is unable to do while allowing the individual to tell a full and complete story from the beginning to the end (Olmstead, 2013).

Policy practice has its own words and phrases that make sense in the federal offices in Washington, DC, state capitols, or in local governmental offices. Some of the definitions might seem contrary or differ from those typically associated with a word (see *casework*) but recognize the definitions reflect the word or phrase within the social policy arena. As with words and phrases in general, misusing a term or expression in policy practice can result in negative outcomes.

This glossary is not a complete comprehensive listing of all policy terms nor is it meant to be an end in itself. The glossary does list the more common words and terms a social worker will hear and use. A Web search will result in similar glossaries to help build the social worker's policy lexicon.

A final recommendation for all social workers. A useful and very helpful text is the *Social Work Dictionary*, which defines numerous terms that are common to all social workers. In a manner of speaking, the *Dictionary* provides a shared language for social workers. The *Dictionary*, published by NASW, has evolved through a number of editions with leading social work scholars and practitioners adding and defining words and phrases that are applicable to the social work profession. Every practitioner should have a copy of the *Dictionary* on her or his desk: Barker, Robert L. (ed). *The social work dictionary* (6th ed.). Washington, DC: NASW Press.

Accessibility   The extent to which a facility is readily approachable and usable by individuals with disabilities, particularly such areas as the personnel office, worksite, and public areas.

Accommodations for Individuals with Disabilities (ACE)   ACE providers must ensure that individuals with disabilities are not excluded from services, programs, and courses because of existing disabilities. Accessibility accommodations may apply to circumstances other than wheelchair access.

Adjournment   Termination of a session for that day, with the hour and day of the next meeting being set.

Adjournment sine die   Final termination of a regular or special legislative session.

Adoption   Approval or acceptance; usually applied to amendments, committee reports, or resolutions.

Advocate   Someone who speaks up for herself/himself and members of his or her identity group; e.g., a woman who lobbies for equal pay for women.

Affirmed   Upheld, agreed with (e.g., The Appellate Court affirmed the judgment of the City Court).

Ally   A person of one social identity group who stands up in support of members of another group; typically member of dominant group standing beside member(s) of targeted group; e.g., a male arguing for equal pay for women.

Amendment   Any alteration made (or proposed to be made) to a bill or clause thereof, by adding, deleting, substituting, or omitting.

- *Committee amendment*—an alteration made (or proposed to be made) to a bill that is offered by a legislative committee.
- *Floor amendment*—an alternation offered to a legislative document that is presented by a legislator while that document is being discussed on the floor of that legislator's chamber.

American conservatism   The belief that freedom trumps all other political considerations; the government should play a small role in people's lives.

American exceptionalism   The view that the United States is different from other countries.

American liberalism   The belief that the government should promote equality in politics and economics.

Amicus curiae   A friend of the court. A non-party to a proceeding that the Court permits to present its views.

Appropriation   The act of a legislative body that formally specifies the amount of authorized money that an agency can spend.

Ascribed status   A trait or characteristic people possess as a result of the circumstances of birth.

Assimilation   The process whereby members of a group give up parts of their own culture in order to blend in to a new culture.

Author   The person (usually a legislator) who presents a bill or resolution for consideration; may be joined by others, who are known as coauthors. *See also* introducer, patron, sponsor.

Belief   A specific idea that people feel to be true.

Best practices   Clinical, practical, educational and/or research services based on appropriately documented and accountable professional and scientific materials.

Bias   A tendency to assume a certain viewpoint or answer is correct. Supporting or opposing a particular person or thing in an unfair way, because of allowing personal opinions to influence your judgment.

Bicameral   A legislature consisting of two separate chambers, each serving as a check on the other's power.

Biennium   Two-year term of legislative activity.

Bill   A bill is the form used for most legislation, whether permanent or temporary, general or special, public or private. A bill originating in the House of Representatives is designated by the letters "H.R.," signifying "House of Representatives," followed by a number that it retains throughout all its parliamentary stages; a bill in the Senate is designated by "S.R." followed by a number that it retains throughout all its parliamentary stages. Bills are presented to the President for action when approved in identical form by both the House of Representatives and the Senate.

Bill of Rights   The first 10 amendments to the Constitution, which identify specific rights of the American people and the states.

Block grant   A grant-in-aid with few restrictions or rules about how it can be spent.

Blog   A website updated frequently by an individual or group to record opinions or information.

Brief   In law, a written or printed document prepared by the lawyers on each side of a dispute and submitted to the court in support of their arguments. (*See* policy brief.)

Budget   (1) The suggested allocation of state moneys presented to the legislature for consideration; (2) a formal document that reflects the authorized expenditures of the state.

Bureaucracy   A type of formal organization in which a rational approach is used for the handling of large tasks.

Calendar   (1) A printed list of proposals that are arranged according to the order of business and are scheduled for consideration by a chamber; (2) agenda of daily legislative business in a chamber.

Casework   Work done by an elected legislator or her/his staff on behalf of constituents.

Categorical grant   Money given for a specific purpose that comes with restrictions concerning how the money is spent. *See* project grants and formula grants.

Caucus   An informal meeting of a group of the members; most commonly based on political party affiliation, but it may have other bases, such as gender, race, geographic location, or specific issue.

Checks and balances   The ability of different branches of government to stop each other from acting; designed to prevent one branch from gaining too much power.

Child nutrition   These are food programs administered by the USDA (United States Department of Agriculture) which include school lunch, breakfast, and after-school programs. They target children from low-income households and provide free or reduced price meals.

Child protection worker   Refers to a worker who is mandated under government policy or legislation to provide service to families where a child has been identified either at risk of maltreatment or as being maltreated.

Child tax credit   A tax credit given to a taxpayer for each dependent child who is under the age of 17 at the end of the tax year. In the U.S., families making less than $110,000 per year may claim the full credit. After $110,000 it phases out at the rate of $50 for each additional $1,000 (or portion of $1,000) earned above $110,000. *See* Negative income tax.

Child welfare   A term used to describe a set of government and private services designed to protect children and encourage family stability. The main aim of these services is to safeguard children from abuse and neglect. Child welfare agencies will typically investigate allegations of abuse and neglect, supervise foster care, and arrange adoptions. They also offer services aimed to support families so that they can stay intact and raise children successfully and to remedy risks in families where the child has been removed so reunification can occur.

Chronic unemployment   The rate of unemployment attributable to persons who have persistent trouble finding work because of the absence of low-skilled jobs or because they have severe deficiencies in basic educational, social, and work skills.

Civil liberties   Individual freedoms that cannot be taken away, including free speech, freedom of religion, and the rights of the accused.

Class   A group of people with similar levels of wealth, influence, and status.

Coalition   A collection of different people or groups, working toward a common goal.

Code   A compilation of laws and their revisions according to subject matter (usually arranged by title, chapter, and section); the official publication of the statutes.

Code of Ethics   A Code of Ethics is intended to serve as a guide to the everyday professional conduct of social workers (e.g., NASW's Code of Ethics: http://www.naswdc.org/pubs/code/default.asp) and delineates the standards and principles that guide the conduct and professional practice of social workers.

Committee   A body of members appointed by the presiding officer (or another authority specified by the chamber) to consider and make recommendations concerning disposition of bills, resolutions, and other related matters.
- *Conference committee*—A committee composed of members from the two houses specifically appointed to reconcile the differences between House and Senate versions of a bill or bills.
- *Interim committee*—A committee established to study or investigate certain matters between annual or biennial legislative sessions and to report to the next regular session.
- *Joint committee*—A committee composed of members from both chambers.
- *Standing committee*—A committee appointed with continuing responsibility in a general issue area or field of legislative activity.

Committee of the whole   Either house of the legislature sitting in its entirety as a committee to consider bills or issues.

Committee report   Official release of a bill or resolution from committee with (or without) a specific recommendation, such as "pass," "pass as amended," or "do not pass."

Committee substitute   A bill offered by a committee in lieu of another bill that was originally referred to the committee for consideration; technically, the committee substitute is an amendment to the original bill.

Concurrent resolution   Matters affecting the operations of both the House of Representatives and Senate are usually initiated by means of concurrent resolutions. A concurrent resolution originating in the House of Representatives is designated "H.Con.Res." followed by its individual number; "S.Con. Res." Designates the resolution began in the Senate. On approval by both the House of Representatives and Senate, they are signed by the Clerk of the House and the Secretary of the Senate. They are not presented to the President for action.

Conflict theory   Theory that in any capitalist society there is eternal conflict between the owners of the means of production and the workers.

Convene   When the members of a chamber gather for the meeting of the legislature daily, weekly, and at the beginning of a session as provided by the constitution or law.

Crime against the person   An act of violence either threatened or perpetrated against a person.

Crime against property   The theft of property or certain forms of damage against the property of another person.

Culture of poverty   Describes the idea that poor people do not learn the norms and values that can help them improve their circumstances and hence get trapped in a repeated pattern of poverty

Debatable   Open to parliamentary discussion or argument.

Debate   Discussion of a matter according to parliamentary rules.

Debt   Cumulative annual deficit money owed by a government.

Decorum   Proper order, etiquette, and conduct of members during a floor session.

Deficit   The annual difference between the money a government takes in (e.g., receipts) and what the government spends (e.g., outlays).

Deregulation   The repeal or reduction of regulations in order to boost efficiency, increase competitiveness, and benefit individuals.

Died in committee   The defeat of a bill by not returning it from committee to the the full legislative body for further action.

Discouraged workers   Individuals who have stopped looking for a job because they are convinced that they will not find a suitable one.

Discrimination   The unequal treatment of members of various groups based on race, gender, social class, sexual orientation, physical ability, religion, and other categories.

Dissent   Difference of opinion; to cast a negative vote.

District   That division of the state represented by a legislator distinguished numerically or by geographical boundaries.

Diversity   Differences in and among societal groups based on race and/or ethnicity, gender, age, physical/mental abilities, sexual orientation, religion, size, and other distinguishing characteristics.

Divided government   One political party controls the executive branch of government, while another political party controls at least one chamber of the legislative branch.

Division of a question   Procedure to separate a matter to be voted upon into two or more questions.

Earned income tax credit   The EITC or EIC is a refundable tax credit for low- to moderate-income working individuals and couples, particularly those with children. The amount of EITC benefit depends on a recipient's income and number of children. In 2017, a two-parent, two child family maximum adjusted gross income was $50,597. *See* Negative income tax.

Enabling legislation   A law passed by a legislative body that lays out the general purposes and powers of an agency but grants the agency the power to determine the details of how it implements policy.

Entitlement   Name for social programs that benefit certain individuals who meet certain requirements, regardless of need.

Equality   Access or provision of equal opportunities, where individuals are protected from being discriminated against.

Equal opportunity   Principle of nondiscrimination which emphasizes that opportunities in education, employment, advancement, benefits and resource distribution, and other areas should be freely available to all citizens irrespective of their age, race, sex, religion, political association, ethnic origin, or any other individual or group characteristic unrelated to ability, performance, and qualification.

Equity   A state in which all people in a given society share equal rights and opportunities.

Ethnocentrism   The tendency to believe that one's ethnic or cultural group is centrally important and that all other groups are measured in relation to one's own.

Exempt 501(c)(3) organization   Commonly referred to as *charitable organizations* and fall into one of three primary categories: public charities, private foundations, and private operating foundations. No part of the activities or the net earnings can unfairly benefit any director, officer, or private individual affiliated with the organization. The 501(c)(3) faces stringent rules regarding lobbying or other legislative activity while direct engagement in political campaigns or endorsing (or antiendorsement) a candidate for public office is strictly prohibited.

Extended family   Refers to persons who have a significant and/or meaningful relationship with a child or adult but are not related by blood or marriage and are typically from the same community.

Federalism   A system of government (i.e., United States), in which power is shared by national and state governments.

Filibuster   The prolonged discussion of a bill to delay legislative action.

First reading   The first presentation of a bill or its title for consideration. In some states, the first reading is done at the time of introduction.

Fiscal   Dealing with state revenues and expenditures.

Fiscal note   A fiscal note seeks to state in dollars the estimated amount of increase or decrease in revenue or expenditures and the present and future implications of a piece of pending legislation.

Fiscal year   An accounting period of 12 months; federal government fiscal year is September 1–August 31; local governments and nonprofit agencies have various beginning and ending dates for their fiscal years.

Formula grant   Grants in which a formula is used to determine how much money each state receives.

Gender role   A set of behaviors, attitudes, and personality characteristics expected and encouraged of a person based on his or her sex.

Government   The institution responsible for making and enforcing the rules of society and for regulating relations with other societies.

Groupthink   Refers to the tendency of people in positions of power to follow the opinions of the group, to the point that there is a narrow view of the issue at hand.

Hate crime   Hate crime legislation often defines a hate crime as a crime motivated by the actual or perceived race, color, religion, national origin, ethnicity, gender, disability, or sexual orientation of any person.

Head Start   This is a preschool program available to children in low-income families. The US Department of Health and Human Services administers it.

Health   The well-being of people.

Hearing   Public discussion and appearance on a proposal or bill; usually scheduled by a committee.

House   Generic term for a legislative body; usually the body in a bicameral legislature that has the greater number of members; shortened name for House of Representatives or House of Delegates.

Housing assistance   Various housing programs are administered by the Department of Housing and Urban Development (HUD), including rental assistance, public housing, and various community development grants.

Idealism   The view that states should act in the global arena to promote moral causes and use ethical means to achieve them.

Ideology   A set of values that people devise to rationalize a particular social custom.

Income transfer   A government action that takes money from one part of the population and gives it to another part.

Incrementalism   View change as occurring in small steps based on a series of compromises.

Indefinite postponement   A form of adverse disposition of a proposal for that session of the legislature.

In-group bias (favoritism)   The tendency for groups to "favor" themselves by rewarding group members economically, socially, psychologically, and emotionally in order to uplift one group over another.

Injustice   The practice of being unfair or unjust. The word *injustice* generally refers to abuse, misuse, neglect, or malfeasance that is sanctioned by a legal system.

In-kind   Assistance, generally to the poor, that is not given as cash but in forms such as SNAP and rent vouchers.

Insert   Add language to a bill or resolution.

Interim   The interval between regular sessions of the legislature.

Job training programs   These are the myriad of training programs administered by the Department of Labor (DOL) to provide job training, displacement, and employment services generally targeting low-income Americans.

Joint resolution   Joint resolutions may originate either in the House of Representatives or in the Senate. There is little difference between a bill and a joint resolution. Both are subject to the same procedure, except for a joint resolution proposing an amendment to the Constitution. A joint resolution originating in the House of Representatives is designated "H.J.Res.," S.J.Res. if started in the Senate and is followed by its individual number. Joint resolutions become law in the same manner as bills.

Joint session   A combined meeting of the Senate and House in one chamber.

Jurisdiction   The geographical limits or territory within which specific power, rights, or authority may be exercised.

Law   A norm that is written down and enforced by an official agency

Lawful alien status   Refers to people admitted to the United States who are granted permanent authorization to work by the United States Citizenship and Immigration Services (USCIS) (formerly INS) or admitted to the United States on a temporary basis with USCIS (INS) authorization to work.

Legislative day   A day on which either chamber convenes (or both chambers convene) to conduct official business.

Legislative intent   Purpose for which a measure is passed.

LGBTA   Acronym encompassing the diverse groups of lesbian, gay, bisexual, transgendered populations and allies and/or lesbian, gay, bisexual, and transgender alliances/associations.

LGBTIQQ   Lesbian, gay, bisexual, transgender, intersex, queer, and questioning.

LIHEAP   This is a program to aid low-income households that pay a high proportion of household income for home energy, either heating or cooling a residential dwelling. LIHEAP stands for Low Income Home Energy Assistance Program and is administered by the Department of Health and Human Services.

Limited government   A government that places few restrictions on its citizens' choices and actions, and in which the government is limited in what it can do.

Line item   Numeric line in an appropriation or budget bill.

Line item veto   A special type of veto that the chief executive officer can use to strike the specific parts of the bill he or she dislikes without rejecting the entire bill.

Lobby or lobbyist   Promoting, opposing, or in any manner influencing or attempting to influence the introduction, defeat, or enactment of legislation before any legislative body. The term does not include providing public testimony before a legislative body, a regulatory body, or any committee.

Majority leader A member of the majority political party designated to be a leader. (The procedure for designating the majority leader and other officers varies from state to state.)

Majority party The political party with more than half of the seats in a legislative body.

Majority report Recommendation of action on a measure that is submitted by a majority of the members of a committee.

Markup The action taken by a legislative committee to amend or revise a bill.

Measure General term for bill, resolution, or memorial.

Medicaid A joint federal and state program that helps with medical costs for people with low incomes and limited resources. Medicaid programs vary from state to state, but most health care costs are covered if you qualify for both Medicare and Medicaid.

Medicare The federal health insurance program for people 65 years of age or older; certain younger people with disabilities; and people with permanent kidney failure with dialysis or a transplant, sometimes called ESRD (end-stage renal disease).

Melting pot (*See* multiculturalism.) A term used to refer to a pluralistic society in which people who originally come from different societies blend together to form a new society.

Minority leader A member of the minority political party designated to be leader. (Process of designation varies from state to state.)

Minority party The political party with fewer than half of the seats in a legislative body.

Minority report A report that reflects the thinking of the members not favoring the majority position or action on an issue.

Minutes Accurate record of the proceedings of a meeting in chronological order.

Motion Formal proposal offered by a member of a deliberative assembly.

Multiculturalism A term often used instead of "melting pot" to denote a pluralistic society in which the original cultural heritages of its citizens are recognized and respected.

National origin The political state from which an individual hails; may or may not be the same as that the person's current location or citizenship.

Negative income tax Two tax credit programs are administered by the Internal Revenue Service (IRS) to distribute money to low-income Americans. The tax credits include a "refundable" portion which is paid to individuals and families that owe no income tax for the year. Therefore, this portion of the tax credits act as "negative income tax." The two programs are the Earned Income Tax Credit (EITC) and the Child Tax Credit.

Nongovernmental organizations Nongovernmental organizations (NGOs) are private or nonprofit institutions and agencies that work to serve some public interest independently from a national or local government entity. NGOs often seek to improve social problems that exist internationally; enhance the rights, knowledge, and economic opportunities of all people; and help nations and cultures in development efforts. Nonprofit and private social service organizations are typically referred to as an NGO in the global community.

Nonpartisan   Having no association or affiliation with a political party or caucus.

Norm   A guideline or an expectation for behavior.

Nutrition Assistance Programs   The US Department of Agriculture program that helps needy families buy food.

OASDI (Old Age, Survivors, Disability Insurance)   Social Security programs that provide monthly cash benefits to workers and their dependents when they retire, die, or become disabled.

Oppression   Results from the use of institutional power and privilege where one person or group benefits at the expense of another. Oppression is the use of power and the effects of domination.

Order of business   The defined routine of procedure in the legislative body each day.

Out of order   Not being conducted under proper parliamentary rules and procedures.

Parliamentary inquiry   Question posed by a member to the presiding officer for clarification of the procedure or business before the House.

Partisan   Associated or affiliated with a single political party or caucus.

Party platform   The collection of issue positions endorsed by a political party.

People of color   A collective term for men and women of Asian, African, Latin, and Native American backgrounds; as opposed to the collective "White" for those of European ancestry.

Per diem   Literally, per day; daily expense money rendered to legislators or staff.

Petition   Formal request submitted by an individual or group of individuals to the legislature.

Platform   Any hardware of software t hat hosts a system. For instance, WordPress is a platform that manages a community of blogs.

Pluralism   A society contains numerous centers of power and many people participate in making decisions for society.

Point of information   A request from a legislator to the presiding officer for clarification of a procedural matter.

Point of order   A question by a member to the presiding officer calling attention to a breach of order or of the rules.

Policy brief   A written document that synthesizes existing research knowledge on a policy or practice issue of importance. Written in language an interested nonexpert would find accessible, policy briefs answer the questions: "What is the research evidence related to a given policy or practice option—and what policy recommendations follow from that evidence?"

Policy goal   Desired state of affairs that is hoped to be achieved by the policy.

Political action committee (PAC)   An organization whose purpose is to raise and distribute campaign funds to candidates seeking political office. PACs are generally formed by corporations, labor unions, trade associations, or other organizations or individuals and channel the voluntary contributions they raise to candidates for elective offices. PACs may also spend their funds on what are termed "independent expenditures"—defined in law as a message that advocates the election or defeat of a clearly identified candidate who has no relationship with the PAC.

Political party   An alliance of like-minded people who work together to win elections and control of the government.

Politics   The processes by which government decisions are made.

Postpone indefinitely   A means of disposing of an issue by not setting a date on which to consider it again.

Precedent   Interpretation of rulings by presiding officers on specific rules; unwritten rules that are established by custom.

Prefile   Ability to introduce a measure before the opening of the session.

Prejudice   A preconceived opinion that is not based on reason or actual experience. It is a conscious phenomenon when an individual or group chooses to degrade another person or group, using specific and identifiable reasons. Typically these are irrational reasons. Often they develop when biased ideas are reinforced repeatedly.

Presiding officer   Person designated to preside at a legislative session.

Poverty guidelines   A federal measure that is different from the poverty threshold. They establish a financial level to determine eligibility for certain federal programs.

Poverty threshold   A federal measure that is different the poverty guidelines. The threshold allows the government to quantify (count) the number of people in poverty.

Power   The ability to control others, events, or resources.

Power elite   Theory that the United States is actually run by a small group representing the most wealthy, powerful, and influential people in business, government, and the military.

Prejudice   A prejudgment or unjustifiable, and usually negative, attitude of one type of individual or groups toward another group and its members.

Primary election   An election within a party to choose its nominee for an elected office.

Primary sources   Records made at the time of the event and by participants or direct observers of the event. (*See* Secondary sources.)

Privilege   A special advantage, immunity, permission, right, or benefit granted to or enjoyed by an individual because of class, caste, gender, or racial/ethnic group.

Progressive tax   A tax that takes a larger percentage of a larger income and a smaller percentage of a smaller income.

Project grant   Categorical grant programs in which states submit proposals for projects to the federal government and the national government chooses which to fund on a competitive basis.

Proposed rule   The official document that announces and explains an agency's plan to address a problem or accomplish a goal. All proposed rules must be published in the *Federal Register* to notify the public and to give them an opportunity to submit comments. The proposed rule and the public comments received on it form the basis of the final rule.

Public good   Services that benefit everyone, not just some. Fire and police departments and infrastructure services are examples.

Quorum   When a legislative body is assembled, the minimum number of members required to transact business.

Quorum call   A method used to establish the presence of a majority for the lawful transacting of business.

Racial justice   A proactive reinforcement of policies, practices, attitudes, and actions that produces equitable power, access, opportunities, treatment, impacts, and outcomes for all.

Racial profiling   The discriminatory practice by law enforcement officials of targeting individuals for suspicion of crime based on the individual's race, ethnicity, religion, or national origin.

Ratify   To approve and make valid.

Rational decision making   A systematic process of defining problems, evaluating alternatives, and choosing optimal solutions.

Reapportionment   Redrawing legislative district boundaries to provide equality of representation.

Recess   Intermission in a daily session; intermission from one day to the next.

Referral   The assigning or referring of a bill to committee.

Regressive taxes   Takes a larger percentage of income from low-income earners than from high-income earners. It is in opposition with a progressive tax, which takes a larger percentage from high-income earners.

Republic   A government that runs by representative democracy.

Resolution   A document that expresses the sentiment or intent of the legislature or a chamber, that governs the business of the legislature or a chamber, or that expresses recognition by the legislature or a chamber.

Retirement Earnings Test   If you receive monthly Social Security benefits before your full retirement age and work, your earnings from wages and/or self-employment cannot exceed a certain amount without reducing your monthly benefits.

Role   A set of norms, values, and personality characteristics expected of a person based on the setting he or she is in.

Role conflict   The conflict that can result from the competing demands of two or more roles.

Rule making   The administrative processes to create, amend, and circulate regulations. Legislatures first pass a bill that is a broad policy statement and outlines program mandates. The bill, which is signed by the respective chief executive (President, Governor, Mayor) is then assigned to the appropriate agency where the detailed, explicit rule-making process occurs.

Rules   Regulating principles or methods of legislative procedure.

Secondary sources Reconstructions of an event by a person without first-hand knowledge of it. (*See* Primary Sources.)

Segregation A system that keeps different groups separate from each other through physical dividers, social pressures, or laws.

Self-determination A characteristic of a person that leads them to make choices and decisions based on their own preference and interests, to monitor and regulate their own actions and to be goal oriented and self-directing.

Senate A legislative body; usually the body in a bicameral legislature having the fewer number of members.

Seniority Recognition of prior legislative service.

Separation of power Dividing up governmental power among several branches.

Session (1) Period during which the legislature meets; (2) the daily meeting of the Senate or House.

- *Regular session*—the annual (or biennial) meeting of the legislature required by the Constitution.
- *Special (or extraordinary) session*—a special meeting of the legislature that is called by the governor (or the legislature itself) and limited to specific matters.

Simple majority One more than half of those voting on a question.

Sine die Literally, "without day"; usually, adjournment without a day being set for reconvening; final adjournment.

SNAP (Supplemental Nutrition Assistance Program) Food program for low-income individuals and families. SNAP used to be called the food stamp program. It is run by the United States Department of Agriculture. Participants receive a debit card, which is accepted in most grocery stories for food purchases.

Social control The ways a society devises to encourage conformity to norms.

Social insurance Programs in which eligibility is based on prior contributions to government, usually in the form of payroll taxes.

Social justice Access to resources that enhance one's chances of getting what one needs or influencing others in order to lead a safe, productive, fulfilling life.

Social problems The activities of individuals or groups making assertion of grievances and claims with respect to some putative conditions

Social Security Retirement Social Security is based on a simple concept: While one works, he or she pays taxes into the Social Security system, and when the person retires or becomes disabled, the person, his or her spouse, and dependent children receive monthly benefits that are based on the reported earnings. Also, survivors can collect benefits if the beneficiary dies. Also, known as Old Age Benefits.

Social Security Survivors Benefits Benefits based on your record (if you should die) are paid to: widow/widower age 60 or older, 50 or older if disabled, or any age if caring for a child under age 16 or disabled before age 22; children, if they are unmarried and under age 18, under 19 but still in school, or 18 or older but disabled before age 22; and parents, if you provided at least one half of their support. An ex-spouse could also be eligible for a widow/widower's benefit on your record. A special one-time lump sum payment of $255 may be made to the spouse or minor children.

Social welfare   Nation's system of programs, benefits and services that help people meet those social, economic, educational, and health needs that are fundamental to the maintenance of society

Social worker   Graduates of CSWE accredited schools of social work (in the United States with either bachelor's, master's, or doctoral degrees) who use their knowledge and skills to provide social services for clients (who may be individuals, families, groups, communities, organizations, or society in general). Social workers help people increase their capacities for problem solving and coping, and they help them obtain needed resources, facilitate interactions between individuals and between people and their environments, make organizations responsible to people, and influence social policies.

Socialism   A system under which resources and means of production are owned by the society as a whole, rights to private property are limited, the good of the whole society is stressed more than individual profit, and the government maintains control of the economy.

Speaker   Usually the title given to the person elected as the presiding officer of the House or Assembly; in some states, the title given to the presiding officer of the Senate.

Sponsor   The person (usually a legislator) who presents a bill or resolution for consideration; may be joined by others, who are known as cosponsors. *See also* Author, Introducer, *and* Patron.

Split ticket voting   A ballot cast by a voter who votes for candidates from more than one political party.

Staffer   A person who works for a legislator in a supporting capacity.

Status of bill   The progress of a bill at any given time in the legislative process. It can be in committee, on the calendar, in the other house, etc.

Statute   A law passed by Congress, a state legislature, or some other government body.

Stereotype   Blanket beliefs and expectations about members of certain groups that present an oversimplified opinion, prejudiced attitude, or uncritical judgment. They go beyond necessary and useful categorizations and generalizations in that they are typically negative, are based on little information, and are highly generalized.

Stigma   A trait that we possess that causes a person/group to lose prestige in the eyes of others.

Stratification   A societal system in which there is an unequal distribution of society's rewards and in which people are arranged hierarchically into layers according to how many of society's rewards they possess.

Structural unemployment   Reflects an imperfect match-up of employee skills and the skill requirements of the available jobs or a permanent reduction in demand for an industry's output (e.g., advances in technology).

Stakeholders   All people interested in and potentially affected by a policy such as interest groups or public officials

Sunset   Expiration date of a bill, a particular agency, benefit, or law unless it is reauthorized by the legislature.

Supplemental appropriation Adjustment of funds allocated by the original appropriation.

Supplemental Security Income (SSI) A federal supplemental income program funded by general tax revenues (not Social Security taxes). It targets aged, blind, and disabled people who have limited income and resources by providing monthly cash payments to meet basic needs for food, clothing, and shelter.

Suspension of the rules Parliamentary procedure whereby actions can be taken that would otherwise be out of order.

TANF This is a combined federal and state program that pays cash to low-income households with the goal of moving individuals from welfare to work. TANF stands for *Temporary Assistance for Needy Families* and is administered by the US Department of Health and Human Services.

Terrorism A politically motivated violent attack on civilians by an individual or group.

Totalitarianism A political system under which the government maintains tight control over nearly all aspects of citizens' lives.

Underemployed Working at a job for which one is overqualified, or working part-time when full time work is desired.

Unicameral A legislature with only one chamber (e.g., Nebraska is the only state with one chamber).

Unincorporated nonprofit association Forms whenever at least two people agree to pursue a common lawful purpose that is not for profit. Funds are raised for a limited purpose such as helping a neighbor or sending the local high school group on a trip. An unincorporated association can operate as a tax-exempt nonprofit as long as the purpose of its activity is of public benefit and annual revenues are less than $5,000.

Veto The power of the chief executive (e.g., president or governor) to stop a bill passed by Congress or a state legislature from becoming law.

Veto override Vote by the legislature to pass a bill over a chief executive officer, such as the U.S. president or a state governor veto.

Voice vote Oral expression of the members when a question is submitted for their determination. When asked by the presiding officers, members respond "aye" or "nay." The presiding officer then decides which side prevailed.

Voluntary association A group people choose to join, in which members are united by the pursuit of a common goal.

Vote Formal expression of a decision by the body.

Whistleblower A person who reports wrongdoing in a government agency.

WIC This is a program to provide healthy food to pregnant women and children up to 5 years of age. WIC stands for *Women, Infants and Children* and is available to low-income households.

Working poor The class composed of people whose work leaves them vulnerable to falling below the poverty level.

Xenophobia   A culturally based fear of outsiders. Xenophobia has often been associated with the hostile reception given to those who immigrate into societies and communities.

Yays and nays   Recorded vote of members on an issue.

SOURCES

Association of Social Work Boards. (2017). Retrieved from www.aswb.org/.../2013/10/ASWB_ACE_Glossary.pdf;

Canadian Human Rights Commission. (2016). Glossary. Retrieved from http://www.chrc-ccdp.gc.ca/eng/content/glossary;

Center for the Study of Social Policy. (2017). Race equity-glossary of terms. Retrieved from www.cssp.org/about/race-equity/GLOSSARY-OF-TERMS.pdf;

Federal Safety Net. (2017). U.S. welfare programs, antipoverty programs. Retrieved from http://federalsafetynet.com/us-welfare-programs.html;

Foundation Group. (2017). What is a 501(c)(3)? Retrieved from https://www.501c3.org/what-is-a-501c3/.

National Association of Social Workers. (2017). Definitions. Retrieved from http://www.naswdc.org/practice/intl/definitions.asp;

National Conference of State Legislatures. (2016). Glossary of legislative terms. Retrieved from http://www.ncsl.org/research/about-state-legislatures/glossary-of-legislative-terms.aspx.

National Education Policy Center (2016). Policy Briefs. Retrieved from http://nepc.colorado.edu/publications/policy-briefs;

Quizlet Inc. (2017). Social welfare policy terms. Retrieved from https://quizlet.com/35272883/social-welfare-policy-terms-flash-cards/.

Social Security Administration. (2017). Glossary of Social Security terms. Retrieved from https://www.ssa.gov/agency/glossary/;

Sparknotes. (2017). Sociology glossary. Retrieved from http://www.sparknotes.com/sociology/glossary/terms.html;

Sparknotes. (2017). U.S. Government and politics glossary. Retrieved from www.sparknotes.com/.../glossary/terms.htm.

REFERENCES

Judythemorgan. (2014, September 10). Word magic—one word Wednesday. View from the front porch. Retrieved from http://judythewriter.com/word-magic-one-word-wednesday/ on February 25, 2017.

Moos, J. (2012, December 15). School shooting front pages show the power of a single word, a name. Poynter Institute. Retrieved from http://www.poynter.org/2012/school-shooting-headlines-show-the-power-of-a-single-word/198386/ on February 25, 2017.

Olmstead, G. (2013, August 30). 5 reasons why words matter. The American Conservative. Retrieved from http://www.theamericanconservative.com/2013/08/30/5-reasons-why-words-matter/ on February 25, 2017.

Planas, R. (April 2, 2013). AP drops term "illegal immigrant" from style guide (UPDATED). *The Huffington Post*. Retrieved from http://www.huffingtonpost.com/2013/04/02/ap-drops-term-illegal-immigrant_n_3001432.html on February 25, 2017.

Toobin, J. (August 5, 2015). Should I use the term illegal immigrant. *The New Yorker*. Retrieved from http://www.newyorker.com/news/daily-comment/should-i-use-the-term-illegal-immigrant on February 25, 2017.

CHAPTER 12

Final Thoughts

Social issues and problems are threaded throughout the 200-plus years of US history. And there is every reason to believe that many of these and other unknown difficulties will continue in the future. Policy practice provides the social work profession an important opportunity to promote and advocate for just and fair policies while working to create environments where all people can realize their individual and collective aspirations.

Policy practice just does not happen because a social worker wants to create some sort of change. There is a clearly identified knowledge base and skill set that is unique to policy practice. This is no different from any form of social work practice; clinical social work requires a mastery of core and advanced skills and an understanding of human behavior theories that are different from macro and mezzo work. The social worker whose primary work focus is in the social policy arena develops expertise in a number of advanced topics such as cost–benefit models, fiscal notes, multivariate analysis, environmental risk analysis, qualitative methods for policy analysis, or geographic information systems. Although these subject areas are important for the policy practice specialist, they are not part of the core knowledge and practice behaviors that every social worker should be versed in, no matter his or her work setting.

Briefly revisiting the critical fundamental areas of policy practice is an important reminder of the essential knowledge and skills that require ongoing professional development to sharpen and hone. Paying attention to postgraduate, continuing education opportunities in policy practice will help the social worker develop new and relevant expertise necessary for successful interventions in our fast, ever-changing global community.

SOCIAL WORK PRACTICE AND SOCIAL POLICY

A major premise in the *Handbook* is that all forms of social work practice are directly related to, framed by, and regulated by one or more organizational or public policies. All one needs to do is look at any public or nonprofit social services agency; most are open Monday through Friday, from 8:00 a.m. to 6:00 p.m. and maybe to 8:00 p.m. one weekday evening. However, how do these hours affect a family? Are the adult caretakers required to take unpaid leave or vacation time to access an agency? Why isn't the agency open every night and on weekends? Do the operating hours unintentionally create a barrier for some persons due to work obligations? How do extended hours reflect the agency's mission and purpose?

What some might consider being a minor but fair and just operational change, however, has other implications for the agency. What are the additional financial costs to the agency to extend its hours, including professional and support staff (salaries or hiring additional personnel); are there additional expenses related to the facility operations (heat, electricity); are extra dollars needed to cover these costs, or can existing programs be eliminated with cost savings redirected?

Policy practice attends to a wide swath of organizational matters: who is eligible to participate in a program; how services are paid for; where programs are offered; whether new programs should be added; and whether existing programs should be modified or eliminated.

Without a doubt, all organizational policies directly influence the level and quality of the social worker's services as well as those programs offered by an agency. All social workers, including the BSW generalist practitioner, the MSW clinical social worker, and the PhD/DSW researcher/administrator/practitioner, must engage directly in policy practice; otherwise they do a disservice to their clients and the broader community.

CRITICAL THINKING, A PATHWAY TO TRUTH

One of the most difficult tasks a person faces is to recognize and admit that his or her personal opinion or viewpoint is wrong. A personal belief or conviction is a central driving force in what an individual believes is right and just. These attitudes and preferences can be, and sadly often are, blind to the evidence. "Alternative facts," a new phrase reflecting such positions, emerged shortly following the presidential inauguration in January 2017 and reflects the idea, "I believe this to be true because I have always believed it to be true, or I believe this to be true because others believe it to be true." In the end, ignoring conclusions and findings of rigorous research only hurts clients. Critical thinking is a basic skill that forces the social worker to seek out verifiable information no matter where the information may lead the practitioner or the client. The objective is not to affirm what one believes, but it is a process that leads to the best solution for a particular situation (see Box 12.1).

Most social policy positions are based on the majority's perceptions. Former President Ronald Reagan once stated that people purposefully choose to be homeless and, as a result, the government should do little for them (Roberts, 1988). Yet research around the reasons that lead to homelessness clearly shows direct linkages with mental health, dual-diagnosis issues, domestic violence, and a lack of affordable housing. But ignoring the research allows people to justify falsely that homeless persons simply choose to live under bridges and, as a result, the larger community has no obligation to help them.

Finally, critical thinking is not a one-time or periodic skill that a social worker employs in certain work situations. All forms of social work practice, including micro, mezzo, and macro interventions, are built around and firmly rooted in critical thinking. This is a constant, persistent process common in every social work intervention with each client and advocacy activity.

UNDERSTANDING SOCIAL JUSTICE

An agency's set of policies as well as those of public organizations are a direct statement of a community's view of social justice. Social justice is not limited to a liberal or progressive belief system as there are numerous justice philosophies that reflect contrasting philosophies. Understanding the various, often dichotomous, perspectives of social justice helps the social worker acquire a clearer picture of a situation. A good test for a policy practitioner is to frame an issue or social policy analysis from two different justice positions, such as a libertarian and feminist frameworks. This CT exercise forces the social worker to understand the issue from alternative positions. As a result, the policy practitioner is in a stronger position to propose a comprehensive change strategy that accounts for a variety of possible challenges. Simply outright rejecting one particular philosophy without understanding its basis or addressing the differences in perspectives is nothing more than demagoguery and reinforces political partisanship.

Box 12.1

NO LABELS

Labels allow for quick, snap judgements to be made about people or groups. Labeling in the political world is common—conservative, liberal, moderate, radical, Democrat, Tea Party, Republican, Green—and results in combative, partisan politics. A national advocacy group No Labels typifies the growing number of organizations that promote problem solving over political identify. No Labels sees itself as a peoples' "movement" to support "elected officials who combine ideological independence and common sense with a willingness to reach across the aisle to get things done." See https://www.nolabels.org/.

IDENTIFY CONSTITUENCY GROUPS AND CREATING COLLABORATIONS

Successful policy practice rarely results from an individual's solo effort. Building collaborations and broadening constituency bases are vital in policy practice. The broader and larger the constituency group and collaborative partners, the greater the chance the policy issue will be resolved in a proactive manner. Town hall meetings, voter registration campaigns, testifying in front of elected and voluntary groups, and speaking in public forums at every opportunity help build and strengthen collaborations.

The role of social media, however, is essential in today's 24/7 communication world. Research shows that more and more people, young and old alike, are becoming adept with various social media platforms. Tapping into social media and building a strategy that includes multiple *virtual rooms* helps individuals identify with others while sharing information in nearly real time. Understanding various social media platforms, which work best for which group, and remaining up to date on the infusion of new virtual rooms is essential for the policy practitioner. The social worker must have the expertise to move around several virtual rooms at any one time. Staying wed to a particular technology at the expense of ignoring new, alternative platforms will quickly make the social worker obsolete while potentially eliminating some people from the effort.

A key important axiom for the social worker to remember when building collaborations and engaging constituents is that *constant and persistent communication helps maintain and foster a community's support.*

COMMUNICATING WITH BOARDS, LEGISLATIVE GROUPS, AND THE PUBLIC

Policy practice involves direct engagement with boards of directors, legislators, and the public. Providing testimony, writing a succinct issue analyses, crafting targeted policy briefs and memos, preparing info and fact sheets, developing dashboard indicators, and using social media platforms are separate pieces for a robust and well-rounded policy practice communication strategy. Success in any policy practice initiative requires full understanding of various communication avenues, their respective strengths and limitations, and which work best, either singularly or in combination with others, in a given situation. The social worker need not be an expert in every communication method but can, and should, rely on others who are capable to be the "issue's voice" with particular techniques. Knowing the limits of one's skills and what she or he is good at doing reflects the profession's belief of "professional use of self." The policy practitioner who taps into everyone's strengths and expertise has the greatest chance of achieving their advocacy objectives.

VÉRIFIER, ПРОВЕРИТЬ, VERIFICAR, ÜBERPRÜFEN SIE, 验证, KONTROLLERA

The 21st century is built around immediate and continual communications; people today become easily impatient and frustrated without ongoing digital or media interactions. Just observe a group of people or a family eating dinner in a restaurant, walking down the street, or sitting on a bench. What are they doing? In all likelihood, each person is looking at his or her mobile device, texting someone or responding to a Tweet. Today, we live in an expanding house of "virtual rooms" that are significant and integral parts of the human experience.

People now rely on social media for the majority of their information. Social workers are no different from the public as they too rely on Web sources and social media for news, research, and other informational pieces. Digital-based information now is firmly embedded in policy briefs, issue analyses, and public presentations. However, how does the policy practitioner conclude that the posted information is reliable? What is the outcome if the digitally based data, stories, and reports are incorrect; what impact does this have for the social worker's recommendations and to what extent does presenting inaccurate and false information damage a social worker's credibility?

The policy practitioner must always verify—*Vérifier, Проверить, Verificar, Überprüfen Sie, 验证, Kontrollera*—evidence gleamed through websites to promote an issue, a proposed policy change, or an agency's redirection. Any Web search results in millions of sites posting information and data. The information is quickly retrieved, cut and pasted onto an info sheet, or Tweeted out in a matter of minutes. The social worker must remember a fundamental rule when it comes to any Web or social media posting: *Just because something is written on the Web or sent out on a social media platform doesn't mean it is necessarily true.*

Assessing a site's authenticity, the reliability of the information, and the extent the site is politically biased is important. The accuracy, or lack thereof, of material distributed to the public dramatically influences the potential success or failure of a policy practice initiative. Promoting a position based on faulty data or research will assuredly derail the prospects of achieving the desired outcome. Additionally, the social worker credibility will quickly diminish; he or she will not be recognized as a competent, trusted professional if his or her position is based on faulty, inaccurate data.

PRACTICE CHANGES OVER TIME

When the author first began his work in the early 1970s, copies of a handout were made from a mimeograph that produced about 25 legible prints of one page in a purplish color ink; a two-page handout required two mimeographs sheets and so on. Written issue or policy briefs were carefully typed on a nonelectric typewriter;

spelling and typographical mistakes had to be carefully hand-erased lest the paper be torn. Over time, the electric typewriter with different color ribbons and interchangeable font heads became commonplace while copy machines made it possible to quickly make multiple reprints of a document. By the early 1990s, the desktop computer was becoming commonplace and the advent of the World Wide Web changed how people communicated with each other and increased their capacity to access information. Cellular telephones and paging devices, once limited to physicians and wealthy people, became common fixtures in American households. By 2017, the total communications environment was dramatically different compared to 40 years earlier. The author could have remained steadfastly attached to his manual typewriter and mimeograph copies, but his work would also have become ineffective, and he would have been left on the sideline wondering what was taking place.

Successful practice recognizes that what one knows and is skilled at doing today will change tomorrow. Flexibility and a willingness to grow and change are integral; remaining in a fixed place and being unwilling to consider new alternative practice methods or digital platforms will quickly result in a professional's self-state of obsoleteness.

CHANGE HAPPENS

Change is a constant in the human experience. Yet people generally fear change because it is creating a new, unknown environment and set of relationships. The experienced social worker can share story after story about clients enmeshed in horrible situations, but they could always find a reason to resist change and remain in their current state.

Any change effort is a slow process, and modifying or creating new policies is not immune to what seems to be a sluggish, repetitive process. Most proposed bills in the US Congress and state houses across the United States are defeated and most never get a vote by the full legislative chamber. It is common for a proposal to be introduced and reintroduced session after session.

Boards of directors of local nonprofit agencies too are reluctant and reticent to add new programs or alter existing programs. A common remark voiced by board members is, "If it ain't broke, don't fix it." Or, "This is the way we have always done it."

Policy practice is a slow process, and the social worker must resist the temptation to become frustrated and throw one's hands in the air saying something like, "Well, we gave it a try," and move on to another project. The social worker must help the constituency understand that change is a deliberative process and takes time; change can happen with persistence and a willingness to comprise. The attitude "it's my way or the highway" only creates a we-they scenario, which most often leads to defeat. Finding partners and areas of agreement, no matter how small, keeps the door open for future change efforts.

WHO WRITES THE NEXT CHAPTER

A student stopped by my office asking if she could talk with me for a few minutes. She was in her second year of the MSW program, a clinical major who came to graduate school so she could set up a private practice after graduation. She was perplexed. She said she came to graduate school knowing "exactly what I wanted to do." In her first semester, she had no interest in nor knew anything about policy, but after taking her first policy course she admitted to being somewhat intrigued with the area. Now in her last semester of studies, she had enrolled in my political social work elective course. She said that policy practice was something she would like to do but had not heard of any social workers doing such things nor did she know if there were jobs for social workers in that area. I remember her saying something like, "You know, most people think social workers just give out food stamps or work in child welfare."

After talking a bit, I gave her a list of names of people, told her to go to the library (this was precomputer and World Wide Web days) to see what she could learn about them, and then meet with me the following week. The list included the following individuals:

- Jeannette Rankin
- Frances Perkins
- Maryann Mahaffey
- Whitney Moore Young Jr
- Barbara A. Mikulski
- Ronald V. Dellums

The student came back the following week quite excited and said, "Wow!" And just who were these people?

> *Jeannette Rankin*—a social worker; first woman to hold national office in the United States when, in 1916, she was elected to the US House of Representatives. She was elected as a representative from Montana before the 19th Amendment (e.g., extending the right to vote to women) had passed the US Congress and became the law of the land in 1920.
>
> *Frances Perkins*—a social worker; appointed by President Franklin D. Roosevelt as Secretary of Labor in 1933 and served until 1945; she was the first women appointed to a president's cabinet and was responsible for initiating a number of the New Deal programs, including Social Security, the 40-hour workweek, unemployment insurance, worker's compensation, and the minimum wage.
>
> *Maryann Mahaffey*—a social worker; first elected to the Detroit City Council in 1974. She served as a council member, president pro-tempore, and was

president from 1990 to 1998. She also was the first women elected president of the National Association of Social Workers in 1975.

Whitney Moore Young Jr—a social worker; was executive director of the National Urban League and received the Presidential Medal of Freedom from President Lyndon Baines Jonson.

Barbara A. Mikulski—a social worker; first elected to Baltimore City Council in 1971. In 1976, she won a seat in the US House of Representatives and 10 years later, in 1986, she was elected to the US Senate. In 2011, Mikulski became the longest serving woman senator in US history, and in 2012 she became the longest serving woman in the history of the US Congress.

Ronald V. Dellums—a social worker; represented Oakland California in the US House of Representatives from 1970 to 1998. He chaired the Congressional Black Caucus and was a leading voice calling the government to curb and reverse its military spending and the nuclear arms race; he was a leader in the effort to terminate US government support for the racist regime in South Africa.

The student was right: Wow! There are scores of social workers who have and continue to make their imprint in the policy world. We find social workers engaged in policy practice in the US Congress; in state houses across the country; and in local, state, and national policy advocacy organizations. There are other unsung heroes whose names are not archived in books nor in "Halls of Fame" such as the National Association of Social Workers Social Work Pioneers (NASW Foundation, 2016). In fact, every day social workers in their agencies carry out the majority of policy practice. Their objective is simple: How do we make our agency, its programs, and resulting services more relevant for our community?

The daily encounters of social workers with clients provide irreplaceable insight into the consequences of issues that people deal with on a daily basis. From the personal to societal, all people, no matter where they live, what their socioeconomic status, their race, ethnicity, gender, or age are dealing with social concerns each day. Some are so large that they immobilize the person, family, or community; others are quickly resolved, and the people move on with their lives. But each day, every person is confronted with an issue that potentially can radically change his or her life.

Each individual social worker, based on the profession's mission and beliefs, is positioned to provide important leadership in strengthening or redirecting agency-based and public social policies. The accumulated experiences, knowledge, and expertise of the human condition, resulting from more than a century of social work practice, empower the policy practitioner to be a proactive leader of change. From the US Congress to a local school board, from large national NGOs to small neighborhood-based nonprofits, social workers can and are continuing to make significant differences in the policies that frame practice.

There will never be a final chapter for a policy handbook; but we do know that the next chapter will be authored by the next generation of social work policy practitioners. Some of their names and pictures will be added to the various social work Hall of Fames. Although honors are nice, most important is to understand, believe, and recognize that one social worker, through policy practice, can make a neighborhood, town, village, city, state, or our nation a better place for all people. And what will result in the broader community from that one social worker's activities? All people will have the opportunity to realize their full potential and live their dreams in a community built around and supported by fair and just policies.

REFERENCES

NASW Foundation. (2016). NASW social work pioneers. Retrieved from http://www.nasw-foundation.org/pioneers/default.asp on April 18, 2016.

Roberts, S. (1988, December 23). Reagan on homelessness: Many choose to live in the streets. *The New York Times*. Retrieved from http://www.nytimes.com/1988/12/23/us/reagan-on-homelessness-many-choose-to-live-in-the-streets.html on February 18, 2017.

Appendices

Congressional Caucuses, 115th Congress (Updated July 7, 2017)

This appendix lists the US House of Representative formal caucuses of the 115th Congress, which convened on January 3, 2017. A caucus does not automatically carry over from one congressional session to the next, as each caucus is required to register with the US House of Representatives Committee on House Administration (see https://cha.house.gov/member-services/congressional-memberstaff-organizations). As of July 1, 2017, there were 386 congressional caucuses formally organized by the House Committee on Administration for the 115th Congressional session; the number of caucuses is down from 454 caucuses registered with the Committee on Administration by the end of the 114th session. Visit https://cha.house.gov/member-services/congressional-memberstaff-organizations for the most current posting of US House of Representatives caucuses.

CONGRESSIONAL CAUCUSES, 115TH CONGRESS, JANUARY 3, 2017 TO JANUARY 3, 2019 (UPDATED JULY 7, 2017)

- 115th Class Caucus
- Ad Hoc Congressional Committee for Irish Affairs
- Agriculture and Rural America Task Force
- American Sikh Congressional Caucus
- Americans Abroad Caucus
- Asia-Pacific Economic Cooperation (APEC) Caucus
- Assyrian Caucus
- Auto Care Caucus
- Bipartisan Congressional Task Force to Combat Identity Theft and Fraud
- Bi-Partisan Congressional Pro-Life Caucus
- Bipartisan Disabilities Caucus
- Bipartisan Heroin Task Force
- Bipartisan Historically Black Colleges and Universities Caucus
- Bipartisan Taskforce for Combating Anti-Semitism
- Bipartisan Task Force to End Sexual Violence
- Blue Dog Coalition
- California Democratic Congressional Delegation
- California Public Higher Education Caucus
- Carbonated and Non-alcoholic (C.A.N.) Caucus
- Caucus for the Humane Bond
- Cement Caucus
- Chesapeake Bay Watershed Caucus
- Climate Solutions Caucus
- Congressional 4th Amendment Caucus
- Congressional 21st Century Skills Caucus
- Congressional Academic Medicine Caucus

- Congressional Access to Civil Legal Service Caucus
- Congressional Addiction, Treatment and Recovery Caucus
- Congressional Adult Literacy Caucus
- Congressional Afghan Caucus
- Congressional Agriculture Research Caucus
- Congressional Air Force Caucus
- Congressional Aluminum Caucus
- Congressional American Religious Freedom Caucus
- Congressional Animal Protection Caucus
- Congressional Arctic Working Group
- Congressional Army Caucus
- Congressional Arthritis Caucus
- Congressional Article I Caucus
- Congressional Artificial Intelligence (AI) Caucus
- Congressional Arts Caucus
- Congressional Asian Pacific American Caucus (CAPAC)
- Congressional Assisting Caregivers Today Caucus
- Congressional Asthma and Allergy Caucus
- Congressional Azerbaijan Caucus
- Congressional Baseball Caucus
- Congressional Beef Caucus
- Congressional Bike Caucus
- Congressional Biofuels Caucus
- Congressional Biomass Caucus

- Congressional Biomedical Research Caucus
- Congressional Black Caucus
- Congressional Blue Collar Caucus
- Congressional Border Caucus
- Congressional Border Security Caucus
- Congressional Bourbon Caucus
- Congressional Brain Injury Task Force
- Congressional Building Trades Caucus
- Congressional Buy American Caucus
- Congressional Cambodia Caucus
- Congressional Cancer Prevention Caucus
- Congressional Cancer Survivors Caucus
- Congressional Candy Caucus
- Congressional Cannabis Caucus
- Congressional Career and Technical Education Caucus
- Congressional Caribbean Caucus
- Congressional Caucus for Competitiveness in Entertainment Technology (E-TECH)
- Congressional Caucus for Effective Foreign Assistance
- Congressional Caucus for Women's Issues
- Congressional Caucus on Black Women and Girls
- Congressional Caucus on Bosnia
- Congressional Caucus on Brazil
- Congressional Caucus on California High-Speed Rail

- Congressional Caucus on Ethnic and Religious Freedom in Sri Lanka
- Congressional Caucus on Foster Youth
- Congressional Caucus on Hellenic Issues
- Congressional Caucus on India and Indian Americans
- Congressional Caucus on Intellectual Property Promotion and Piracy Prevention (IP Caucus)
- Congressional Caucus on International Exchange and Study
- Congressional Caucus on Korea
- Congressional Caucus on Long-Range Strike
- Congressional Caucus on Maternity Care
- Congressional Caucus on Parkinson's Disease
- Congressional Caucus on Poland
- Congressional Caucus on Public–Private Partnerships (P3)
- Congressional Caucus on the Association of Southeast Asian Nations (ASEAN)
- Congressional Caucus on the Deadliest Cancers
- Congressional Caucus on Macedonia and Macedonian-Americans
- Congressional Caucus on Modern Agriculture
- Congressional Caucus on Multicultural Media
- Congressional Caucus on the Netherlands
- Congressional Caucus on Prescription Drug Abuse

- Congressional Caucus on Urban Regional Studies
- Congressional Caucus on Vietnam
- Congressional Caucus on Virtual, Augmented and Mixed Reality Technologies ("The Reality Caucus")
- Congressional Caucus on Youth Sports
- Congressional Central America Caucus
- Congressional Chemistry Caucus
- Congressional Chicken Caucus
- Congressional Children's Caucus
- Congressional Childhood Cancer Caucus
- Congressional Children's Health Care Caucus
- Congressional Citizen Legislature Caucus
- Congressional Citrus Caucus
- Congressional Census Caucus
- Congressional Coal Caucus
- Congressional Coalition on Adoption
- Congressional Coastal Communities Caucus
- Congressional Coast Guard Caucus
- Congressional Colombia Caucus
- Congressional Community College Caucus
- Congressional Congenital Heart Caucus
- Congressional Cooperative Business Caucus
- Congressional Corrosion Prevention Caucus
- Congressional Cranberry Caucus

- Congressional Cyber Security Caucus
- Congressional Cystic Fibrosis Caucus
- Congressional Czech Caucus
- Congressional Dairy Farmer Caucus
- Congressional Deaf Caucus
- Congressional Defense Communities Caucus
- Congressional Diabetes Caucus
- Congressional Dietary Supplement Caucus
- Congressional Digital Trade Caucus
- Congressional Direct Selling Caucus
- Congressional Directed Energy Caucus
- Congressional Diversifying Tech Caucus
- Congressional Dyslexia Caucus
- Congressional E-Learning Caucus
- Congressional Electronic Warfare Working Group
- Congressional Emergency Medical Services (EMS) Caucus
- Congressional Energy Savings Performance Caucus
- Congressional Energy Storage Caucus
- Congressional Estuary Caucus
- Congressional Everglades Caucus
- Congressional Explosive Ordnance Disposal (EOD) Caucus
- Congressional Fertilizer Caucus

- Congressional Financial Security and Life Insurance Caucus
- Congressional Fintech and Payments Caucus
- Congressional Fire Services Caucus
- Congressional Flat Tax Caucus
- Congressional Food Safety Caucus
- Congressional Former Mayors Caucus
- Congressional Fragile X Caucus
- Congressional Franchise Caucus
- Congressional French Caucus
- Congressional Friends of Australia Caucus
- Congressional Friends of Denmark Caucus
- Congressional Friends of Egypt Caucus
- Congressional Friends of Ireland Caucus
- Congressional Friends of Liechtenstein Caucus
- Congressional Friends of New Zealand Caucus
- Congressional Friends of Norway
- Congressional Friends of Spain Caucus
- Congressional Friends of Wales Caucus
- Congressional Full Employment Caucus
- Congressional Future Caucus
- Congressional Georgia Caucus
- Congressional German-American Caucus
- Congressional Global Health Caucus

- Congressional Global Road Safety Caucus
- Congressional Green Schools Caucus
- Congressional Grid Innovation Caucus
- Congressional Hazards Caucus
- Congressional Hearing Health Caucus
- Congressional Heart and Stroke Caucus
- Congressional Hellenic Israel Alliance
- Congressional High Performance Building Caucus
- Congressional High-Speed & Intercity Passenger Rail Caucus
- Congressional Hispanic Caucus
- Congressional Hispanic Conference
- Congressional Hockey Caucus
- Congressional Home Health Caucus
- Congressional Home Protection Caucus
- Congressional Homelessness Caucus
- Congressional House Cancer Caucus
- Congressional House Manufacturing Caucus
- House Congressional Mobility Air Forces Caucus
- Congressional Human Trafficking Caucus
- Congressional Humanities Caucus
- Congressional Hungarian Caucus
- Congressional Independent Colleges Caucus
- Congressional Innovation Caucus
- Congressional International Basic Education Caucus
- Congressional Internet Caucus
- Congressional Internet of Things Caucus
- Congressional Interstate 11 Caucus
- Congressional Interstate 73/ 73/75 Caucus
- Congressional Invasive Species Caucus
- Congressional Inventions Caucus
- Congressional Iraq Caucus
- Congressional Kidney Caucus
- Congressional Labor and Working Families Caucus
- Congressional Latino-Jewish Caucus
- Congressional LGBT Equality Caucus
- Congressional Life Sciences Caucus
- Congressional Long Island Sound Caucus
- Congressional Lung Cancer Caucus
- Congressional Lupus Caucus
- Congressional Maker Caucus
- Congressional Media Fairness Caucus
- Congressional Men's Health Caucus
- Congressional Mentoring Caucus
- Congressional Middle Class Jobs Caucus
- Congressional Microbusiness Caucus
- Congressional Military Family Caucus
- Congressional Military Mental Health Caucus
- Congressional Military Sexual Assault Prevention Caucus
- Congressional Military Veterans Caucus
- Congressional Military Youth Programs Caucus
- Congressional Mississippi River Caucus
- Congressional Modeling and Simulation Caucus
- Congressional Morocco Caucus
- Congressional Motorcycle Caucus
- Congressional Motorsports Caucus
- Congressional Multiple Sclerosis Caucus
- Congressional National Guard and Reserve Components Caucus
- Congressional National Parks Caucus
- Congressional Native American Caucus
- Congressional Navy and Marine Corps Caucus
- Congressional Neuroscience Caucus
- Congressional New Americans Caucus
- Congressional NextGen 9-1-1 Caucus
- Congressional Nigeria Caucus
- Congressional Nuclear Security Working Group
- Congressional Nursing Caucus
- Congressional Oceans Caucus
- Congressional Ohio River Basin Caucus

- Congressional Open Source Caucus
- Congressional Opportunity Action Group
- Congressional Oral Health Caucus
- Congressional Organ and Tissue Donation and Transplantation Awareness Caucus
- Congressional Out of Poverty Caucus
- Congressional Peace Corps Caucus
- Congressional Peanut Caucus
- Congressional Pediatric & Adult Hydrocephalus Caucus
- Congressional Pension Protection for Working Americans Caucus
- Congressional Pilots Caucus
- Congressional Pollinator Protection Caucus
- Congressional PORTS Caucus
- Congressional Portuguese Caucus
- Congressional Post-9/11 Veterans Caucus
- Congressional Prayer Caucus
- Congressional Pre-K Caucus
- Congressional Primary Care Caucus
- Congressional Privacy Caucus
- Congressional Prize Caucus
- Congressional Progressive Caucus
- Congressional Propane Caucus
- Congressional Public Broadcasting
- Congressional Public Health Caucus
- Congressional Public Transportation Caucus

- Congressional Puget Sound Recovery Caucus
- Congressional Rare Earth Caucus
- Congressional Ready Mixed Concrete Caucus
- Congressional Recycling Caucus
- Congressional Reentry Caucus
- Congressional Research and Development (R&D) Caucus
- Congressional Resilient Construction Caucus
- Congressional Rugby Caucus
- Congressional Rural Caucus
- Congressional Rural Veterans Caucus
- Congressional School Choice Caucus
- Congressional Scouting Caucus
- Congressional Second Amendment Caucus
- Congressional Semiconductor Caucus
- Congressional Serbian Caucus
- Congressional Sharing Economy Caucus
- Congressional Shellfish Caucus
- Congressional Shipbuilding Caucus
- Congressional Sindh Caucus
- Congressional Singapore Caucus
- Congressional Ski and Snowboard Caucus
- Congressional Skin Cancer Caucus
- Congressional Slovak Caucus
- Congressional Small Business Caucus
- Congressional Smart Transportation Caucus

- Congressional Social Work Caucus
- Congressional Soils Caucus
- Congressional Special Operations Forces Caucus
- Congressional Sportsmen's Caucus
- Congressional STEAM Caucus
- Congressional Sudan and South Sudan Caucus
- Congressional Taiwan Caucus
- Congressional Telehealth Caucus
- Congressional Term Limits Caucus
- Congressional Texas Maritime Caucus
- Congressional Tourette Syndrome Caucus
- Congressional Trademark Caucus
- Congressional Transparency Caucus
- Congressional Transatlantic Trade and Investment Partnership (TTIP) Caucus
- Congressional Travel and Tourism Caucus
- Congressional Tuesday Group Caucus
- Congressional Unmanned Systems Caucus
- Congressional US Cargo Airship Caucus
- Congressional US–Lebanon Friendship Caucus
- Congressional US–Mexico Friendship Caucus
- Congressional Urban Caucus
- Congressional US–China Working Group
- Congressional Valley Fever Task Force Caucus

- Congressional Values Action Team
- Congressional Veterans Jobs Caucus
- Congressional Victims' Rights Caucus
- Congressional Voting Rights Caucus
- Congressional Warrior's Caucus
- Congressional Wildlife Refuge Caucus
- Congressional Working Forests Caucus
- Congressional Writers Caucus
- Congressional Youth Challenge Caucus
- Congressional Zika Caucus
- Congressional Zoo and Aquarium Caucus
- Connecting the Americas Caucus
- Conservative Opportunity Society
- Creative Rights Caucus
- Crime Prevention and Youth Development Caucus
- Democratic Israel Working Group
- Distributed Generation Caucus
- Electromagnetic Pulse Caucus
- European Union Caucus
- Florida Ports Caucus
- Friends of Finland Caucus
- Friends of Kazakhstan Caucus
- Friends of Switzerland Caucus
- Global Investment in America Caucus
- Government Efficiency Caucus
- Historic Preservation Caucus

- House Aerospace Caucus
- House Automotive Caucus
- House Baltic Caucus
- House Decentralized Wastewater Recycling Caucus
- House Ethiopian-American Caucus
- House Farmer's Cooperative Caucus
- House Freedom Caucus
- House General Aviation Caucus
- House Liberty Caucus
- House Organic Caucus
- House Outdoor Recreation Caucus
- House Paper and Packaging Caucus
- House Republican Israel Caucus
- House Rural Education Caucus
- House Specialty Crops Caucus
- House Sugar Caucus
- House Textile Caucus
- House Trails Caucus
- House UK Caucus
- House Whistleblower Protection Caucus
- House Wire and Wire Products Caucus
- Hydrogen and Fuel Cell Caucus
- I-69 Congressional Caucus
- Immigrant Servicemembers and Veterans Caucus
- International Conservation Caucus
- International Religious Freedom Caucus
- Israel Allies Caucus
- Kurdish-American Congressional Caucus
- Land Conservation Caucus
- Law Enforcement Caucus

- Medical Technology Caucus
- Mental Health Caucus
- Missile Defense Caucus
- Municipal Finance Caucus
- National Heritage Area Caucus
- National Service Caucus
- New Democrat Coalition
- Northeast-Midwest (NEMW) Congressional Coalition
- Northern Border Caucus
- Northwest Energy Caucus
- Oil and National Security (ONS) Caucus
- Olympic & Paralympic Caucus
- Problems Solvers Caucus
- Public Works and Infrastructure Caucus
- Purple Heart Caucus
- Rare Disease Caucus
- Real Estate Caucus
- Recording Arts and Sciences Congressional Caucus
- Romanian Caucus
- Skilled American Workforce Caucus
- Small Brewers Caucus
- Sri Lanka Caucus
- Task Force on Anti-Terrorism & Proliferation Financing
- Taxed Enough Already Caucus
- Tuberculosis (TB) Elimination Caucus
- Tunisia Caucus
- US–Japan Caucus
- US–Philippines Friendship Caucus
- Veterinary Medicine Caucus
- Work for Warriors Caucus

Example of Federal Register Publication Call for Proposed Rule Change

This appendix includes an example of a formal announcement for a proposed rules change, which is required for all federal and state policy actions. Only during an emergency may a rules change occur without a formal public hearing.

Request for Public Comment on the Proposed Adoption of Administration for Native Americans Program Policies and Procedures
Source: https://www.federalregister.gov/documents/2017/01/23/2017-01418/ request-for-public-comment-on-the-proposed-adoption-of-administration-for-native-americans-program

A Notice by the Children and Families Administration on 01/23/2017

Document Details
Publication Date: 01/23/2017
Agencies: Administration for Children and Families
Dates: The deadline for receipt of comments is 30 days from the date of publication in the Federal Register. No Funding Opportunity Announcement (FOA) will be published prior to 30 days from publication of this Notice.
Document Type: Notice
Document Citation: 82 FR 7834
Page: 7834-7836 (3 pages)
Agency/Docket Number: CFDA Numbers: 93.581, 93.587, 93.612
Document Number: 2017-01418

Published Document
AGENCY: Administration for Native Americans, ACF, HHS.
ACTION: Notice for public comment.

SUMMARY:

Pursuant to Section 814 of the Native American Programs Act of 1974 (NAPA), as amended, the Administration for Native Americans (ANA) is required to provide members of the public an opportunity to comment on proposed changes in interpretive rules and general statements of policy and to give notice of the final adoption of such changes no less than 30 days before such changes become effective. In accordance with notice requirements of NAPA, ANA herein describes proposed interpretive rules and general statements of policy that relate to ANA's funding opportunities beginning in fiscal year (FY) 2017 related to the following programs: Environmental Regulatory Enhancement (HHS-2017-ACF-ANA-NR-1221), Sustainable Employment and Economic Development Strategies (HHS-2017-ACF-ANA-NE-1225), Native American Language Preservation and Maintenance-Esther Martinez Immersion (HHS-2017-ACF-ANA-NB-1226), Native American Language Preservation and Maintenance (HHS-2017-ACF-ANA-NL-1235), Social and Economic Development Strategies (HHS-2017-ACF-ANA-NA-1236), and Economic Development Strategies-Alaska (HHS-2015-ACF-ANA-NK-0960), and Native Youth Initiative for Leadership, Empowerment, and Development (HHS-2017-ACF-ANA-NC-1263). This notice of public comment also provides additional information about ANA's plan for administering grant programs.

DATES: The deadline for receipt of comments is 30 days from the date of publication in the **Federal Register**. No Funding Opportunity Announcement (FOA) will be published prior to 30 days from publication of this Notice.

ADDRESSES: Comments in response to this notice should be addressed to Camille Loya, Director of Policy, Administration for Native Americans, 330 C Street SW., Washington, DC 20201. Delays may occur in mail delivery to federal offices; therefore, a copy of comments should be emailed to *ANAComments@acf. hhs.gov.* Comments will be available for inspection by members of the public at the Administration for Native Americans, 330 C Street SW., Washington, DC 20201.

FOR FURTHER INFORMATION CONTACT: Camille Loya, Director, Division of Policy, Administration for Native Americans, (877) 922-9262.

SUPPLEMENTARY INFORMATION: Section 814 of NAPA, as amended, incorporates provisions of the Administrative Procedure Act that require ANA to provide notice of its proposed interpretive rules and statements of policy and to seek public comment on such proposals. ANA has also decided to provide notice and seek comments on proposed new rules of agency organization, procedure, or practice. The proposed interpretive rules, statements of policy, and rules of ANA procedure and practice reflected in clarifications, modifications, and new text will appear in the seven FY 2017 FOAs: Environmental Regulatory

Enhancement (ERE), Sustainable Employment and Economic Development Strategies (SEEDS), Native American Language Preservation and Maintenance-Esther Martinez Immersion (EMI), Native American Language Preservation and Maintenance (P&M), Social and Economic Development Strategies (SEDS), Social and Economic Development Strategies-Alaska (SEDS-AK), and Native Youth Initiative for Leadership, Empowerment, and Development (I-LEAD). This notice serves to fulfill the statutory notice and public comment requirement.

A. FUNDING OPPORTUNITY ANNOUNCEMENTS

For information on the types of projects funded by ANA, please refer to the following for information on current and previously funded ANA grants at http://www.acf.hhs.gov/ana/grants.

B. INTERPRETIVE RULES, STATEMENTS OF POLICY, PROCEDURES, AND PRACTICE

1. The following is applicable to all ANA FOAs published beginning in FY 2017:
    a. Pre-application trainings, teleconferences, or webinars. It is government-wide policy and practice that each FOA contain all of the detail needed for an applicant to fully understand the funding opportunity and submit a complete and compliant application. ANA has historically conducted in-person pre-application trainings through its Regional Technical Assistance (TA) Centers and now proposes possible additional pre-application teleconferences or webinars related to its FOAs beginning in FY 2017. Joining and participating in any pre-application in-person training, teleconference, or webinar is voluntary and only information provided in published FOAs will be presented. ACF policy requires that no additional information that is not already provided in the FOA can be disseminated after FOAs have been published. Participation in any of the pre-application training or informational opportunities is voluntary and will not affect award selection. Participants will remain anonymous and, in the case of in-person training, names of participants will not be retained after the training. Opting not to participate in a pre-application in-person training, teleconference, or webinar will not affect eligibility, application scoring, or the selection process. Applicants unable to attend pre-application teleconferences or webinars will be able to access materials, recordings, or transcripts on the ANA Web site at on the Events section of the ANA Web site at http://www.acf.hhs.gov/ana/events after the teleconference or webinar has concluded and no later than 30 days prior to the application due date. ANA has historically posted its *Pre-Application Guide to Developing and Writing Your ANA Application* that

is used in in-person pre-application meetings and will continue to do so. This resource can be found at http://www.acf.hhs.gov/ana/resource/pre-application-training-manual. For the dates, times, registration, and other information for scheduled pre-application in-person trainings applicants should contact the appropriate regional Training and Technical Assistance Provider at http://www.acf.hhs.gov/ana/t-ta-regions-map. This proposed policy and practice will be reflected in *Section I. Program Description—Pre-Application Teleconferences or Webinars* of the FOAs.

b. Application periods. ANA proposes to reduce from 90 to 60 days the time period applicants have to respond to all FY 2017 FOAs because we have determined, based on experience and feedback provided by prior applicants Start Printed Page 7835 and TA providers, that a 60-day period to prepare, finalize, and submit applications responsive to the FOAs is a sufficient period of time. In addition, a 60-day application period will help ANA to ensure grants are awarded timely given the time required for competitive panel review, internal review, award decisions, and administrative processing of grant awards. This proposed policy and practice will be reflected in the *Overview Section* of the FOAs.

c. Application Toolkit. ANA proposes to add a link in all FOAs to allow applicants to access ANA's newly established ANA Application Toolkit. The purpose of the Application Toolkit is to provide examples and templates to assist eligible applicants to navigate the application requirements detailed in FOAs. As a collection of otherwise available tools, use of the ANA Application Toolkit is voluntary. This proposed practice will be reflected in *Section VIII. Other Information, Reference Web sites* in the FOAs.

2. The following is applicable to Social and Economic Development Strategies (SEDS) FOA (HHS-2017-ACF-ANA-NA-1236), including Social and Economic Development Strategies for Alaska (SEDS-AK) (HHS-2015-ACF-ANA-NK-0960), beginning in FY 2017:

New Program Area of Interest. In response to the enactment of the Native American Tourism and Improving Visitor Experience Act (NATIVE Act), Public Law 114-221, in September 2016, ANA proposes to include a new economic development program area of interest under the SEDS and SEDS-AK FOAs. The new program area of interest is proposed as:

Tourism—Planning or developing resources, services, and businesses that promote travel, recreation and tourism, or branding to tell the story of Native Americans as the First Peoples of the United States. Projects may use the arts or other cultural resources to help revitalize Native communities, promote economic development, increase livability, and present the uniqueness of the Native communities to visitors in a way that celebrates the diversity of the United States.

Even though ANA has previously funded economic and social development projects broadly falling under tourism, the new program area of interest is proposed in response to new specific statutory authority under the NATIVE Act. This proposed policy will be reflected in *Section I. Program Description, Program Areas of Interest* in the SEDS and SEDS-AK FOAs.

3. The following is applicable to Native Youth Initiative for Leadership, Empowerment, and Development (I-LEAD) (HHS-2017-ACF-ANA-NC-1263) FOA beginning in FY 2017:

   a. Application due dates. ANA proposes to modify the application due dates for I-LEAD applications because ANA anticipates earlier publication than in FY 2016. In addition, ANA proposes a 60-day application period for all FY 2017 FOAs. These two factors combine to result in earlier I-LEAD application deadlines.

   b. Grants as the instruments of I-LEAD financial assistance. In 2016, ANA awarded I-LEAD financial assistance as cooperative agreements. We propose, beginning in FY 2017, to award I-LEAD financial assistance as grants instead of cooperative agreements because we do not believe the level of substantial federal involvement associated with cooperative agreements is necessary for successful future I-LEAD projects. Both cooperative agreements and grants are legal instruments of financial assistance, but cooperative agreements are distinguished from grants in that cooperative agreements provide for substantial federal involvement between the federal awarding agency (ANA) and the non-federal entity (I-LEAD awardee) in carrying out the activity(ies) contemplated by the federal award. In general terms, "substantial federal involvement" refers to the degree to which federal employees (or technical assistance providers) are directly performing, implementing, or directing parts of the funded program. In a cooperative agreement, federal employees and their agents participate more closely in performance under the financial assistance award including mandated collaborations and activities with other entities. In contrast, with grants, the federal government is limited to an oversight and monitoring role but does not direct grant performance. ANA has determined that I-LEAD projects do not require the level of "substantial federal involvement" contemplated by cooperative agreements. While ANA intends to continue to develop and refine technical assistance resources, materials, and opportunities for all recipients of I-LEAD awards and to encourage and facilitate communities of practice across funded projects serving Native youth, we have determined that the oversight and monitoring role is sufficient to ensure the purposes of I-LEAD projects are adequately supported while, at the same time, allowing I-LEAD grant recipients to determine how to implement their grants within the terms and conditions of their grant awards.

   c. Length of project periods. ANA proposes to shorten the project period for I-LEAD awards beginning in FY 2017 from no more than 60 months to no more than 48 months because we have determined that project periods of up to 48 months better position I-LEAD projects for long-term success.

Based on ANA's experience with the first recipients of I-LEAD financial assistance, we believe slightly more compressed I-LEAD project periods will facilitate greater emphasis by I-LEAD grantees, at the beginning their projects, on the efficient implementation of culturally relevant evidence-based programming as well as a greater emphasis at end of I-LEAD project periods on activities to ensure financial and programmatic sustainability of project outcomes. We believe there is an inherent momentum in 48-month project periods that will carry I-LEAD projects forward from planning, implementation, and continuous quality improvement to long term sustainability at the end of 48-month I-LEAD project periods. This proposed policy will be reflected in the *Executive Summary* of the I-LEAD FOA.

d. Project Description—

   i. Objective Work Plan. ANA proposes requiring submission of the Objective Work Plan (OWP) as part of the initial application submission and reflecting the entire project period of up to 48 months. When I-LEAD projects were funded as cooperative agreements, part of ANA's substantial federal involvement included post-award development of the OWP in partnership with I-LEAD recipients. Since ANA proposes to award I-LEAD financial assistance as grants, without the substantial federal involvement entailed by joint development of OWPs, submission of the OWP as an application requirement beginning in FY 2017 has been determined necessary to support adequate project planning and post-award monitoring. This proposed policy will be reflected in *Section IV.2. Content and Form of Application Submission—Project Description—Objective Work Plan* in the I-LEAD FOA.

   ii. Outcome oriented project objectives. ANA proposes outcome oriented objectives that are Specific, Measurable, Achievable, Relevant, and Time-bound (S.M.A.R.T.) be included in funding applications because it is our experience that objectives that are S.M.A.R.T. are more likely to be achieved and are more likely to be useful to gauge project progress. This change for I-LEAD projects would also make the requirements for I-LEAD applications consistent with the Start Printed Page 7836 application requirements for ANA's other funding opportunities. This proposed policy will be reflected in *Section IV.2. Content and Form of Application Submission—Project Description—Expected Outcomes— Objectives and V.1. Criteria—Outcomes Expected* in the I-LEAD FOA.

   iii. Impact Indicator. ANA proposes applications for I-LEAD financial assistance include at least one impact indicator: a qualitative measure that defines factor(s) the project needs to benchmark and monitor. Impact indicators also provide the means for measuring and evaluating an I-LEAD project's progress and impact. This proposed policy will be reflected in the *Section IV.2. Content and Form of Application*

Submission—*Project Description—Expected Outcomes—Impact* in the I-LEAD FOA.

e. Project Budget and Budget Justification. I-LEAD applicants are required to attend ANA's annual grantee meeting. We propose to add a new requirement of attendance for an additional day to convene with I-LEAD projects funded by ANA and the youth involved in project implementation. This proposed policy will be reflected in *Section IV.2. Content and Form of Application Submission—Project Description—Project Budget and Budget Justification* in the I-LEAD FOA and will also reflect suggested travel costs increased by $500 per region for additional estimated lodging and per diem.

f. Review Criteria—

i. limination of Bonus Points. ANA proposes to remove the bonus points that were authorized in FY 2016 I-LEAD FOAs because our experience with the prior year's application review demonstrated the allocation of up to 5 bonus points for letters of support from youth is not necessary to ensure applications reflect support from youth involved in the development of the project proposal as well as in project implementation. The proposed application point allocation reflecting the discontinued use of bonus points is found at *Section V.1. Criteria* of the I-LEAD FOA.

ii. Allocation of points across I-LEAD application evaluation criteria. ANA proposes to modify the point allocation across I-LEAD application review criteria to ac\count for the proposed elimination of bonus points as well as the proposed OWP application requirement. We propose, beginning in FY 2017, the following evaluation criteria point allocations: Needs for Assistance up to 10 points; Outcomes Expected up to 25 points; Approach up to 35 points; OWP up to 20 points; and the Budget and Budget Justification up to10 points. The proposed modification to the point allocation can be found at *Section V.1. Criteria* for the I-LEAD FOA.

Statutory Authority: Section 814 of the Native American Programs Act of 1974 (NAPA), as amended.

Kimberly Romine,
Deputy Commissioner, Administration for Native Americans.
[FR Doc. 2017-01418 Filed 1-19-17; 8:45 am]
BILLING CODE 4184-34-P

Social Workers in Congress, 115th Congress and Social Workers in State and Local Offices

This National Association of Social Workers collects information regarding social workers who hold elective offices at the local, state, and federal levels of government. Check the NASW website for the most up-to-date available information regarding social workers serving in Congress and holding state and local offices: https://www.socialworkers.org/pace/state_swers.asp.

SOCIAL WORKERS IN CONGRESS, 115TH CONGRESS, JANUARY 3, 2017–JANUARY 3, 2019

Name	Web Address
Senator Debbie Stabenow (D-MI)	www.stabenow.senate.gov/?p=contact
Representative Karen Bass (D-CA)	https://bass.house.gov/
Representative Susan A. Davis (D-CA)	http://susandavis.house.gov/
Representative Luis V. Gutierrez (D-IL)	https://gutierrez.house.gov/
Representative Barbara Lee (D-CA)	https://lee.house.gov/
Representative Carol Shea-Porter (D-NH)	https://shea-porter.house.gov/
Representative Kyrsten Sinema (D-AZ)	https://sinema.house.gov/index.cfm/home
Representative Niki Tsongas (D-MA)	https://tsongas.house.gov/#dialog

Source: National Association of Social Workers (2016). Social workers in Congress, 114th session. Retrieved from https://www.socialworkers.org/pace/state_swers.asp on February 17, 2017.

SOCIAL WORKERS IN ELECTED STATE AND LOCAL OFFICES BY STATE, REPORTED BY NASW, FEBRUARY 7, 2017

State	Name	Party	Office Level	Gender	Credential	Race/Ethnicity
AK	Betty Davis	D	State legislature	F	BSW	African American
AZ	Celeste Plumlee	D	State legislature	F	MSW	Caucasian
AZ	Paul Cunningham	D	City/ municipal	M	MSW	Caucasian
AZ	Katie Hobbs	D	State legislature	F	BSW, MSW	Caucasian
AZ	Pete Rios	D	County/ borough	M	MSW	Hispanic/Latino
AZ	Kyrsten Sinema	D	Congress	F	BSW, MSW	Caucasian
AZ	Ralph Varela	D	City/ municipal	M	MSW	Hispanic/Latino
CA	Fernando Armenta	D	County/ borough	M	MSW	Hispanic/Latino
CA	Ruth Atkin	D	City/ municipal	F	MSW	Caucasian
CA	John Avalos	D	County/ borough	M	MSW	Hispanic/Latino
CA	Susan Davis	D	Congress	F	MSW	Caucasian
CA	Susan Eggman	D	State legislature	F	MSW	Hispanic/Latino
CA	Monica Garcia	D	School board	F	MSW	Hispanic/Latino
CA	Genoveva Garcia-Calloway	D	City/ municipal	F	MSW	Hispanic/Latino
CA	Jorge Gonzalez	D	School board	M	MSW	Hispanic/Latino
CA	Cheryl Heitmann	D	City/ municipal	F	MSW	Caucasian
CA	Barbara Lee	D	Congress	F	MSW	African American
CA	Victor Manalo	D	City/ municipal	M	MSW	Asian/Pacific
CA	David Mineta	D	Other	M	MSW	Asian/Pacific
CA	Nayin Nahabedian	D	School board	F	MSW	Other
CA	Bill Rosendahl	D	City/ municipal	M	MSW	Caucasian
CA	Al Rowlett	D	School board	M	MSW	African American

State	Name	Party	Office Level	Gender	Credential	Race/Ethnicity
CA	Ann Tanner		School board	F	MSW	Caucasian
CA	Tony Thurmond	D	City/ municipal	M	MSW	African American
CA	Clark Williams	D	County/ borough	M	MSW	Caucasian
CA	Mariko Yamada	D	State legislature	F	MSW	Asian/Pacific
CO	Tracy Kraft-Tharp	D	State legislature	F	MSW	Caucasian
CO	Judy Montero	D	City/ municipal	F	MSW	Hispanic/Latino
CO	Jonathan Singer	D	State legislature	M	MSW, BSW	Caucasian
CT	Julie Cooper Altman	D	School board	F	MSW	
CT	Lucille Brown		School board	F	MSW	
CT	David Burgess	D	City/ municipal	M	MSW	Caucasian
CT	Diane Cady	D	City/ municipal	F	MSW	Caucasian
CT	Steve Cassano	D	State legislature	M	MSW	Caucasian
CT	Christopher Donovan	D	State legislature	M	MSW	Caucasian
CT	Toni Edmunds- Walker	D	State legislature	F	MSW	African American
CT	Glen Gemma	D	School board	M	MSW	Caucasian
CT	Rick Lopes	D	State legislature	M	MSW	Caucasian
CT	Mary Jane Lundgren	D	City/ municipal	F	MSW	Caucasian
CT	Christopher Lyddy	D	State legislature	M	MSW	Caucasian
CT	Edith Prague	D	State legislature	F	MSW	Caucasian
CT	Pedro Segarra	D	City/ municipal	M	MSW	Hispanic/Latino
CT	Kim Shepardson Watson	D	School board	F	MSW	

State	Name	Party	Office Level	Gender	Credential	Race/Ethnicity
CT	Robert J. Wolf	D	City/municipal	M	MSW	
DC	Tommy Wells	D	City/municipal	M	MSW	Caucasian
DE	Ted Blunt	D	City/municipal	M	MSW	African American
FL	Suzanne Gunzburger	D	County/borough	F	MSW	Caucasian
FL	Steve Kornell	D	City/municipal	M	MSW	Caucasian
FL	John Legg	Reform	State legislature	M	BSW	Caucasian
FL	Diane Scott		School board	F	MSW, DSW	Caucasian
GA	Pam Stephenson	D	State legislature	F	MSW	African American
GA	Renee Unterman	R	State legislature	F	BSW	Caucasian
GA	Evelyn Winn Dixon	D	City/municipal	F	MSW	African American
HI	Haunani Apoliona	I	County/borough	F	MSW	Asian/Pacific
HI	Ryan Yamane	D	State legislature	M	MSW	Asian/Pacific
IA	James Anderson	D	Human Rights Commission Chair	M	MSW	Caucasian
IA	Martha Anderson	D	State legislature	F	MSW	Caucasian
IA	Mark Cowan		School board	M	MSW	
IA	Joni Dittmer	R	School board	F	MSW	Caucasian
IA	Joel Fry	R	State legislature	M	MSW	
IA	Susan Kosche Vallem		City/municipal	F	MSW	Caucasian
IA	Rebecca Schmitz	D	County/borough	F	MSW	Caucasian

State	Name	Party	Office Level	Gender	Credential	Race/Ethnicity
IA	Mark Smith	D	State legislature	M	MSW	Caucasian
ID	Cherie Buckner-Webb	D	State legislature	F	MSW	African American
IL	John Del Genio	I	School board	M	MSW	Caucasian
IL	Lori DeYoung	D	County/ borough	F	PhD	Caucasian
IL	Kenneth Dunkin	D	State legislature	M	MSW	African American
IL	Luis Gutierrez	D	Congress	M	MSW	Hispanic/Latino
IL	Jane Herron	D	School board	F	MSW	Caucasian
IL	Christine Radogno	R	State legislature	F	MSW	Caucasian
IL	Susan Rose		City/ municipal	F	MSW, PhD	Caucasian
IL	Edie Sutker	I	City/ municipal	F	MSW	Caucasian
IN	Oliver Davis	D	City/ municipal	M	MSW	African American
IN	Joe Micon	I	State legislature	M	MSW	Caucasian
IN	Gail Riecken	D	State legislature	F	BSW	Caucasian
KS	Robert Byers		School board	M		African American
KS	Becky Fast		City/ municipal	F	MSW	Caucasian
KS	Vanessa Sanborn		School board	F		Caucasian
KY	Shevawn Akers		City/ municipal	F	MSW	Caucasian
KY	Diane Lawless		City/ municipal	F	BSW; MSW	Caucasian
KY	Tina Ward-Pugh	D	City/ municipal	F	MSW	Caucasian
KY	Jim Wayne	D	State legislature	M	MSW	Caucasian

State	Name	Party	Office Level	Gender	Credential	Race/Ethnicity
KY	Susan Westrom	D	State legislature	F	MSW	Caucasian
LA	Carolyn Hill	D	School board	F	MSW	African American
LA	LaVonya Malveaux	D	City/ municipal	F	BSW	African American
MA	Michael Ashe	N/A	County/ borough	M	MSW	Caucasian
MA	Sally Bleiberg	N/A	City/ municipal	F	BSW, MSW	Caucasian
MA	Henrietta Davis	D	City/ municipal	F	MSW	Caucasian
MA	Susan Falkoff	D	City/ municipal	F	MSW	Caucasian
MA	Sheila Harrington	R	State legislature	F	BSW	Caucasian
MA	Denise Hurst	D	School board	F	MSW	African American
MA	Johnathan Lothrop	D	City/ municipal	M	MSW	Caucasian
MA	Alison Malkin		City/ municipal	F	MSW	Caucasian
MA	Marc McGovern	D	School board	M	MSW	Caucasian
MA	Jennifer McKenna	N/A	City/ municipal	F	MSW	Caucasian
MA	Sarai Rivera	D	City/ municipal	F	MSW	Puerto Rican
MA	Karen Spilka	D	State legislature	F	BSW	Caucasian
MA	Niki Tsongas	D	Congress	F		Caucasian
MA	Judy Zabin	N/A	City/ municipal	F	MSW	Caucasian
MD	Melony Griffith	D	State legislature	F	MSW	African American
MD	Barbara Mikulski	D	Congress	F	MSW	Caucasian
ME	Michael Brennan	D	City/ municipal	M	MSW, BSW	Caucasian
ME	Adam Goode	D	State legislature	M	MSW	Caucasian

State	Name	Party	Office Level	Gender	Credential	Race/Ethnicity
ME	Joyce McCreight	D	State legislature	F		Caucasian
ME	Melanie Sachs	D	City/municipal	F	MSW, BSW	Caucasian
ME	Charlotte Warren	D	State legislature	F		Caucasian
MI	Theresa Abed	D	State legislature	F	MSW, BSW	Caucasian
MI	Terry Brown	D	State legislature	M	MSW, BSW	Caucasian
MI	Marcia Hovey-Wright	D	State legislature	F	MSW, BSW	Caucasian
MI	Barbara Levin Bergman	D	County/borough	F	MSW, BSW	Caucasian
MI	Debbie Stabenow	D	Congress	F	MSW	Caucasian
MI	Jacquelin E. Washington		School board	F	MSW	African American
MN	Lawrence Hosch	D	State legislature	M	MSW	Caucasian
MN	Sheldon Johnson	D	State legislature	M	BSW	Caucasian
MN	Rafael Ortega	D	County/borough	M	MSW, BSW	Hispanic/Latino
NC	Alan Beck		School board	M	BSW	
NC	Donna Bell		City/municipal	F	MSW	African American
NC	MaryAnn Black		County/borough	F	MSW	
NC	Jaquelyn Gist	N/A	City/municipal	F	MSW	Caucasian
NC	Michelle Johnson		City/municipal	F	MSW	African American
NC	Graig Meyer	D	State legislature	M	MSW	
NC	Paige Sayles		School board	F	MSW	
NC	John I. Steele		City/municipal	M	MSW	Caucasian
NC	Tom Stevens		City/municipal	M	MSW	Caucasian

State	Name	Party	Office Level	Gender	Credential	Race/Ethnicity
ND	Tim Mathern	D	State legislature	M	MSW	Caucasian
NE	Kate Bolz	D	State legislature	F	MSW	Caucasian
NH	James MacKay	R	State legislature	M	DSW	Caucasian
NJ	Sheila Oliver	D	State legislature	F	MSW	African American
NM	Mary Jane Garcia	D	State legislature	F		Hispanic/Latino
NV	Teresa Benitez-Thompson	D	State legislature	F	MSW	Hispanic/Latino
NV	Carolyn Edwards	I	School board	F	MSW	Caucasian
NV	David Humke	R	County/borough	M	MSW	Caucasian
NV	Annie Wilson	I	School board	F	MSW	African American
NY	Patricia Eddington	D	State legislature	F	MSW	Caucasian
NY	Earlene Hill Hooper	D	State legislature	F	MSW	African American
NY	Fran Knapp	D	County/borough	F		Caucasian
NY	Henrietta Lodge		School board	F	MSW	
NY	Vito Lopez	D	State legislature	M	MSW	Hispanic/Latino
NY	Katharine O'Connel	D	City/municipal	F	MSW	Caucasian
NY	Angela Petty	D	County/borough	F	MSW	Caucasian
NY	Joseph Sanfiliippo	D	City/municipal	M	MSW	Caucasian
OH	Jacqueline Bird		City/municipal	F	BSW	Caucasian

State	Name	Party	Office Level	Gender	Credential	Race/Ethnicity
OH	Patricia Britt	D	City/ municipal	F	BSW	African American
OH	Thomas West	D	City/ municipal	M	MSW	African American
OH	Tina Wozniak	D	County/ borough	F	MSW	Caucasian
OR	Joseph Gallegos		State legislature			
OR	William Shields	D	State legislature	M	MSW	Caucasian
OR	Carolyn Tomei	D	State legislature	F	MSW	Caucasian
PA	William Amesbury	D	County/ borough	M	MSW	Caucasian
PA	John Blake	D	State legislature	M	MSW	Caucasian
PA	Diane Ellis-Marsegila	D	County/ borough	F	MSW	Caucasian
PA	Maria Weidinger	D	City/ municipal	F	MSW	Caucasian
RI	Michael Burk	D	School board	M	MSW	Caucasian
RI	Maria Cimini	D	State legislature	F	MSW	Caucasian
RI	Gary Cournoyer	D	City/ municipal	M	MSW	Caucasian
RI	Stephen Mueller	D	School board	M	MSW	Caucasian
RI	Roger Picard	D	State legislature	M	MSW	Caucasian
RI	Michael Reeves	D	School board	M	MSW	Caucasian
RI	Rita Williams		City/ municipal	F	MSW	Caucasian
SC	Gilda Cobb-Hunter	D	State legislature	F	MSW	African American
SC	Jim Manning	D	County/ borough	M	MSW	Caucasian

State	Name	Party	Office Level	Gender	Credential	Race/Ethnicity
SD	Joni Cutler	R	State legislature	F	BSW	Caucasian
TN	Dr. Carol B. Berz		City/municipal	F	MSW	Caucasian
TN	Michelle Holt-Horton		School board	F	MSW	Caucasian
TN	Joe Pitts	D	State legislature	M	BSW	Caucasian
TX	Sylvia Garcia	D	County/borough	F	BSW	Mexican American
TX	Elliott Naishtat	D	State legislature	M	MSW	Caucasian
UT	Francis D. Gibson	R	State legislature	M	MSW	Caucasian
UT	Sandra Hollins	D	State legislature	F	MSW	African American
UT	Christine Passey	D	State legislature	F	BSW	Caucasian
VA	James Fitzsimmons		School board	M	MSW	Caucasian
VT	Janet Ancel	D	State legislature	F	MSW	Caucasian
VT	Diane Bugbee	D	School board	F	MSW	Caucasian
VT	Sandra Dooley	D	City/municipal	F	MSW	Caucasian
VT	Michael Fisher	D	State legislature	M	MSW	Caucasian
VT	Ann Denison Pugh	D	State legislature	F	MSW	Caucasian
VT	Sarah Kunz Robinson	D	City/municipal	F	MSW	Caucasian
WA	Mary Lou Dickerson	D	State legislature	F	MSW	Caucasian
WA	Connie Ladenburg	D	State legislature	F	MSW	Caucasian
WA	Tina Orwall	D	State legislature	F	MSW	Caucasian

State	Name	Party	Office Level	Gender	Credential	Race/Ethnicity
WA	Eric Pettigrew	D	State legislature	M	MSW	African American
WI	Tamara Grigsby	D	State legislature	F	MSW	African American
WI	Mark Schmitt		County/ borough	M	MSW	Caucasian
WI	Nick Smiar	D	County/ borough	M	PhD	Caucasian
WV	Cathy Gatson	D	County/ borough	F	MSW	Caucasian
WV	Becky Jones Jordan		School board	F	MSW	Caucasian
WV	Robert Musick	D	City/ municipal	M	MSW	Caucasian
WV	John David Smith		City/ municipal	M	MSW	Caucasian
WY	Georgia Broyles		City/ municipal	F	MSW	Caucasian
WY	Floyd Esquibel	D	State legislature	M	MSW, BSW	Hispanic/Latino
WY	Jerry Iekel	R	State legislature	M	MSW, BSW	Caucasian

Note. The list is outdated as some of those individuals identified on the NASW website were not in office at the time when the information was downloaded from the Web. For example, former Texas legislator Elliott Naishtat did not seek re-election in 2016, and four Vermont legislators (Diane Bugbee, Sandra Dooley, Michael Fisher, and Sarah Kunz Robinson) were not in office.

Source: National Association of Social Workers (2016). Social workers in state and local office. Retrieved from https://www.socialworkers.org/pace/state.asp on April 16, 2016.

Three Examples of Op-Eds Written by Social Workers

The op-ed, the opinion editorial opposite the editorial page, is an excellent opportunity to advocate or support a position. The narrative is compelling and driven by clear evidence. Social workers, through their daily practice experiences, are in a unique position to share their insights on the human condition, social issues, and emerging problems.

Box A4.1

ARE RACE RELATIONS WORSE UNDER OBAMA? PERHAPS, BUT THE PRESIDENT HAS LITTLE TO DO WITH IT

Pittsburg Post-Gazette, April 19, 2015

By Larry E. Davis

Are race relations worse today than they were before America elected its first black president?

Yes and no.

But the yes has little to do with President Barack Obama, as is often the accusation or insinuation in the asking of this question. I believe three factors contribute to our present state of race relations.

Our society does seem to be experiencing more racial turmoil today than it has in the last few decades. Not since the civil rights movement of the 1960s and the conflicts that accompanied it have we seen our country so gripped by the issue of racism. Why is this the case?

Beginning, perhaps, with the beating of Rodney King by white Los Angeles police officers in 1991, the modern-day abuse of black people has become steadily more exposed. This has culminated in the recent police killings of black men in New York, South Carolina and elsewhere that have become known to almost everyone due to the ubiquity of smartphones and social media.

Social media have made racism more audible and more visible. They have enabled acts of racism to be captured and carried instantly to millions of people. Social media are doing exactly what television did in the civil rights era—exposing injustice.

This is a good thing. Exposure can help curb racial bigotry. But social media have the added benefit of allowing millions to participate in that exposure by posting and reposting videos, interviews, news articles and commentary.

Behavior not only reflects attitudes, it can change attitudes. And research suggests that once we cease to engage in a given behavior there is less reason to maintain the thinking that supported it. Hence, by exposing, thereby discouraging, thereby reducing racist behavior, social media may also help to reduce racially biased attitudes.

Most of the racist practices we witness today have a long history. One case in point is the recent incident in Oklahoma, where students from a college fraternity were exposed reciting a racist fraternity chant. This was captured on video.

At a press conference, the young man who led the chant was asked where he learned it. He declined to respond, but reporters later confirmed that it had been passed down by prior generations of fraternity members.

So no, the number of race-related incidents probably has not increased, but we do have a vastly heightened awareness of them through their media exposure.

Yet yes, race relations are probably worse today than they have been in our most recent past. Actually, this is predictable since race relations have historically worsened in difficult economic times.

Our country has lost much of its manufacturing base over the last few decades. This has dramatically hurt working-class families. Among whites, males in particular have lost economic ground since the 1980s. Hence, white males and their families, in particular, feel betrayed by our society. Unfortunately, blacks and other nonwhites are frequently viewed as the reason for these job losses or, at a minimum, perceived as competitors for the few jobs that are available.

The thing is, blacks too depended on manufacturing to live middle-class lives and have experienced devastating economic losses—perhaps more than any other group. Indeed, one in five auto workers was black in the 1960s. So they also feel abandoned by society.

In addition, blacks are all too aware of the long history of racial exploitation and maltreatment they have experienced in virtually all sectors of employment. So, like whites, today's working-age blacks are pessimistic about their employment futures—and they too are angry about it. The result is that we have problematic race relations grounded in economic failings and perceived competition among groups—a common cause of racial conflict.

Another reason we now are experiencing less-than-harmonious race relations is the changing racial demographics of the country. In 1970, nonwhites comprised just 20 percent of the population. Today nonwhites make up slightly over 30 percent.

This demographic change has resulted in a waning of many of the advantages whites enjoyed through their sheer numbers. For some, President Obama is the manifestation and embodiment of these demographic changes. To many whites, he is seen as what is wrong with the country.

Indeed, things have changed: More nonwhites are eligible to vote, and they are voting more. The civil rights movement eventually helped put more minorities in positions of power and wealth as barriers that excluded minorities and women from opportunities have fallen.

While these changes have made our country more just, they also have eliminated some "white privileges." Sociologist Michael Kimmel has suggested that the removal of these privileges has outraged some whites, placing them in what he calls a state of "aggrieved entitlement."

As Americans, we will adapt to these new realities. As we did with the racial strife brought on by the civil rights movement, we will work through the trauma of exposed racism, economic strife and changing demographics. Few among us can imagine going back to separate black and white restrooms or water fountains.

As my colleague professor Jennifer Hockchilds has said, "The memories of what once was will be replaced with memories of how things are, and how things are soon come to be the way things ought to be."

Larry E. Davis is dean of the School of Social Work, Donald M. Henderson Professor and director of the Center on Race and Social Problems at the University of Pittsburgh (ledavis@pitt.edu).

Source: Davis, L. E. (2015, April 19). Are race relations worse under Obama?" *Pittsburgh Post-Gazette*. Retrieved from http://www.post-gazette.com/opinion/Op-Ed/2015/04/19/Are-race-relations-worse-under-Obama-asks-Larry-E-Davis-of-the-University-of-Pittsburgh/stories/201504190077 on December 2, 2016.

Box A4.2
ON WORLD AIDS DAY, LET'S CONFRONT
THE CHALLENGING PROBLEM OF HIV/AIDS IN THE BLACK
GAY COMMUNITY WITH RENEWED HONESTY AND ACTION

By Gary Bailey

Huffington Post, November 30, 2016

In the spring of 1986, I found myself in the intensive care unit at Boston's Tufts New England Medical Center. I was the only person visiting a friend who just five days prior had been diagnosed with pneumocystis pneumonia. At the time, this type of pneumonia was known as a difficult to treat, opportunistic infection. It was also an indicator that my friend had AIDS. I listened to the respirator that helped him breath, and watched helplessly as his life ebbed away. I had no idea that this was not to be just one heartbreaking loss, but rather the beginning of a period of intense grief that would last for years, as countless of my friends died of the disease.

In those very early days, there was little outreach being done about AIDS in the Black community. In fact, it was hard to find any information at all. But then I met Larry Kessler, who had founded the Boston AIDS Action Committee. I first became involved as a volunteer, specifically to get the word out into communities of color.

There I met other Black gay men and we formed support groups specifically for Black gay men. It was so desperately needed. Due to the stigma of AIDS, many of my friends' families were unwilling to admit what was happening to their loved ones when they got sick. After they died, family members often refused to acknowledge the cause. My friends and I quickly learned to speak in code about "cancer funerals" when we were with our extended families, in our churches, or out in the community.

When we were in more inclusive and safer gay spaces, such as local gay bars and clubs, we found that there too, few people wanted to talk about AIDS. Although the intersection of race and AIDS was acknowledged at AIDS Action, it was obvious that Black gay men were more likely to get sick and die faster than White gay men. We needed to give each other support and help find ways to get around some of the race-based barriers we faced in getting information, much less access to healthcare.

Three decades later, that greater vulnerability to HIV among Black gay men still exists. Last year, the U.S. Centers for Disease Control reported great news: rates of new HIV diagnoses had dropped 19 percent between 2005 and 2014. But new diagnoses were up among Black gay men by 22 percent, and had increased an astounding 87 percent for young Black gay men aged

13–24 years old. If current HIV diagnoses rates persist, about 1 in 2 black men who have sex with men (MSM) and 1 in 4 Latino MSM in the United States will be diagnosed with HIV during their lifetime, according to a new analysis by researchers at the Centers for Disease Control and Prevention (CDC).

The offensive trope that Black gay men are more likely to contract HIV because they take greater sexual risks has been thoroughly debunked by careful study. The simple truth is that racism has played, and continues to play, a significant role in the lives of Black gay men making them more vulnerable to HIV. Historically, as a community, Black gay men have had much lower rates of health insurance coverage, and when the coverage was there, the role that implicit bias plays in some parts of the healthcare delivery system resulted in poorer health outcomes for people of color generally.

Practically speaking, this means that Black gay men living with HIV are less likely to have suppressed the virus with medication and are more likely to transmit HIV to a sexual partner. This helps explain the higher rates of HIV among gay men of color.

The work of raising awareness, and eliminating barriers to healthcare and medicine is far from over. Here's where we must do better:

- Getting Black gay & MSMs tested for HIV and treated with culturally sensitive and informed medical interventions is critical to lowering rates of HIV.
- Encourage sexually active Black gay men who do not have HIV to ask their doctor about PrEP (pre-exposure prophylaxis), an anti-retroviral medication that, if taken daily, makes it nearly impossible to acquire HIV.
- Just as important, although more difficult to achieve, is reducing racism and homophobia, both explicit and implicit, among healthcare providers and support staff. A 2015 study published in the American Journal of Public Health found that nearly a third (29 percent) of Black gay and bisexual men said that they had encountered racist or homophobic behavior in healthcare settings. As a result they were much less likely to seek out preventive care, such as HIV testing and treatment, on a timely basis.

People who *know* better *do* better. We owe it to those who didn't make it, to do what we can now to end this disease, once and for all.

Gary Bailey M.S.W., A.C.S.W. Professor of Practice, Simmons College School of Social Work, SocialWork@Simmons, and Simmons College School of Nursing and Health Sciences.

Source: Bailey, G. (2016, November 30). On World AIDS Day, let's confront the challenging problem of HIV/AIDS in the black gay community with renewed honesty and action. *Huffington Post*. Retrieved from http://www.huffingtonpost.com/gary-bailey-msw-acsw/on-world-aids-day-lets-co_b_13312506.html on December 2, 2016.

Box A4.3
HOMELESS DESERVE MORE THAN RHETORIC

By Ira Colby

Houston Chronicle, November 30, 2013

More than a month has passed since I saw the police cars' blue lights blinking. The traffic had come to a crawl, and I knew something bad had happened. The intersection was quickly filling with onlookers. Yellow police tape cordoned off the bus stop's waiting booth where inside, a white blanket covered a body.

I immediately knew that Ms. Cleo was under the nondescript blanket.

Ms. Cleo was a homeless woman who sat day in and day out at a corner that I drove by to and from work. She had been there for years, sitting on a small chair. I don't know how old Ms. Cleo was; the stress and pain of the streets seems to make people look older than they really are. She wasn't a large woman, maybe 5 foot, 5 or 6 inches, and she walked with a slow shuffle. Ms. Cleo was always there with a smile and a wave even on those days when I didn't stop the car to roll down my window to give her some spare change or my sack lunch.

I have no idea how many thousands of cars passed by Ms. Cleo each week or how many people passed her by over the years. But that day, Ms. Cleo lay slumped over on the bus stop seat under an everyday blanket.

The homeless are everywhere—they're not just an urban phenomenon. In Houston, we see the homeless on our street corners with cardboard signs— "Homeless, Hungry, Please Help, God Bless." We see them in our parks, sometimes sleeping on a bench with a shopping cart holding their life's possessions; we see homeless people in the library, riding Metro trains and buses, at night on the sidewalk curled up under a blanket, or standing in a food line outside of a church hall. For the most part, we see them but we also avoid making eye contact or saying hello.

Our government leaders ask how many homeless people are there, but do the numbers really matter? Has it made a difference knowing a number? The National Alliance to End Homelessness reports that in the nationwide January "point-in-time count," there were 633,782 homeless persons in the United States. But is this number even close to being exact?

Because there is no consensus around the U.S. Department of Housing and Urban Development's definition of homelessness, I would say probably not. And this number is even more suspect in light of the U.S. Department of Education's October report that identified slightly more than 1.1 million homeless youth enrolled in public schools during the 2011–2012 academic year.

The homeless in our communities have complex problems with no easy, one-size-fits-all solution. The U.S. Conference of Mayors' 2012 Status Report on

Hunger and Homelessness noted that 30 percent of homeless adults were severely mentally ill, 18 percent were physically disabled, 17 percent were employed, 16 percent were victims of domestic violence, 13 percent were veterans, and 4 percent were HIV-positive.

And sadly, as Ms. Cleo attests, 44 percent of the homeless, according to the National Coalition for the Homeless, are unsheltered; they will not be in a safe, secure, housing environment tonight.

Our national, state and local homeless policies are convoluted and disjointed, firmly built on a foundation that lacks compassion and understanding of the multi-dimensional, complex issues faced on a daily basis by homeless persons.

How often do we hear someone minimizing the issue of homelessness by claiming affected persons "choose" to live on the streets? Is it really "freedom of choice" when a comprehensive supportive system is simply not available? Or, how often have we heard someone say, don't give them any food or money, you're only encouraging them to beg? It is certainly easy to justify not doing anything when much needs to be done.

Houston Mayor Annise Parker is aggressively tackling homelessness among veterans. The city's Housing Houston's Heroes initiative is part of a nationwide partnership between public agencies and area nonprofit organizations. Initial reports are encouraging as homeless veterans move from the streets into safe, secure housing.

But much more must be done for all of those people whose homes are the streets, parks and underpasses. The time has come for the elected local, county, state and federal officials to work directly with the leaders of nonprofit and public agencies to create an aggressive homeless prevention program, one that provides safe and secure living spaces. A place that is easily accessible and affordable, staffed by qualified professionals who can provide critical behavioral health care case-management services.

A comprehensive shelter program must create pathways from the insecurity of the streets to the safety of a permanent home. Just as important is to establish programs that ensure unaccompanied youth on the street have a place to spend the night.

Let me pose a simple question: Would you be fine and supportive if your son or daughter, brother or sister, mother or father, aunt or uncle said they were going to live on the streets?

Ms. Cleo was someone's daughter, granddaughter, maybe a niece and a sister. She deserved better.

Ira Colby is Dean and Professor of Social Work, Graduate College of Social Work, University of Houston.

Source: Colby, I. (2013, November 13). Homeless deserve more than rhetoric. *Houston Chronicle*. Retrieved from http://www.chron.com/opinion/outlook/article/Homeless-deserve-more-than-rhetoric-5022745.php on May 22, 2016.

Op-Ed and Letters to the Editor Guidelines: 100 Online and Print Publications

Most newspapers provide space for individuals to submit Op-eds (see Appendix 4) and letters to the editor. This information is typically found on the newspaper's editorial page and/or the paper's website. A person does not need to be a newspaper subscriber or live in the paper's hometown/distribution area in order to submit an op-ed or letter to the editor. This appendix includes guidelines and links to 100 online and printed newspapers with the largest circulations.

Source: The Oped Project. (n.d.). Submission information. Retrieved from http://www.theopedproject.org/index.php?option=com_content&view=article&id=47&Itemid=54#50 on July 29, 2016.

1. **USA Today**

   Op-Eds: 650–900 words. They want pieces that address issues now at the top of the news in an incisive, compelling way or introduce wholly new subject matters and insights of interest to readers. Do not attach the op-ed but paste it into the body of the email. Include background information, like your qualifications for writing about the subject and your basic contact information. E-mail the Forum Page Editor at theforum@usatoday.com. A response may take up to a week.

   Letters: 200 words or fewer have the best chance of being published. Letters that include a name, address, day and evening phone numbers, and that are verified by USA TODAY, are considered for publication. Send it to letters@usatoday.com or by fax to 703-854-2053 or by mail to 7950 Jones Branch Drive, McLean, VA 22108.

2. **Wall Street Journal**

   Op-Eds: 600–1,200 words, double-spaced. The piece must center on a strong argument about an issue in the news and not be a response to a Journal article. Please use jargon-free language. Exclusive use of your article is required and the paper reserves 10 working days to keep it under consideration. In your e-mail, include a brief summary of your article, your name and day and evening phone numbers. Do not send your op-ed as an attachment but paste it below your summary and contact information. E-mail the Editorial Features Editor Mark Lasswell, edit.features@wsj.com. Authors whose submissions are selected will be notified as soon as possible. Authors whose articles will not be used will be contacted within 10 business days. Do not call to confirm receipt or check for a status until 10 business days have passed.

   Letters: 300-word limit. If responding to a letter that has appeared already, send comments to Timothy Lemmer (letters editor) at wsj.ltrs@wsj.com or fax to (212)-416-2255. Include date, city where writer is located.

3. **New York Times**

   Op-Eds: 400–1,200 words but any length will be considered. All submissions must be original and exclusive to the Times and they will not consider pieces that have been already published. Do not send attachments if submitting by email. You can submit pieces to opinion@nytimes.com, by fax to 212-556-4100 or by mail to The Op-Ed Page, 620 Eighth Ave, New York, NY 10018. If you do not hear back within 3 business days, please assume they are passing and you can submit it elsewhere.

   Lives Column: 800 words, the "Lives" column features an essay by an outside contributor each week on the last page of The New York Times magazine. Columns are in the form of personal essays. Send it to lives@nytimes.com Read more details on how to write and submit a "Lives" column.

   Letters: 150–175 words. Must be exclusive to the NYTimes. Send e-mails letters@nytimes.com and for the International NYT, send to inytletters@nytimes.com. No attachments. Only letters selected for publication will be notified within a week. Letters may be edited and shortened for space.

4. **NY Daily News** (New York, NY)

   Op-Eds: 650–750 words and must be offered exclusively to the Daily News. They will not consider articles that have been published elsewhere. Do not send attachments. E-mail submissions to Josh Greenman, oped@nydailynews.com. If you do not hear back within 5 business days, assume they have declined.

   Letters: The shorter the letter, the more likely to get published. Include name, address, and phone number. Submit by e-mail to voicers@nydailynews.com

5. **Los Angeles Times** (MO)

   Op-Eds: 750 words average and 1,200-word pieces are sometimes run on Sundays. List the name of author followed by the topic in the subject line; paste the text of the article into the body of the message. Include day and evening phone numbers and short biography of writer. You will hear from the editor within 5 days if it's accepted. Send to oped@latimes.com. Call 213/237-2121 for complete submission information. Nicholas Goldberg, the former Op-Ed editor (now editor of the Editorial Pages), explains how the opinion pages work and what their goal is in the article, Op-Ed, explained.

Letters: 150 words or fewer. Letters that do not contain full contact information cannot be published. Letters may be edited. You will be contacted if they wish to publish your letter. Submit via an online form.

6. **Washington Post**

Op-Eds: 800 words maximum. Articles already in other publications or posted online (including in blog form) will not be accepted. You don't need to have special expertise, but if you do, elaborate on it. If you do not hear back in a week, it's safe to assume your piece will not be used. The best way to submit article is using the online form. You can submit personal essay op-eds to the Outlook section, outlook@washpost.com.

Letters: 200 words or fewer. Do not send attachments, include contact information and, if sending by mail, signature. Submit by e-mail (preferred) to letters@washpost.com or mail to Letters to the Editor, The Washington Post, 1150 15 St. NW, Washington, DC 20071. The Post is unable to acknowledge letters it does not publish.

7. **New York Post** (New York, NY)

Op-Eds: Send to online@nypost.com or call to pitch by phone, 212-930-8288. No other information listed.

Letters: Send to letters@nypost.com. Include name and basic contact information with all submissions.

8. **Chicago Tribune** (IL)

Op-Eds: 500–600 words. Not looking for "Ax-grinding, spleen-venting tirades," nor for direct rebuttals of news stories or other op-ed articles. They also will not consider "self-serving advocacy pieces." Completed op-eds should be sent with your name, address, day and evening cell phone numbers, and your credentials for writing on the topic. You must have either expertise in the field or a relevant personal experience. E-mail is preferred method of submission ctc-comment@tribune.com. Mailing address: "Op-ed submission, 435 N. Michigan Ave., TT-400/Chicago, IL 60611." Cannot accept telephone, mail or e-mail queries. Articles are edited as little as possible, but right is reserved to do so. If you do not hear back within a week, assume they do not plan to use your piece.

Letters: 400 words or fewer about timely topics. Preferred submission method is by e-mail: ctc-TribLetter@Tribune.com. You may also submit it by fax: 312/222-2598, mail to Voice of the People, Chicago Tribune, 435 N. Michigan Ave., Chicago, IL, 60611 or submit it via an online form. Include your contact information as well as your city and state.

9. **Houston Chronicle** (TX)

Op-Eds: 700 words or less. The essay should be written persuasively and not be promotional. No attachments, please. Include name, Twitter handle if you have one, day and evening phone numbers, and byline identification with affiliation or expertise that is related to the essay. Send articles to outlook@chron.com. Authors of essays chosen for publication will be contacted.

Letters: 250 words or less, must have all contact information including your Twitter handle, if relevant. Letters are subject to editing. Send by e-mail to viewpoints@chron.com. No attachments.

10. **Philadelphia Inquirer** (PA)

Op-Eds: 500–800 words. Include name, e-mail address, day and evening phone number/s, and mailing address. Submissions by e-mail: oped@phillynews.com, by mail: Commentary Page Editor, The Inquirer, Box 41705, Philadelphia, PA 19101 or by fax: 215-854-4483. Previously unpublished pieces are preferred. They only respond to those whose pieces they will accept.

Letters: Approx. 200 words. Authors' e-mail addresses are published only with their consent. Letters may be edited for clarity, length, and accuracy. Preference for publication goes to letters sent exclusively to The Inquirer. Because of the volume, we cannot confirm receipt of each letter. Letters become the property of The Inquirer and may be republished in any medium. Include your name, e-mail address, home address, and day and evening phone numbers should be included for verification purposes. E-mail to Inquirer.Letters@phillynews.com; mail to Readers Editor, The Inquirer, Box 41705, Philadelphia, PA 19101; or faxed to 215-854-4483. Questions? Call 215-854-4215.

11. **Newsday** (Long Island, NY)

Op-Eds: 700–800 words. They occasionally publish unsolicited opinion essays. Include your name, phone numbers, address and e-mail address with your article. Submit it to oped@newsday.com. The editor will contact you if your essay is to be published.

Letters: 5,000 characters or less. Submit using this form (go to newspaper website) and following the instructions.

12. **Denver Post** (CO)

Op-Eds: 650 words or fewer. They favor columns on public policy, social issues and current news and give preference to local and regional writers and to local and regional issues. They do not publish organizational statements, business pitches or political campaign promotions as guest commentaries. They reserve the right to edit columns for style, grammar, length, taste, libel and general readability. Writers retain the rights to their work after publication but they cannot consider pieces that have been published previously. E-mail the piece to columns@denverpost.com with "guest commentary" in the subject line, include a high-resolution photo of the author and a short biographical paragraph.

Letters: Email or mail to: openforum@denverpost.com, Letter to the Editor, The Denver Post, 101 W. Colfax Ave, Denver CO 80202.

13. **Arizona Republic** (Phoenix)

Op-Eds: 600 words. "My Turn" columns from individuals and organizations in Arizona are given priority. Designed to provide a forum for "untitled" Arizonans. If your submission is under consideration you will receive a telephone call or e-mail requesting a photograph (color or black and white; standard head-and-shoulder shots). Give name, phone number, city of residence and email address. List expertise. Contact opinions@arizonarepublic.com, 602-444-8292, or My Turn, The Arizona Republic, PO Box 1950, Phoenix, AZ 85001.

Letters: 1000 characters or fewer. Subject matter should be relevant to readers, provocative, constructive, timely. Passion is good. So is humor. Letters criticizing The Republic are OK, even encouraged, so long as the criticism is constructive and not mean-spirited. Letters that disagree with editorial stances are every bit as valuable for publication, if not more so, than letters that agree with them. Letter writers may have no more than one letter published per month. Only signed letters are published. Submit using an online form or send via US mail to: Letters to the Editor, The Arizona Republic, P.O. Box 1950, Phoenix, AZ 85001. Letters may also be faxed to (602) 444-8933.

14. **The Christian Science Monitor**

Op-Eds: As of spring 2014, CSM is not accepting general, unsolicited op-eds. They are now accepting topic specific commentary submissions for their Energy Voices and New Economy blogs. Please see the criteria on this page for submissions to Energy Voices and New Economy. Doors may be opening for submissions to other sections in the near future.

Letters: 200 words or fewer. Letters need to refer to a specific article that appeared in a weekly magazine issue of the Monitor within the past two months. It must be your original work and have not been published anywhere else. Include your full name, address, and phone number. Submit to letters@csmonitor.com. They will only contact people whose letters they will publish.

15. **Chicago Sun Times** (IL)

Op-Eds: 600-word limit. They favor op-eds about local Chicago-area and Illinois issues. Please include full name, address and telephone number. Submit it online using an online or by mail: Chicago Sun-Times, 401 N. Wabash, Chicago, IL 60611. They will only contact writers of op-eds that they are interested in publishing.

Letters: Letters must be written exclusively for this paper. Include full name, phone number and address. Submit using an online form. Read their submission guidelines.

16. **Plain Dealer** (Cleveland, OH)

    Op-Eds: 700-word limit. Include your daytime phone number. Email submissions are preferred forum@plaind.com. Include daytime telephone number. Letters are edited for length and clarity. You will typically hear back on Thursdays if your piece has been accepted.

    Letters: 200 words or fewer. They want letters that comment on and further the public debate on topics of general interest. Include full contact information. Submit via an online form by mailing it to Letters to the Editor, Cleveland Plain Dealer, 1801 Superior Ave., Cleveland, OH 44114 or faxing 216/999-6114.

17. **Detroit Free Press** (MI)

    Op-Eds: 550 words or less. They will consider pieces that are newsworthy, factual and make a compelling argument. Include relevant links to sources for information used in the commentary. Please include a complete address and both day and evening telephone numbers. E-mail: oped@freepress.com.

    Letters: 150 words or less. Subject to editing for length, accuracy and clarity. Must include full mailing address and phone numbers. Submit using an online form, or mail: Editor, Detroit Free Press, 600 W. Fort, Detroit, MI 48226 or fax: 313/222-6774

18. **Boston Globe** (MA)

    Op-Eds: 700 words or less. Fax to 617-929-2098 or e-mail it to oped@globe.com. They will only contact people whose pieces they will publish. If you have not heard back in 5 days, you can assume they are passing on it.

    Letters: Limit 200 words. Include all contact information. Submit via an online form or mail to Letters to the Editor, Boston Globe, P.O. Box 55819, Boston, MA 02205-5819.

19. **Dallas Morning News** (TX)

    Op-Eds: Less than 650 words. They like to publish columns about state and local issues that are written by those with specific knowledge about the topic. Include a "tagline" for yourself, daytime phone number and mailing address as well as a JPG photo of yourself. Submit by e-mail: viewpoints@dallasnews.com.

    Letters: Less than 200 words. Your topic should be about something in the news in the last few weeks. Focus on one thing you want to say. They edit for clarity and length. Include your name, address and phone number. Submit using an online form or by mail: Letters from Readers, The Dallas Morning News, Box 655237, Dallas, TX 75265.

20. **Seattle Times** (WA)

    Op-Eds: 650-word maximum, must be exclusive to Seattle Times. Preference given to local writers and issues. They prefer e-mail submissions, opinion@seattletimes.com. You can also submit by mail, The Seattle Times, P.O. Box 70, Seattle, WA 98111 or by fax to 206/382-6760. Include basic contact information.

Letters: 200 words or less. The decision to publish a letter is based on clarity of thought, response to current events and the graceful art of letter writing. Opinions that differ from those presented elsewhere on the editorial and opinion pages are also given priority. If submitting a letter, please include the topic or headline and date of the article, editorial or opinion piece to which your letter refers. Submit the letter with contact information to letters@seattletimes.com, or Letters Editor, Seattle Times, PO Box 70, Seattle, WA 98111 or fax 206/382-6760. For more information, call 206/464-2132.

21. **San Francisco Chronicle** (CA)

Op-Eds: "Open Forum" pieces are 500 words or fewer. Submissions for the "Sunday Insight" can be up to 700 words. Have a piece about an issue in the news that's unusual in its approach and uncommonly well-written? Mad? Outraged? Have an only-in-the-Bay-Area story? Do you know someone who is tackling a problem or meeting a challenge in a particularly innovative way? They don't run one writer's work more often than every 6 months. Use an online form for both types of commentary.

Letters: 200 or fewer words. Comment on news stories in the main section of the newspaper or to opine on views expressed on the Opinion pages, contact Letters to the Editor. Shorter letters have a better chance of being selected for publication.

22. **Oregonian** (Portland, OR)

Op-Eds: 500 words or fewer preferred. They are interested in highly topical issues or themes of particular relevance to the Pacific Northwest, Oregon, and the Portland metropolitan area. On matters of national or international scope, special expertise is generally a prerequisite. Many pieces are turned down because they lack universal interest or repeat a point of view that has already been aired recently in letters or op-ed pieces. Many unsuccessful submissions lack appeal to a wide range of readers or delve into nonlocal subjects that we prefer to leave to the national columnists. Best way to submit is via email sent to commentary@news.oregonian.com either as an attachment in word or in a message field. Or mail to Op-Ed Editor, The Oregonian, 1320 S.W. Broadway, Portland, OR 97201. If possible, include photo of self, preferably in color.

Letters: Max 150 words. Send to letters@news.oregonian.com, fax: 503/294-4193 or by mail: Letters to the Editor, The Oregonian 1320 SW Broadway Portland, OR 97201.

23. **Star-Ledger** (Newark, NJ)

Op-Eds: 675 words or fewer. Include name, address, and phone number. Submissions may be sent to The Star-Ledger, 1 Star-Ledger Plaza, Newark, NJ 07102-1200, or e-mailed to oped@starledger.com. E-mail submissions must be text submissions, not attachments.

Letters: 200 words or fewer. Submissions may be sent to The Star-Ledger, 1 Star-Ledger Plaza, Newark, NJ 07102-1200, or e-mailed to eletters@starledger.com. E-mail submissions must be text submissions, not attachments.

24. **San Diego Union-Tribune** (CA)

    Op-Eds: No length specified. Submissions should be about something in the news that would be of interest to area resident. Send commentaries to Community Opinion Editor Blanca Gonzalez at **blanca.gonzalez@ utsandiego.com.** You can also fax it to (619) 260-5081 or send it to Community Opinion Editor Blanca Gonzalez, U-T San Diego, P.O. Box 120191, San Diego, CA 92112-0191.

    Letters: 125 words or fewer. Exclusive to Union-Tribune. Preference is for letters that reference items published in the Union-Tribune within the past month. Include full name, address, phone number, must be signed if faxed or mailed. Send it to **letters@utsandiego.com** or fax it to (619) 260-5081. You can also send it to Letters Editor, U-T San Diego, P.O. Box 120191, San Diego, CA 92112-0191.

25. **Tampa Bay Times**

    Op-Eds: The Times very rarely uses op-eds, but those submitted should be 750 words or less. Submit by e-mail, text only, to: local@tampabay.com.

    Letters: 250 words max. Complete an online form.

26. **San Jose Mercury News** (CA)

    Op-Eds: 600 words or fewer. Please provide your full name, address, and telephone number with all submissions, but only your name and district where you live will appear in print. No attachments. Preferred submission method is by e-mail to opinion@bayareanewsgroup.com or US mail to P.O. Box 1189, Pacifica, Calif. 94044 or fax 359-3821 or in person to 59 Bill Drake Way (formerly Aura Vista Drive).

    Letters: 250–300 words. Please provide your full name, address, and telephone number with all submissions, but only your name and district where you live will appear in print. No attachments. Preferred submission method is by e-mail to mnletters@bayareanewsgroup.com or US mail to P.O. Box 1189, Pacifica, CA 94044 or fax 359-3821 or in person to 59 Bill Drake Way (formerly Aura Vista Drive).

27. **Sacramento Bee** (CA)

    Op-Eds: 600 words. They are seeking well-written pieces that make people think or that provide new insight into a familiar problem. They're especially interested in articles on local, state or Western regional issues. They will call within 5 working days if they are interested in the submission. Submit using an online form.

    Letters: 150-word limit. Reference article in Bee if possible, refer to issue covered within last two weeks, include name, mailing address, daytime phone. Submit via an online form.

28. **Kansas City Star**

    Op-Eds: Up to 600 words. Be sure to include a one-sentence author description, including city of residence, and daytime phone number. All submissions are edited, may be republished in any format and become property of The Star. An essay and color phot of the writer should be emailed to oped@kcstar.com or mailed to: The Star, Opinion Page Editor, The Kansas City Star, 1729 Grand Blvd., Kansas City, MO 64108.

Letters: Up to 200 words. Letters are subject to editing and writers may not appear more than once a month. Submit using an online form or by mail to The Kansas City Star, Letters, 1729 Grand Blvd., Kansas City, MO 64108. Please include your full name, address and daytime phone number with anything you send.

29. **St Louis Post-Dispatch** (MO)

Op-Eds: Should be approximately 500 words. Preference given to Illinois and Missouri authors, others not ruled out. E-mail as text: letters@post-dispatch.com or fax 314/340-3139.

Letters: 250 words or fewer. The best letters are timely, straightforward and focused on a single issue. All letters are subject to editing for fact, grammar, length, clarity and taste. It's fair to criticize the ideas and arguments of others, but we don't allow name-calling. If you are responding to a specific article, letter or editorial, please include the date of its publication. Your letter must include your address and a daytime phone number. Only your name and city of residence—not your address—will be published. If we're considering your letter for publication, we will call you to verify your authorship and your willingness to see it in print. Mail to Letters to the Editor, St. Louis Post-Dispatch, 900 North Tucker Blvd., St. Louis, MO 63101, e-mail letters@post-dispatch.com.

30. **Orange County Register** (CA)

Op-Eds: 625 words or fewer. They look for timely and well written op-eds on public policy issues, especially state and local. They give preference to local writers. Submissions should be accompanied by the writer's headshot, title, city of residence, phone number (not for publication) and any other relevant information, such as your expertise or experience in the subject. They cannot respond to everyone personally. Email submissions to commentary@ocregister.com.

Letters: 200 words or fewer or videos of 30 seconds. Provide your name, city and telephone number. Submit it by email to letters@ocregister.com.

31. **Atlanta Journal-Constitution** (GA)

Op-Eds: 450 to 600 words. Preference is given to Atlanta and Georgia writers who focus on local and regional issues, especially education, transportation, economy, leadership and quality of life. Op-eds should be sent as MS Word attachments as well as pasted into the body of the email. Please include the name of the author and a brief bio on both the attachment and the body of the email, with day and evening phone numbers. Columns submitted to the AJC may be published, republished and made available in the AJC or other databases and electronic formats. Submit via e-mail to Tom Sabulis, tsabulis@ajc.com, Opinion Editor.

Letters: 150 words or fewer e-mail letters@ajc.com. Include basic contact info. Bio information on employment/experience is suggested but optional

32. **Indianapolis Star** (IN)

Op-Eds: 600 words. Prefers local writers, but people writing about topics of relevance to Indiana are okay too. Include name and contact information. Submit via e-mail: stareditor@starnews.com.

Let it Out is a regular column in The Star featuring reader feedback on a variety of topics. The comments can be funny, critical, inspiring and even poetic. If you'd like to submit your thoughts, please use an online form. All comments remain anonymous.

Letters: 200 words or fewer. Submit using an online form or mail to Letters to the Editor, The Indianapolis Star, P.O. Box 145, Indianapolis, IN 46206-0145. By submitting your work, you grant The Indianapolis Star the rights to publish, distribute, archive and use the work in print, electronic, online or other formats.

33. **Milwaukee Journal Sentinel** (WI)

Op-Eds: 500–600 words, or longer at paper's discretion. Opinion articles published in the Sunday Crossroads section and the Perspectives page. Timely, well-written, provocative opinions on topics of local interest are given first preference for publication. All submissions are subject to editing. Name, street address and daytime phone number are required. They will only contact people whose pieces are selected for publication. Submit via e-mail to jsedit@journalsentinel.com, mail to Crossroads/Perspectives, Milwaukee Journal Sentinel, P.O. Box 371, Milwaukee, WI 53201-0371, or by fax: (414) 223-5444.

Letters: 200 words or less. Timely, well-written, provocative opinions on topics of interest in Milwaukee and Wisconsin are given first preference. All letters are subject to editing. Submit via an online form or by email to jsedit@journalsentinel.com. Each writer is limited to one published letter every 2 months.

34. **Baltimore Sun** (MD)

Op-Eds: 650–750 words. Local topics and authors are preferred. Submit using an online form

Letters: The Sun welcomes letters of 250 words or less. All letters become property of the Sun, which reserves the right to edit them. Include name, address, day and evening telephone numbers. Submit via e-mail, talkback@baltimoresun.com or by fax, 410-332-6977.

35. **Pioneer Press** (St. Paul, MN)

Op-Eds: Maximum of 750 words. Preference to regional issues, writers and communities typically underrepresented on opinion pages. E-mail your article to Pat Effenberger, peffenberger@pioneerpress.com, 615-228-5016.

Letters: 150 words or fewer. Include full name, city of residence, street address and phone number. All letters subject to editing. Must be exclusive. Send, as body of the email—not as an attachment, to letters@pioneerpress.com, or to Opinion Pages, Pioneer Press, 345 Cedar St., St. Paul, MN 55101, or by fax, 651-228-5564. Direct questions to 651-228-5545.

36. **Pittsburgh Post-Gazette** (PA)

Op-Eds: 600–800 words. They publish longer pieces in the Sunday Forum. They give priority to local writers writing on local topics. They generally don't use unsolicited freelance pieces on national and international issues from outside the region unless the writer has special knowledge or the topic is of local interest. They welcome query letters. They will contact people about accepted pieces right away. They pay between $50 and $100 for most pieces. Submit via e-mail to opinion@post-gazette.com, by fax (Attn: Opinion Page) to 412-263-2606, or by mail to Opinion Page, Pittsburgh Post-Gazette, 34 Boulevard of the Allies, Pittsburgh, PA 15222.

Letters: 250 words or fewer. Letters that are concise have a better chance of being used. E-mail letters@post-gazette.com Address letters to: Letters to the Editor, Pittsburgh Post-Gazette, 34 Blvd. of the Allies, Pittsburgh, PA 15222, or fax to 412/263-2014.

37. **The Columbus Dispatch** (OH)

Op-Eds: Op-Eds: 700–800 words. Submit via e-mail to the Forum Page Editor at forum@dispatch.com. No attachments.

Letters: 200 words or fewer. Each letter must include name, home address and daytime phone number. Dispatch.com also posts letters that don't make it to print in *The Dispatch*. Submit using an online form or mail to Letters to the Editor, The Dispatch, 34 S. 3rd St., Columbus, OH 43215, or fax it to 614-461-8793.

38. **Orlando Sentinel** (FL)

Op-Ed: 700 words maximum. Typically the views of an expert in a particular field, this column includes a head-and-shoulders picture and a short bio. Send by e-mail: insight@orlandosentinel.com, or mail to Letter to the Editor, Orlando Sentinel, 633 N. Orange Ave. MP-218, Orlando, FL 32801 or by fax to 407-420-5286.

New Voices: This is a forum for readers from high-school age through 29, with a maximum of 630 words. Include a head-and-shoulders picture, and send to **newvoices@orlandosentinel.com** or by mail.

Letters: 250 words or fewer. Letters should be brief and to the point and must include your name, address and daytime and evening telephone numbers. Submit it via an online form or mail to Letter to the Editor, Orlando Sentinel, 633 N. Orange Ave. MP-218, Orlando, FL 32801 or by fax to 407-420-5286.

39. **Louisville Courier-Journal** (KY)

Op-Eds: 500–700 words. Include contact information. Submit via e-mail to Pam Platt, pplatt@courier-journal.com. For questions, call her at 502-582-4578.

Letters: 200 words or fewer. The letter must include your full name, address (e-mail address also, if you have one) and a daytime phone number. Please also type your letter's topic or subject in the space provided. Submit using an online form

40. **Las Vegas Review Journal** (NV)

Op-Eds: 600–700 words. They prefer shorter pieces focused on or with a tie to local issues. Submit it by e-mail to letters@reviewjournal.com and write "Op-Ed Submission" in the subject line. You can cc Patrick Everson, peverson@reviewjournal.com, and also leave him a voicemail to let him know you submitted a piece: 702-383-0353.

Letters: You must include your name and phone number. Submit your letter via an online form.

41. **Contra Costa Times** (East Bay area of CA)

Op-Eds: 750 words maximum. Provide your full name, address, and telephone number with all submissions. E-mail by Friday noon of the week preceding publication to elarsen@bayareanewsgroup.com, or mail to P.O. Box 1189, Pacifica, CA 94044 or fax 359-3821 or in person to 59 Bill Drake Way (formerly Aura Vista Drive).

Letters: 250–300 words. Provide your full name, address, and telephone number with all submissions. E-mail by Friday noon of the week preceding publication to elarsen@bayareanewsgroup.com, or mail to P.O. Box 1189, Pacifica, Calif. 94044 or fax 359-3821 or in person to 59 Bill Drake Way (formerly Aura Vista Drive).

42. **Arkansas Democrat-Gazette** (Little Rock, AR)

Op-Eds: Should be 650–800 words and written by Arkansas residents. Include name, address, a note of bio and a daytime telephone number. E-mail Voices@arkansasonline.com. With questions, call Brenda Looper, 501-378-3481.

Letters: 250 words or fewer. Clarity, brevity, and originality are valued. You must include the writer's real name, mailing address and a daytime telephone number for verification. Submit using an online form.

43. **Cincinnati Enquirer** (OH)

Op-Eds: 400–450 words. Use the same e-mail address as letters: letters@enquirer.com. Require a photo and a two-line bio about the author in order to be published. Also include a daytime phone number for the author.

Letters: Limited to 100 words, submit via e-mail: letters@enquirer.com, mail: Cincinnati Enquirer, Letters to the Editor, 312 Elm St., Cincinnati, OH 45202, an online form, or fax: (513) 768-8569. May be edited for space and clarity. Longer letters may be considered for other features on the Editorial Page, Opinions Page, or in Sunday Forum.

44. **Greensburg Tribune-Review** and **Pittsburg Tribune-Review** (PA)

Op-Eds: Send to opinion@tribweb.com or fax to 724/838-5171.

Letters: 200 words or fewer. No writer will be published more than once every 30 days. We reserve the right to accept or reject any letter for publication, and also to edit for grammar, length and accuracy. All letters must list the author's name, address and telephone number for verification purposes. E-mail: opinion@tribweb.com or mail to Letters to the Editor, Tribune-Review, 622 Cabin Hill Drive, Greensburg, PA 15601 or fax 724/838-5171

45. **The Detroit News** (MI)

    Op-Eds: 600–750 words for pieces of "Commentary" on current public policy and societal issues on the local state, national and international scene. First priority given to local and state topics written by Michigan writers. Must be exclusive in Detroit metro area. Send by email to comment@detnews.com or fax to 313/222-6417or mail to James David Dickson, The Detroit News, Editorial Page, 615 W. Lafayette Blvd., Detroit, MI 48226.

    Letters: 250 words maximum. Direct rebuttals to editorials may be up to 300 words. Include all contact information. E-mail: letters@detnews.com, or fax 313/222-6417, or mail: The Detroit News, Letters, Editorial Page, 615 W. Lafayette, Detroit, MI 48226. Letters are subject to editing. Letters already submitted to other publications are not considered.

46. **The Charlotte Observer** (NC)

    Op-Eds: Up to 750 words. Submit your op-ed pieces to the same mailing address, fax number and e-mail as letters to the editor with "op-ed" in the subject heading.

    Letters: Letters typically address a single idea and do not exceed 150 words. Please sign (unless you are using e-mail or computer fax) and include your address and daytime telephone number. They edit for brevity, grammar and clarity, and they reject letters published elsewhere. Send letters to The Observer Forum, The Charlotte Observer, P.O. Box 30308, Charlotte, NC 28230-0308 or fax them to 704/358-5022. Letters can also be emailed to opinion@charlotteobserver.com.

47. **Fort Worth Star-Telegram** (Fort Worth, TX)

    Op-Eds: 750 words or fewer, prefers timely issues that are of particular interest in the region. Include your contact information. Mail: Op-Ed Page Editor, Box 1870, Fort Worth, TX 76101, fax: 817/390-7831. Submissions via e-mail are preferred: letters@star-telegram.com.

    Letters: Suggested length is 200 words or less. May be edited for pace, clarity, civility and accuracy. Letters must include author's full name, address and day and home phone numbers for verification purposes only. Submit via e-mail: letters@star-telegram.com, fax: 817-390-7688, and mail: Box 1870, Fort Worth, TX 7101. Questions call 817-390-7830 to speak with Mike Norman, Editorial Page Director.

48. **The Buffalo News** (NY)

    Op-Eds: "My View" is 600 words. Personal narrative, open to all Western New York writers. "Another Voice" is 475 words. Issue-oriented that requires background or expertise on the topic. Submit either, with your contact information, to editpage@buffnews.com.

Letters: Up to 250 words. Must include the writer's name, address, and phone number. Email to lettertoeditor@buffnews.com

49. **Virginian-Pilot** (Norfolk, VA)

    Op-Eds: 750 words or less. Local interest is key to getting your op-ed printed. Be sure to include your name, address and phone number. E-mail letters@pilotonline.com by fax at 757/446-2051.

    Letters: 150 words. They want concise letters on public issues. Letters may be edited for length, style and clarity and writers are limited to one published letter every month. Please add your name, city, street address and daytime telephone number for confirmation. E- mail: letters@pilotonline.com or fax at 757/446-2051, or mail to Letters to the Editor, P.O. Box 449, Norfolk, VA 23501-0449.)

50. **Miami Herald** (FL)

    Op-Eds: Under 650 words. Published submissions are to be used exclusively for the Miami Herald. E-mailed submissions are preferred. Send by e-mail to oped@MiamiHerald.com. Include a head-shot. Provide e-mail address or a website to run with the column. If you do not hear within 10 days, safely assume submission has been declined.

    Letters: Include contact information. They only publish writers once per 60 days. Submit by email to HeraldEd@miamiherald.com, by fax to 305-376-8950, or mail to the Readers' Forum, The Miami Herald, 1 Herald Plaza, Miami, FL 33132.

51. **The Times Picayune** (New Orleans, LA)

    Op-Eds: Limit 700 words. Articles should have a strong Louisiana angle. They edit for length and clarity. All submissions become the property of The Times-Picayune and will not be returned; they may be published or otherwise reused in any medium. Submit an online form

    Letters: 200 words maximum. All submissions must include a daytime phone number and full name. Initials and pen names are not accepted. Do not send a letter as an email attachment such as.doc or.txt. All submissions become the property of The Times-Picayune and will not be returned. Submissions may be edited and may be published or otherwise reused in any medium. Submit via e-mail to letters@nola.com, or by mail to Letters to the Editor, The Times-Picayune, 365 Canal Street, Suite 3100, New Orleans, LA 70130

52. **South Florida Sun-Sentinel** (FL)

    Op-Eds: You can submit two types of pieces. "Viewpoints" are 450 words and it's easier to get placement. Op-Eds are 650 words but are harder to place because the paper runs their own opinion pieces on certain days. Include contact information, a short byline and a high resolution JPG photo of the author and note in the subject line it's a submission. E-mail submission to Diana Mellion, dmellion@sun-sentinel.com.

Letters: 200 words maximum and 100 words or fewer stands the best chance of being published. Include your name, address and daytime phone number. All letters are subject to editing. MOST letters are edited for clarification and length. They only contact people they will publish. You can submit via e-mail (no attachments) letter@sun-sentinel.com or submit via an online form.

53. **Omaha World-Herald** (NE)

    Op-Eds: 700–800 words. In the subject line write, "Another Point of View" and send to pulse@owh.com, or mail to Omaha World-Herald, 1334 Dodge Street, Omaha, NE 68102, or fax to 402-345-4547.

    Letters: 200 words maximum. Letters must include the writer's first and last names as well as the writer's address and telephone number. Letters must be in the original words of the writer and may be edited for reasons including taste, accuracy, clarity and length. Send by e-mail to pulse@owh.com

54. **The Record** (Bergen County, NJ)

    Op-Eds: 700 words. E-mail: oped@northjersey.com or fax: 201/646-4749. http://www.northjersey.com/

    Letters: 200 words maximum. Please be brief and include all contact information. Submit via e-mail to letterstotheeditor@northjersey.com or by fax to 201-457-2520.

55. **The Tampa Tribune** (FL)

    Op-Eds: 500–750 words. Submissions should be about an issue that is of interest in the local area. Include name, address, title, phone number and "any information that you think would be needed for footer info." Submit via an online form and indicate it's an op-ed at the top of the submission.

    Letters: 150-word limit, include daytime phone and address. Submit your letter via an online form.

56. **San Antonio Express News** (TX)

    Op-Eds: The shorter the better. All letters and guest commentaries are subject to editing for style, spelling and libel. They must include the author's full name (no initials or pseudonyms), place of residency and phone number. Submit by 5 p.m. on Fridays for consideration in the next editing to eortiz@primetimenewspapers.com.

    Letters: The shorter the better. All letters and guest commentaries are subject to editing for style, spelling and libel. They must include the author's full name (no initials or pseudonyms), place of residency, and phone number. Submit by 5 p.m. on Fridays for consideration in the next editing to eortiz@primetimenewspapers.com.

57. **The Oklahoman** (Oklahoma City, Oklahoma)

    Op-Eds: 500 words. Preference given to Oklahoma authors and topics of interest to people in Oklahoma. Include a biographical byline and attach a high-resolution photo of the author. Submit via e-mail to J. E. McReynolds, jmcreynolds@opubco.com. Questions? Call him at 405-475-3469.

Letters: 250-word max. Cover your topic in the fewest possible words. Get to your main point quickly. Stay focused on your key points. Include full name, address and e-mail. Submit letters to the editor via an online form.

58. **The Hartford Courant** (CT)

Op-Eds: Limit 700 words. Pieces should be provocative, highly opinionated, easy-to-read essays, usually on a public policy issue, although personal pieces are also welcome. Those who wish to write op-eds for the Other Opinion page should have expertise or personal experience with the subject they are writing about. We give priority to locally written pieces on statewide or regional issues. They pay $40 for op-ed pieces, slightly more for Commentary cover articles. We do not pay for essays by think tanks, advocacy groups, government officials, commercial concerns. Read the full guidelines. Submissions should be sent via e-mail to oped@courant.com (preferred method), pasted into the body of the email, or by fax to 860-520-6941.

Letters: 200-word maximum. Letters require full name, mailing address, phone numbers and e-mail address for verification. Your letter should be exclusive to The Courant. Your submission may be edited and shortened. Writers will ordinarily be limited to one published letter every 2 months. Submit via an online form.

59. **The Commercial Appeal** (Memphis, TN) *Op-Eds*: 700-word limit. They are looking for pieces that has relevancy and a connection to the Memphis area. Include a short byline and attach a high-resolution JPG photo. Send submissions to Jerome Wright, wright@commercialappeal.com. Questions? Call him at 901-529-5830.

Letters: 200–250 words. Must be timely and relevant to the Memphis area. All letters must include the writer's name, full home address and daytime and evening phone numbers for verification. Send submissions to letters@commercialappeal.com. Questions? Call 901-529-5830.

60. **Austin American-Statesman** (TX)

Op-Ed: 600–650 word maximum. Include a one-sentence biography and attach a JPG photo of yourself. Submit via e-mail to views@statesman.com.

Letters: 1,000 characters. Letters are edited for brevity, grammar, and clarity. Letters typically address a single idea. Submit via an online form. You can also submit via mail to Letters to the Editor, P.O. Box 670, Austin, TX 78767.

61. **News & Observer** (Raleigh, NC)

Letters: 200-word limit. Include name, mailing address, email address, and daytime phone number. Letters may be mailed to "The People's Forum, PO Box 191, Raleigh, NC 27620," faxed to (919) 829-4872, or submitted via an online form.

62. **Investor's Business Daily** (Los Angeles, CA)

    Op-Eds: To submit an Op-Ed article for consideration for IBD's Editorial page, email it to letters@ibdeditorials.com

63. **Boston Herald** (MA)

    Op-Eds: 650–800 words. Include contact information. Send via e-mail to oped@bostonherald.com or fax to 617/542-1315.

    Letters: E-mail to Letterstoeditor@bostonherald.com or submit using an online form.

64. **Times Dispatch** (Richmond, VA)

    Op-Eds: 800 words or less. Rarely accept unsolicited op-eds, and the ones they use must be specifically Virginia- and/or Richmond-related, as well as exclusive to the Times-Dispatch. This excludes most pieces dealing with national or international subjects. E-mail Cindy Paris, cparis@timesdispatch.com.

    Letters: Submit signed letters by fax: 804/-819-1216 or e-mail letters@times-dispatch.com or Todd Culbertson, TCulbertson@timesdispatch.com.

65. **The Tennessean** (Nashville)

    Op-Eds: 600–700 words. E-mail submission to voices@tennessean.com. Questions? Call Ted Rayburn, 615-259-8063.

    Letters: Preference will be given to letters of less than 250 words. To be considered for publication, letters must include the writer's name, street address and daytime telephone number. Only the name, hometown and ZIP code will be published. Letter writers who would like their e-mail addresses published should include that address with the letter. Submit via an online form. Letters may also be mailed to Letters to the Editor, The Tennessean, 1100 Broadway, Nashville, TN 37203. They may be e-mailed to letters@tennessean.com or faxed to 615-259-8093.

66. **Fresno Bee** (CA)

    Op-Eds: Submit 750 words for Valley Voices, E-mail to letters@fresnobee.com and write "Valley Voices" submission in the subject line.

    Letters: 200 words maximum. Submit via an online form.

67. **Rochester Democrat & Chronicle** (NY)

    Speaking Out: 400 or fewer words. All letters and essays chosen for publication are subject to editing for length, clarity and accuracy. For questions about essays, call 258-2250. Submit via an online form.

    Letters: 150 words or fewer. All letters and essays chosen for publication are subject to editing for length, clarity and accuracy. For questions about essays, call 258-2250. Submit via an online form.

68. **Asbury Park Press** (NJ)

    Op-Eds: 400 words or less, prefer writers with expertise in the area they are writing about. Submit all pieces to Op-Ed Editor, Randy Bergmann. E-mail: rbergmann@app.com or fax: 732/643-4014.

Letters: 200 words maximum. Send via email to Linda Reddington, lreddington@app.com, or via regular mail: Your Views, Asbury Park Press 3601 Highway 66, Box 1550, Neptune, NJ 07754-1551 or by fax (732) 643-4014.

69. **Birmingham News** (AL)

Op-Eds: 600 words. Send pieces to letters@al.com and indicate in the subject that it's an op-ed. You can also cc or send questions to KA Turner, Director of Opinion and Commentary, kturner@al.com, 205-325-3387.

Letters: 250 words maximum. The letter should express opinions on topics of local interest. Letters may be edited for clarity or shortened for publication. Submit usingan online form or by emailing bhamletters@al.com.

70. **Des Moines Register** (IA)

Op-Eds: 700 words on topics related to Iowa and of interest to our readers. If published, a head shot and a signed essay agreement form is necessary. E-mail to revans@dmreg.com. Questions? Call Randy Evans, 515-284-8118.

Letters: 200 words or fewer. Include your name, complete address and daytime phone number. All submissions may be edited for length, accuracy and clarity and may be published or distributed in print, electronic, or other forms. Send via an online form, or e-mail letters@dmreg.com or fax 515-286-2504.

71. **West Palm Beach Post** (FL)

Op-Eds: 600–700 words, must be timely, a strong opinion and well stated. E-mail to letters@pbpost.com and indicate it's an op-ed in the subject line.

Letters: The Palm Beach Post welcomes letters about issues of current interest and material that has appeared in the newspaper. Maximum of 250 words, all are subject to editing for brevity and clarity. Send to letters@pbpost.com.

72. **Honolulu Star-Advertiser** (HI)

Op-Eds: 500–600 words. The article may be edited for clarity and length. Include your name, address, and phone number. E-mail to letters@honoluluadvertiser.com or mail to Letters to the Editor, Star-Advertiser, 7 Waterfront Plaza, 500 Ala Moana, Suite 7-210, Honolulu, HI 96813.

Letters: 200 words or fewer. Letters must be in good taste on any topic. Submissions must include writer's true name, address, and telephone number. Submit via an online form. E-mail: letters@honoluluadvertiser.com or mail to Letters to the Editor, Star-Advertiser, 7 Waterfront Plaza, 500 Ala Moana, Suite 7-210, Honolulu, HI 96813.

73. **Riverside Press-Enterprise** (CA)

Op-Eds: Manuscripts must be brief. Submit by fax: 909/368-9022 or e-mail: letters@pe.com.

Letters: 200 words. Include contact information. To improve the likelihood of publication, please cite sources, if appropriate, to support claims involving events or statistics. Submit via an online form.

74. **Salt Lake City Tribune** (UT)

   Op-Eds: 600 words. All submissions should include name, address, telephone number and some information on the author so that it can be included on the end of the piece. E-mail Tim Fitzpatrick, editor of the editorial page, at fitz@sltrib.com (no attachments); send the typed, double-spaced submission to Tim Fitzpatrick, The Salt Lake Tribune, 90 S. 400 West, Suite 700, Salt Lake City, UT 84101; or fax 801/257-8515.

   Letters: 200 words. Include full contact information. Concise letters developing a single theme are more likely to be published. For printed submissions, please type and double space throughout. Letters are condensed and edited. Because of the volume of mail received, not all submissions are published. Submit by email to letters@sltrib.com (no attachments), by fax to 801-257-8950 or by mail to Salt Lake Tribune, 90 S. 400 West, Salt Lake City, UT 84101.

75. **Daily Herald** (Arlington Heights, IL)

   Letters: 300-word max. Attach digital photograph of yourself, at least 300 dpi, for publication. All submissions must include your name, town, and day and evening phone numbers. All submissions are considered for publication in print and online. No letter will be published anonymously. All letters are subject to editing. Submit via an online form.

76. **Florida Times-Union** (Jacksonville)

   Opinion Blog: Create an account with the website and you can submit an opinion blog post.

   Letters: 250 words. To increase the chances of a letter being used, choose one topic and make the point succinctly. Broad topics such as the future of the human species generally are less likely to be used than specific topics such as a pending issue in the City Council that is nearing final action. Include contact information and name. Send via email to letters@jacksonville.com (no attachments) or via an online form.

77. **Providence Journal** (RI)

   Op-Eds: 800 words. If you refer to a published piece, please include the headline and date of the article. Please include a line at the bottom identifying you and any special expertise you have in the topic. They may edit opeds for length and clarity. You must include your full address and phone number for confirmation purposes. They do not accept faxed columns. Submit via e-mail to letters@providencejournal.com or by mail to Op-ed Submission, The Providence Journal, 75 Fountain Street, Providence, RI 02902.

   Letters: They strongly favor letters of 150 words or fewer. Include contact information. They may edit letters for length and clarity. No faxed letters. Submit via email to letters@providencejournal.com or by mail to Letters to the Editor, The Providence Journal, 75 Fountain Street, Providence, RI 02902.

78. **Toledo Blade** (OH)

    Op-Eds: 750 words. Include full name, address and daytime phone number. Submit via e-mail to David Kushma, dkushma@theblade.com. Call with any questions: 419-724-6170.

    Letters: 200 words. Must include name, day phone and an address. Submit via an online form, or by mail to Readers' Forum, The Blade, 541 North Superior Street, PO Box 921, Toledo, OH 43697, or by fax to 419/724-6191.

79. **Dayton Daily News** (OH)

    Op-Eds: 700–750 words, include daytime phone numbers with all submissions. E-mail: edletter@coxohio.com.

    Letters: 250 words. Include your full name and a daytime telephone number. To publish as many letters as possible, they may be edited. No attachments, please. Submit via an online form, or fax your letter to (937) 225-7302, or mail: Letters to the editor, 1611 S. Main St., Dayton, OH 45409.

80. **Grand Rapids Press** (MI)

    Op-Eds: 750 words or less, Press prefers that the author be both an area resident and an expert on the issue. Prefers e-mail submissions. E-mail (no attachments) to grletters@mlive.com or fax to 616/222-5212.

    Letters: 200 words. Include your full name, home address, and phone number. All submissions are subject to condensation and editing. Writers are limited to one letter every 60 days. E-mail a letter to the editor for publication online and in print: grletters@mlive.com.

81. **Tulsa World** (OK)

    Op-Eds: 650 words. Include contact information. Send via e-mail to letters@tulsaworld.com.

    Letters: 250 words. Include contact information. Letters may be edited for length, style, and grammar. Submit via an online form.

82. **Allentown Morning Call** (PA)

    Op-Eds: 700 words maximum. Pieces should be on a topic in your area of expertise and of local, regional, or state interest. Include your background, affiliation, address, and phone number. Submit "Your View" pieces to townsquare@mcall.com, or mail to Town Square, The Morning Call, Box 1260, Allentown, PA 18105.

    Letters: 200-word limit. Include contact information. Because of the volume of letters, unpublished letters cannot be acknowledged or returned. The Morning Call reserves the right to edit and condense all letters. Submit via an online form, by e-mail: letters@mcall.com, fax: (610) 820-6693, or mail: Letters to the Editor, The Morning Call, Box 1260, Allentown, PA 18105.

83. **Knoxville News-Sentinel** (TN)

    Op-Eds: 600–700 words. E-mail to letters@knoxnews.com and indicate that it's intended to be an op-ed submission. Include a bio and contact information.

Letters: 300 words maximum. The letter should be sent only to the News Sentinel. It should be signed and include a street address and phone number. All letters are subject to editing and condensing. Submit via e-mail to letters@knoxnews.com, by fax 865-342-6265, or by mail, Letters to the Editor, News Sentinel, 2332 News Sentinel Drive, Knoxville, TN 37921

84. **Lexington Herald-Leader** (KY)

Op-Eds: 700 words max and writer must have demonstrated special interest. Include name, address, and phone number. Submit via e-mail to hleditorial@herald-leader.com

Letters: 250 words. Include your name and contact information. They may edit the letter for brevity, content and clarity. Submit via this an online form or submit by fax to 859-231-3332 or by mail to Letters to the Editor, Lexington Herald-Leader, 100 Midland Ave, Lexington, KY 40508.

85. **Akron Beacon Journal** (OH)

Op Eds: 500–750 words. Guidelines listed daily in print edition of paper. Author should include bio. E-mail: vop@thebeaconjournal.com.

Letters: Send emails without attachments to vop@thebeaconjournal.com. You must include your name, address and phone number to be considered for publication.

86. **Daily News** (Los Angeles)

Op-Eds: 600–700 words. Submit an essay with your contact information to Mike Brossart, mike.brossart@langnews.com. Call him with any questions, 909-483-9313.

Letters: 150 words. Letters must be signed and include a daytime phone number and the community or city in which the author lives. Submit via e-mail (no attachments) to dnforum@dailynews.com.

87. **Albuquerque Journal** (NM)

Op-Eds: Prefers locally written commentaries and a limit of 750 words. Send to Dan Herrera, dherrera@abqjournal.com. Call with questions, 505-823-3810.

Letters: Preference is given to letters that are fresh, brief, clear and that don't require factual verification. Letters must include writer's signature, home address and telephone, and a daytime number. Submit via an online form.

88. **Arizona Daily Star** (Tuscon, AZ)

Op-Eds: 600 words. Pieces should express ideas, viewpoints, criticism and news analysis that encourage discussion on issues with an impact on the community. When writing, authors should fully disclose their relationship with an issue and their expertise on the topic. This is particularly relevant when writing about a political campaign or candidate. Facts must be annotated. Please include a head-and-shoulders photograph, first saved as a high-resolution jpg and then attached to the form. Submit via an online form.

Letters: 150 words. Letters should have ideas, viewpoints, criticism and news analysis that encourage discussion on issues impacting the community.

Submissions may be edited for clarity or length. All submissions become the property of the Arizona Daily Star. Submit via an online form.

89. **The Post Standard** (Syracuse, NY)

Op-Eds: 750 words. Essays should be about issues directly affecting Central New York. Include contact information and a short bio. E-mail to letters@syracuse.com.

Letters: 250-word limit. Anything you send becomes property of The Herald Co., publishers of The Post-Standard. Material may be excerpted, edited for length or content, and may be published or used in any other way. Due to the volume of submissions, you may be limited to one entry per month. Submit via an online form.

90. **The Press Register** (Mobile, AL)

Op-Eds: 650 words. Submit essay with contact information to the Director of Commentary and Opinion, kturner@al.com.

Letters: 250 words maximum. The letter should express opinions on topics of local interest. Letters may be edited for clarity or shortened for publication. Submit using an online form or by emailing mobileletters@al.com.

91. **The Oakland Tribune** (CA)

My Word (Op-Eds): 550 word limit. Include name, home address, and a day-time phone number. All essays are subject to verification and editing for legal aspects, style, clarity and brevity. The Opinion Editor is Dan Hatfield, who can be reached at 925-977-8430, dhatfield@bayareanewsgroup.com. You can submit your My Word article via an online form

Letters: 250 words or less. You can submit your letter via an online form.

92. **Wisconsin State Journal** (Madison, WI)

Letters: 250 words. The writer's name and hometown will be published, but not the personal contact information. The Wisconsin State Journal does-n't print letters that have been copied from advocacy websites or organizations. Submit via an online form.

93. **La Opinion** (Los Angeles, CA)

Letters: Spanish newspaper in Los Angeles. Send by e-mail to editorial@laopinion.com or tribuna@laopinion.com.

94. **News Journal/Delaware Online** (Wilmington, DE)

Letters: 250 words. It should be brief as possible, about an issue important to the greater Delaware community, and please include full contact information. Submit via an online form or mail to Letters to the Editor, Box 15505, Wilmington, DE 19850 or fax to 302/324-2595.

95. **Tacoma News Tribune** (WA)

Op-Eds: 500 words. Pieces are selected based on a personal experience or expertise and must be of unusual interest to readers. Send via an online form, by email to Patrick.ocallahan@thenewstribune.com.

Letters: 200-word limit and those less than 150 words will receive priority. Include your contact information. Send via an online form.

96. **The Advocate** (Baton Rouge, LA)

    Letters: 450 words. Submit via an online form.

97. **Post & Courier** (Charleston, SC)

    Op-Eds: No more than 700 words. Include contact information. Send to Charles Rowe, Opinion Page Editor, crowe@postandcourier.com.

    Letters: Submissions are subject to editing for length, clarity. Include contact information. Submit via e-mail: letters@postandcourier.com.

98. **The Journal News** (White Plains, NY)

    Op-Eds: 750 words. Essays should deal with a timely, and preferably local, issue of public interest. They should be well-composed essays on points of view that merit more detailed discussion than is available in briefer letters to the editor.

    You must include your name, address and daytime telephone number to permit verification. Be sure to let them know if you have particular experience, training or expertise that is relevant to the subject matter of your essay. Submit via e-mail to letters@lohud.com (with "Community View" in the subject line), by fax to 914-696-8396, or by mail to Community View, The Journal News, 1133 Westchester Ave., Suite N110, White Plains, NY 10604.

    Letters: Letters may be edited for length. Please provide name, address and telephone number for verification. Letters may be published in print and/or distributed electronically. Submit via an online form, by e-mail to letters@lohud.com, or by mail to Letters to the Editor, The Journal News, 1133 Westchester Ave., Suite N110, White Plains, NY 10604.

99. **The State** (SC)

    Op-Eds: Op-ed writers are expected to bring a knowledge or expertise to the topic. Columns should not merely state the writer's opinion, but should put forth information-backed arguments that are likely to persuade readers. They do not generally publish out of state authors. Submit via an online form.

    Letters: Should be concise and legible. Letters will be edited. They do not generally accept pieces from people outside the state. Submit via an online form.

100. **The Times of Northwest Indiana** (Munster, IN)

    Op-Eds: 450-word limit. Send either to letters@nwi.com or doug.ross@nwi.com.

    Letters: 150-word limit. Submit via an online form.

Example of Policy Issue Brief

A Policy Brief or Policy Memo is a short, one- to two-page narrative that succinctly outlines the key dimensions of an issue and recommendations to address the matter. A well-crafted brief does not generally include tables, graphs, or data; this information is supplemental and is better communicated via an Info Sheet or Dashboard (see Chapter 10).

Source: Katherine Barillas, PhD, Director of Child Welfare Policy, One Voice Coalition, received January 2017.

SUPPORTING KIN WHO CARE FOR RELATIVE CHILDREN

Issue/Concern

There are over 250,000 children in the state of Texas living in an informal arrangement with a relative who is typically a grandparent and low-income.[1] In 2016, there were over 12,000 children living with a relative through placement by the Department of Family and Protective Services (DFPS).

Research shows relative placements to be successful with the right amount of financial resources and access to services and information. These caregivers prevent their relative children from coming into foster care or being homeless and they

---

1. Kids Count Data Center, 2011–2013.

provide savings in both financial and emotional terms. However, to do so, they need guidance and financial support to strengthen their ability to take care of the children living in their homes.

Policy/Budget Recommendations

- Support short-term, voluntary kinship arrangements known as Parental Child Safety Placements by:
  - Allowing PCSPs the option of receiving benefits and caseworkers from DFPS by adding this population to statute;
  - Requiring DFPS to assist caregivers in arranging for necessary resources to care for the child before closing the case;
  - Requiring a plan for closure of a PCSP placement or transfer of the case to Family Based Safety Services to be due no later than day 30 of the case instead of day 60; with extensions for extenuating circumstances approved by a CPS Program Administrator (PA);
  - Requiring a PCSP used during the investigation stage to be closed or the case transferred to FBSS no later than 60 days after the start of the case; with extensions for extenuating circumstances approved by a PA (rather than a soft guideline of 90 days) given that most placements of this kind deteriorate around 60 days and this is the latest timeline for investigative closure;
  - Altering the Chapter 34 agreement to:
    - Add obtaining original or copies of documentation including birth certificates, social security cards etc.;
    - Remove requirements that:
      - The agreement is not valid if there is a court of continuing jurisdiction involving the child in question;
      - A relative must attempt to notify the other parent at least twice: first by certified mail and then by first class mail
- Require the grandparent grant of $1,000 to be provided within 60 days of the child's placement in the home instead of the 120 days that is currently set in policy and the reimbursement of $500 to be provided within 6 months of the child's placement instead of the year anniversary of the child's placement in the home;
- Raise the reimbursement payments so that kin can address the basic needs of the relative children in their care;
- Remove the Sunset provision attached to the Permanency Care Assistance Program so it can continue to allow children to exit to permanency with relatives;
- HHSC should establish an information, referral and outreach collaborative for kinship caregivers through a Kinship Navigator Program;

- Grandparents are frequently denied TANF because their car is valued at over $4,650, but they need a care to transport their grandchildren to doctor and other necessary appointments depriving them of a needed financial benefit. Texas should exempt grandparents (age 60 and older) who are currently caring for a relative child (birth to 18th birthday) an exemption from vehicles that are currently part of an asset test

For more information contact:
Katherine Barillas, PhD, Director of Child Welfare Policy
Kbarillas@onevoicetexas.org; 713-480-3937

INDEX

Tables, figures, and boxes are indicated by an italic t, f, and b following the page number.